The Irish Buddhist

The Irish Buddhist

*The Forgotten Monk Who Faced Down the
British Empire*

ALICIA TURNER, LAURENCE COX,
AND BRIAN BOCKING

OXFORD
UNIVERSITY PRESS

OXFORD
UNIVERSITY PRESS

Oxford University Press is a department of the University of Oxford. It furthers
the University's objective of excellence in research, scholarship, and education
by publishing worldwide. Oxford is a registered trade mark of Oxford University
Press in the UK and certain other countries.

Published in the United States of America by Oxford University Press
198 Madison Avenue, New York, NY 10016, United States of America.

© Alicia Turner, Laurence Cox and Brian Bocking 2020

CIP data is on file at the Library of Congress
ISBN 978–0–19–007308–4

1 3 5 7 9 8 6 4 2

Printed by Integrated Books International, United States of America

This book is dedicated with love to our partners, who have patiently tolerated our obsession with Dhammaloka for many years, as well as helping with this project in ways too numerous to be counted:
Michelle
Órfhlaith
Shelagh

Contents

Illustrations

Maps

Acknowledgments

Like Dhammaloka's own projects, this book was made possible by the support and collaboration of many academic researchers, independent scholars, Buddhists, librarians, friends, and family around the world, who enabled us to track him through many different countries, languages, disciplines, and perspectives.

In particular we would like to record our thanks to those colleagues who have been a close part of this network of "Dhammaloka Studies" specialists over the years:

Thomas Borchert
Phibul Choompolpaisal
Kate Crosby
Tadhg Foley
Maria Griffin
Jasmine Jasani
Rachel Pisani
Mihirini Sirisena
Andrew Skilton
Thomas Tweed
Shin'ichi Yoshinaga.

We want to thank the many other people who have supported this project in many different ways over the years and without whom we would have been unable to complete this project:

Akshobin, Aung Soe Min, Jyoti Atwal, Tim Barrett, Stephan Bean, Sangeeta Besoya, Robert Bickers, Anne Blackburn, Sarah Blake, Bo Bo Lasin, Marion Bowman, Bénedicte Brac de la Perrière, Erik Braun, Colm Breathnach, John Breen, Ian Brown, Chang Qing, Tim Colton, Chris Connolly, Michael Cooke, Marian Cotter, David Cox, Richard Cox, Wendy Cox, John Crow, Erik Davis, Mahinda Deegalle, Marc Demarest, Lucia Dolce, Wendy Doniger, Philip Douglas, the Duggan family, Terry Dunne, Yulia Egorova, Audrey Elliott, Gilles de Flogny, David Fahey, Richard Fardon, Caroline Fennell, Alicia Filipowich, Fiona Fitzsimons, Keith Flett, Bernie Gardiner, Richard Gombrich, Jan Graham-Clark, Charles Guard, Naoko Gunji, Lydia Guzy, Anna Halahoff, Elizabeth Harris, Helen Doxford Harris, Paul Harrison, Simone Heidegger,

Ian Herbertson, Adrian Hermann, Michael Holland †, Cheryl Hoskin, Chad Hubert, Michael Hutt, Vivian Ibrahim, Mami Iwata, Richard Jaffe, Vicky Janssen, Michael Jenkins, Joyce Jenkins, Bob Jones, Shane Kilcommins, James Kapalo, Steven Kemper, James Ketelaar, Mathew Kidwell, Hwansoo Kim, Audrey Kinch, Alexey Kirichenko, Orion Klautau, Hilary Lawson, Ian Lawton, Ken Lennan, Clement Liang, Amarjiva Lochan, Johnsen Low, Tomás MacSheoin, Maung Maung Thein, John May, Anna Mazzoldi, Barbara McCormack, Sharman Minus, David Wynne Morgan, Hiram Morgan, Loreley Morling, Steve Mullins, John L. Murphy, Alf Nilsen, Nyanatusita, Douglas Ober, Eunan O'Halpin, Emma Okada, Yoshiko Okamoto, Seamus O'Tuama, Chris Powell, Timothy Pwee, Michael Pye, Pyi Phyo Kyaw, Ted Rausch, Andrew Rawlinson, Michael Roberts, Oliver Scharbrodt, Gaynor Sekimori, Yafa Shanneik, Jill Shaw, Christopher Shepard, Laurence Singlehurst, Sue Spelling, Irene Lin Stanford, Emma Sweeney, Francois Tainturier, Francesca Tarocco, Alan Taylor, Rosemary Taylor, Stefania Travagnin, Katja Triplett, Eleonore Tuohy, Joe Tuohy, Geoffrey Turner, David Twomey, John Twomey, Galia Umansky, Les Valentine, Jean van Sinderen-Law, Ven. Veera Vingvorn, Jane Clarke Wadsworth, Wai Phyo Maung, Youxuan Wang, Judy Webster, Paul Whitaker, Jo Wildy, and archivists and librarians at institutions on four continents for their amazing patience and generosity.

Our thanks go to the organizers, staff, and student helpers and all participants of Dhammaloka Day (2011) and the "South-East Asia as a Crossroads for Buddhist Exchange" conference (2012), both at University College Cork; the "Bordering the Borderless" conference (2013) at Duke University; and the "Asian Buddhism: Plural Colonialisms and Plural Modernities" conference (2014) in Kyoto, who helped us tease out the ideas in this book.

We also want to thank our colleagues and staff of the Department of Humanities, York University; the Department of Sociology and the Library, Maynooth University; and the Study of Religions Department, University College Cork.

Our special thanks go to Cynthia Read and Hannah Campeanu at Oxford University Press, to Tharani Ramachandran and her team at Newgen, and to Eric Rayman of Miller Korzenik Sommers Rayman.

Funding for the research in this book has included an Irish Research Council Advanced Collaborative Research Project Grant; a Canadian SSHRC Insight Development Grant; a Dhammakaya International Society of the UK grant; a Robert H. N. Ho Foundation/ACLS Fellowship; an IAHR/AAR Collaborative Research Grant; and conference and research support from University College Cork, Maynooth University, and York University, Toronto.

Our sincere apologies to anyone we've forgotten!

Abbreviations

BTS	Buddhist Tract Society
IOGT	International [before 1906 Independent] Order of Good Templars
IYMBA	International Young Men's Buddhist Association
SPB	Society for Promoting Buddhism
Ult.	Ultimo, last [month]
YMBA	Young Men's Buddhist Association
YMCA	Young Men's Christian Association
YWCA	Young Women's Christian Association

Introduction

A Courtroom in Rangoon

On Friday, January 20, 1911, two Irishmen, one saffron-robed and shaven-headed and the other black-robed and wearing an elaborate wig, faced each other in the heat of the Chief Court of Rangoon, in British-ruled Burma.[1] The figure in black was the Chief Court Judge, the Honourable Daniel Harold Ryan Twomey, forty-six years old, a native of Carrigtwohill, County Cork, and by 1911 one of Burma's best-known judges, with a reputation for severity.

Looking up at Twomey from the dock was the "Irish Buddhist" U Dhammaloka, whose original name—as far as the court knew—was William Colvin (shown in Figure I.1). In truth, no one in the packed courtroom, apart from Dhammaloka himself, knew his pre-monastic name, reported elsewhere as Larry O'Rourke and Laurence Carroll, among others, nor his age, which contemporaries estimated at anything between the late thirties and mid-fifties.[2] Alongside Dhammaloka were his legal representatives—the dashing figure of the celebrated nationalist lawyer U Chit Hlaing (Figure I.2) and his learned colleague, Mr. Harvey.

Whether either Twomey or Dhammaloka was in the least impressed by the other's ritual garb is doubtful. Twomey was used to having Buddhist monks before him in court, whether for family property disputes or criminal charges, while Dhammaloka, as a temperance campaigner and Buddhist renunciant, probably regarded himself not only as Twomey's moral superior but also as a fellow upholder of the law, having brought to justice corrupt officials who might otherwise have escaped the courts. According to a correspondent in Calcutta who had known him since 1903,

> Dhammaloka was, indeed, a terror to evil-doers, and many have been the sensational exposures that he has been instrumental in effecting. . . . He took a keen pride in his work, and often would walk the streets in the dead of night or in the early morning in order to obtain some particular information which would enable him to bring some wrong-doer to task. . . . During a visit paid by Dhammaloka, while in Singapore, the writer casually mentioned that a

The Irish Buddhist. Alicia Turner, Laurence Cox, and Brian Bocking, Oxford University Press (2020)
© Alicia Turner, Laurence Cox and Brian Bocking.
DOI: 10.1093/oso/9780190073084.001.0001

RKV. U. DHUMLOKA.
(An Irish Buddhist Priest.)

Figure I.1. A Celebrity Preacher: Photograph of U Dhammaloka taken in 1901–2, sent in 1907 to the Calcutta illustrated magazine *The Empress*, with the comment that "he is much stouter now and apparently in the best of health."
National Library of India.

Figure I.2. Dhammaloka's defender: U Chit Hlaing, UK-trained barrister and future Burmese nationalist who led Dhammaloka's defense at the 1911 appeal hearing in Rangoon.
Wikimedia Commons/Public Domain.

municipal officer residing in the vicinity appeared to be living beyond his means. "He must be a scoundrel," burst forth Dhammaloka, "and he must be living on the proceeds of blackmail. I shall give him my attention." Nothing more was said, and within a fortnight the writer was astonished to read a lengthy report in the local papers of a charge of receiving bribes brought against the municipal officer concerned, in the Police Court.[3]

Judge Daniel Twomey, born near the great harbor city of Cork, educated at St. Stanislaus Jesuit school in Tullamore and a graduate of University College London, began his career in Burma in 1882 as a government officer in the Indian Civil Service, retrained as a lawyer by 1895, and worked his way to a senior judicial position. In Burma, Twomey liked to appear tough. According to future Burmese president U Ba U, Twomey used to say to his junior officers:

What do you think of me? Look at my name. It is Twomey. *Two* (pronounced *tu*) means "hammer" [in Burmese], *mey* (pronounced *mee*) means "fire." My name is thus a combination of hammer and fire. True to my name I will first smash you up with a hammer and then scorch you with fire if you don't do your work properly.[4]

Despite his reputation as a colonial "diehard," the Catholic Twomey was sensitive to non-Christian religious values and appreciated Buddhism's role as the main-stay of Burmese society. Indeed, in an influential 1904 paper he had set down a proposal for British colonial recognition of Buddhist monastic authority.[5] However, the case he was about to hear in the packed courtroom had little to do with Buddhism as traditionally known in Burma. Dhammaloka, being both white and a Buddhist monk, was a rarity. As a European Buddhist monk who specialized in publicly challenging Christian missionaries and thereby defying European colonial hierarchies, he was unique. Under the Indian Penal Code, as local district magistrate Ernest Neufville Drury had ruled two months earlier, Dhammaloka's preaching constituted seditious libel and could be prevented by law.

Burma was, in those days, governed from the Indian capital, Calcutta, under laws designed in London for British India. In Drury's judgment, Dhammaloka's anti-missionary diatribes fell under Section 153A of the Indian Penal Code, which "provides for the punishment of any person who by words spoken or written, promotes or attempts to promote feelings of enmity or hatred between different classes of His Majesty's subjects"—meaning, in this case, between Christians and Buddhists.[6] This and similar "preventive" acts such as the Indian Press Act were not, of course, applied to the frequent European (including missionary) attacks on Asian religions, nor to racist commentary in the colonial press, any more than the use of troops to conquer new territories and put down uprisings was seen as criminal. The laws were directed at "native" anti-colonial agitators who might threaten the imperial order. As the Moulmein correspondent for the *United Burma* newspaper put it,

Hundreds of Christians have preached and published blasphemous books, pamphlets and leaflets about non-Christian religions, but in all these years no-one has yet been arrested or bound over. It is a crying injustice to close the mouth of anti-Christian preachers, when these highlight the seamy sides of the Christian religion, while the Christian preachers can both preach and write the most abominable nonsense against our religion.[7]

After his brief hearing in November 1910, Drury concluded that Dhammaloka had mounted a scurrilous attack on the Christian religion delivered, through interpreters, to large Burmese audiences in the port city of Moulmein. He ordered him to be bound over for a year against two sureties (bonds) of 1,000 rupees each for good behavior (or, as the accused later put it, "not agitate against the preachers of the bleeding lamb").[8] The funds were presumably provided by Dhammaloka's lay supporters.[9] Dhammaloka disagreed with the ruling, but rather than risk his supporters' money and his own freedom by resuming his preaching, he had asked for a "criminal revision" of the order; in effect appealing against it. This was the case now to be heard in the Chief Court of Rangoon by his fellow countryman, Judge Twomey.

The Bible, the Bottle, and the Gatling Gun

The court came to order. U Chit Hlaing, speaking on behalf of Dhammaloka, opened by arguing that Dhammaloka as a European subject was entitled to a full trial by jury.[10] This was dismissed by Mr. Rutledge, for the Crown, who argued that Drury's judgment had been the result of an "inquiry," not a full trial. Drury, as a European (i.e., white) British subject and a magistrate, could legitimately hold an inquiry against another European British subject, Dhammaloka.

Rutledge then came to the heart of the matter. What had Dhammaloka actually said? Witnesses to Dhammaloka's sermons now read their statements out in court. Over the course of three public meetings, Dhammaloka had reportedly declared that:

> The American Missionary Baptists are the biggest blackguards that ever existed. . . . If any Christian minister comes to you, you should repeat what I have told you. . . . Christian ministers [are] addicted to immorality and go about each with a Bible, a bottle of whisky and a knife.

Similar statements certainly appear regularly in Dhammaloka's sermons, more precisely as a three-part critique of the missionary (the Bible), the problems of alcohol (the bottle), and the British military presence (the Gatling gun).[11] This critique formed the core of his political program. He allegedly went on:

> Burmese Christians should return to Buddhism. . . . The Christian missionary has come to Burma to convert the people to Christianity and secondly to destroy the customs of the people, to destroy everything that has been in Burma for 2,000 years.[12]

In Burma, as in British-ruled Ireland, there were limits to how far the colonial power could be seen to repress local religion. However, given the British empire's ideological links with missionary Christianity, Dhammaloka's overt condemnation of the Bible could be readily understood by all concerned as an implicit critique of the colonial power—direct attacks on which could, of course, be treated as treason. Elsewhere he had argued that "Burmese people used never to drink alcohol . . . [the] customs of Christian countries arrived together, so there are now people who smoke opium and whatnot,"[13] while in a previous run-in with the colonial justice system, he was accused of saying that the British "had taken Burma from the Burmans and now desired to trample on their religion" and had had to deny this.[14] The witness testimony from Moulmein reported even fiercer rhetoric by Dhammaloka, identifying Christianity as a devilish threat:

> [Under] the Inquisition thousands of men, women and children were killed every month and hundreds and thousands of young girls taken by the priests for immoral purposes. . . . Nine million women were put to death on accusation of witchcraft by the Christian Church. . . . Christianity is to-day the same devil as it was 2,000 years ago, but at present its power has gone, its wings having been clipped by science.[15]

These and similar comments reflected not traditional Buddhist teachings but the writings of contemporary Western freethinkers (atheists), with whom Dhammaloka maintained a lively correspondence and from whom he drew his arguments; indeed, his thriving Buddhist Tract Society devoted itself largely to republishing atheist texts useful for defeating missionaries in public arguments.[16]

Chit Hlaing responded that, as a Buddhist monk, Dhammaloka did not at all intend to incite hatred, merely to deter Burmese Buddhists from becoming Christians and to induce Burmese Christian converts to return to Buddhism. Moreover, all of these statements, however provocative they might sound, were taken by Dhammaloka from various books—they were already public knowledge.

Rutledge riposted that while Dhammaloka's language was highly *offensive* to Christians, this was not the issue. Nor did he need actually to have *generated* feelings of hatred or enmity toward Christians. Instead, Drury's order against Dhammaloka was correctly issued because he had deliberately *intended* to excite such feelings. The end, argued Rutledge, does not justify the means: the aim of restoring Christian converts to Buddhism may be entirely laudable, but it cannot be achieved by unlawful means, in this case *intending* to incite feelings of enmity between different classes of his Majesty's subjects.

Turning to Chit Hlaing's second claim, that anything Dhammaloka said was already in the public domain, Rutledge argued that a statement may be harmless when merely printed in an English book but seditious in a speech to a native audience.

Bringing Dhammaloka to Book?

Dhammaloka and his supporters had to wait until January 31, for Judge Twomey to deliver his judgement. We will discover Dhammaloka's fate in Chapter 10. Whatever the verdict, the authorities were eager to keep matters low-key. Charges such as those faced by Dhammaloka in 1910–11 entailed relatively simple magistrate- or judge-only "inquiries," with penalties meant to restrict the defendant without making a martyr of him. A spectacular jury trial would have benefited both Dhammaloka's and Chit Hlaing's radical careers. In this context Twomey no doubt wished to keep things sober, mundane, and manageable, a wise colonial tactic in Burma as much as in his and Dhammaloka's native Ireland.

In Burma, Dhammaloka had been a thorn in the colonial authorities' side since at least 1901, when he had avoided another trial for sedition and successfully challenged the authorities at the country's most revered Buddhist site: the Shwedagon pagoda (see Chapter 3). By 1910 the authorities—or the wider colonial establishment from which they could hardly be separated, missionaries included—may have decided that the time had come to do something about this turbulent monk.

Dhammaloka would claim correctly that this confrontation with the law only boosted his cause. In the longer term, the efforts, like his, that contemporaries collectively referred to as the Buddhist revival played a major role in the anticolonial movements that hastened the end of empire in Asia. In Burma, some of the approaches and issues which Dhammaloka pioneered would become central planks of nationalist agitation in the decades following his death and played an important part in ending British rule—while bequeathing future problems to Burma's many ethnic and religious minorities.

The Hunt for Dhammaloka: A Detective Story across Two Centuries

The courtroom drama in Rangoon was readily understood as symbolizing something much larger. As Dhammaloka's American freethinking sympathizers editorialized,

> The intruders, for it is thus the missionaries and their helpers are perceived, have money and office. The natives seem nowhere to have so little say as in their own land. If they were to persecute missionaries, Christian nations would at once fill their countries with soldiers to back them. But when the missionaries, having gained power, oppress the natives, these latter can secure no redress.[17]

While "the natives" (including not just Burmese but much of Rangoon's Indian and Chinese populations) undoubtedly saw Dhammaloka as being on their side, this particular confrontation is not as straightforward as it seems. Why—given that, as Dhammaloka himself noted, this trial gave him "a big boost in the eyes of the Burmese people" [18]—did he apparently go quiet and then, once the year's binding-over ran out, leave Burma for good? If the British were trying to avoid creating a martyr, would he not have benefited from becoming one?

Perhaps threats of more severe charges were conveyed privately, or some of the colonial officials whose activities Dhammaloka had denounced may have threatened other kinds of retaliation. Yet if we consider that Dhammaloka had at least five different aliases; that Colvin was almost certainly not his real name; that around a quarter of a century is missing from his biography before he became a monk; and that we have no secure record of him after 1913, we might also wonder whether there was more to it than this. Did he have a past that might come back to haunt him if he had been imprisoned?

Certainly, for us as researchers a century later, Dhammaloka has proved every bit as elusive, confusing, and hard to pin down as he was for colonial authorities in his own time. Utterly implausible stories about him turn out to be true, while apparently straightforward accounts wither under scrutiny. He disappears from one place and reappears in another, for no readily apparent reason. While we have far more material on his life than did any colonial official of the day, our interest and sympathy only helps us so far in getting beyond the defenses he used to protect himself.

In fact, it was by luck as much as anything that we managed to identify Dhammaloka as "a person of interest" at all. Alicia, researching the history of Buddhism in colonial Burma, had been struck by reference to an Irish monk in the colonial newspapers and set it aside for possible future exploration. Laurence, working on the history of Buddhism in Ireland, came across a mention of Dhammaloka in the *Blue-Grass Blade*—a Kentucky freethinking journal whose founder was jailed twice for blasphemy—and initially assumed the editor had invented Dhammaloka as a convenient Buddhist "sock puppet" to serve his own rhetorical purposes, until he found an envelope from Dhammaloka's Buddhist Tract Society postmarked Rangoon (Figure I.3). Brian, who had just founded University College Cork's Study of Religions department, made the connection. While reviewing a book, he came across a footnote by Alexey Kirichenko referencing Alicia's Irish Buddhist monk.[19] He brought the three of us together and set us off on a ten-year journey together in belated pursuit of this fascinating character.

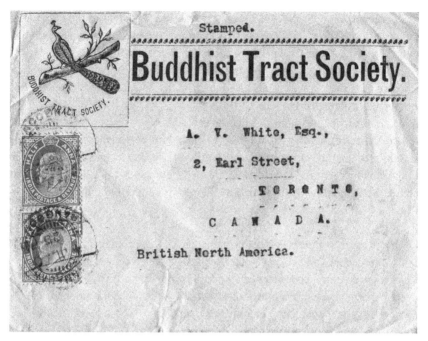

Figure I.3. From Burma to Canada: Buddhist Tract Society envelope from Rangoon, addressed to A. V. White in Toronto, 1907–10.
Authors' collection.

Who Was Dhammaloka?

We are reasonably certain that Dhammaloka was born in the Dublin area in the 1850s, crossed the Atlantic to become a hobo (migrant worker) across the United States, and then worked his way across the Pacific to Japan as a sailor. He was already a self-educated radical when he took higher ordination as a Buddhist monk in Rangoon, Burma, in 1900, formalizing a rejection, perhaps many years in the making, of Christianity and of colonialism's racial boundaries. As a monk, he was a highly visible and provocative critic of Christian missionaries, active in the networks that were making Buddhism a global religion and repeatedly at the forefront of religiously charged confrontations with the colonial powers.

Dhammaloka was an effective and immensely popular organizer in Burma (Myanmar), Siam (Thailand), the Straits Settlements and Federated Malay States (today's Singapore and Malaysia), and Ceylon (Sri Lanka). He was active in India, Japan, Australia, and perhaps Cambodia and China, and a minor celebrity in the global media, as well as in Asian politics. His allies included leading Buddhist monks and laity in several countries, Chinese and Sinhalese diaspora merchants, members of the Tavoy minority in Burma and Siam, Indian migrant laborers, and "poor whites." During his spectacular Buddhist career spanning more than a dozen years, we can see encapsulated many of the struggles that shaped the period of high colonialism in Asia.

As an organizer and agitator, Dhammaloka cut a bombastic public figure, but in person his formation as a Buddhist monk and his personality present a more complicated picture of the man. On the Buddhist Vesak festival in 1902, the Canadian journalist and novelist Sarah Jeanette Duncan, writing as Mrs. Everard Cotes, met Dhammaloka in Rangoon. Along with a photograph (Figure 2.1 in Chapter 2), she gave us a remarkable pen-portrait:

> I had seen many priests of Buddha, poonghees . . . he would not, I thought, be like those. But he was curiously like them. His shaven head was as disconcertingly smooth, the sun had tanned his skin almost as dark as an olive. In his eyes, which were blue, sat the same look of withdrawal and of concentration, as if his spirit, intent upon inner examination, had turned its back upon the world. When he spoke or answered it looked over his shoulder. And all with the strangest Hibernian echo, not only in his voice, but on his long upper lip, in the way his eyes darkened when he smiled. . . .
>
> The mere spectacle of him was too dramatic, too absorbing—the wide gulf he had stepped across on the bridge of his yellow robe. It was as though I hailed him, with my questions, from the other side, as if he shouted to answer me, though his voice was soft.[20]

Yet, this was not the only image Dhammaloka conveyed. Another side of Dhammaloka is revealed in a Singapore newspaper's description in the following year:

> Like most Irishmen, he has a ready tongue, a vivacious manner, and wonderful powers of "blarney." He could charm the heart of an old wheelbarrow.[21]

The Wider Imperial Context

Some readers will be familiar with the history we have gestured at in the preceding pages; others may be completely lost, in place as well as time. One of the single most important historical facts of the twentieth century is this: in 1900, as still today, an absolute majority of the human race lived in Asia, but in 1900, most of Asia, like most of Africa and parts of Europe and the Caribbean, was colonized

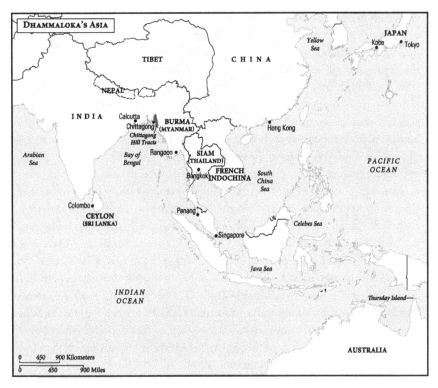

Map I.1. Dhammaloka's Asia.

by the major European powers, Britain above all. During the nineteenth century the European presence in Asia grew from highly localized to the governing power almost everywhere except Tibet, Siam, and Japan (see Map I.1). Yet by 1950 most of Asia was independent, following decades of nationalist, peasant, communist, and other movements.

This future of independent nation-states was hardly visible in 1900, when most of Europe comprised dynastic multiethnic states, such as the Ottoman, Romanov, and Hapsburg empires, the German empire with its Polish, Danish, and Alsatian fringes—or the United Kingdom of Great Britain and (all of) Ireland. Yet Asians could certainly imagine a future beyond colonialism, and did so in many different ways. Some sought a return to their own ancient empires; some imagined a future shaped by socialism or anarchism; some foresaw a happy world built by science and education alone.

In this context, religion became a mechanism for mobilization that could draw on long-standing discourses and affiliations for both local and pan-Asian movements and held out its own promises for a post-colonial world. The late nineteenth century saw a flurry of new Buddhist movements across Asia that elites and organizers dubbed a "Buddhist Revival." Their organizations ranged wildly, from locally based lay associations for study, moral reform, or, later, meditation, to ambitious pan-Asian visions of a "United Buddhist World." While the term "revival" evoked a sense of reinstating the Buddhism of a pristine past, the Buddhists involved were constantly and often consciously engaged in innovations. Many of these movements have been labeled as "modernist" by later scholars due to their engagement of new technological (print capitalism, etc.) and social formations (lay authority, increasing roles for women, and eventually the nation-state). Yet many of the Buddhists active at the time saw their goal not as transformation, but the preservation of the tradition in changing times.

This was a time of "great men" (and women) whose work would shape Buddhism for the next century. Some had international ambitions and scope, such as the indefatigable Sinhalese activist Anagarika Dharmapala and Japanese Buddhist representatives Shaku Soen and D. T. Suzuki, connected through the 1893 World's Parliament of Religions in Chicago.[22] But others had more local and traditional monastic agendas, such as Ledi Sayadaw in Burma who initiated a movement for Abhidhamma study and lay meditation, or Hikkaduve Sumangala, the most senior and committed monastic advocate of the Buddhist revival in Ceylon.[23] Moreover, while the history of this period is often written about elite figures and interaction with "the West," it was a time of key intra-Asian interactions and (mis)communications, such as the Japanese Buddhists traveling to India to "discover" the land of the Buddha.[24]

Buddhist intellectuals in the 1900s could successfully present Buddhism as a modern, "scientific" religion on a world stage. Buddhism was authentically Asian in origin and—in the vision presented by some Buddhist organizers—connected the whole continent, from Sri Lanka to Japan. In this context, Japanese sects invested in overseas missions as a sort of Buddhist soft power strategy, Indian intellectuals might oscillate between Buddhism and Marxism as alternative possibilities for an Asian modernity,[25] and the Buddhist monarch of independent Thailand could be proposed as the head of a new, combined, Buddhism including Ceylon and Burma. The movements and initiatives intersecting Dhammaloka's life thus stood at the origins of Buddhism's globalizing moment.

In later decades, as it became increasingly clear that the future lay with independent nation-states, Buddhism would often become an ethno-nationalist project, attractive to the educated urban elites who would take over after empire. Yet this was not the world of 1900. In the early years of the twentieth century covered by this book, native elites still mostly sought advancement through empire or, at most, local "Home Rule" autonomy, and Buddhist monks were mostly content to build their power locally. It was thus a diffuse network—of religious reformers, political radicals, creative writers, local patrons, organizational entrepreneurs, sophisticated scholars, and dislocated Westerners—who together constructed and contested the pan-Asian aspect of movements that they labeled as a revival of Buddhism, attempting to mold numerous local attempts at Buddhist organization-building into something far more ambitious. Dhammaloka inhabited these networks and helped to shape them. His story gives us an insight into this remarkable moment of Asian modernity, when imperialism's hold on the world was weakening but the future was far from clear.

At the center of global European-style imperialism was the British empire. Yet its dominant presence in Asia was shaped very differently in different places: in Ceylon, long a Dutch colony before it became British; in India, only slowly absorbed into empire up to the 1857 Rebellion, which brought more direct control and intervention; in the bustling trading ports of the Straits Settlements; in Tibet, opened by force in 1904; in the opium trade and Treaty ports of China (notably Hong Kong); in Kobe and the other ports of "Great Japan"; in the Australian settlement; and so on. Some places saw a lone diplomatic officer or only traders. Others had vast garrisons stationed, were dominated by officers, judges, and missionaries, or saw whole new extractive industries created, together with entire populations of "poor whites" and mixed "Eurasians."

The British empire also stretched across the sea to another colony, Ireland, where an educated, urban elite largely sought Home Rule rather than independence and brandished its own local religion, Roman Catholicism, as a tool of ethnic self-assertion. In decades to come, Irish independence, seized from under the shadow of Britain, would fascinate many Asian nationalists. In the years around 1900, however, alongside radicals like Dhammaloka we find many more Irish figures, like Judge Twomey, making a career or at least a living in Asia, from the heights of the Indian Civil Service to the ranks of the colonial army. Ireland— impoverished under union with Britain since 1800 and following the devastating famine of the 1840s—exported its landless and urban poor and its well-educated alike throughout the empire. Often more linguistically adept than their English counterparts, their familiarity with the daily complexities of colonial life served the Irish well in Asia.

Burma, where our story starts, had its own complexities. Conquered in three separate wars between 1824 and 1885 and now a province of British India, it had been a multiethnic empire comprising a Burman core and a wide range of subordinate ethnicities, from "hill tribes" to once-major kingdoms like the Mon and Arakanese. A centralizing Burman Buddhist order was flanked by new reformist sects within the sangha, by sangha groups associated with minority identities, such as Dhammaloka's own Tavoy monastery in Rangoon, and by other religions. The Chinese diaspora, British (including Irish) colonists and sailors, and Indian merchants and laborers all added to this picture. The historic inland capital Mandalay, conquered in 1885, contrasted with the port of Rangoon, seized thirty years earlier and now a key multiethnic node in the booming colonial export of rice, teak, rubies, oil, and other resources shipped by rail, river, and sea.

In Burma, as elsewhere in the empire, the vast majority, whether in the forests, the paddy fields, or the docks, suffered poverty and exploitation and also experienced rapid change—expropriation, the birth and collapse of industries and towns, the reshaping of daily life in a thousand ways—not only through colonialism, technology, and capitalism, but also through local people's own intensive organizing in many different forms, particularly religious. Perched on top of all was a relatively small, geographically concentrated, colonial establishment—with courts and prisons, police, and military at its disposal and the memory of a bloody counterinsurgency campaign, only concluded in the late 1880s. With this coercive power came a sharp racial divide and complex genderings, in which "natives" and "English" were treated as radically distinct, with very different roles, privileges and power.

Why Dhammaloka?

At this point we might ask, "why should we be interested in Dhammaloka?" Why not just dismiss his activities as marginal, as many of his contemporaries did? Or, as one reader asked us, why should we care about yet another white man in Asia?

We can answer by noting the complex ways in which class, race, religion, and nation combined to connect personal identity, cultural boundaries, and imperial power in the colonial heyday, and how Dhammaloka's boundary-crossing threatened an order far more fragile than it may have seemed. In his person—white, Irish, working class, Buddhist, freethinking, teetotal, and deeply anticolonial, he defied the myths that undergirded the colonial project—myths of racial and cultural difference and the "civilizing" mission. Moreover, while histories of colonialism and anti-colonial nationalism have overwhelmingly focused on middle-class and educated elites, Dhammaloka's story allows us to see *plebeian* cosmopolitan interactions across Asia—not least networks among Asian Buddhists—that facilitated both the operation of colonialism and resistance to it. Finally, his life compels us to reconsider the history of Buddhism in the West—revealing not just early failures in founding sangha lineages of Europeans, but looking well beyond the interests of middle-class and intellectual European Buddhists.

In earlier centuries, before the main political colonial intervention in the nineteenth century, European traders operated as one among other ethnic trading communities vying for prominence in the lucrative and cosmopolitan ports of the Bay of Bengal. Like other traders, they intermarried and created lives in Asia. In this era not only wealthy European traders and adventurers came to Asia, but also large numbers of plebeian Europeans, especially sailors and soldiers. With British dominance in India and Southeast Asia, the trade ports of Singapore and Penang generated some of the most diverse and cosmopolitan populations in the world—mingling Chinese, Arab, Tamil, European, and Southeast Asian populations.

The mid-nineteenth century saw these indirect trading-based interventions give way to direct rule in most of South and Southeast Asia, changing the British approach to the politics of colonial rule in important ways. An Orientalist policy, which had emphasized indigenous language, text, and law, shifted to the Utilitarian liberal model of the "civilizing mission" as a justification for conquest. This brought greater interventions in the daily lives of colonial populations, with distinctions of race and religion increasingly sharpened in teaching Indians and Burmese the ways of civilized modernity. The colonial administration encouraged English education and European dress among Asians, while Europeans were now penalized for adopting native clothing and manners. These interventions into the lives of the colonized were paralleled by efforts to police the behavior of poor whites in Asia, including Sailor's Homes, laws against European vagrancy, and policies against intermarriage.[26]

The new emphasis on racial divisions was intended to bolster the solidarity of Europeans and to induce native respect and deference. The conduct of "poor whites" and Europeans "going native" undercut this. Although Empire celebrated its civil servants, officers, capitalists, professionals, missionaries, and philanthropists,[27] it needed its ordinary soldiers and sailors, barmaids, tally clerks, and minor officials, and created the unemployed or destitute, the bankrupt, and alcoholics. Mixed-race children, and the children of Europeans who could not afford to send them "home" for education (thus slipping down the hierarchy), added to the difficulties of sustaining "whites" as a race apart.

Poor whites' "beachcombing" and "loafing" (casual labor and idleness) undermined the elevated status which colonial elites sought to associate with whiteness, as did dressing like natives. Indigent whites filled the new workhouses and jails as they drank, stole, idled, dissembled, and otherwise brought "the European race" into disrepute. "Going native," in both the cultural and sexual senses this phrase implied, was a source of horrified fascination for the higher classes. Even today, academic studies focus almost entirely on elite responses to those who "went native," rather than on the lives of the many poor whites who actually *did* go native.[28]

Going Native

A European Buddhist monk in 1900 was a paradigm of "going native." Not only did Dhammaloka dress in local clothes when many middle-class Asians were donning European dress, he went barefoot (a marker of subordinate racial and religious status), and practiced poverty and begging, epitomizing everything that industrious Victorian Europeans were supposed to shun. Of course, he also breached the fundamental Christian/heathen religious boundary that justified empire (and intensive missionary fundraising) back home. And the ritual submission—noted in colonial accounts of ordination ceremonies—of a white man to an Asian religious hierarchy provided a dangerous reversal of the expected colonial order of things.

The opening of the Suez Canal in 1869 and the arrival of new technologies— railroads, steamships, and telegraphs—not only expanded colonial interventions in Asian lives, it created insatiable demands for labor. Sunil Amrith has documented the massive migration of South Indian Tamils across the Bay of Bengal to Ceylon, Burma, Singapore, and Malaya to provide labor for the colonies and plantations, mirrored by the westward migration of Hokkien and Cantonese Chinese workers and traders to the same areas.[29] Internal migration in India, Burma, and Malaya brought people from the countryside to colonial port cities and new areas of agricultural production.

What is often missed in this story is a major movement, from the 1850s to the 1870s, of working-class European (including Euro-American) men to British colonial Asia. These were soldiers, sailors, railway workers, and so on—who mostly remained in Asia after their discharge. Nearly half the European population of India was made up of such "poor whites."[30] Inter-racial and inter-religious interaction were inescapable in the daily lives of the migrant poor and working classes, especially in the port cities. Together, waves of labor migrants, Chinese, Indian, and European—laborers, carpenters, petty traders, dock workers, and sailors— constructed the colonial port cities of Asia, produced its goods, and moved them across the seas. They built not just the physical networks that undergirded empire, but also the personal, social, and cultural networks of interactions that made all this activity possible. While the "white" status of European working- class migrants brought them certain privileges in the colonial hierarchies, plebeian whites had far greater daily interactions with Asian workers than the elites who commanded their labor.

The ideological apparatus of empire—with its myths of strict racial, colonial, ethnic, and religious divisions—was only ever a thin veneer over the pluralist and cosmopolitan interactions taking place at the height of British colonialism.[31] While the European elite tended its myth of superiority and separateness, poor whites, much more integrated into the multiethnic operations of the colonial engine-room, were correspondingly less likely to respect the practices of division. Colonialism in reality ran on interactions and interconnections between different ethnic and religious groups. Thus, Dhammaloka's story is not just the story of an unusual European monk, but reveals the hugely varied interactions among people of different ethnic, religious, and class backgrounds. These networks, interactions, and solidarities also belie the narratives of inviolable ethnic, religious, and national identities that have come to dominate in the post-colonial period.

Moreover, Dhammaloka's story lets us see the fragility of the British empire and the extent of anti-imperial organizing around the world in the early twentieth century. After the 1857 Rebellion in India, the British empire in Asia faced substantial contradictions as subaltern classes drove struggles for national independence in the global South and for democracy, welfare states, or state socialism in the global North. It was not just Dhammaloka's status as white and Buddhist: his *Irishness*, too, was problematic for colonial officials. Much of the army in India and Burma, from privates to officers, was Irish, and mostly Catholic.[32] Their loyalty to an imperial British Anglican elite was a source of well-founded anxiety. "Back home" in Ireland, the imperial center had been threatened by Fenians (the conspiratorial and insurrectionary Irish Republican Brotherhood), the resurgence of organized Catholicism, the boycotts and other direct action of the 1879–82 Land War that led to the dis-possession of the landholding aristocracy, and now Irish Home Rule nation-alism. Since the 1845–1849 Great Famine, Ireland had been exporting labor power along with cattle on the hoof; yet with people came ideas. Irish radicals were to be found at the heart of British and American socialism and trade un-ionism, while their more conservative, but equally nationalist, counterparts were "becoming white" and taking over the police departments and city halls of New York, Boston, and Chicago, and were visible in Singapore, Rangoon, and Calcutta.[33]

In the extensive fictional literature on *imagined* "going native," religious conversion to an Asian tradition plays a major role. Two of the best-known colonial novels show Irish or part-Irish men with military links becoming Buddhists: Rudyard Kipling's *Kim* (1900) and Bithia Croker's *The Road to Mandalay* (1917).[34] Both authors knew the Irish in the Indian Army well. Whether or not their Irish Buddhists were directly inspired by Dhammaloka (which is not impossible), both authors—and huge numbers of readers across the world—found the idea strangely attractive. The combination of "poor whites," "going native," and "Irish Buddhists" provoked a mixture of unease and fascina-tion in Britain and Ireland, as among whites in Asia.

Meanwhile, from the Asian perspective, a variety of Asian groups were not only comfortable with Dhammaloka as a poor white gone native, but, recog-nizing the strategic value of his challenge to the colonial boundaries of race and religion, readily included him within their networks and strategies. Thus when we study the unusual figure of Dhammaloka, his conflicts and complexities, we are studying a challenge to some of the core power relationships of the period of high imperialism.

They Seek Him Here, They Seek Him There...

It is testament to Dhammaloka's genius for combining self-publicity with avoiding self-incrimination that, after nearly a decade of work, we are still unsure of his real name or date of birth, and the circumstances of his death remain a mystery. As we shall see in Chapter 1, working-class people in Dhammaloka's time could evade surveillance far more easily than we might suppose. Much of today's armory of fingerprints, photographs, and so on was constructed precisely to deal with the difficulties of tracking the Victorian-era poor, while travel documents and national borders were nowhere near as effective as they are today.

Transnational history, too, has its own challenges. Just as Dhammaloka, moving from one country to another, needed a linguistic connection, a network of contacts, and an understanding of how Buddhism worked locally and how it connected to the wider world of globalizing Buddhism, so too our research has involved an extensive network, at times rivaling the international Buddhist organizations that Dhammaloka moved through or invented. We have called on colleagues working in or on at least a dozen countries for advice, translations, sources, and contacts. In the true spirit of academic *dana* (generosity), they have not held back.

Historical and Buddhist studies expertise is traditionally national in focus for good reason: so much knowledge and linguistic skill is needed to understand even a single context, not least mastery of the relevant archives. It would have been impossible in practice, before the advent of widespread digitization, to track a single person across all these different contexts to the extent we have done, especially when his names are reported in so many different forms. In addition to traditional research methods, this project has deployed new approaches to the use of digital methodologies in tracking Buddhist movements from Ceylon to Japan.

Most of the sources we have used to track Dhammaloka are newspapers in English, Burmese, and Japanese, along with tracts, pamphlets, and journals from Buddhist associations. Many were published in Asia, but Dhammaloka's reputation also spread far and wide—from a German atheist journal to a Mormon newspaper from Utah. The nature of newspaper publishing in Asia at this time shaped the nature of the research as well. This was a time of booming newspaper circulations and the proliferation of multiple newspapers in each city. A city like Rangoon in 1900 had multiple papers in Burmese, English, Chinese, and Indian languages, serving different constituencies. The English-language papers should not be understood to represent a homogenous European colonial voice, however. Different papers represented gradations of class and rank, with Burmese, Chinese, and Indian intellectuals and merchants frequently conversing in middle- and lower-level English papers. The elite voice of the *Rangoon Gazette* reproduced the interests of colonial officials and the richest Europeans, but most in the middling ranks of colonial service, commerce, and education found the *Times of Burma* or the *Burma Echo* much more in tune with their sensibilities.

Proliferating newspapers did not mean an equivalent increase in paid reporters. Many newspapers relied on "correspondents"—readers in smaller towns or further ports who wrote columns anonymously in exchange for merely seeing their ideas in print—often reflecting their own interpretation of local events. While telegraphic wire services were available to the more elite papers, journalistic standards were much less concerned with originality than today: they often reprinted *verbatim* the previous day's news reported in papers from other places, with or without attribution. Thus while the newspapers from smaller colonial towns or in minority Asian languages have often been lost to history, their reporting has often been preserved for those who read the more metropolitan newspapers carefully. In this context, it is not surprising that Dhammaloka became closely acquainted with newspaper editors in his quest to gain support for his Buddhist projects, serving as a correspondent on his travels either in his own name or through an alias.

What gets preserved or digitized today is as socially selective a process as what got printed in early twentieth-century Asia. The largest English-language papers from India and Singapore, as well as the books, journals, and missionary reports now in US and European libraries, are easily available. Copies of smaller religious and political periodicals and tracts, however, have vanished as the world has changed; through wars, the fall of empires, and the coming and going of dictatorships. Material in colonial languages (particularly English and French) is more likely to be digitized than that in dominant local languages (like Burmese or Sinhala), while minority-language texts are even less likely to be preserved or digitized. Within a predominantly English-language corpus, it is still the voices of Dhammaloka's white opponents—the colonial establishment and the missionary press—which are best recorded, followed by those of the elite (urban, educated, Anglophone) nationalist groups who would take over these states in the 1940s.

Finally, source criticism—understanding *who* is writing this, *why*, and *for whom*—is a significant challenge, particularly when a news clipping is discovered out of context. Like witness statements, such material about a hugely controversial figure can never be taken at face value. Social movements challenge official "common sense" and are often misrepresented in turn. It would, after all, be surprising if many of the gossipy local correspondents for the colonial press were familiar with the language, debates, or symbolism animating the worlds of pan-Asian Buddhist organizers, poor whites, or ethnic diasporas. Moreover, the casual racism of the sources conveys not just the racism of the time, but the multiple sets of divisions that Dhammaloka overcame. Even as they depict him bridging worlds between Asian ethnicities, two of our key sources report Dhammaloka's speech in "stage Irish," a stereotypical and condescending depiction of Irishness common in the period. We have changed quotations from these sources into standard English because they were frankly unreadable in the original, but we also note the ways in which the racism of even sympathetic sources colors the image of Dhammaloka that we can access.

For example, American author Harry Franck in his 1910 *A Vagabond Journey Around the World* has Dhammaloka saying "Well, 'twas on the Acme thot I picked oop with a blessed ould sea dog of the name of Blodgett, and we shipped out of Frisco fer Japan. Blodgett, poor b'y, died on the vi'age, and after payin' off I wint on alone, fitchin' oop at last in Rhangoon."[35]

We have rendered this and all comparable examples in standard English. In this case: "Well, it was on the *Acme* that I picked up with a blessed old sea-dog of the name of Blodgett, and we shipped out of Frisco for Japan. Blodgett, poor boy, died on the voyage, and after paying off I went on alone, fetching up at last in Rangoon."

For nearly a decade, the three of us have been piecing together the evidence for Dhammaloka's life, from the first apparently unconnected snippets to what has become a flood of data as digitization has increased. At times, a single source has given us a lead that opened up events in a whole country, or across a year, enabling us to fill in the blanks. In doing this, our picture of Dhammaloka has filled out, as has our understanding of the different ways his opponents responded to him, how different Asian organizations and networks engaged with him, and what the hobo on the road—or the supporter in the crowd—said and did when they met him.

Yet many, many things remain uncertain, open to discussion. To take just one example: for the first draft of this book we translated a Swedish-language anarchist publication from Minnesota, containing clippings Dhammaloka had sent to the freethinking *Truth-Seeker* newspaper in New York about his hearing before Judge Twomey in Rangoon. Those pieces showed us that *United Burma* was not, as we had believed, a single pamphlet, but a significant political periodical of the day, allied to Dhammaloka. Because of its politics—on the radical wing of Indian nationalism, but based in Burma, then a province of India—it was of interest neither to the librarians of the later Indian state nor to those of the Burmese, since these are now typically represented as separate national struggles. We have not located any archive for *United Burma*, despite the prominence of its editor, a close associate of Gandhi. It is not so much that the victors always write history; rather, the victors preserve the voices they approve of and the ones that serve their story.

Buddhist Studies and Dharma Bums

Anxieties provoked by "going native" would resurface in postwar America, at the foundation of Buddhist studies as a separate academic discipline. Western studies of Buddhism through the nineteenth and twentieth centuries had been dominated by gentleman scholars studying Buddhist texts. But as Donald Lopez has shown, many of the founding postwar generation of US Buddhologists had been "journeyers to the East."[36] An interest in Buddhism was strongly associated with peace during the period of US warfare in Asia from the mid-1950s to the 1970s, with the hippie trail, and before that with the Beats; Jack Kerouac's novel *The Dharma Bums*, for example, fictionalized the real-life Gary Snyder.[37] This was not the best image for a serious new academic discipline, and Buddhist studies has struggled with the pull between gentleman scholar and dharma bum in telling its own history.

Dhammaloka was self-taught rather than a scholar, and no gentleman; in fact, he was uncomfortably similar to Gary Snyder. Both had been sailors and hoboes, had radical politics, were hostile to imperialism abroad, and were unusually close to "natives" in their personal lives. Dhammaloka's focus on temperance, ethics, freethought, and countering the civilizational threat of missionary Christianity did not fit well with the modern Western Buddhist reader's ideal of a *bhikkhu* (the widely used Pali term for a Buddhist monk) as a serene contemplative. The pallor of the saint could be discerned far more readily in another European ordained as a Buddhist monk in this period, Ananda Metteyya (Allan Bennett)—and he brought his understanding of Buddhism back to London, rather than remaining in Asia.

Hence, in Buddhist studies histories, Ananda Metteyya became "the first" Western Buddhist monk and Dhammaloka was forgotten. This was despite the Singapore *Straits Times* report in 1904 of "an Irishman, who was stated to be the first white man to enter the Buddhist brotherhood, and who was entitled the Lord Abbot Right Reverend U. Dhammaloka" ordaining another European at his Buddhist mission in Singapore.[38] This account, published four years before Ananda Metteyya arrived in London, reappeared in 1923 in the best-known history of Singapore and again in 1976 in Heinrich DuMoulin's widely read *Buddhism in the Modern World*—its significance studiously ignored.[39] Researching Dhammaloka, then, helps us put our finger on some strategic problems both in the racial power relationships of imperial Asia and in how Buddhist history has been represented in Western contexts.

In tracing Dhammaloka's life, this book uncovers relationships of transnational solidarity across race and class within the globalizing moment of Buddhist mobilization at the turn of the twentieth century, as well as between Western radicals and Asian anti-colonial movements. With Thomas Tweed,

we can consider the meanings that religion comes to carry in the highly mo-
bile worlds of globalizing Buddhism in this period.[40] As with Leela Gandhi's
Affective Communities, Dhammaloka's life enables us to see how cultural,
personal, and religious transformation cut across the colonial attempt to
"modernize" Asia according to a Western template.[41] It also brings an often-
overlooked dimension of social class to these questions. The imperial world
was organized by race and class; in Asia, as in Ireland, the varied relationships
between the struggles of social subalterns (workers, peasants, women, minority ethnic groups) and the struggles of race and nation in this period shaped
long subsequent histories.

What is more, once we began looking, we discovered there were many
more "lost" eccentric, radical, disreputable, obscure, or subversive early global
Buddhist figures to be found. Dhammaloka takes center stage only because—
for a non-elite figure—he is unusually well documented. We have unearthed
accounts of his conversations and public talks, newspaper writings, texts he edited for publication, and commentary from contemporary critics and friends
alike. As mentioned, only digitization has made it possible to recover such a
substantial part of his history, incidentally demonstrating that, at the time,
Dhammaloka was anything but obscure. Like other "forgotten" early Western
Buddhists such as Charles Pfoundes or Salvatore Cioffi, he was very well known
in his day.[42]

Historians of religions are rightly wary of reproducing the "origin myths" of
present-day traditions as if they were history. Yet in the case of modern global
Buddhism there remains a strong tendency to project back into the past only
what is of interest to the present. Buddhist history is still being written by the
"winners," and sometimes historical "facts" turn out to be no more than venerable fictions. Many things, perhaps, are missed thereby, but one of the most
important is failure. Buddhists of the decades around 1900, whether Asian
reformers or Western converts, often had grandiose plans, most of which naturally came to nothing.

Yet if we are to understand in depth both how Westerners converted to
Buddhism in the earliest phase of Western Buddhism in the late nineteenth
and early twentieth centuries and—equally interestingly—why more did not,
despite Buddhism's widespread cultural resonance at the time, the study of
failure, in the short or long term, becomes fundamental.[43] Rather than reproducing a narrative in which the *Zeitgeist*, or the simple availability of Buddhist
texts, or the unique personal qualities of a particular figure, "explain" such
processes of globalizing Buddhism, we can begin to ask more systematically
why some attempts at dissemination and conversion undertaken in often vo-
latile and fast-changing colonial environments were successful, while others
were not.

Politics in the Long Term

The post-1945 transition of Asian countries into independent nation-states was one of the largest historical changes of the twentieth century, casting long shadows on the present. In 1901, colonial elites responded to Dhammaloka with anxious sneers, but twenty years later, Burmese nationalists were using methods he had pioneered, around issues he had highlighted, in a strategy of "Buddhism against empire." Within thirty-five years of Dhammaloka's own disappearance, Britain's empire in Asia had virtually vanished.

While some of what he thought, said, and did at the time later became common sense, there were important differences. Dhammaloka himself would be erased not only in the history of *Western* Buddhism but also in *Burmese* narratives of the early anti-colonial struggle, because that narrative soon became nationalist, lauding the ethno-religious supremacy of Burmese Buddhists within the state of Burma. That narrative had no place for an Irish Buddhist—nor for his Tavoyan, Indian, Chinese, Siamese, Sinhalese, Singaporean, or Japanese friends from multiple religious backgrounds.

At the other end of the British empire, in Ireland, early resistance to British rule (partly inspired, like many of Dhammaloka's activities, by the republican humanist Tom Paine) was ultimately replaced by ethno-nationalist organizing, resulting in a partitioned and sectarian modern Ireland. Perhaps such modern ethno-religious nationalisms were an inevitable outcome of the intertwining of empire, religion, and ethnicity. Maybe an effective anti-colonial movement had to take shape within the structures bequeathed by colonialism. Yet the relationships of cosmopolitan solidarity with Asian anti-colonial movements—exemplified in Dhammaloka's story—suggest that these outcomes were not the only possibilities. Other, more multicultural, polyglot—and humane—futures were imagined and, to some extent, attempted.

Religious fundamentalism and ethnic supremacism were not inevitable within post-colonial Buddhism. Part of the value of identifying hidden pasts is to stress the possibility of other presents. In the 1900s, a zealous and opinionated Irish atheist and temperance campaigner could be embraced by traditional Burmese Buddhists and cooperate with multiple ethnic minorities across Southeast Asia and modernizing Buddhists in Japan with no sense of incongruity. The current shape of Asian national polities and sanghas—in Asia and in the Asian diaspora—is not written in stone. It was a different world when a Buddhist in Burma could write to a Kentucky atheist about their shared celebration of Paine:

> There were sold in Burma over 10,000 copies of the "Age of Reason" last year, as well as some copies of the "Rights of Man." . . . You will convey the greetings of ten millions of Buddhists of this province to your Association on the occasion

of the great celebration of that grand Hero of Freethought. . . . it is time that we should show the bigots and the ministers of every church that Thomas Paine was the real friend of man—in fact, we can call him a Humanitarian of the loftiest type.[44]

The radical cosmopolitanism that Dhammaloka expresses here grew out of his multiple connections spanning many countries and contexts: the worlds of American hoboes and freethinking sailors, Shan opium barons and Sinhalese gem merchants, rural Burmese devotees and Indian railway policemen, Japanese Buddhist missionaries and ethnic minorities in Bangkok. Dhammaloka's extraordinary life defied conventional boundaries between colonizer and colonized, enacting a politics of direct relationships across divides, and stressing common humanity against brute power and racial hierarchy.

Dhammaloka's life is thus a window into the relationships at the heart of empire, a glimpse into alternative possibilities of the struggle against colonialism. It is a way of thinking about the meaning of "Buddhism" at the start of its modern globalization. It is also, of course, a remarkable tale told by an extraordinary storyteller who was able to cross the world—and challenge power—on the strength of his wits alone.

1

Dhammaloka before Dhammaloka

Before 1900

Dhammaloka had an extraordinary life, even by the standards of his contemporaries. And he made good use of his adventures—including, on occasion, adding in some he had not himself experienced. Reading through the various accounts of his earlier life—all dating from after his ordination in 1900—we are presented with a bewildering variety of tales: had he been a pearl-diver, a Catholic priest, a mining engineer, a migrant worker, a sailor, a Salvation Army exhorter—or perhaps many of these?

Who was Dhammaloka? It has been a ten-year detective project trying to track his past through many different kinds of records. To misquote E. P. Thompson, if it was hard to identify someone who wanted to hide his past a hundred years ago, it will be even harder to identify him today.[1] Harald Fischer-Tiné, studying poor whites in Asia during the colonial period, writes,

> In spite of the recently increasing sensibility towards this topic, the existing literature is still very fragmentary and . . . the white "underdogs" of colonial India still can be ranked among the "people without history". . . . Apart from a few scattered nuggets in the notes of ex-convicts or workhouse-inmates, most of the sources were mediated, altered or censored by colonial authorities. . . . Thus a good deal of the analysis had to rely on the "reading against the grain" of official reports and elite writings.[2]

Fortunately, we now have quite a bit of what Dhammaloka said and wrote himself. An adult learner, he became a celebrity preacher, a publisher, a frequent newspaper correspondent, and a subject of media comment. Thus we have a substantial body of sources documenting his life once he became a very public figure as a monk after 1900. However, his pre-1900 past remains obscure, and we can only make various kinds of identification with different levels of probability.

The Irish Buddhist. Alicia Turner, Laurence Cox, and Brian Bocking, Oxford University Press (2020)
© Alicia Turner, Laurence Cox and Brian Bocking.
DOI: 10.1093/oso/9780190073084.001.0001

Tracing a Life through Unreliable Accounts

The question of Dhammaloka's identity prior to his conversion excited much curiosity among both critics and friends, especially in the early years after 1900. Several sketchy accounts of his early life were published by supporters, journalists, and missionaries. Most reflect what Dhammaloka said about himself, while others claim to reveal a hidden past. None can be taken as completely reliable. What we have are fragments and assertions, suggestions, observations, and asides, all to be taken with a pinch of salt unless proved otherwise. Unfortunately, no one who claimed to know Dhammaloka's premonastic identity appears to have known him personally before 1900. The only witness who could (and did) provide convincing details was Dhammaloka himself.

We might seem to be on fairly firm ground when we ask what Dhammaloka told others, because he was a dedicated self-publicist who very often used the narrative of his own life to make a point. What better than a firsthand account? However, Dhammaloka gave contradictory accounts to different people, and this of course casts doubt on everything he said. His description of how he became a Buddhist well before 1900 and then rose through the Buddhist ranks, for example, constitutes a kind of "auto-hagiography"—a pious tale of a saint's life told, somewhat unusually, by the "saint" himself. One report even suggested a Celtic Buddhist nativity; in 1902, an art collector who encountered Dhammaloka in Tokyo passed on the intriguing (and highly improbable) news that Dhammaloka's parents had themselves been Buddhists, "members of a little Buddhist church in Ireland."[3]

We found eight extended versions of Dhammaloka's early life and a few seemingly reliable snippets of information from other sources, like an aside from an Irish newspaper editor in Singapore. However, comparison shows that a number of these accounts are dependent on each other, so that we are going back to a handful of separate reports from friends or acquaintances. The most detailed account of Dhammaloka's early life comes from a young American college graduate, Harry Franck, who in 1904–5 circled the globe as a penniless beachcomber, recounting his travels in a 1910 bestseller entitled *A Vagabond Journey around the World*. Franck spent many hours with Dhammaloka when traveling from India to Burma in 1905 and he devotes several pages to the story of "Damalaku's" earlier life. In July 1911, the *Atlanta Constitution* and the *San Francisco Examiner* simultaneously published a sensational double-page spread entitled "Solved! The Riddle of 'Dama Laku, the Wise One,' the Buddhist Abbot of Rangoon—Once an American Tramp."[4] This repeats Franck's 1910 *Vagabond Journey* account but adds extra details, suggesting that Franck had been interviewed for the piece. The Dublin *Sunday Independent* of August 6, 1911, and subsequently other newspapers in different parts of the world, soon reprinted elements of the story.

A second pair of accounts of Dhammaloka's early life, occasioned by news reaching India of his death in Melbourne, is represented by an obituary in the Calcutta *Englishman* of April 11, 1912, "From Catholic Priest to Buddhist Monk," written by a resident of India who had known Dhammaloka for at least a decade (that is, after Dhammaloka became a monk). Some of its content reached the United Kingdom. A subsequent obituary in the *American Theosophist* magazine of September 1913 draws on both *Vagabond Journey* and some of this 1912 account, adding further information of its own.[5]

Finally, we have the two earliest detailed accounts, both from women. In December 1901, the Canadian journalist and author Sara Jeanette Duncan, writing as Mrs. Everard Cotes, interviewed Dhammaloka in Rangoon for *Harper's Monthly Magazine*.[6] Cotes's article includes one of only two known photographs of Dhammaloka.[7] And in 1906, Gertrude Adams Fisher published *A Woman Alone in the Heart of Japan*, with a section entitled "An Irish Buddhist," reporting two encounters with Dhammaloka in Tokyo in October 1902.[8]

Piecing together Dhammaloka's biography before 1900 from these various sources has proven particularly challenging, necessitating research that goes well beyond these specific accounts into broader historical and cultural contexts. By most accounts, Dhammaloka's life before ordination spanned four decades and at least three continents. Our research required understanding historical events and popular movements in Ireland, England, the United States, Japan, India, Australia, and Southeast Asia, and social forces ranging from the development of railroads and intercontinental shipping to hobo culture in the United States and poor white beachcombers in Asia. Laurence Cox, together with research assistants Mihirini Sirisena and Rachel Pisani, pursued a year-long research project looking in the United States and Ceylon for, among other things, traces of the man who would become Dhammaloka.[9] We have supplemented the sources mentioned earlier with research into social history and details from administrative and shipping records of the period, to produce a composite of the possible lives Dhammaloka may have led.

This chapter presents a story that weaves the aspects we can document with some certainty into the stories recounted by possibly unreliable narrators. While flagging those aspects that are very unlikely to be true or are certainly fabricated, we include them where they may give the reader a fuller understanding. Our aim is to present a picture of the most probable version of Dhammaloka's altogether very improbable life.

An Irish Sailor and Hobo

Interviewing Dhammaloka by the banks of the Ganges in 1905, Harry Franck received a compelling account of Dhammaloka's life, from his birth in Dublin via a migrant worker's life in the United States to sailing between San Francisco and Japan, and finishing up a relatively well-paid "tally-man" checking cargo in Rangoon before he turned to Buddhism.[10] However, Dhammaloka also backed up this life-story with a thick book of newspaper clippings covering "ten years" (more likely five) of Dhammaloka's travel and missionary work as a monk, including a riveting account of his trip to Tibet. This journey later caused a splash in the Western press, but we now know that it never took place, which casts doubt on everything else Dhammaloka told Franck about his pre-monastic life.[11] Of course, if Dhammaloka had spent decades traveling in America and Asia before 1900, he would have heard dozens of life-stories both similar and dissimilar to his own and amassed a wealth of useful details of names, places, and events which he could reuse with different audiences to answer questions about his own past life.

The time and place of Dhammaloka's birth remain open questions. Franck recounts, "He was born in Dublin in the early [eighteen] fifties."[12] Birthdates, either specified or derived from his supposed age, vary from 1850 to 1870. Most people, including Dhammaloka himself, felt he looked young for his age. In 1912 the Burma Railway Police described him as "about 42," while his obituarist friend in Calcutta in the same year thought him "quite 55 years old, if not more."[13]

Dhammaloka was universally known as "the Irish Buddhist" (and as late as 1907 was described by the *Rangoon Times* as "the only Irish Hpoongyi in the world"), but ethnic identifications can be misleading. In Burmese he was sometimes referred to as *Ingale* [lit. "English"] but this was a generic Burmese term for white Europeans; Dhammaloka sometimes used "English Buddhist" for himself.[14] If he was occasionally described as "American" or "Australian," this did not imply that he was *born* in either country, simply that he had spent time there.

A far more solid indication is that the Killarney-born editor of the Singapore *Straits Times*, Edward Alexander Morphy, after falling out with Dhammaloka, identified him as "of Booterstown, or Blackrock, or whatever adjacent spot in the County of Dublin he may hail from."[15] Morphy, Irish himself, is a trustworthy witness to the fact that Dhammaloka was Irish, and, as all sources agree, from Dublin.[16] The locations fit with a Laurence Carroll (one of Dhammaloka's aliases), born in Booterstown Avenue, Blackrock, which is indeed "county Dublin" rather than the city. Other Irish people recognized his Irishness—from the Cork-born Judge Twomey to an Irish policeman who paid Dhammaloka's fare for him in Penang, taking him for a Catholic priest.[17]

As for Dhammaloka's original name, we have half a dozen possible candidates (all may, of course, be false), which we have pursued through birth, education, census, shipping, and other records.[18] The idea of concealing or reinventing one's identity was in the air in the late nineteenth century, a period of extensive migration and social mobility. This is when criminal authorities, in colonial Asia as elsewhere, introduced "mugshots" (where the subject would "mug," or grimace, in order to make the photograph as unrecognizable as possible) and fingerprints, to fix an individual's identity.[19] European passports did not come into use until the 1914–18 war.

When pressed for his pre-monastic name, Dhammaloka most often replied "William Colvin." This name features regularly—but only after 1900—in newspaper, missionary, and court reports written by people who lived in Rangoon or Singapore and knew Dhammaloka. An early (1901) Rangoon newspaper story talks of "U Dhammaloka the English Hpongyi (Mr. Colvin)."[20] Morphy, the newspaper editor, in 1905 fulminated in Singapore against "William or Bill Colvin," and the sedition case presided over by Judge Twomey in 1911 was that of "U Dhammaloka *alias* Colvin vs. Emperor."[21]

In an Irish context, "William Colvin" is immediately recognizable as a Protestant name,[22] a few notches on the social scale above an Irish Catholic of the same class (so a more useful alias when dealing with officialdom). Other William Colvins include Presbyterian ministers and judges. One report even had him as Calvin.[23] There is, however, no suitable William Colvin in the many pre-1900 records we have searched to match our man, nor does this name "fit" in terms of how other Irish people saw him, in terms of his political leanings or his limited formal education.

"Larry (i.e., Laurence or Lawrence) O'Rourke" is attested only once, by Harry Franck, whose engaging account of his meeting with Dhammaloka in 1905 includes the following exchange:

> "Aye, but we'd have to know your name," I suggested.
> "As I was going to tell you, it's U (oo) Damalaku."
> "Don't sound Irish," I remarked.
> "No, indeed," laughed the priest, "that's my Buddhist name. The old one was Larry O'Rourke."[24]

As a consequence, "Larry O'Rourke" was the name repeated in dozens of newspapers around the globe after Franck's *A Vagabond Journey Around the World* hit the bookshops in 1910–11.

Laurence O'Rourke (and variants Lawrence and Larry) is a far more plausible name for a working-class Dublin Catholic, but again there are no good candidates to be found in the extant census, birth, and marriage records. Larry O'Rourke's is a well-known Dublin pub and the name had appeared in novels such as Thomas Aldrich's *A Rivermouth Romance* (1873) and songs such as *A Bull's Not a He-cow* (discussing a shillelagh fighter), so it is perhaps an obvious alias. Or Franck may simply have misheard or misremembered the name, as he did with "Damalaku." Three further names also appear only fleetingly: "Collins" in a Catholic newspaper in Kansas (perhaps a misprint, yielding a more Catholic name than Colvin), "Collin" in a Ceylon report, and "Mr. Kelly" in an unreliably recorded anecdote told by the tea magnate Sir Thomas Lipton.[25]

Another Laurence, "Laurence Carroll," turns up quite late in Dhammaloka's career, in the *American Theosophist*.[26] This is our best candidate, appearing in a number of independent records prior to 1900 which could match our man. Laurence Carroll's is thus the story we will tell in this chapter.[27] If we are wrong, the story of emigration and hobo life is nevertheless close enough to experiences Dhammaloka must surely have shared for the story to be told as his.[28]

Laurence Carroll's Early Years

Laurence Carroll, then, was baptized on May 6, 1856, in Booterstown's Catholic church, South Dublin. Laurence was the youngest of six children of Timothy Carroll and Catherine Hogan.[29] Their father Timothy was fifty-two when his first child arrived; his wife Catherine was much younger, born sometime before 1830.[30] By 1861, Timothy was running a provision shop on Booterstown Avenue, the family having moved into no. 85 Booterstown Avenue some time between 1850 and 1856.[31] Their small house stood just in front of the Catholic church, built by Viscount Fitzwilliam in 1812–13 for his Catholic tenants, but deliberately unobtrusive to avoid offending Protestants. Laurence literally grew up in the shadow of the church.

Booterstown would have been an interesting place for a child growing up in the 1850s and 1860s. Booterstown Avenue today shows many different periods of building, from old cottage or farmhouse to middle-class suburban home; there was clearly a lively social mix. Ireland's first railway stopped at the end of the avenue, which slopes down toward the sea. The railway connected Dublin to the newish (1820s) mail and ferry port at Kingstown (today's Dún Laoghaire), but the distance could easily be walked in an hour. Dublin's docks, with their ships from near and far, were also within easy reach.

In the 1860s and 1870s, Asia—even Buddhism—was in the air in Ireland.[32] Irish people were part and parcel of the British empire at all levels, from eminent administrators, diplomats, and missionaries to ordinary soldiers and sailors. Newspapers and museums, popular literature, and exhibitions made reference to Buddhism, and still more to "India," loosely conceived. If Asia was exciting and mysterious, it was not terrifyingly distant.

While mid-nineteenth-century Ireland had little space for overt opposition to religion, there was plenty of scope for anticlericalism, particularly in politically radical families.[33] The anti-colonial and republican United Irishmen had been active up to 1798 in southeast Dublin, including Booterstown and Blackrock. From 1816, laborers poured into the area as the harbor was being built, giving rise to strikes and riots.[34] In the later nineteenth century the Fenians were active in nearby Kingstown. The teenage Carroll could quite readily have found a political language for his feelings.

And Carroll perhaps had cause for discontent. The school registers have Laurence present at age six in 1863, and leaving at thirteen or fourteen because "employed at home," presumably in the shop.[35] With two elder brothers, Laurence's chances of inheritance (and thus of being able to support a family) were minimal. For him, as for millions like him, emigration was almost inevitable: roughly one in two Irish people emigrated at the time, giving rise to vast Irish diasporas abroad and strong connections to back home.[36]

The *Atlanta Constitution*'s account of Dhammaloka's early life has him emigrating in two stages; from Dublin to Liverpool and then

> Some time after experiencing the pangs of hunger in the streets of Liverpool the youth secured a berth in the pantry of a packet steamer, and in due time found himself in New York.[37]

Liverpool in the 1870s was an increasingly Irish city, with riots pitting Catholic Irish against Protestant English. The Irish community was desperately poor, and it is unsurprising that Laurence could not find work. Experience in his father's "provision store" could qualify him for similar work aboard ship, and this US immigration record offers corroboration:

> Laurence Carroll, arrival date: 13 May 1872; birth: 1853; place of origin: Ireland; port of departure: Liverpool, England; port of arrival: New York.[38]

This adds another few years to his age, common enough in the period.

Hoboing across the United States

Arriving in New York, one of tens of thousands of poor Irish emigrants arriving every year, Laurence did not face an easy time.[39] The *Atlanta Constitution*'s account has him working on coastal ships for some time. Being Irish, and having worked his passage from Liverpool, probably helped Laurence get a sailing job out of New York, a city notoriously structured on ethnic lines:

Several trips along our coast in a schooner taught young Larry that the life of a seaman on a wind-jammer was very hard. He gave up the sea for the time being and decided to see what the interior of the country looked like.[40]

After the schooner, Harry Franck's account has Dhammaloka move from sailing to the newer transport technology: the railroad.

He beat his way on a freight train to Buffalo. Soon tiring of a dish-washing position in that city he boarded a "side-door Pullman" for Chicago. After a few weeks in the Windy City during which he was unable to find work and was obliged to beg for food, he continued on westward.[41]

A "side-door Pullman" means illegally jumping a freight train—our first introduction to the hobo life to come. Laurence's time in Chicago, a city still being rebuilt after the fire of 1871, probably coincided with the city's first bread riots in 1873.[42] Most workers had been let go that year and a young, unconnected Irishman with no relevant skills would move on quickly.

More than thirty years later, on the banks of the Ganges, Dhammaloka's tales of his hobo days carried conviction with two expert witnesses—Clarence Rice of Chicago and Harry Franck.

He was not long in convincing both Rice and me that he knew the secrets of the "blind baggage" and the ways of railroad "bulls." More than once he growled out the name of some junction where we, too, had been ditched, and told of running the police gauntlet in cities that rank even to-day as "bad towns."[43]

It was a common shared experience. Hoboes were everywhere: a "tramp army" traveled the United States during the demobilization and recession following the end of the Civil War in 1865. Contemporary observers thought that "the methods of the bivouac"—learning how to travel fast, find temporary shelter, forage for food, and "trust tomorrow to take care of tomorrow"—had been generalized by the military lifestyle in the Civil War.[44] Todd DePastino argues that while working men of many backgrounds became tramps, new immigrants "followed their own distinct patterns of group migration," leading by the later nineteenth century to an increasing identification between Irishness and tramping.[45] Tramping could also express a form of resistance to wage labor and social control:[46]

Tramps stood at the center of a swirling vortex of concerns about the new corporate industrial order coming into being after the Civil War. Americans in these years saw the rise of large-scale manufacturing and mass production, the spread of railroads and continental markets, and the creation of strict work-place hierarchies based on a universal system of wage labor.[47]

From Chicago, Dhammaloka told Franck that he had briefly engaged in shepherding in Montana and was soon again on the move.

> By that time the young fellow had learned the ropes of "getting over the road." He knew how to "deck" passenger trains, to ride the rods and brake beams, and the mysteries of the "blind baggage" were as an open book to him.
>   Side by side with Chinese coolies he picked fruit in California, little thinking that day would come when thousands of Chinese Buddhists would gather in Singapore to do him honor upon his triumphant return from Japan.[48]

Franck was thunderstruck to discover that his and Dhammaloka's paths had crossed in California:

> "Two years after landing in the States," [said Dhammaloka] "I hit California and took a job trucking on a blessed fruit-boat in the Sacramento River—the Acme."
>   "What!" I gasped, "The Acme? I was truckman on her in 1902."
>   "Bless me eyes, were you now?" cried the Irishman. "'Tis a blessed small world."[49]

"Trucking" meant carrying. We have not found an *Acme* that Dhammaloka could have served on in the 1870s, but Franck must have worked on a later *Acme*, built in 1899 and dismantled in 1911.

Franck continues the tale:

> Then followed a residence of some months in San Francisco. A man of strong physique and blessed with brawny arms, O'Rourke found work on the docks. He admits that he drank as hard as he worked, and that on dozens of occasions his heavy fists made themselves felt along the "Barbary Coast."[50]

Unsurprisingly, we could find no records for an itinerant like Carroll (or Franck's "O'Rourke") in the inland United States. However, in 1874 two Lawrence O'Rourkes are listed in San Francisco: a gardener and a laborer, the latter living on Jessie Street, not far from the Pacific Mail's wharf for its Japan/China ships, and at one end of San Francisco's red light district, the Barbary Coast.[51] This O'Rourke was gone by 1875. If he was our Laurence Carroll under an alias, we know why; he had taken a ship for Japan.

A Trans-Pacific Sailor

The same pattern of drinking and fighting reappears as an explanation for "O'Rourke" leaving ship in Japan, at least in the racier *Atlanta Constitution* account:

> A captain of one of the Pacific Mail steamships took a fancy to the powerful young wanderer and offered him a berth as quarter-master.[52] Two round trips to the Orient followed, but on the first leg of the third trip O'Rourke found himself "on the beach" at Yokohama after a brawl which caused him to lose his steamer. Shipping out of Yokohama as a foremast hand on a Dutch tramp, he made his way to Singapore and ultimately drifted up to Rangoon.[53]

For his *Vagabond Journey* book, Franck had selected a more affecting dimension of the story.

> [I]t was on the Acme that I picked up with a blessed old sea-dog of the name of Blodgett and we shipped out of Frisco for Japan. Blodgett, poor boy, died on the voyage, and after paying off I went on alone, fetching up at last in Rangoon.[54]

If Laurence Carroll/O'Rourke left Ireland in the early 1870s, nearly three decades are unaccounted for before his 1900 higher ordination in Rangoon. A 1913 account in the *American Theosophist* speaks of Carroll encountering Col. Olcott's 1881 *Buddhist Catechism* in the United States and going to Asia for religious reasons:[55]

> He determined to seek further employment in a Buddhist country and crossed to Japan as a sailor before the mast. There he stayed but a short time, as Japanese Buddhism did not appeal to his ascetic mind.[56]

Interviewed in Japan in 1902, Dhammaloka claimed to have been a mining engineer in Australia, though we have found nothing to confirm this.[57] At any rate, he eventually ended up in Rangoon (Figure 1.1), seemingly now sober and earning a decent wage, and gradually turning Buddhist. The *Atlanta Constitution* writes:

> Offered a position at the chief seaport of Burma, he settled down to work as a tally clerk for a British timber concern. He had abandoned his old drinking habits and was drawing a good salary when an English pamphlet on Buddhism fell into his possession. Its contents fascinated him.[58]

Figure 1.1. A working port and hub of empire: Rangoon harbor, where Dhammaloka had a job as a tally-man checking cargo.
Photograph ca. 1900 by Felice Beato. © Collection of Gilles de Flogny.

But when did this gradual conversion take place? To Franck, Dhammaloka said,

> The English were not holding Burma then [implying a pre-1885 date]. . . . Up to the day of my confirmation I was drawing a hundred rupees a month. I quit my job.[59]

In 1902, journalist Sara Jeanette Duncan (Mrs. Everard Cotes) sought more details of Dhammaloka's past, before his arrival in Rangoon.

> Earlier he had been indicated by another [name], which implied, to those who knew it, an Irish diver employed in the pearl fisheries of Ceylon.[60]

When she asked him why he had become a monk, he said,

> It first came before me, as you may say, in Ceylon. I studied it a bit there, and then I came up here to Burma to one of these *kyaungs*, which is Burmese for monasteries, and the priests they took me in hand and learned me till I was ready to enter the priesthood myself.[61]

Other accounts, too, place Carroll in Ceylon before Burma. In the spring of 1905, a Dublin graduate and beachcomber John Askins in Colombo, Ceylon, told Harry Franck of an Irish friend who was a sincere Buddhist monk, and "currently in Nepal."[62] At the time, this could only have been Dhammaloka.[63] In a 1902 interview with the *Nipon* newspaper in Tokyo, he claimed extensive first-hand knowledge of Ceylon:

> I have heard that there is a plan in Japan to send migrants to Ceylon. I have travelled to most places in Ceylon, so I know the situation there well. Ceylon is certainly a beautiful country, but it is not a place to which you send emigrants. The productive areas are already occupied by people, and unoccupied areas facing the north are not productive. The people of Ceylon are poor, so Japanese people cannot go there and get hired.[64]

In the same interview, Dhammaloka revealed a good practical grasp of the issues facing a poor immigrant in Burma, with further asides on Siam, Australia, and America:

> Unlike, say, America, where an immigrant only serves others and simply gets paid or becomes a slave, Burma is the only country I know where, after several years of settlement, an immigrant can become independent, by staying there and even obtaining their own land.[65]

He went on to praise the higher wages and low cost of living in Burma, with positive comments too on housing, clothing, climate, and health, and warnings against tricksters and slave traffickers en route. He provided a detailed account of Burmese agriculture, industry, and trade from the worker's point of view: seasonality, migrant labor, gendered division of labor, and so on. Dhammaloka clearly had a good sense of the differences among Asian countries, from the viewpoint of a poor migrant.

Conversion to Buddhism and Ordination

The surviving accounts differ on how Dhammaloka came to Buddhism. Was he in his late twenties, or nearer forty-five, when he found his vocation? Most locate it after his arrival in Asia. The *Atlanta Constitution* says that he got serious about Buddhism while still working as a tally-man on the Rangoon docks:

> He then devoted his spare moments to the study of the sacred Pali language of the Buddhists of southern and eastern India [Ceylon and Burma]. The simple but beautiful story of Gautama Buddha appealed to O'Rourke.

The yellow-robed priests of Rangoon assisted him in his studies, and night by night he pondered over the sacred leaves of the Dhammapadra [*sic*] until he felt that he had indeed found the Noble Path.[66]

It might seem unusual for an Irishman to study in a Buddhist monastery but, as we shall see, the Tavoy monastery in Rangoon where Dhammaloka ordained was used to European beachcombers and their ways. The moment of conversion is represented thus in Franck's *Vagabond Journey*:

> When I was sure it was right I took orders among them, being the first blessed white man to turn Buddhist priest. . . . I gave every blessed thing I owned to a friend of mine, even to my socks. At the temple, an old priest made me a present of a strip of yellow cloth, but they tore it into three pieces to make it worthless, and then sewed the pieces together again for a robe, and I've worn it, or one like it, ever since. . . .
>
> When I took the robe, and that's twenty years and gone, I became a novice in the famous Tavoy monastery.

The timings, however, seem exaggerated. We know Dhammaloka took higher ordination in 1900, while the figure of twenty years given to Franck in 1905 would suggest 1885. It is just possible that Dhammaloka was ordained many years before 1900, disrobed temporarily, perhaps in order to travel somewhere, and in July 1900 was being *re-ordained*, but we have no sightings whatsoever of him before 1900, as a monk or otherwise, to confirm this.

An extended novitiate is easy enough to imagine, and could push his entry to the monastery back into the 1890s. However, speaking to Cotes in December 1901, Dhammaloka claimed to have been going on alms-rounds for just three years, which suggests a novitiate no earlier than 1898.[67] Dhammaloka was never one to downplay his claims, so we should probably take this reply seriously. Interviewed by the *Nipon* newspaper later in the same year, Dhammaloka said, "I have been in Burma for ten years, so I have been everywhere in those years," but when he goes on to describes his tours and organizing activities as a monk, they all belong in the period 1900–2.[68]

Our sketch of a late nineteenth-century Irish emigrant's life fits with the near-certainties of Dhammaloka's past (an Irish-born hobo and sailor). It shows us a young man traveling and living on his wits during an economic depression, picking up a small amount of land-based work without ever settling, and moving from a major eastern port (New York) to a major western one (San Francisco) and thence to Asia, which would become his home. The strong possibility is that Dhammaloka did not become a novice monk until at least 1898. If so, this raises some important questions: about timings, about his politics, and about ethnic frontiers.

Four Competing Chronologies

In Franck's account, young Larry's various sojourns in the United States are said to be brief: "Several trips along our coast in a schooner," "Soon tiring of a dishwashing position," "a few weeks," "until the wanderlust laid hold of him again," "working here and there," "he drifted to California."[69] All this fits with the relatively short period most migrant workers spent as hoboes:

> For most homeless wanderers, the road represented a brief stage of poverty, an episodic experience rather than a permanent condition. Almost 90 percent of those migrants who applied for public aid in New York State in 1874–75 had been on the road for less than one month. Fewer than 5 percent of police station lodgers surveyed in 1891–92 had been tramping for more than one year.[70]

And within three years of arriving in New York, it seems, Laurence was sailing between San Francisco and Japan, before he was either paid off or thrown off in Yokohama. The difficulty is that we have up to twenty-five years to account for before he appears as a fully ordained monk in Rangoon. What on earth was he doing all that time? We have come up with four plausible versions of his life-story in this period.

The first is that he remained a sailor for a quarter-century, traveling around the world. An early (1901) Burmese account says that having encountered Buddhist teachings, he went on "an investigating tour round the world," taking in "China, Japan, America (North and South), Europe, Africa, and finally Ceylon where he became a Buddhist soon after."[71] A sailor's life would fit with his known skills and the absence of records—not that we know his alias(es)—but begs the question of why he had so little to say about the experience. Can we really imagine this arch-raconteur having no interesting mariner's stories to tell after a quarter-century traveling the globe?

A second possibility is that these years were lost to drink. By the time of his ordination in 1900 he was a strong temperance advocate, probably already an active member of the International Order of Good Templars (IOGT).[72] Linking these facts with his own comments about his past suggests a recovered alcoholic. He could well have spent much of that quarter-century as a drunken hobo in the United States, or perhaps a drunken sailor in Asia. Perhaps he spent the 1890s in Burma getting sober, with the help of the IOGT or the Tavoy monastery. His evasiveness when asked his "real" name—as well as his silence about the years 1875–1900—could then be due to shame.

The United States or Asia?

A third possibility is a "short US, long Asian" career. But if he spent only a few years in America, what did he do in Asia? We have not come across other whites in Asia telling interesting (or discreditable) stories about Dhammaloka's past, as might be expected if he had lived somewhere where the white colonial population was relatively small—or if he had been part of a tight-knit group like the military, or (as some suggested) the Salvation Army. Everything we know about him suggests that he found it hard *not* to be noticed. He might, then, have been working on local tramp steamers around Asia, like the autobiographical hero of Conrad's *The Shadow-Line*; just one among the masses of anonymous "poor whites" in India—sailing, but not to anywhere very interesting.[73] He could have been in Ceylon for a long period. There were enough "poor whites" there for the future Dhammaloka not to have stood out. He later demonstrated strong ties to people originally from the Burmese seaport town of Tavoy; maybe he spent significant time there.

There are indications of a period in Australia. Dhammaloka said as much to the *Kobe Herald* on his arrival in Japan in August 1902, and told the *Nipon* newspaper in December 1902, and the *China Mail* in Hong Kong shortly afterward, that he was born Irish, had emigrated to Australia, worked there as a mining engineer and "explored Buddhistic literature, some fifteen years ago."[74] An experienced French diplomat in Bangkok, Charles Lemire, similarly pegged "Damalouka" as an Irish-born Australian.[75]

If he had been either a miner in Australia or a pearl diver in Ceylon, that could explain his reported connection with Thursday Island (Australia), a hub of the pearl industry with gold mining on the adjacent Horn Island.[76] In 1904 Dhammaloka, in Singapore, was reportedly planning a Buddhist missionary visit to Thursday Island. An advance notice sent to the local *Torres Straits Pilot* newspaper explained that he had been there before and, although a Buddhist priest, was a European, so the new "White Australia" policy would not prevent him from visiting the island.[77]

Franck, in his 1910 book, faithfully reported Dhammaloka's 1905 account of being ordained before 1885 and then spending fifteen years rising through the ranks in the Tavoy monastery before traveling as a "Buddhist bishop" to Tibet and most recently to Nepal. After his ordination, recounted Dhammaloka,

> I was made an elder, then the abbot of the monastery, then after fifteen years, the Bishop, as you would call it, of Rangoon. . . . It's the bishop's place to travel, and in these six years gone I've visited every blessed Buddhist kingdom in Asia, from Japan to Ceylon; and I was in Lhasa talking with the Dalai Lama long

before Younghusband would have dared to show his face there [i.e., before 1903–4]. There's not a Buddhist king nor prince that hasn't treated me like one of them, though they'd have cut the throats of any other European. I'm coming back now from three months with the prince of Nepal, teaching his priests, him giving me the ticket to Chittagong.[78]

The *Atlanta Constitution* version embellished Franck's account even further:

He was [after ordination] given travelling orders [within Burma] by his abbot, but unbeknown to himself was watched secretly to see whether he was as sincere in his beliefs as he professed to be. Larry O'Rourke, now named "Dama Laku," stood every test. He had mastered the Burmese and Tibetan dialects while undergoing his novitiate, and went from village to village on foot, teaching the gospel of Buddha, the Perfect One. He was created an elder. Then, in rapid succession, came his advancement to an abbacy and a bishopric. . . . As the devout Mohammedan must at some time during his life make the pilgrimage to Mecca, so must every Buddhist priest above the rank of abbot make the pilgrimage to Lhassa.[79]

Could *any* of this be true? We have found no evidence to support either the Tibet or Nepal trips, despite plenty of evidence that Dhammaloka during 1902–3 planned to go to Lhasa. He would have been entitled to the honorific "U" (arguably "elder") after five years as a fully ordained monk—but only in 1905, the year he spoke to Franck. In 1902, the *Kobe Herald* had him ordained "five years ago," around 1897, which could be his novice ordination or sheer invention.[80] There is no indication in any Burmese source that he was given the title of abbot, nor any title that could be translated as bishop. And while Burmese and Tibetan share a linguistic family, in this period there was little other connection between the two Buddhist traditions.

Nonetheless, some of the travels mentioned here *are* attested. By 1905 Dhammaloka had certainly traveled to Japan (whence he returned claiming the Japanese title "Lord High Abbot"), and he clearly knew Ceylon. "Every blessed Buddhist kingdom in Asia" is an only slightly exaggerated description of his travels, which, when Frank met him in 1905, had also included India, Burma, the Straits Settlements, the Federated Malay States, Siam, and China. Fantasy, then, but with more than a grain of truth—and perhaps the self-representation of a man who understood himself as part of a pan-Asian Buddhism, not simply the Burmese kind.

A fourth possible career trajectory involves a "long US, short Asian" chronology, offering the possibility of substantial past careers in the West, before Laurence arrived in Asia. Among the least credible claims made by different people about Dhammaloka's former career is that he had been a Catholic priest. We know enough about his educational level to be confident that he was no graduate of a clerical seminary. Cotes, likewise, in 1902, discerned in Dhammaloka's pattern of speech a certain refinement, but she knew it was not of the kind bestowed by education:

> his voice was soft and his speech illiterate. That was extraordinary, his ignorant manner of speaking, quite discounted and as it were, neutralised, by the refinement he had gathered somewhere—not in Dublin.[81]

Gertrude Adams Fisher, an American staying in Tokyo the following year, described "the Irish Buddhist" as an ex-priest—information that likely came from Dhammaloka himself. Three accounts (Indian, British, and American) of his life, written more than a decade later, concurred.[82] It seems to be a claim he made from time to time, perhaps to emphasize the distance he had traveled from Christianity to embrace Buddhism. Rather more plausibly, following Dhammaloka's 1900 ordination, local Christian missionaries suggested he had once been an "exhorter" in the Salvation Army, again in Australia.[83] This seems more in keeping with his boldness as a public speaker and intimate Bible knowledge. However, Dhammaloka's well-attested ability to quickly pinpoint passages in the Bible—particularly its most "immoral" and "offensive" passages—may simply have been part of his self-education as a militant atheist.

Far more pressing in considering a "long US, short Asian" chronology is, again, why he was silent about this period. This links with the questions of how and where he learned his political organizing skills and why he used aliases. As we shall see, the newly ordained Dhammaloka had limited writing skills but was a very effective public speaker, deft at using the media, able to set up organizations, willing to engage in direct action and use the courts for his purposes, inspirational before crowds of different ethnicities, and capable of attracting a remarkable range of generous supporters and funders. Skills of this kind are not simply picked off the shelf: they are earned through experience and practice, or through working with others who have mastered them. In other words, the best explanation available within a "long US" chronology is one that gives him an active political past in the United States that he kept quiet about once in Asia.

These four options are not, of course, mutually exclusive. We can readily imagine a young and politically active Laurence Carroll in the States migrating, willingly or not, to Asia under a different name, becoming a sailor who called at Thursday Island or was a worker there, having problems with the bottle, becoming a beachcomber and occasional pearl-diver in Ceylon and finally a tally-clerk in Burma, drying out and embracing temperance, being gradually drawn by propinquity to Burmese Buddhism, and finally taking novice ordination in the dying years of the nineteenth century—to emerge in July 1900 from the chrysalis of his obscured past as U Dhammaloka, "the Irish Buddhist."

Dhammaloka's Political Skills

We can say little with certainty about Dhammaloka's political formation. Laurence Cox and Rachel Pisani were unable to locate any concrete evidence of the pre-Buddhist Dhammaloka in any social movements in the United States, which at this time hosted several movements with links back to Ireland. Most obvious is the Fenianism of the Irish Republican Brotherhood, which saw risings, military responses, and repression in Ireland, England, and Canada in the 1860s.[84] After 1871, the Fenians were increasingly replaced in the United States by Clan na Gael ("Family of the Gaels"), which by the 1880s included labor and socialist tendencies.

A less formal tradition was that of Irish secret societies and factions.[85] Back in 1821, the building of Dublin's Kingstown harbor saw troops brought in to deal with striking quarrymen, some of them living in Booterstown and Blackrock, who brought their own traditions of effective clandestine organizing from the Wicklow hills.[86] The secret society tradition was transplanted to Liverpool and became the subject of a moral panic in the Pennsylvania coalfields in the 1870s. Real or not, the "Molly Maguires" came to stand for a particularly brutal phase in the development of the US labor movement, facing off against Pinkertons, private guards, and state forces and using various forms of clandestinity and violence in self-defense.[87]

In the United Kingdom and United States during the 1870s, a new wave of labor radicalism, socialism, and anarchism was gathering force. In the United States in the late 1860s, the 640,000-member National Labor Union was calling for an eight-hour day; from the 1870s the Knights of Labor reached even larger numbers of workers, collaborating with the Irish Land League and organizing US Irish workers on a non-sectarian basis.[88] American socialism and anarchism thrived among immigrant and migrant groups, not least hoboes, coming to a head around the 1886 execution of anarchists accused of the Haymarket bombing in Chicago.[89]

The 1877 countrywide general strike in the United States saw 100,000 workers in many different occupations put down their tools. More than a hundred people were killed in repression that took on the character of class warfare:

As corporations and state governments created new armed forces to meet growing civil unrest, workers themselves formed their own militias, drilling, marching, and parading under both republican and socialist banners. Posed before this smoldering background of violence, the tramp assumed a menacing profile. . . .

Tramps emerged from the ashes of 1877 as the primary scapegoats for the uprising. . . . By fingering tramps for blame, observers such as [Francis] Wayland explained away not only the strike's unusual levels of violence but also its extraordinary geographic breadth.[90]

If our Laurence, as an Irish hobo, was suspected of involvement in anti-state violence of these Fenian, secret society, radical labor, or left-wing kinds, he had good reason to hide his identity in later years.

While we have found no specific records to pinpoint Laurence's affiliations or activities, we can say that in his later writing and organizing Dhammaloka appears steeped in the radical culture of his day. This was a self-taught, largely working-class culture that was strongly internationalist, and combined an interest in socialist, anarchist, or nationalist politics with an openness to self-improvement, spiritualism, and theosophy, and issues such as feminism and birth control, vegetarianism and dietary reform, anti-colonialism and anti-imperialism.[91] As a monk, Dhammaloka confidently deployed much of the radicals' "repertoire of contention," including the mass meeting and the speaking tour, the founding of formal organizations and development of informal networks, the publication of "gray" literature (self-published leaflets, posters, anonymous tracts), use of polemic in the general media, tactics of what we might now call civil disobedience, and an openness to political trials.

Soapboxing, that is, outdoor public speaking, was a major pastime, and US hoboes were connected to a broad radical culture—in the mid-1870s this included sympathetic commentary from labor periodicals such as the *National Labor Tribune* and *Workingman's Advocate*.[92] Frank Higbie has aptly described hoboes as "unschooled but not uneducated." Working men could share cheap newspapers, pamphlets, and tracts, while social movements created spaces where workers could debate, whether in workhouses, union libraries, boxcars, bunkhouses, or on park benches.[93] All this paralleled the "Workers' University" of the British proletariat, whose effects were also felt in Asia.[94]

Nels Anderson's slightly later participant observation research into Chicago hobo life in the 1910s and 1920s, published in *The Hobo: The Sociology of the Homeless Man*, shed entirely new light on the world of the American hobo, particularly on hobo intellectual life.[95] While the details differed, much of what Anderson observed would have been recognizable in the last quarter of the nineteenth century. Anderson describes some hoboes' haunts as

the rendezvous of the thinker, the dreamer and the chronic agitator . . . the stronghold of the more or less vagabond poets, artists, writers, revolutionists of various types. . . .

Around the edges of the Square the curbstone orators gather their audiences. Religion, politics, science, the economic struggle—these are the principal themes of discussion in this outdoor forum. Often there are three or four audiences gathered at the same time in different parts of the park, each carrying on a different discussion.[96]

Anderson notes that hoboes passed on reading material to one another, devouring but not endorsing "the so-called 'capitalist' press" but alive to a wider milieu of radical publications.[97] In his period, books read included not just "sex stories," detective tales, and jokes, but radical novelist Jack London and pocket-sized editions on sociology, economics, politics, and history.[98] If Dhammaloka was able to challenge college-educated missionaries in debate, the chances are that he learned this skill from other self-confident working-class thinkers.

A Life among Men?

The interviews with Cotes and Fisher are among the few encounters with women in Dhammaloka's life after his ordination. Later we will meet Burmese Buddhist women as devotees and audience members, and a few other European women— his patron in Tokyo, Letitia Jephson, his Buddhist Tract Society contributor, Sophia Egoroff, and his fellow radical turned Indian Theosophical opponent, Annie Besant. We also encounter him campaigning against injustices to women; but other than Jephson and perhaps Egoroff, he never appears personally close to women. Some part of this was good Burmese monastic conduct; but it is likely that Dhammaloka was uncomfortable around women, and this may have colored his interviews.

In post-Famine Ireland, tenant farmers had rapidly moved from multiple to single inheritance of their tenancies, meaning that (with unchanged family sizes) most men and women would not inherit and thus (where access to land was the prerequisite for starting a family) were condemned to lifelong celibacy unless they emigrated. Marriage now came very late, even for first sons, and a Catholic "devotional revolution," with vast numbers becoming nuns, monks, and priests, helped to absorb some of the rest—who then took on the task of policing their siblings' sexuality. Irish Catholicism in this period thus became obsessively oriented toward sexual control.

Emigrant Irish men, too, often wound up in deeply single-sex environments, in the short or long term: laboring gangs, the British army, sailing, or Catholic religious orders. These reproduced a discomfort with women, and a premium on being at ease with other men. Dhammaloka's life of sailing, migrant labor, and Buddhist monasticism could fit into this pattern; but we cannot be certain.

Crossing Ethnic Boundaries

We are on safer ground when it comes to Dhammaloka's ethnic identifications, and how he seems so readily to have crossed the line between white colonizer and Asian colonized, by ordaining as a Buddhist monk. Ethnicity (for example, being recognizably "Irish") often operates as a means of social closure, meaning that it is seen as an unchangeable feature of a social group; a community may bond around shared ethnicity when everything else has fallen away. This is particularly true for migrants, for whom the "imagined community" of people from one's own ethnic group, landed in a strange place, makes it possible to build the relationships that give access to work, housing, political connections, and other types of mutual support. If by 1900 Dhammaloka could turn his back on all of this, and repudiate his white, European, Catholic Irish identity by changing his name, religion, dress, and way of life to join with fellow Asians, what does this say about his earlier identifications?

By his own account, the European/Asian racial frontier that Laurence so definitively crossed by ordaining as a Buddhist monk was only the latest in a long series of ethnic frontiers he had crossed, or at least seriously questioned. In colonial Burma, "Europeans" and "natives" were separated by dress, schooling, language, and marriage conventions intended to set up Europeans (i.e., whites) as a race apart. Alarmingly (in the eyes of the white establishment), these stratagems of division were constantly challenged by the behavior of "poor whites" who failed to dress correctly, to maintain respectability in areas such as sobriety, financial probity, or sexual morality, or to insist on their privileged status as Christians and so on—so that the Irish bhikkhu acted as a living incarnation of a series of ethnic anxieties.

If, immediately prior to becoming a monk, Laurence was a tally-clerk in Rangoon, checking goods coming off ships and into warehouses, he would have supervised "natives" closely and would have needed some basic Burmese or Hindustani. If he was earlier a quartermaster (responsible for a watch) on a mail ship plying between San Francisco and Yokohama, the young man would have been in close contact with the largely Chinese crew. The Pacific Mail line's San Francisco–Hong Kong–Yokohama run became the first regular steam service across the Pacific, carrying Chinese and Japanese immigrants to California. Quartermasters and other officers on these ships were white, while the crews were Chinese. As both quartermaster and later tally-man, Dhammaloka had a foreman-like role, requiring him to communicate across ethnic lines—in contrast with the classic land-based Irish "gang" of railway or construction workers, put together precisely on grounds of ethnicity.

Rising racism and anti-East Asian immigrant sentiment in the western United States targeted the Pacific Mail specifically. In July 1877, whites leaving an "anti-coolie club" and a union meeting broke into Chinese homes in San Francisco; the next night a number of Chinese people were murdered and there were clashes between rioters and police. On the third night, the lumber yard opposite the Pacific Mail's wharf was set on fire in hope of burning down the wharf, and the militia were called out.[99]

Working our way backward through Dhammaloka's own account, he had earlier worked with Chinese coolies transporting fruit in California. Sacramento had California's largest population of Chinese at the time. Chinese temples, often combining Buddhist, Confucian, and Daoist strands, sprang up across northern California from the 1850s onward.[100] If Dhammaloka had been drawn by a "Theosophist pamphlet" such as Olcott's *Buddhist Catechism*, extolling the merits of Buddhism as an Asian religion, that then had immediate practical implications for him, working alongside Chinese colleagues, especially given the frequent conflicts between white (often Irish) and Chinese workers.

Conflicts over labor were deeply racialized. The 1870 census lists 1,949 Chinese people in Montana Territory out of nearly 20,000;[101] the Central Pacific Railroad was largely built by Chinese labor. In the post–Civil War downturn, Chinese laborers became a scapegoat for rising unemployment.[102] In California especially, the emergent (white) labor movement overlapped with anti-Chinese agitation;[103] Irish drayman Denis Kearney's Workingman's Party ran under the slogan "The Chinese must go." In 1878 and 1882, the US Congress passed Chinese exclusion laws.

Going further back, the story Dhammaloka told Franck places him crossing the tense ethnic frontier between white colonizers and Native Americans in Montana in the period between Red Cloud's War (1866–68), which revolved around settler access to the gold fields, and the Great Sioux War (1876–77), famous for Custer's defeat at Little Bighorn, also in Montana.[104]

Before that again, we find Laurence as a hobo in the post–Civil War period, with Irish hoboes pitted against Blacks. DePastino observes that

> [t]he large number of Irish immigrants in America's tramp army suggests that the road itself may have served as a critical racial proving ground for poor white men. Notorious for their particularly virulent brand of white supremacy, Irish immigrants accounted for almost one-half of police station lodgers and vagrants.[105]
>
> For the Irish, preserving the road as a domain of white men was one of these key privileges, even if it confirmed among elites that the Irish were a race apart, sharing the same vagrant characteristics as African Americans.[106]

The Irish competed with Blacks for unskilled work, particularly in the period of high emigration from Ireland and the US South after the 1845-9 Irish Famine and the US Civil War.[107] Further back still, we find Carroll in a Liverpool that saw Catholic-Protestant street conflicts, and a Dublin shaped by related tensions.[108]

For a working man in this period, it was virtually impossible to avoid such conflicts. The Irish diaspora in the United States and elsewhere has been routinely thought of in terms of particular occupations (police, firemen), religious power (priests, nuns, Catholic-only schools), and racism (we Irish versus the rest); and there is much truth to all of this.[109] However, not all those born in Ireland chose (or choose) to identify in this way.

Rejecting Racialization

At some point in his repeated crossing of these ethnic frontiers, we have to imagine the future Dhammaloka ceasing to draw on Irishness, whiteness, or Christianity as a primary resource for solidarity, support, and work opportunities, refusing hostility to Protestants, Blacks, Native Americans, Chinese, or Asians, and becoming the figure we see in the 1900s—readily able to move from one country and culture to another, at home in several languages, abandoning the Catholic identity central to the Irish diaspora, and becoming a "friend of all the world." Thus he earnestly warns prospective Japanese emigrants to the United States in 1902 that "in recent years, if one goes to America or Australia, these and other countries have vehement movements to drive out immigration of Japanese laborers."[110]

Everything we know of Dhammaloka's later time as a monk suggests a broad vision of a shared humanity, coupled with an (Irish-flavored) hostility to imperial structures of racial power and cultural oppression. The far-flung network of allies, supporters, hosts, and patrons he nurtured clearly depended on his genuine friendliness and appreciation for individuals who, to most Irishmen at home or in the colonies, would have been the "Other." When Dhammaloka does come into the public eye in 1900, it is as an Irishman who has "gone native" in dress, religion, and behavior and has repudiated his supposed Irish ethnic Christianity. Somewhere along the line between the Liverpool docks, hoboing across the States, leaving ship in Yokohama, beachcombing through Asia, and finally turning Buddhist lies a complete disenchantment with ethno-religious identification; an inability or unwillingness to behave in ways that would signal loyalty to the ethnic "clan."

We might imagine Dhammaloka saying, with the anonymous white sailor who wrote in 1927 about "How I Became a Buddhist,"

> when away in the west with my ship, I feel as if I am away from home; and begin to feel bright and cheered again, as soon as I have passed Aden, and know

I am getting nearer again to the home of Buddhism, Ceylon, where I now have
among the Buddhists of the Island all the best, most real friends I have in this
world. For the people you happen to have been born among are not your real
friends unless they and you think alike.[111]

Dhammaloka's past life, before he became the Buddhist monk Dhammaloka,
remains a mystery. Comprising many good tales of varied degrees of believa-
bility, it is supported by contradictory details supplied by Dhammaloka himself
and by others. Nevertheless, this attempt to tell the story of the man before he
took the robes, imperfect though it may be, offers an important window into the
social and political worlds of white migrant men of Dhammaloka's kind in the
United States and Asia in the second half of the nineteenth century. Moreover,
the stories he told offer a portrait of a man whose traits in his earlier life are un-
mistakably reflected in the later monk. Dhammaloka was bold, adaptable, resourceful, and reflective. He was critical of the power structures around him, and
he built networks of solidarity across the boundaries of race and colonial status.

2

The Irish Buddhist Wins Burmese Hearts

1900–2

On Sunday, July 8, 1900, at 8:15 in the morning, Dhammaloka entered the *sima* (ordination ground) at the Kyaikmantan Kyo monastery in Rangoon, for a historic event.[1] He was already a novice, so he appeared shaven-headed and wearing monk's robes.[2] Dhammaloka's ordination was no ordinary ordination ritual. It was administered by more than twenty senior monks, four times the usual quorum of five. The ceremony entailed him reciting the *Kammavaca* ordination text in the Pali language. As a novice, Dhammaloka would have been expected to memorize this text, and to learn from his preceptor the rules and responsibilities of a fully ordained monk. The Burmese monastic establishment recognized and accordingly celebrated the significance of the ordination of a European. Of the nine monks who administered his recitation, eight were senior Burmese abbots (*sayadaw*), including U Vicitta, the Sayadaw of the Tavoy monastery in Rangoon, U Dhammaloka's base for the next decade (the photograph in figure 2.1 was taken in Rangoon). The chief officiant, the Myataung Sayadaw, was a particularly prominent figure, having published learned Pali treatises and negotiated with the British on behalf of the Buddhists of Lower Burma.[3]

The event was entirely orthodox, the same as for any fully ordained monk. However, this was no simple and quiet affair; it attracted a substantial audience. A further 100 monks were in attendance, and 200 laypeople came to see the auspicious ordination of a European into the Buddhist order. Afterward, there was a ceremony of donating umbrellas, fans, towels—and copies of a bilingual Burmese-English book on Buddhism—to all the monks, a means for the lay patron to make merit.

The wealthy sponsor who funded this lavish event and Dhammaloka's subsequent needs as a monk was not Burmese, but a Chinese businessman given the Burmese name Ko Ing Myaing. He was joined by other members of a Chinese Buddhist association, one of many lay Buddhist groups active in Rangoon. Thus the highly orthodox Burmese ordination of an Irishman was sponsored by Chinese Buddhists. Little wonder that Dhammaloka went on to be an advocate for multiethnic Buddhism.

The Irish Buddhist. Alicia Turner, Laurence Cox, and Brian Bocking, Oxford University Press (2020)
© Alicia Turner, Laurence Cox and Brian Bocking.
DOI: 10.1093/oso/9780190073084.001.0001

OO-DHAMMA-NANDA

Figure 2.1. Dhammaloka in late 1901 (a year after his ordination), misnamed "Oo-Dhamma-Nanda," in *Harper's Magazine*, October 1902.

Photo by Philip A. Klier, Rangoon. *Harper's Magazine*.

With this auspicious event, Dhammaloka would launch his illustrious career as a champion of Buddhism, and Burmese Buddhists, in Burma. He would become famous across the length and breadth of the British colony, drawing crowds of thousands of villagers and townspeople on his preaching tours and attracting the ire of Christian missionaries and British colonial officials, as reflected in the court case that opened this book. The ordination prefigured other aspects of his career as well. The multiethnic Asian solidarity displayed at his ordination—from orthodox Burmese monks to Chinese businessmen—would become characteristic of both his milieu and the connections he actively cultivated. Moreover, it seems clear that Dhammaloka was not the single author of this historic occasion: the presence of so many senior monks indicates that the Burmese sangha, too, saw the ordination of a European as a means to further their own projects and agenda in a period of instability and change.

Burma, today known officially as Myanmar, had come under colonial rule in stages over the previous seventy-five years, culminating in the fall of the Burmese monarchy in Mandalay in 1885. Two regions claimed by the Burmese had come under British rule in 1824: Arakan, in the west, was home to Buddhist and Muslim populations and polities that bordered the British territories of Bengal and Chittagong, while Tenasserim, in the southeast, was home to the port towns of Tavoy and Moulmein and linked by trading routes to the entrepôts of Malacca and Singapore to the south.[4] In 1852, these regions were brought together with the rest of the southern portion of the Burmese empire, to be ruled as part of British India—and Burma would remain a part of India until 1935.

Colonial Burma was a deeply multicultural society. In addition to the more than one hundred "indigenous" ethnic groups, the parts of Burma along the Bay of Bengal had long been host to a diverse population of traders and migrants, including South Indians, Bengalis, Punjabis, Hokkien and Cantonese Chinese, Malays, and those from much further afield, including Arabs and Europeans. This meant that the colonial cities Dhammaloka frequented were cosmopolitan and religiously plural places, filled with temples, mosques, and churches alongside Buddhist pagodas and monasteries. By Dhammaloka's time, Rangoon was home to more Indians and Chinese than Burmese inside the city limits. Multiethnic interactions would play a key role in Dhammaloka's career.

The period since 1885 had been felt as a moment of crisis and transition. In addition to the myriad material changes brought by British rule, many were concerned that the loss of a Buddhist king was a sign that Buddhism itself could soon be lost. In response, Buddhist laypeople across the country rallied themselves in associations to preserve Buddhism. It was in this moment of increasing Buddhist activity, labeled by locals as a revival, that Dhammaloka was ordained.

A Novice at the Tavoy Monastery in Rangoon

It is not clear how long Dhammaloka spent as a novice monk (*samanera*) prior to full ordination. Many years later, in 1909, Dhammaloka claimed that he became a novice because of missionary attacks on Buddhism in Rangoon, seemingly those happening around 1900.[5] However, in 1902, he offered a different account to a journalist in Japan, suggesting a long period spent in a monastery before his full ordination:

> I just wanted to study Buddhist doctrine, but I was not initially thinking of en-
> tering a monastery or anything like that. But when I went [to Burma], I was
> deeply moved by the really good conduct and purity of Burmese monks, so it
> occurred to me to enter a monastery and become a devout follower. Originally
> I did not intend to become a Buddhist monk, but as I gradually developed, be-
> came a monk, entered a monastery and tried the ascetic life of a high priest,
> because it was so genuinely pure and upright it reinforced my desire to become
> one myself, so I finally became a real monk.[6]

Dhammaloka's home, the Tavoy monastery, was part of Rangoon's Thayettaw Kyaung Taik monastic complex, which has a colorful history. Originally founded in a quiet grove of mango trees (*thayettaw*) on the outskirts of the pre-colonial city, when the British demolished the city to lay out the regimented grid of their new colonial capital, Thayettaw became home to all of the displaced Buddhist monasteries. By 1900 the complex had become a warren of more than fifty mon-asteries and their *zayats* (rest houses)—each with its own complicated history and regional affiliations. Connected by winding paths, the Thayettaw Kyaung Taik was the antithesis of the ordered colonial structure expanding all around it.

The Thayettaw monasteries and rest houses became places of refuge for sailors and travelers from throughout colonial Burma and beyond. The Tavoy monastery in particular became known as a place that would take in not just other monks and laypeople from the town of Tavoy, but travelers of all stripes, including beachcombers from well beyond Asia. Monasteries often provided shelter to migrants connected by a hometown, whether monks looking to learn in the capital or laypeople traveling for trade or advancement. In this way, they pro-vided a nexus for mobility. But the Tavoy monastery included in its remit many more than just those from the sailing port of Tavoy. The "vagabond traveler" Harry Franck describes arriving at the monastery to find "a burly negro, dressed in an old sweater of the White Star line," and another white American, this one ordained as a monk but with the marks of a long life as a merchant seaman.[7] The Tavoy monastery thus became a place for interactions across a range of racial and ethnic divides—welcoming constituencies from the large Chinese population in the immediately adjacent Chinatown and the nearby Indian neighborhoods, as well as those from much farther afield.

The welcoming attitude of the Tavoy monastery was in keeping with the Thayettaw complex in the way it often challenged the boundaries of conventional Burmese society. The resthouses hosted theatrical performances and, it is rumored, the first films in Burma, attracting criticism from conservatives while drawing a diverse crowd of Chinese, Indians, Europeans, and Burmese, reflecting the multiethnic makeup of the new colonial capital. Located on bustling Godwin Road leading up from the docks, the monasteries were also immediately adjacent to a vibrant Chinatown. The monastery complex, itself a place of boundary crossings, readily embraced Dhammaloka, whose very existence as a European Buddhist monk transgressed rigid ethnic and religious boundaries.

In this context, Dhammaloka's ordination lay sponsor, the layman Ing Myaing, is of particular interest. The Burmese-language newspaper report describes him as a rich Chinese man, accompanied by the good men of his Buddhist association. He was quite possibly a Sino-Burmese businessman from the port of Tavoy. The report also includes a long Pali-Burmese preamble about the karmic reasons for sponsoring ordinations—one that offers valuable insights into the nature of the boundaries drawn and crossed.

The newspaper article recounts the scriptural story of the Buddhist elder Moggaliputta, who explains to a king that donating great wealth counts less than sponsoring an ordination. By donating money, "You are merely a benefactor of the four requisites [clothing, food, medicine, and lodging]. By sponsoring the ordination of your son and daughter, or the son and daughter of others, you will be able to inherit and conquer the true wealth of *sasana* [Buddhism]." Ing Myaing and the members of his association "have not sponsored the ordination of their own sons as monks," the article explains, but, "the merit of sponsoring the higher ordination of an English novice Dhammaloka into monkhood makes them inheritors of the true wealth of *sasana*."[8]

A Chinese merchant, whose sons were raised as Chinese rather than Burmese, would not have the opportunity to sponsor the ordination of his own flesh and blood, yet this event brought him into the Burmese Buddhist community as an ordination sponsor. In Burma, a key motivation for ordination was to transfer merit to one's parents out of gratitude, but Dhammaloka, of course, had no parents available to sponsor his ordination. Both Ing Myaing and Dhammaloka were outsiders in this sense, unable to participate fully in the norms of Burmese Buddhist tradition. However, their devout conduct made them "true inheritors of the *sasana*" and thus very much insiders of the community. In this way, their actions redrew and expanded the boundaries of that community.

Public interest in Dhammaloka's ordination ceremony may have been heightened because Dhammaloka was the first European to receive higher ordination in Burma, but he was not the first European monk seen in Burma. Eighteen months earlier, in February 1899, an Englishman, Gordon Douglas, had been ordained in Ceylon by a visiting senior Burmese monk.[9] Douglas, who received the Buddhist name Asoka, toured Burma in early 1900 with great fanfare but by April that year had died from cholera. Asoka's example may have paved the way for Dhammaloka's ordination, but Dhammaloka's personal charisma, extensive preaching tours, and massive popularity with Burmese Buddhists would soon eclipse the local memory of Asoka.

Dhammaloka's Meteoric Rise to Fame

Not long after his ordination, Dhammaloka made his first public move, aimed at defending Burmese Buddhist spaces.[10] A small advertisement appeared low down on page six of the *Times of Burma* on Saturday, November 3, 1900. It read:

> NOTICE—Will all Christian Missionaries take warning that you are hereby informed that you must not distribute tracts pamphlets or other Christian literature during the coming full Moon festival on the Shwe Dagon Pagoda or Zayats [rest houses] or other religious buildings. By Order; (Sd.) U Dhammaloka, Tavoy Kyoung, Godwin Road, Rangoon.[11]

The declaration, bold in its sweeping authority and its direct confrontational tone, gives an excellent introduction to the public persona Dhammaloka created. Directed at other Europeans (though many English-speaking Burmans would have noted it, too), it clearly announced what Dhammaloka saw as one of his prime tasks in Burma: to foil the advances of missionary Christianity and preserve Buddhism for the good of the Burmese people. Another brief item announced a lecture by "U Dhamma Soka" (his name evidently not yet well known to the paper) at the Shwedagon Pagoda the following day on "What has Christianity done for civilization?" The marginal positioning of the items, low down on an inside page of an English-language newspaper among miscellaneous items of "Local News," also tells us something about Dhammaloka's claim on European attention four months after his ordination; he was visible, but on the margins; noticeable, but not important.

On February 6, 1901, following a visit to Rangoon in January by the seasoned Sinhalese Buddhist activist and founder of the pan-Asian Maha Bodhi Society, Anagarika Dharmapala,[12] the ban was extended countrywide, warning Christian missionaries "By order, U. Dhammaloka, English Hpoongyee," against distributing tracts "in any Pagoda, Kyoung [monastery] or Zayat in the Province of

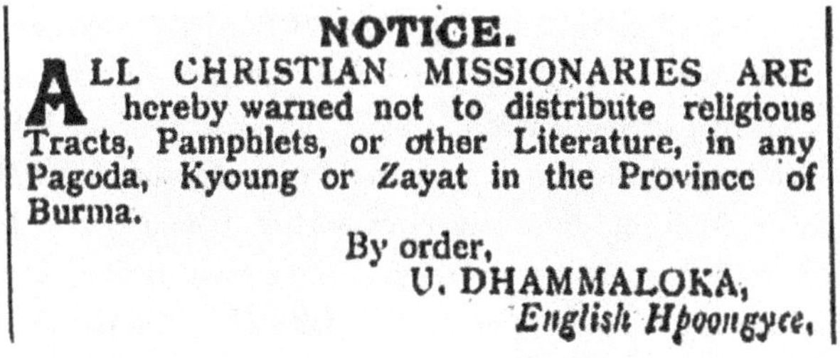

> **NOTICE.**
>
> **A**LL CHRISTIAN MISSIONARIES ARE hereby warned not to distribute religious Tracts, Pamphlets, or other Literature, in any Pagoda, Kyoung or Zayat in the Province of Burma.
>
> By order,
>
> U. DHAMMALOKA,
>
> *English Hpoongyee,*

Figure 2.2. Dhammaloka's warning to missionaries in the *Times of Burma*, February 6, 1901.

Authors' collection.

Burma" (see Figure 2.2).[13] By this time, Dhammaloka was nearly two weeks into an extensive preaching tour of Burma, drawing large and enthusiastic crowds.

Even before the earlier November 1900 warning notice appeared, Dhammaloka had penned a longer piece directed at fellow Buddhists and sent to Dharmapala at the *Journal of the Maha-Bodhi Society* in Calcutta, where it was published in December 1900.[14] It offered a robust analysis of the dangers to Buddhism from the colonial powers, symbolized by Christianity, exhorting Burmese Buddhists to recognize both the modernity and superiority of Buddhism and to resist the menacing advances of Christianity. The headline reads: "Buddhists of Burmah! Be warned in time! Do your Duty!" and the piece starts "The Christian belief is slowly spreading. . . . "

From this beginning, we might expect Dhammaloka to caution his readers against the insidious power of Christianity. Instead, drawing on Western atheist and agnostic critiques, he argues that science has exposed Christian beliefs as fallacious and that Christianity is internally divided, weak, and in terminal decline. Nevertheless, he says, Europeans are funding missionaries to impose this failing religion on the Burmese. Why? Only to hinder the global rise of Buddhism, which is entirely compatible with science. Dhammaloka declares that

> Christianity, as a system of religion, is sorry stuff. . . . As science advances, belief in Christianity is fading in Europe. Christianity spreads in this country, not because it has any intrinsic worth—for science has shown it has none—but because its Missionaries are backed up by the powers of the purse. Of our own great religion, a European scientist has said: "Buddhism is perfectly compatible with science: Christianity is diametrically opposed to it. Scientific thought has made its way in spite of Christianity; and it is by means of scientific thought that Christianity is ultimately destined to perish." It is perishing in Europe, but money makes it thrive here, while our own scientific Gospel—Buddhism—is

daily being robbed of its votaries. Buddhists of Burma! Reflect well on our dangers. Can you bear to see sacrilegious hands deface or destroy our holy inheritance? The star-like Buddhas are calling upon you to proclaim from housetop and hill-side, from meadow and valley, the sacred gospel which they have entrusted to you. Will you show yourselves worthy of the trust? We have slept long enough, shall we not at last, with a great and grave danger looming before us in all its huge and hideous proportions, shake off our lethargy? Buddhists of Burma! Rise then and gird up your loins for the coming struggle. May the Blessed Lord Buddha guide your efforts, prosper them and crown them with reward![15]

Dhammaloka explains in an accompanying letter to Anagarika Dharmapala that the piece had already been circulated as a printed leaflet in Burmese and English around Burma. It would soon gain much broader exposure through the Burmese newspapers. On December 29, the *Arakan Times* published a copy, explaining that it had been widely circulated in Arakan, and the Rangoon *Times of Burma* ran it on January 9, 1901.[16] The tract would gain even greater notoriety: by June 1901 it would be republished in a journal in Frankfurt, Germany.[17] This piece stands as Dhammaloka's manifesto: it speaks to a particular Burmese concern with the decline of Buddhism under colonialism that would bring him fame among Burmese Buddhists.

Dhammaloka's name would soon be familiar in elite Burmese Buddhist circles, too. Toward the end of December 1900, he made a trip to Mandalay (see Map 2.1), the former Burmese royal capital and seat of monastic authority. Traveling from Rangoon, he reached Mandalay on December 30. There he was hosted by the Mandalay "Society for Promoting Buddhism" (SPB), a key institution of the recent Burmese Buddhist organizing. The SPB was focused both on preserving monkhood in face of the loss of royal funding and on teaching Buddhism to students attending the new government schools. The organization had only recently been founded, in April 1900, and Dhammaloka's early affiliation with it certainly helped his future work in Burma. In Mandalay, he offered advice on the work ahead to preserve Buddhism, and lectured on the topic of temperance to thirty Buddhist nuns visiting from the nearby monastic enclave of Mingun.[18]

Preaching Tour Draws Thousands

By mid-January 1901, Dhammaloka had returned to Rangoon. The newspapers show him embroiled in a controversy that highlighted a cause almost as dear to him as the preservation of Buddhism, and one he would champion throughout

Map 2.1. Dhammaloka's Burma Tours, 1900–2.

his career: opposition to alcohol. He was, perhaps even before his ordination, an officer of the Burmese Grand Lodge of the Independent Order of the Good Templars (IOGT),[19] a worldwide ecumenical temperance organization. In December 1900 a Christian minister who supported moderation rather than complete abstention had chaired an IOGT meeting in Rangoon. Dhammaloka had objected that someone who was not a total abstainer had been given authority. The tensions ran particularly high, and a meeting in January provoked a complaint about Dhammaloka's behavior to the IOGT's regional superiors in India.[20]

On January 26, 1901, Dhammaloka began a first extensive preaching tour to spread his message of the threat to Buddhism. He left Rangoon for a journey that would last until March. It would take him through the delta region of southern Burma and then to the southeast, covering the major towns in those areas of Burma that had been longest under British control and missionary influence.[21] The months from January to March are the best for travel in Burma and thus the traditional season for itinerant preachers. Dhammaloka would prove himself extremely popular with Buddhists in the smaller towns across colonial Burma (Figure 2.3). His preaching tours became central to his work and he crisscrossed the province—at the invitation of local Buddhists—multiple times; including in 1901, 1902, 1907, 1908, and 1910.

The highlight of the 1901 tour was a stop in Bassein, where Dhammaloka was greeted by the still-grieving supporters of the late Bhikkhu Asoka. The *Times of Burma* reported that Dhammaloka was greeted as a hero:

> The members of the [local Buddhist] Society, specially dressed in all-white, as well as many others, received him and paid their respects at the wharf, with feelings of deepest joy and thankfulness; for never, since the death of Bhikkhu Asoka (the late Hpoongyi Mr Douglas) has a more generous open-hearted sympathy with the cause of Buddhism in Burma been shown by any other [of a] western nation.[22]

Asoka's brief career as a white monk seems to have laid the groundwork for Dhammaloka to be recognized as a worthy successor. The Irishman was escorted

Figure 2.3. En route to hear the Irish Phongyi: A Burmese festival carriage, the kind that would have carried the thousands to hear Dhammaloka's sermons.
Photo by Philip A. Klier, Rangoon, 1907. The National Archives (UK).

to a monastery building specially reserved for his visit. "During the fourteen days that he was here, the people from six o-clock in the morning to ten o-clock at night went in a stream as it were pouring up and down the road leading to the boarding place of the white bhikkhu without cessation."[23] Addressing the local press, Dhammaloka described his mission as bringing "home to the Burmese the conviction that Buddhism is the only Truth, far superior to other religions."[24] In the report of a lecture he gave through an interpreter, we gain a picture of his appeal to the Burmese.[25] The content of Dhammaloka's talk would have come as a surprise to his audience.

> I believe some of you are very anxious to hear my lecture on the Noble Dhamma tonight; but I see little benefit in doing so as long as you are already faithful followers of Lord Buddha. Because you may rest assured that there are here Burmese bhikkhus who know Buddhism as much as I myself know. Nay, perhaps more; and I know for certain that I cannot preach you a new and better Dhamma. . . . Yet, I have much to inform you. There are at present, you know, many Christian missionaries in Burma, trying to pick holes in your Blessed Religion and convert you, Burmans, into Christianity.
>
> You should always be on your guard against the preaching of those missionaries. If they apprise you that they have brought to you what they call western Civilization, or Religion of Peace, do not hesitate for a moment to reply that you would rather call it western Attraction, or Religion of Blood shed.[26]

He thus sidestepped the usual sermon on the *dhamma* (Buddhist teachings) expected from a revered Buddhist monk and instead emphasized Buddhism as an entity under threat. Rather than expound the virtues of Buddhist philosophy or ethics, Dhammaloka instead described the faults of Christianity and the danger it posed to the Burmese.

Dhammaloka's theme of Buddhism under threat resonated with Burmese audiences because it aligned particularly well with local Burmese concerns of the day. The Buddhist tradition had long held that Buddhism itself is impermanent and had been in constant decline since the Buddha's passing. This grand theme had spurred various Buddhist reforms and revivals over the past two and a half millennia, with kings, monks, and laypeople inspired to examine their contemporary situation for signs of deterioration and to purify their Buddhist practices and redouble their efforts to resist the decline as much as possible. Burmese interpreted the loss of their Buddhist king in 1885 and the arrival of the new colonial political and cultural conditions as clear signs of the decline of Buddhism. Dhammaloka had thus arrived in the middle of what locals termed a Buddhist revival in Burma. An irony of his intervention, however, is that few Burmese had actually converted to Christianity and few Burmese Buddhists identified

Christianity as the key threat to the future of Buddhism. The secular schools and their own co-religionists' lax morals in changing times were of more concern.[27]

Dhammaloka's anti-Christian rhetoric naturally caught the attention of local missionaries, and an American Christian soon visited him to engage him in debate.[28] The missionary incidentally brought with him two Europeans said to be freethinkers (i.e., atheists or agnostics) who wanted to observe the debate and who probably relished much of what Dhammaloka had to say. Though the missionary was said to be well versed in Buddhist doctrine, he was reportedly unable to best Dhammaloka. Decades earlier, in the mid-nineteenth century, debates between Christian missionaries and Buddhist monks had been key to Buddhist anti-colonial politics in Ceylon, but in Burma public confrontations between missionaries and monks were virtually unknown.[29] It seems that after this encounter in Bassein, missionaries in Burma determined that such debates were not in their interests, for this was the first and last time they sought out Dhammaloka for formal debate, although he encountered other vocal Christian opponents. We have a graphic example from 1905 (see Chapter 7) of an impromptu debate on the banks of the Ganges between Dhammaloka and an unfortunate Indian Christian missionary, when Dhammaloka demonstrated in front of a transfixed crowd that he was well practiced in making both the Bible and its advocates appear ridiculous.[30]

Dhammaloka's February 1901 visit to Bassein was followed by appearances in Maungmya, and Maubin in the delta region, then southeast to the seaport town of Tavoy, the home base of the monks from his own Rangoon monastery, then to Mergui and on to the thriving city of Moulmein, before returning to Rangoon in March.[31] The seaport towns would have been well known to a sailor engaged in local trade and might have meant a return to some of his previous haunts. Back in Rangoon, Dhammaloka would again challenge Europeans in defense of Buddhism. This time he would not target missionary Christianity or alcohol, but confront British colonialism itself, through the "shoe" controversy that we discuss in Chapter 3.

Most references to Dhammaloka's activities during the spring and summer of 1901 are tied to this controversy, apart from one report that at the end of March he chaired the anniversary of the Rangoon Theosophical Society, where he appeared to "carry the meeting by storm the way the audience clapped. He seems to be very popular with both the Buddhists and Hindus of Rangoon."[32] During these months, Dhammaloka's fame seems only to have grown, both in Burma and beyond: by August 1901 the content of his sermons and tracts had been published in a New York literary journal, a Mormon newspaper in Utah, and a German freethought magazine.[33]

December 1901 was marked by three events that would shape Dhammaloka's career. The first was the visit to Burma of Lord Curzon, the Viceroy of India, and

its ramifications, discussed in the following section. Second was the novice or-
dination in Akyab, in the west of Burma, of a newly arrived Englishman, Allan
Bennett [MacGregor], who took the monastic name "Ananda Metteyya." Ananda
Metteyya moved to Rangoon and would quickly become Dhammaloka's staunch
critic and rival. Third was the novice ordination, at Dhammaloka's own Tavoy
monastery in Rangoon, of another European, an elderly Englishman called
James Butement (or Butemen) who had arrived in Rangoon on December 3.[34]
Butement took, like the late Gordon Douglas, the monastic name of Asoka.

The novice ordination of this second Asoka (whom we call Asoka II to avoid
confusion), held on December 15, 1901, inaugurated a new and important aspect of Dhammaloka's campaign: the ordination of more European monks to
help carry out his mission of promoting and defending Buddhism—and not just
in Burma.[35] At this point Dhammaloka was not yet senior enough to carry out
ordinations himself in Burma, but it is clear that Asoka II's ordination took place
at his instigation.

> Today took place . . . amid a great concourse of people, the ordination ceremony
> of another European, who had made up his mind to become a hpoongyi, thus
> the sooner to reach the end of miseries, Nirvana. It appears the reverend gen-
> tleman, by name now Asoka, had been for 30 years a prey to harbouring doubts
> and has at last found safe refuge in the calm beatitude of hpoongyihood. . . .
> There were gathered several influential bishops, and the ceremony was
> conducted by Hpoongyi Oo Sanda. A hush fell upon the whole assembly when
> the old gentleman pronounced distinctly the ancient profession of Buddhism.
> Buddham saranam gacchami! I go for refuge to the Buddha, the Law and the
> Brotherhood—which from a Christian turned him a Buddhist and he donned
> the yellow robe. Then, taking his alms-bowl, he went his first round for alms in
> the monastery itself, and the fair sex amid much merriment gave him his first
> meal as hpoongyi.[36]

Following the ordination, Dhammaloka gave a talk about the "Society for the
Propagation of Buddhism," whose object was "that we should spread Buddhism
in all people whatsoever color they are," and referring to Asoka II as "the
society's ripest fruit."[37] The event attracted a large and pious local crowd of "a few
Chinamen mingled with Burmans," as well as some European observers specially
invited by Dhammaloka. Among these was Mrs. Everard Cotes, the Canadian
journalist and novelist, better known today under her maiden name of Sara
Jeanette Duncan. Cotes had traveled with Viceroy Curzon around Burma, but
stayed on in Rangoon after Curzon's departure and interviewed Dhammaloka at
Asoka II's ordination for *Harper's Monthly Magazine*. The *Harper's* article would
undoubtedly have spread the name of Dhammaloka far and wide in Europe and

America if Cotes had not inexplicably referred to him throughout her article as "Oo-Dhamma-Nanda!"[38]

The Name "Dhammaloka"

Our Irish Buddhist would have received the Pali monastic name "Dhammaloka" at his novice ordination. This name might be read as *dhamma* + *loka* "world/ realm of the Buddhist 'law' (dharma or *dhamma*)." However, he understood the name as the more common binary *dhamma* + *āloka* meaning "light (*āloka*) of the Buddhist law." On three occasions, Dhammaloka explained that his name indicates light, either in "the Law of the Light" or "the Light of the World"[39]

Why he chose this particular name is unclear, but he probably did choose it himself. Cotes, interviewing Dhammaloka in Rangoon in December 1901, asked him how he got his name.

> He himself chose the designation, he told me. "You were not afraid," I said, "of such a name?"
>
> "Oh, not at all," he said, "I thought I'd like it." [40]

Cotes also shows us the process for choosing monastic names. When the elderly Englishman Asoka II had been shaved of his hair, received his robe, and recited the precepts . . .

> [t]here was still the selection of a name. The new name on the old tombstone of an Englishman. This, according to the usage, was at the candidate's choice, several being submitted to him. It was plainly an interesting moment; the old abbot leaned forward and whispered, the officiating priest bent down, and the others drew around; even the audience—should I say the congregation?—gathered closer, freely offering suggestions, and Oo-Dhamma-Nanda [Dhammaloka] hovered over all. "Oo-Sri-Visuddha," "Venerable Lord of Purity,"; "Oo-Candima," "Lord of the Moon"; "Oo-Dhamma-Sami," "Lord of the Written Law"; —should it be any of these? The candidate hesitated; his fancy was not caught. "Oo-Asoka!" contributed an intelligent layman in a queue,[41] smiling broadly . . . and the old man turned at the suggestion. "I've heard of Asoka," said he, vacillating. Oo-Dhamma-Nanda settled it. "Call him Asoka," said he with authority, and it was agreed.[42]

Cotes's "Oo-Dhamma-Nanda" undoubtedly takes the prize for mis-spellings of Dhammaloka's name, with Dhamma Soka, Dhammtokd, Damlouka, and "Dam-a-looka" close behind, but there are many contenders. Some records show

"Rev. Damaloka," while the near-correct "Dhamaloka" is common. The Calcutta picture magazine *The Empress*, more interested in showing readers a photograph of an Irish Buddhist monk than getting his name right, captioned their portrait of him "Rev U Dhumloka." In Tokyo, his Japanese hosts rendered his name in phonetic *katakana* script as "Dammarooka," but on occasion settled for the easier-to-remember "D-San" ("Mr. D."). Harry Franck made "Oo Damalaku" famous in his 1910 book. The following year the *San Francisco Examiner* sensationally revealed that "Oo Damalaku" was Dublin-born Lawrence O'Rourke. As this story spread rapidly from America, one well-informed Dublin journalist knew enough to correct Franck's "Oo Damalaku" to "U. Dhammaloka" before the story went out to his discerning Irish readers.[43]

The honorific prefix "U" meant little outside Burma, and Dhammaloka usually translated it as "Rev[erend]" when traveling elsewhere. This title gave him a modicum of respectability in countries where his strict observance of monastic rules was less appreciated than in Burma, but he allegedly underwent a significant promotion during his trip to Japan in 1902, returning as "Lord High Abbot" Dhammaloka. This Japanese rank, Dhammaloka explained, gave him precedence over every monk in South and Southeast Asia, and occasionally in this period he wore the black robes of a Japanese abbot, gifted to him in Japan, to reinforce the point. While in Japan, he had argued rather differently that it was the "U" before his name that indicated his high rank. In an interview with a Japanese newspaper in December 1902, Dhammaloka stated:

> [The name] U Dhammaloka . . . is, of course, a dharma name given after I came to Burma. But once a dharma name is granted, it is prohibited by the rule of the sect to use the former, real name. And "U" in this "U Dhammaloka" is an honorific. . . . Just as we [British] say "Lord" someone, so "U" is given to a person in Burma. It is only given to high priests. . . . One cannot have the letter "U" attached unless they have risen to the highest rank.[44]

The titles preceding Dhammaloka's name were often complemented by a string of initials succeeding it, each suggesting a prestigious office or rank. As early as November 1900, Dhammaloka was signing himself "U. Dhammaloka, P.D.G.C.T., English Buddhist Priest" and over the years the list became more and more elaborate. We find the fullest expression of his tendency to embellishment described in the Singapore *Straits Times*. Its editor, Edward Alexander Morphy, was somewhat skeptical of Dhammaloka's credentials:

> The Right Reverend Lord Abbot U. Dhammaloka F.T.S., M.R.T., P.D.C.C.T.,. K.L., A.G., &c., &c., &c., Irish Buddhist Priest, General Superintendent 'Straits Young Men's Buddhist Association'! —we give this aromatic adventurer's string

of titles precisely as he signs himself, including the three &c's, and the 'Right Reverend Lord,' but we do not pretend to know the meaning of the intermediate string of capitals.[45]

Like Morphy, we cannot be sure of the meaning of all these abbreviations, but F.T.S. probably meant Fellow of the Theosophical Society, while P.D.C.C.T. should be P.D.G.C.T., a distinguished service title used in the IOGT temperance movement meaning "Past Deputy Grand Commander of the Temple." As someone who moved rapidly between cultures and contexts, Dhammaloka attached these honorifics to his name in order to assert his authority and social status across cultural, religious, and geographical borders, no doubt in conscious mimicry of the British empire's custom of awarding a dazzling range of titles and distinctions to its loyal servants and friends—part of what David Cannadine calls the "ornamentalism" of the British empire.[46]

Those who encountered the Right Reverend Lord Abbot U Dhammaloka F.T.S., M.R.T., P.D.G.C.T., K.L., A.G., &c., &c., &c., Irish Buddhist Priest, were meant to understand that they were dealing with no ordinary individual. It didn't always work, as the attitude of the Singapore editor shows, but it is characteristic of Dhammaloka that even though he had chosen his own name, he did not leave it there, but found innovative ways to enhance it and thus put it to work on his behalf.

More Popular than the Viceroy

On the last day of 1901, Dhammaloka left Rangoon for Mandalay to meet with the Society for Promoting Buddhism (SPB), just as he had done the year before. Mandalay was the former royal capital and a major seat of Burmese monastic authority and learning. Events in Mandalay would prove important for Dhammaloka's future work and patronage, in Burma and beyond.

A key project for the SPB in their efforts to preserve Buddhism was to secure official recognition by the British of a *thathanabaing*, a term often glossed as Buddhist archbishop, but who was actually merely the head of the dominant Thudhamma monastic lineage, traditionally appointed by the king. The last royally appointed thathanabaing had died in 1895 and the Pakhan Sayadaw, whom many Buddhists regarded as an unofficial thathanabaing, had recently passed away. In November 1901, senior monks met in Mandalay to elect a new thathanabaing—the Moda Sayadaw.[47]

The SPB now took advantage of the imminent visit of the recently appointed Viceroy of India, Lord Curzon, to petition the government to endorse the newly elected thathanabaing.[48] It would be a symbolic gesture, but important for the stature of the sangha as well as its material support, both of which had suffered from the arrival of British colonialism. The British were notoriously reluctant to endorse any religious figures in their colonies, citing a policy of religious neutrality, but from the Burmese perspective official recognition would undoubtedly help to preserve and promote Buddhism in these changing times.

Dhammaloka arrived in Mandalay on December 29, 1901, a month after Curzon had made his first ceremonial visit to the city. Beyond the meetings on the thathanabaing issue, the highlight of Curzon's visit had been a public reception or *durbar* for the chiefs (known as *saopha*) of the Shan States, including the Saopha of Kengtung, an energetic leader with political and cultural ambitions (see Chapter 5). Arriving in Mandalay, Dhammaloka enjoyed a grand reception from the crowds (later claimed to outdo the welcome offered to the Viceroy), indicating the massive popularity he had accumulated by this time.[49] One report runs:

A double row of dark-haired maidens extended from the doors of the monastery for nearly half a mile along the dusty road. The women, after kneeling, stretched themselves at full length on the ground. Their hair, flowing unbound, was spread across the roadway, and over this silken carpet and down the human aisle strode the bare-footed American Buddhist.[50]

This (probably embellished) account represents a traditional way of showing respect to particularly revered monks, with the laywomen receiving merit by offering a carpet for the monk to walk upon. It is indicative of Dhammaloka's rising popularity among Buddhists of Mandalay.

Dhammaloka's visit was sponsored in Mandalay by the SPB and he was housed in the Society's building, formerly the private home of a Burmese royal minister.[51] Dhammaloka had been in contact with the SPB for the past year, but this was an opportunity for the modernizing organization to publicly claim the European monk, and for Dhammaloka to demonstrate the backing of what would become one of the most important Buddhist associations in the country. He subsequently opened branches of the SPB in Lower Burma and served as president of his own Rangoon branch until it was merged with the Maha Bodhi Society's Rangoon branch in April 1902.[52]

In Mandalay, Dhammaloka preached every night to huge crowds at the SPB headquarters. He was invited to events with the most prestigious monastic leaders. This included a meal at the home of U Tun Min, the assistant superintendent of police, attended by twenty titled monks including the recently elected Thathanabaing Moda Sayadaw. After the meal, the guests had a professional photograph taken at Johannes's studio in the town and Dhammaloka had a private interview with the thathanabaing-elect.[53] That evening Dhammaloka gave a rousing lecture on "Why I Became a Buddhist" to a crowd of three thousand.[54] The following week he traveled across the river to the monastic enclave of Sagaing to visit the highly respected Vajirarama Sayadaw, the same monk who had ordained Bhikkhu Asoka (Gordon Douglas) in Ceylon two years earlier.[55]

That Dhammaloka was welcomed by the most respected monks in Mandalay and Sagaing shows that his monastic credentials were regarded as genuine by the most scrupulous of arbiters, despite his relatively recent appearance on the public scene and his unorthodox exuberance in defending Buddhism against Christianity. These meetings may have been strategic on both sides—the monastic leaders seeking government backing for a new thathanabaing likely thought that contact with a European monk might aid their cause, while for Dhammaloka association with such respected monastic figures could only enhance his credibility. Although Dhammaloka was being denounced by some Christian missionaries and newspapers as a newly ordained charlatan, this was clearly not the view of the Burmese sangha, who valued him as a sincere and influential monk—one of their own.

Another Triumphal Tour

From Mandalay, on January 24, 1902, Dhammaloka set out on a grand preaching tour of Upper Burma. A layman named U Maung Maung, by now acting as Dhammaloka's assistant and publicist, announced the tour in the *Times of Burma* in January with a handy itinerary for those interested in hearing Dhammaloka's lectures.[56] Dhammaloka traveled by train from Mandalay to the towns of Kyoukse, Myittha, Meiktila and Myingyan (see Map 2.1), then by steam ferry down the Irrawaddy river to Pakokku, Minbu, and Thayetmyo, touring the central Burman monastic heartland before returning by train from Prome via Tharrawaddy, reaching Rangoon on March 6.[57]

The Burmese were eager to hear Dhammaloka's message; he was received as a hero in each of the towns he visited. There were other preaching monks on tour, but the enthusiastic turnouts for Dhammaloka stand out. Of Toungoo, his first stop en route to Mandalay an observer wrote, "I must say that the Burmese community gave him a grand reception on the day of his arrival here. Any stranger would have thought it was a heaven-born Potentate who was coming to Toungoo."[58] In Pakokku, "U Dhammaloka, on arrival in this station from Myingyan, was given a grand reception [and] gave a lecture to a congregation of around four thousand people."[59] In Tharrawaddy, "The people clad all in white, the Buddhist emblem of purity, met their esteemed European priest at the railway station and conducted him along the road covered with mats and carpets."[60] The tour gained renown even in India: "The extraordinary success of the tour—a tour at times that suggests a royal progress—of U Dhammaloka through Upper Burma, is one of the most significant features of Burmese society in the last decade," observed *The Times of India.*[61]

The content of Dhammaloka's public remarks reprised themes from the past year, including talks entitled "Union is Strength" (on the need to support Buddhism against the Christian missionary threat) and "Why I Became a Buddhist." The criticism of missionary Christianity now shifted into an active focus on bringing converts to Christianity back to Buddhism. In Myittha, Dhammaloka converted a Burman and his family back to Buddhism[62] and he claimed, "During my tour about 100 Burmans who had embraced Christianity have embraced Buddhism again. One European in Pakokku has been converted to Buddhism."[63] Cotes heard similar claims in Rangoon.[64] In a speech in Tokyo later the same year, Dhammaloka claimed that on one occasion he had converted at least 200 Burmese Christians back to Buddhism.[65]

Allowing for exaggeration, this suggests that he saw his tours as potentially restoring significant numbers of Burmese Christian converts to the Buddhist fold. Moreover, he chided the Burmese for not reaching out more to the Karen ethnic minority, many of whom had been converted by American Baptist missionaries.[66] Dhammaloka also talked of ordaining further Europeans and sending Buddhist missions to Europe and America.[67] On return to Rangoon, he posted the following advertisement in the *Times of Burma*, this time on the front page:

WANTED IMMEDIATELY. Twenty BUDDHIST PRIESTS (Hpoongyis) to proceed to the Moungmya and Bassein Districts for work among KARENS under the auspices of the SOCIETY FOR PROMOTING BUDDHISM. Apply to U Dhammaloka, President S.P.B. Tavoy Monastery, Godwin Road, Rangoon.[68]

Another tour of the southeast, like that of the previous year, to take in Shwegyin, Moulmein, Tavoy, and Mergui, was planned.[69] People from towns across Burma were clamoring to see him:

invitations are being sent to the hpoongyi from all parts of Burma. In one day, telegrams were received from four places—Sandoway, Mergui, Maubin, and Nyounglebin—inviting him to those stations and intimating that all of his first class expenses were already paid. The same day—Thursday—a letter was received from Alon-Monywa, in the Lower Chindwin [a river valley to the north] similarly inviting the Irish hpoongyi to that station."[70]

Dhammaloka acceded to as many of these requests as he was able, finding ever-enthusiastic crowds, which included prestigious local officials and those well beyond the Burmese Buddhist majority.

He went first to Shwegyin, home to a famously strict monastic reform sect, where he received large donations and was then reportedly robbed of them.[71] In April, Dhammaloka's appeal to a multiethnic and multi-religious audience, including local officials, was again demonstrated. "There was a large gathering of Buddhists, men women and children at the wharf to receive the phongyi, amongst them being the Atawun Mg Kyaw Min and an ex-Myook (town leader) Mg Kaing Hla Pru. Several Mahomedans and Hindus were also seen in the crowd assembled at the wharf to greet the priest."[72] In May, he arrived in Zigon with twenty Sayadaws and was received with a procession. "The procession was a grand affair for Zigon and its chief features being the many coloured lanterns and three bands of music."[73] He proceeded on to Gyobingauk where "the road was laid with fancy carpets and silk cloths" and on to Letpadan and Thonze before returning to Rangoon.[74] By the end of May he had returned to Rangoon to be present at the higher ordination of Asoka II on the 21st, Vesak day.

Dhammaloka as *Phongyi*

The enthusiastic receptions accorded to Dhammaloka perhaps owed less to his anti-Christian and pro-Buddhist message than to his status and role as a preaching *phongyi* or monk. In the 1890s Burma had undergone a reform in monastic preaching style. Monks had traditionally preached by reciting Pali Buddhist texts, their view of the laity deliberately obscured by large fans.[75] People attended not so much to comprehend the content as to gain merit by hearing the holy words. In stark contrast, the new reformist preachers spoke colloquial Burmese and made their ideas accessible to ordinary people.[76] Dhammaloka's undoubted personal charisma and the dramatic picture his lectures painted of a Burma threatened by the twin evils of Christianity and colonialism compounded the novelty of this new preaching style, but these factors alone could not guarantee him respect. For many audiences the prospect of an imminent Christian takeover of their town or village was somewhat remote. It is evident that a bit of the older purpose also applied. Buddhists who flocked to hear this unusual monk give unusual sermons thereby gained unusual merit.

It helped that Dhammaloka was orthodox in his monastic conduct. On his tours, his daily morning alms round provided opportunities for demonstrations of merit-making piety and popular support. In Henzada, "he goes out every day to receive his alms from the pious Buddhists every morning and the people spread mats, silk cloths, silk handkerchiefs, silk gaungbaungs [head scarves] for him to walk upon."[77] He was in effect a Buddhist celebrity, whose strict adherence to the details of monastic performance endeared him to the laity. Indeed, what startled and confused other Europeans most about Dhammaloka was how closely he resembled his fellow Burmese monks.

Collecting alms, interacting with laypeople with proper decorum, performing nightly devotions; all were second nature to Dhammaloka after his years at the Tavoy monastery. And these acts of devotion formed a currency that transcended any differences of language or appearance and proved him a worthy recipient of reverence and donations. While the content of his preaching was unusual, Dhammaloka cleaved to tradition in vital ways that made him a reassuringly familiar figure.

Yet in other respects Dhammaloka would have appeared distinctly un-Burmese and un-monastic. Burmese culture valued an attitude of quiet equanimity, particularly from monks. Public expressions of agitation or anger on the part of the laity only elicited bemusement at such an odd breach of decorum, and among monks were unheard of. Here, the limitations of cultural translation failed Dhammaloka. His style of performance as preacher, rocking on his feet while expressing righteous indignation, may have entertained the Burmese, but also marked him as an outsider.

Dhammaloka as a European and a Buddhist monk, foreign yet familiar, challenged his Burmese audiences by breaching the colonial divide, blurring the seemingly clear fault line between Burmese Buddhist and European Christian.[78] More than any other European Buddhist before or since, Dhammaloka was accepted by the Burmese masses across the country. Indeed, he bears comparison with only the most popular and charismatic Burmese monks, then and now. Whether the Burmese showed up for entertainment, for merit, or to be converted to his cause, U Dhammaloka gave them an alternative vision: a European joining with them as a Buddhist in solidarity against any and all threats to their Buddhism and their way of life.

A Sudden Departure

In July 1902, the Rangoon newspapers reported that Dhammaloka had left a few weeks earlier and was headed to Tavoy, presumably following through on the proposed tour of Moulmein, Tavoy, and Mergui. He left Tavoy for Bangkok and Singapore, embarking there for Yokohama on the NDL *Bayern* mail ship on July 18, 1902.[79]

The report in March of all the invitations pouring in had also included a reference to two invitations from Japanese monks. "U Dhammaloka's name has become known outside of Burma, in far-distant countries; even in Japan, whence two invitations have already been sent to the Irish hpoongyi inviting him to visit the land of the Chrysanthemum and promote Buddhism."[80] While some cynics writing to the *Times of Burma* doubted the reality of such invitations, Dhammaloka clearly had some connection drawing him to Japan.[81] The transit through Siam may indicate the link: U Maung Maung, his assistant and publicist, had commented in Mandalay that he had donated some of his own religious possessions to the SPB there because he would soon be traveling to Siam, and Maung Maung later accompanied Dhammaloka to Japan.[82]

In the two years between his ordination in Rangoon and the culmination of his tours in 1902, Dhammaloka had surely achieved all that his ordination sponsors could have hoped for from a "white Buddhist," after the setback of the first Asoka's sudden death. Dhammaloka was recognized as a genuine monk by the most senior monastic authorities. He was venerated to the point of adulation by tens of thousands of ordinary people across Burma. He had spoken out forcibly to Europeans in a style and language they well understood, offering a disparaging critique of "unscientific" Christianity from the standpoint of the "superior" religion of Buddhism, and making impressive use of the English-language newspapers to bring his campaigns to the attention of the wider colonial society. He had cultivated and mobilized a multiethnic crowd of supporters and tapped a network of Asian Buddhists and reformers that would facilitate his career much further afield.

In this respect we can see ordaining Dhammaloka as a gamble that paid off: the extension of monastic legitimacy to a somewhat unpredictable character who was nevertheless capable of taking initiatives that would have been harder for a monk more constrained by conventional ties and less confident in the new arenas of public debate, newspaper polemic, and selective provocation. Moreover, Dhammaloka had a significant impact among Burmese Buddhists. As one critical Christian missionary begrudgingly allowed, "There has never been such a stir among Buddhists as has been wrought at the present time by this obscure but zealous foreigner. High native officials, as well as a great number of the common people, have been quickened in their faith in Buddhism and many of them have become more careful in their observance of its practices, and more ardent in their advocacy of its beliefs."[83]

In later chapters we will discuss Dhammaloka's attraction for the multitudes of people who turned out to hear him on his travels through the Burmese heartlands in 1901–2 and in later years. Had he continued to focus on Burma and repeated his annual tours in successive years, the momentum of his campaigns would surely have increased and perhaps soon led to a major confrontation with the authorities. Yet this is where the Burma part of the story has to be put on hold, for Dhammaloka left Burma and would not return for another two years at least, and then only briefly until he resumed touring the country in 1907. His departure for Japan would launch him on a new path, that of internationalist Buddhist organizing.

However, before turning to Japan, we need to go back a year and return to Rangoon, where in March 1901 Dhammaloka had confronted the authorities over an issue that would become a strategic one for Burmese Buddhist nationalists across the next two decades: shoes.

3

Trampling on Our Religion

1901

On the night of the largest and most important pagoda festival of the year, at the largest and most important pilgrimage site in Burma, U Dhammaloka challenged colonial authority head on in a confrontation that would have long echoes. On March 2, 1901, during the Tabaung full moon festival at the great Shwedagon Pagoda in Rangoon, on the pagoda platform teeming with pilgrims and celebrations, he ordered an Indian police officer to remove his shoes while on the hallowed ground of the Buddhist stupa.

Burmese remove their shoes when they enter homes and offices as an everyday sign of respect. Much more important and imperative, however, is the injunction to remove footwear when walking on the grounds of a pagoda. This is because Burmese pagodas are stupas, that is, reliquaries housing underground the relics of the Buddha. Unlike elsewhere in Southeast Asia and India, Burmese would remove their shoes before entering even the outermost boundary of a pagoda's grounds, let alone the grounds of the hallowed Shwedagon, in which four hairs handed over by the Buddha himself are said to be enshrined. To step with one's dirty shoes on the Buddha's very body would be the ultimate sign of disrespect.

However, Europeans found the practice of removing their shoes disgusting and demeaning—quite literally bringing themselves down to the level of the "natives" they governed. Arguing that they had other ways of showing respect, Europeans exempted themselves from removing their shoes at Burmese pagodas. There was some early dissent around this policy in colonial Burma. In 1875, the Burmese elders of Rangoon had protested that Muslims were wearing shoes at Buddhist pagodas yet removing their shoes in mosques. The Chief Commissioner agreed that this was inappropriate and formalized the rule that "those persons, whose creed required them to show respect by taking off their shoes, should take off their shoes on visiting a pagoda."[1] This meant that Hindus, Muslims, and most other Asians should certainly remove their shoes at the Shwedagon. This compromise seems to have satisfied all parties, for there was little mention of the issue of non-Burmese persons wearing shoes at pagodas for twenty-five years.

The Irish Buddhist. Alicia Turner, Laurence Cox, and Brian Bocking, Oxford University Press (2020)
© Alicia Turner, Laurence Cox and Brian Bocking.
DOI: 10.1093/oso/9780190073084.001.0001

And yet, here in 1901 was an Indian, a police officer, defying policy and desecrating what Dhammaloka would refer to as "the Buddha's blessed religion." Dhammaloka's European status emboldened him to confront the officer in a way few Burmese monks would have dared. The authorities had been wary of crime and unruliness at pagoda festivals, so there were several police in attendance. But this particular officer, though in uniform, was not on duty. And as the news reports noted, in line with the 1875 policy, most Indians, including off-duty officers, would remove their shoes when walking on the pagoda grounds.[2] The challenged officer, however, took offense at U Dhammaloka's request. He left the pagoda to complain to his European superior and, a newspaper claimed, embellished the story of the confrontation. The European officer in charge then threatened to arrest monks on the pagoda platform (see figure 3.1) during the festival.[3]

These events of March 1901 followed immediately after Dhammaloka's first well-received preaching tour in towns across lower Burma. He had gained some fame for his anti-Christian message of saving Buddhism, but in this confrontation we can see for the first time that it was not just missionary Christianity that Dhammaloka opposed. In confronting the police officer, Dhammaloka made explicit his concern, shared by many Burmese, that British rule itself posed a threat to the future of Buddhism. Moreover, in choosing shoes as the point of contention, he was taking up an issue that resonated significantly with the Burmese. There had been an internal doctrinal debate about shoes only eight years earlier, and in another fifteen years this would become a key battleground of the nationalist movement for independence.[4] Even in these early days, only nine months after his higher ordination, Dhammaloka had developed his signature cause: indicting British colonialism as a direct threat to Buddhism.

The event stirred up a storm of letters in the English and Burmese newspapers. The next issue of the *Times of Burma* reported that there would be a public meeting of Buddhists to discuss the issue of "people visiting the pagoda with shoes and boots on."[5] Burmese popular opinion was overwhelmingly in support of U Dhammaloka and against allowing any footwear on pagoda grounds. The pagoda trustees, the elected Buddhist representatives who had official control over policy at the religious site, were set to meet on March 17.

However, despite the rhetoric of open public debate, there were backdoor attempts to silence Dhammaloka on two fronts. First, the police began stirring up a legal case against Dhammaloka for sedition.[6] Second, there were closed-door sessions between the pagoda trustees and government officials, with the latter attempting to dictate policy to the former.

Figure 3.1. The most sacred site in Burma: Devotees and tourists on the platform of the Shwedagon Pagoda for a festival, Rangoon, early 1900s.

Authors' collection.

A Wonderful Dream and a Secret Document

The public got wind of these political machinations through a modern colonial twist on a traditional Burmese Buddhist device: claims of monastic dreams and prophecy. On March 18, the day after the pagoda trustees' meeting, a letter was written to the *Times of Burma* under the pseudonym "A Burmese," saying that the bazaar talk was that a famous monk had had a midday dream in which a god revealed that the government and pagoda trustees were hiding a document.

> It is the talk about town and more especially in the Bazaars about the wonderful dream or vision of a Phongyee who is well known in Rangoon. The nature of this dream is this—that while having a mid-day nap he goes into a reverie and while so dreaming a Nat (or devil) appeared unto him while thus asleep and touched him and he followed the guiding spirit and it took him to a large building and the platform of the great . . . pagoda and revealed to him a wonderful secret; and the contents of a certain document which was not drawn up by Mr Pennell[7] but by another star of less magnitude than Mr Pennell who resides in Rangoon.[8]

Dreams, prophecies, and rumors were standard fare in Burma and long before British colonial times had been understood to provide key information about political events.[9] The colonial archive shows that the government took such prophecies quite seriously as political threats in other instances.

It is hard to know how far to read this letter as a mischievous intervention or whether it was meant to be serious reporting about local gossip. Certainly the controversy was the subject of talk, and any hint of supernatural partisanship on the issue would have spread like wildfire. There is no indication of which monk is alleged to have had the dream, but the most famous monk involved, the "Irish Phongyee," would hardly need to be specified. Moreover, any inkling that the government had an unseen and unspoken hand in the trustees' decision would have been good fodder for the gossip circuit.

A second letter appeared in the same issue. The author, "Justice," claimed to have investigated matters with the pagoda trustees, one of whom confirmed the document's existence.[10] The following issue carried a letter from "Daylight," Dhammaloka's most common pseudonym, claiming he had seen the document and that it revealed underhand activity by government officials.[11] It is by no means impossible that all three letters were written by Dhammaloka.

Within the Burmese episteme of the early 1900s, dreams and prophecies were real, quite powerful, and often had bearing on political events. Each of the letters seems to acknowledge this reality and yet mark that there is something incongruent with contemporary modernity, with phrases like "a 20th century prophecy." Regardless of whether the author(s) were reporting a real dream and bazaar talk occurring prior to their newspaper letters, theirs would certainly have been a self-fulfilling prophecy. There was very little that could generate more fervent rumor in Burma than letters to the editor about bazaar gossip and prophetic dreams.

The question of what covert dealing a secret document might reveal was more awkward. Two of the letters mention Mr. C. S. Pennell, then an Assistant Commissioner, high up in the Secretariat of the Lt. Governor's office, and the son-in-law of the famous Rangoon judge and future Lt. Governor, Herbert Thirkell White.[12] The letters thus imply that the government, through Mr. Pennell, might have been trying to coerce the pagoda trustees or collude with them to hide the issue from the public.

The secret document finally came to light in June. It was a public repudiation of U Dhammaloka, written by the government, handed to the trustees for their signature and promptly leaked by them to Dhammaloka. It was a draft resolution denouncing him for disturbing Buddhist worshipers during the festival and stating that if he continued to do so he would be banned from the pagoda grounds. However, the plan backfired. The trustees proved, at least on this occasion, to have more backbone.

We are informed that the Trustees of the Shwe Dagon Pagoda held a meeting on the 17th of March when they refused to pass the following resolution which was sent to them officially for their approval:

"Resolved—
   That the Phongyi U. Dhammaloka be informed that.
   His conduct on the night of 2nd March, feast of Taboung amount [sic] to interference with the administration of the Pagoda platform and disturbed the devotion of worshippers.
   That if he had any objection to take to any of the present regulations he should have made representations to the Trustees of the Pagoda in whose hands the administration of the Pagoda platform is vested.
   That further interference will not be tolerated and that although it is in no way intended to place any obstacle in the way of any person desirous of worshipping at the Pagoda, he will be refused admission to the platform should his conduct again be such as to give rise to apprehension of disturbances which would inconvenience the general body of worshippers."
   Copy to Phongyi U Dhammaloka
   Copy to the Commissioner Police with request that he will kindly direct the police to carry out the wishes of the Trustees.[13]

This document, if approved, would have given the police the authority to act against Dhammaloka. The pagoda trustees making public their repudiation of the government's wishes represented a strong political statement for a body that had not sought out the front line on this issue. Dhammaloka had a good sense of what ordinary Burmese feelings on the subject were. Furthermore—as this misjudged and personalized overreaction on the part of the colonial authorities shows—he had a good sense of where the fault lines in authority lay.

In all of this, the traditional store of Irish "rebel tales"—and perhaps other radical stories gathered subsequently—would have stood him in good stead. In particular, since the days of Daniel O'Connell's Catholic Emancipation movement of the early nineteenth century, the terrain of religion had proved fertile ground for Irish anti-colonial organizing. The colonial power could not dissociate itself entirely from religious matters, but when it got involved it provoked popular resistance in defense of local religion, as in the Tithe War of the 1830s. Forcing the colonial power to intervene in a way that made it look bad, on an issue where otherwise conservative local forces would ally with radicals, had something of a history in Ireland.

Tommy Atkins and the Trustees

While all of this was going on, the police attempted to bring other charges against U Dhammaloka, accusing him of sedition. As an Irish Buddhist convert, his loyalty to empire could be easily questioned. The *Rangoon Gazette* claimed that he had said, "we have taken Burma from the Burmans and now desire to trample on their religion."[14] Dhammaloka, however, was unperturbed by the allegations. He wrote to the *Times of Burma*,

> If I have used the seditious language that he speaks about, let my enemies come forward to prove the assertion. Somebody was for two days running between the Town of Rangoon and the West Riding Barracks, to get Tommy Atkins to swear that I had been preaching sedition; but Tommy was not going to be trapped so easily. I could startle the public of Burma, and the world, of what I know about the shams who state they are loyal subjects of His Majesty King Edward VII.[15]

"Tommy Atkins" was a venerable generic name for the typical European private in the British colonial army, working-class men who had much in common with the beachcombers and sailors of Dhammaloka's earlier life. In a letter appearing on the same page signed by "Tommy Atkins," who says he is "only a soldier," the writer claimed, "I am personally known to the Irish Pongyee as he calls himself and I have had the pleasure of hearing him in the big pagoda. I am sure I have always heard him speaking or lecturing in praise of the British Government, and of the just laws, and the liberty that the Burmese enjoy under the British flag."[16] With the trustees reluctant to condemn the actions of a monk who had defended the sanctity of the Shwedagon Pagoda and in the face of a hostile public opinion, the police were unable to bring charges.

Unfortunately, the pagoda trustees would turn out not to be very reliable allies. After what was clearly more backroom pressure they issued this statement on June 5, less direct than the secret document the government had written, but to much the same effect:

> All Buddhists who come or worship, on the platform of the Pagoda, should stay quietly and not interfere with Europeans, Englishmen, or persons of any other nations who visits the Pagoda for having a look round the plan [i.e., European tourists], and if they in any way try to make a disturbance that policemen will be called to keep a watch on the pagoda, and the person who raises a disturbance against the wishes of others will be presented according to law; a letter to Government officials has been dispatched that notice has been stuck up on the Pagoda to the above effect.[17]

The trustees lost the respect of many Buddhists in this action, which would go a long way towards establishing them as traitors to the nationalist cause in coming decades. However, it was not just Dhammaloka's action in March that provoked this response, but a further confrontation on the Shwedagon Pagoda platform that also raised issues of colonial authority, the enforcement of Burmese inferiority, and disrespect for Buddhism.

A Brush with an Artist

Buddhist pagodas in Burma are stunning architectural monuments, covered in solid gold through the donations of pious Buddhists. Hence they were not simply isolated places of worship, but had come to attract Europeans as tourists, representing the picturesque vision of Asia for Orientalist fantasies. It was this combination of religious and tourist venue that made them important sites for clashes of culture and power.

On April 8, 1901, there was a confrontation between a Mr. Middleton, a European artist painting on the platform, and a Sino-Burmese Buddhist, Khun

Chwan. According to Khun Chwan, Middleton told him to go away from where he was painting and, when he refused, Middleton began to abuse him with a barrage of obscenities. Khun Chwan then accused Middleton of being a "loafer." "Loafer" was a nineteenth-century term used for the unemployed/hobo/beachcomber class to which Dhammaloka had belonged, but here it was used as a great insult because to "loaf" was a high crime against the Victorian work ethic. Middleton called the pagoda trustees and the police to have Khun Chwan brought up on charges of insult.

At the trial, Middleton alleged that Khun Chwan was "mixed up with the European phongyee who had been agitating against the wearing of shoes on the pagoda platform."[18] A pagoda trustee present at the trial and Khun Chwan himself both testified that Khun Chwan had never heard U Dhammaloka preach and that he, Khun Chwan, was the secretary of the Thamadati Buddhist Association, comprising mainly English-speaking young Burmese and Chinese who maintained a rest house on the Shwedagon platform. From the reports of the trial in Indian English-language newspapers, it seems that only the Crown attorney and the complainant Middleton linked the incident and the shoe question; everyone else saw these as separate issues connected only by their proximity on the pagoda platform and the perceived threats to colonial superiority. Khun Chwan was convicted of insulting Middleton and was sentenced to six months rigorous imprisonment and a one-year bond of one hundred rupees upon his release. He promptly appealed.

Rejecting the first appeal, the judge made it clear that the shoe question had come to overshadow all other issues in the minds of European authorities. He wrote,

It is unnecessary to seek for the reason of the accused's behaviour further than the insolent bluster which may often be noticed among the educated young men of Burmah. With regard to the so-called shoe question, I imagine that such a question could only arise if the leaders of the Bhuddist [sic] religion were to express a desire to restrain Europeans from going on the Pagoda platform with their boots on. I presume that the trustees of the Shwe Dagon Pagoda may properly be considered to be such leaders, and the evidence of Mr. Middleton and of Maung Gyi, who is an Honorary Magistrate and Municipal councillor, and a Pagoda trustee, shows clearly that no such feeling exists at present.... If, therefore in future any irresponsible Burmese or half-Burmese or other persons venture to interfere with Europeans going on the Pagoda platform with their boots on the police should deal with them as brawlers and disturbers of the public peace.[19]

The judge's bias and sense of self-righteous privilege were made quite clear. He went on to say:

> if the European in question had been almost anyone but Mr. Middleton, it is not difficult to imagine that he would have in some way assaulted the half-Burman who had dared talk to him in the tone adopted by the accused. Judging from many years' experience of the country, the accused would then have produced a formidable clasp knife, and the European would have been stabbed, and Rangoon would have been treated to a sensational case of a European murdered on the Pagoda platform.[20]

The appellate judge assumed that Europeans, due to their colonial privilege, had a right to assault Burmese, but saw no irony in going on to accuse the Burmese of being inherently violent. His ruling ignored altogether the insult conviction being appealed and instead offered a verdict and legal precedent on the issue of Europeans wearing shoes on pagoda grounds, underlining Dhammaloka's success in forcing the issue.

Khun Chwan appealed this ruling to a higher court again, and the case was heard in Rangoon on July 4. This time his sentence was overturned and the appellate judge chided the magistrate and lower court appellate judge for inflaming European passions by inserting the shoe issue where it did not belong. Justice Fox wrote,

> I am convinced that the occurrence did not spring from any bad feeling on the part of the accused or of anybody else towards Europeans. As to the shoe-wearing question that was, as the accused's advocate said, literally dragged into the case by the Magistrate himself, and it seems to have acted upon him as a cloud obscuring his power of perception.[21]

No Sole Theory

Throughout April to June the court case had been the talk of the town, following Dhammaloka's earlier shoe confrontation, and while the ruling in early July freed Khun Chwan, it did not settle the issue. The conflict had been noticed far afield: from Baltimore, the *Lutheran Observer* believed that "since [Dhammaloka's] arrival restrictions upon preaching and the distribution of [our Christian] religious literature have been rigorously enforced, and the temples zealously guarded from the intrusion of aliens."[22]

Dhammaloka's original confrontation not only gained him the sympathy of a large number of Burmese Buddhists, but spurred others to action. In May, an English-speaking Buddhist monk from Ceylon confronted a Eurasian and an Indian at the Shwekyimyin Pagoda in Mandalay, asking them to remove their shoes.[23] And in July, after both the ruling in the Khun Chwan case and the pagoda trustees' decision to post signs asking Buddhists not to disturb Europeans, U Dhammaloka returned to the Shwedagon (see figure 3.2), again making headlines beyond Burma. The *Times of India* reported:

> At about 2 p.m. on that day he entered the trustees' room, and asked to see Mg Gyi, one of the trustees who gave evidence in the Middleton case. There were three trustees present—Mg Shwe Waing, Po Lan and Po Oung. Colvin [Dhammaloka] on being told that Mg Gyi was not there, informed Mg Shwe Waing that he had a letter from Lord Curzon forbidding Europeans to come on the Pagoda platform. The trustees asked to be allowed to see the letter, but Colvin refused to show it. They then told him that they did not believe he had such a letter, and he went away after abusing and threatening Mg Shwe Waing. Colvin then went down off the platform and posted himself at the bottom of the steps. Here he stopped Mr. Skeen of Messrs. Watts and Skeen and Mr McGeachin of the s.s. *London*, telling them that they would not be allowed to go up on the Pagoda platform. However, they passed him without taking any notice of him, and Colvin then followed them up, and passing them stopped them again at the drawbridge, telling them there would be trouble if they went on. Here a *durwan* [porter] went up and called the trustees, who told Mr. Skeen and his friend they could go up. Colvin got very angry at this, and told Mg Shwe Waing that he would get him turned out of the trusteeship as he was a Government servant and not elected by the people. Colvin then went up on the platform and continued to annoy the two Europeans. He had a crowd of Burmans round him, whom he addressed. He said he had only been waiting for Mr. Middleton's case to blow over, and intended to institute a campaign against Europeans coming up on the platform. [24]

Despite the rhetoric that Burmese were seeking to reject Europeans wearing shoes, this was one of the very few times in the conflict that Europeans had in fact been confronted over footwear; to date the conflict in Rangoon had involved an Indian policeman, a Sino-Burmese man, and an Irishman (Dhammaloka).

Beyond the Europeans' concern that their authority was being challenged, the significance shoes held for different groups on the pagoda platform is telling. The initial appellate judge in the Middleton case was quick to assert that the shoe question was not a religious issue. He solicited a pagoda trustee to defend this claim, because official British religious neutrality meant that his authority to

Figure 3.2. Southern steps of Shwedagon Pagoda. This is where Dhammaloka would have confronted Europeans who entered wearing shoes.
Photo by Philip A. Klier, Rangoon, 1906. The National Archives (UK).

dictate the rights and wrongs of such interactions would be lost if the case became a matter of religion.

For U Dhammaloka, on the other hand, the issue was clearly the defense of Buddhism. Just before the confrontation, he had published a pamphlet entitled "Unity is Strength," exhorting Buddhists to organize in defense of religion; for him these conflicts were a dramatic manifestation of the larger struggle.[25] His critics were not wrong in seeing that this sentiment was tied in with an opposition to colonial rule: the rest of his career would be devoted to a critique of colonialism through the lens of religion. The later Burmese nationalist movement would coalesce in 1916 around the issue of Europeans wearing shoes on the pagoda, and the nationalists would mark their eventual victory on this issue in 1919 as the beginning of the end of colonial rule. Dhammaloka's contributions have not been remembered in Burmese nationalist histories, but he set the stage for what was to become a central political conflict.

4

Tokyo—An Irish Burmese Monk in Imperial Japan

1902–3

With the shoe conflict, his triumphal Mandalay trips, and his countrywide tours over two years, Dhammaloka was now a celebrity monk in Burma. Yet in July 1902 he unexpectedly abandoned Burma to sail for Yokohama. We have seen reports of invitations to Japan and a possible connection through his colleague U Maung Maung of the Mandalay Society for Promoting Buddhism, who accompanied him in Japan.[1]

Questions remain, however. Dhammaloka's sudden departure for Japan apparently caused quite a stir.[2] Why would he leave Burma at the height of his popularity and in the midst of his activities in 1902 to travel to the other end of Buddhist Asia? And why would Japanese Buddhists invite an Irish Burmese monk to visit Tokyo?

Another World's Parliament of Religions?

One explanation may be found in the biography of the inspirational modern Hindu guru Swami Rama Tirtha (1873–1906). Swami Rama arrived in Japan soon after Dhammaloka, expecting, we are told, a repeat in Tokyo of the famous Chicago World's Parliament of Religions, held as part of the huge 1893 Chicago World's Fair.[3] It seems likely that Dhammaloka had heard of the proposed event and wanted to be there, too. The World's Parliament of Religions is credited with being one of the first platforms for a presentation of world religions by their own practitioners, and on somewhat equal footing. Various representatives of Asian traditions at the event, including the Hindu Swami Vivekananda and the Buddhist campaigner Anagarika Dharmapala, went on to define much of the Western perception of "modern" Hinduism and Buddhism. The event was seen as a historic opportunity both for the advancement of inter-religious dialogue

The Irish Buddhist. Alicia Turner, Laurence Cox, and Brian Bocking, Oxford University Press (2020)
© Alicia Turner, Laurence Cox and Brian Bocking.
DOI: 10.1093/oso/9780190073084.001.0001

and for Asians to represent the modernity, and in some views superiority, of their traditions.

The story of a proposed follow-up parliament of religions in Japan brings together a number of important names in modern religious reform movements in Japan and India. The idea that Japan should be the nation to host a World's Parliament of Religions on the tenth anniversary of the Chicago event was actively promoted during 1901–2 by a number of enterprising figures, among them another pioneering Irish Buddhist, "Captain" Charles Pfoundes. A decade earlier, Pfoundes had launched a Buddhist mission in London sponsored by Pure Land Buddhists in Kyoto. He was now back in Japan, his adopted home, working in various roles as a business and cultural intermediary.[4] Pfoundes's own vision was for a major international exhibition in Osaka, covering everything from science and technology to religion and oriental studies, but his efforts seem to have garnered little local or international support. Other promoters of a second Parliament, far better known and more highly regarded among the Japanese, were the fine arts scholar Okakura Kakuzo (pen-name Tenshin) and the Pure Land Buddhist priest Oda Tokuno (1860–1911).[5]

Early in 1902, Okakura was in Bengal, trying to persuade the ailing Swami Vivekananda, undisputed star of the 1893 Chicago Parliament, to travel to Japan to be guest of honor at a follow-up conference. Oda, who had spent two years (1888–90) in Siam, sailed to India via Rangoon in March 1902 to join Okakura. A definite plan for a congress of religions ten years after Chicago was reportedly hatched during a visit to Bodh Gaya by the two Japanese colleagues. Vivekananda declined to be involved in the project on grounds of ill-health and indeed died a few months later in July 1902.[6]

Rumors about the proposed event soon spread in India, including the idea that it would be held as early as October 1902, although Oda and Okakura were actually planning for the spring of 1903.[7] While a later report from Japan says that Dhammaloka first met Oda in Siam, it is more likely that Dhammaloka learned of the proposed Japanese congress in Rangoon, perhaps during Oda's stopover there en route to India in March. Once he knew of the plan, Dhammaloka headed as rapidly as possible to Tokyo to secure a place at the global religious table. On arrival in Japan, he went first to stay with Oda.

Oda and Okakura were criticized in the Japanese press for their presumption in planning to mount, without official backing, an ambitious, large-scale international event billed as a follow-up to the Chicago Parliament of Religions. If it failed, Japan's national reputation would suffer. Puran Singh (1881–1931), a Sikh who in 1902 was a young chemistry student at Tokyo Imperial University and later destined to become an eminent mystic, writer, and business entrepreneur in his native Punjab,[8] recalled many years afterward:

[A]n announcement was made in India by some of the Bengali friends of the late Mr. Okakura of Japan to hold the next session of a similar [to Chicago] International Parliament in Tokyo. Perhaps this announcement was made prematurely. Mr. Okakura, then, was on a flying visit to India, he might have expressed his wish to the late revered Sister Nivedita[9] and probably wanted to arrange for it on his return. But Mr. Okakura was still in Calcutta, when the news reached the Tokyo Press which stood against the proposal, and unsupported as it was by the presence of Mr. Okakura himself in Japan, the proposal was born dead.[10]

Puran Singh's account is found in his biography of his erstwhile guru, Swami Rama Tirtha, the charismatic Hindu saint mentioned earlier. He relates that the Swami's sudden visit to Japan was sponsored by one of his aristocratic Indian devotees in the belief that a second Parliament was about to be held there.[11] According to Singh, who became an instant devotee of Swami Rama when they met in September 1902 at the Indo-Japanese Club in Yokohama, the Swami was simply amused to discover on his arrival that no Parliament of Religions was happening.[12] Dhammaloka would have been met by the same news on his arrival, but made the best of his time in Japan to build other international connections promoting Buddhism.

Dhammaloka's Japanese Connections

If it was the prospect of an international congress that drew Dhammaloka to Japan in 1902, it was probably not his first visit. Harry Franck, who interviewed him three years later, recounted that Dhammaloka had first sailed to Yokohama, the seaport for Tokyo, from San Francisco as an ordinary sailor (by implication around 1880), was paid off (or thrown off his ship) in Japan, and eventually ended up in Rangoon.[13] It is doubtful whether Dhammaloka would have shared this information with his Japanese Buddhist hosts; in a series of nine interviews in December 1902 with the national newspaper *Nipon* he said only that he had worked previously in Australia as a mining engineer.[14] The 1902 visit was certainly his first to Japan in the monastic *persona* of U Dhammaloka, the Irish Buddhist.

Dhammaloka was in Japan by August 14.[15] As a visiting ecclesiastic, Dhammaloka stayed initially with Oda Tokuno but reportedly felt uncomfortable lodging with a married monk[16] and soon moved, perhaps after a short stay at the Asakusa Honganji temple,[17] to a central Tokyo Shingon (esoteric) Buddhist temple-school, Mejiro Soen. The Abbot there was Shaka Unsho, known for his unusual advocacy of strict *vinaya* rules regulating monks' behavior. This should in theory have suited Dhammaloka's lifestyle as a monk from Burma, where vinaya was a greater concern than in Japanese Buddhism.

Dhammaloka explained to the *Nipon* that he was in Japan "to conduct a comparative study of Southern Buddhism and Northern Buddhism, that is, Hinayana and Mahayana" and a Buddhist university newsletter reported that he studied Japanese language and Buddhism daily at the temple school where he stayed.[18] However, Dhammaloka eventually fell out with Unsho who, he claimed, treated him like a novice,[19] and told the *Nipon* that he had learned nothing worthwhile during his stay with Unsho.[20]

Nevertheless, Shaka Unsho's temple was a logical place to stay for a visiting monk with ties to the international Buddhist revival. Abbot Unsho was the uncle of Shaku Kozen, another Japanese Shingon Buddhist monk who had traveled to Ceylon sixteen years earlier in 1886 in search of "authentic" Buddhism and who is today considered to be the first Japanese monk to receive a full Theravada *bhikkhu* (monk's) ordination.[21] Since his return to Japan in 1893, Kozen had been practicing Sinhalese Buddhism in Yokohama. It might have seemed more appropriate for Dhammaloka to stay in Yokohama with this fellow Theravada monk, rather than with the Japanese traditionalist Shaka Unsho at his temple in central Tokyo. Yokohama is, of course, some way from Tokyo, but the likely reason was that Unsho was one of the vice presidents of the Maha Bodhi Society, of which Dhammaloka was a member.[22]

It would also be clear that Unsho in his own temple ranked above the visitor Dhammaloka, an important consideration for the Japanese, who had trouble placing an Irish Burmese Buddhist monk in a recognizable category. Dhammaloka did not take kindly to being treated as an inferior, and Unsho and Dhammaloka soon fell out because Dhammaloka did not display the Japanese-style level of deference demanded by his eminent host. Indeed, Dhammaloka later described him as a danger to true Buddhism, and wrote to Burma from Japan withdrawing his support for Unsho to be listed alongside the Dalai Lama as a vice president of the Society for Promoting Buddhism.[23] Dhammaloka nevertheless learned a thing or two about hierarchy from the Japanese; on his return to Southeast Asia he claimed to have been promoted in Japan to "Lord High Abbot," thus outranking any other monk in the region.

Launching an International Buddhist Association

If a Japan-based World's Parliament of Religions had failed to materialize, Dhammaloka's first public appearance in Japan was at the birth of another institution seeking to promote international Buddhist cooperation and revival. On

September 23, 1902, he was on stage in the auditorium of Takanawa Buddhist University, a progressive Jodo Shinshu (True Pure Land Sect) college,[24] to give one of the talks at the crowded launch of the *Bankoku bukkyo seinen rengokai*, the International Young Men's Buddhist Association (IYMBA).[25] The *Takanawa University Gazette*[26] gave a brief account of the gathering, explaining that while the founding of the Association had been announced in May, with the intended participation of Anagarika Dharmapala, the Buddhist reformer from Ceylon, the inaugural ceremony had been delayed until September.[27]

The first speaker discussed how Takanawa Buddhist University was particularly well poised to found an International Buddhist Association, given it and its predecessor's history of international Buddhist missions.

> Mr Sakurai Gicho[28] [spoke] in detail about the activities of the students at Nishiyama, the predecessor to the present college, and at the Normal School;[29] he spoke too about the history of the Overseas Mission Society[30] and the state of affairs concerning students from this college active overseas now, and of young Otani [Shinshu] priests presently active overseas; he spoke about how great a need there was for a Global Youth Buddhist League, and how ideally placed Takanawa university was to serve as a mediating agency for such.[31]

This was particularly true if the intention of an International Buddhist Association was to promote Japanese Buddhist ideals overseas, and the next few speakers concurred with congratulatory words. The exception to this program was "a lecture in English by Mr Dhammaloka." The *University Gazette* continued,

> Regarding Mr D, he is an Irishman who believes profoundly in Buddhism; after coming to Burma he became extremely devoted to the study and propagation of Buddhism. On one occasion he brought back to their original Buddhist faith two hundred converts to Christianity. He is now, moreover, here in Japan where he is engaged in the daily study of Japanese language and Buddhism at the Mejiro Soen [Shaku Unsho's temple]. This gentleman is shaven-headed, wears a Buddhist robe and has a reverential appearance. In fact, this man is reputedly the pioneer genuine Buddhist monk among Euro-Americans.[32]

A "Euro-American Child"

Dhammaloka was a curiosity and the only non-Japanese among the speakers. His background and approach were not in keeping with the rest of the event, but

Figure 4.1. "My beard is white, but my heart is still red." Shimaji Mokurai, elected by acclaim as president of the IYMBA in Tokyo.
Source: Wikimedia Commons/Public Domain.

his presence would be interpreted as an auspicious sign for the new mission of the International Association, if not perhaps in the most flattering way:

> Lastly, when Mr D's [Dhammaloka's] speech was over, Shimaji Mokurai,[33] employing the clever and witty oratory for which he is renowned, celebrated the establishment of the Association. He declared that when the Buddha's light dwelt in the heart of a Euro-American, this was indeed the coming to fruition of a child, so to say, among the billions of sentient beings; there was no greater example of the working of *ho-on* [repayment of the blessings of the Buddha].[34]

The sixty-four-year-old Shimaji Mokurai (see Figure 4.1) was clearly the most respected authority at the event, and both his personal history and his enthusiasm led the group to adopt him as their natural leader:

> By way of conclusion Prof. Shimaji spoke of his personal association at the time of the Meiji Restoration with the imperial-minded patriots, and how he had survived the terrorism of those years; he also spoke of his planning, at that time,

of the reform of the Honganji sect. This was all of great interest. Above all, when he declared vigorously to us that "my beard is white, but my heart is still red," one could only reflect that his energy was vastly greater than that of many a young man.

He was proposed as President of the IYMBA. His response was: "Could there be anybody less suitable than me!" Upon which the meeting erupted into applause, and during this time Prof. Shimaji got down from the stage.[35]

That Dhammaloka was the only foreign Buddhist—indeed the only foreigner—to speak at this "international" event suggests that his availability for an otherwise all-Japanese event was fortuitous rather than planned. Dhammaloka was a choice not in keeping with Japanese ideas of modern Buddhism at the time. While the innovative, lay/monastic "anagarika" role pioneered by Anagarika Dharmapala, who had visited Japan in May, played to modern Japanese hopes and expectations of Buddhism, Dhammaloka's espousal of Burmese-style celibacy and renunciation hardly matched up to the IYMBA's ideal of a "modern" Buddhist. Indeed, Dhammaloka outspokenly criticized Japanese priests for not being celibate and for drinking alcohol.[36]

In addition, of course, Dhammaloka was not a young man (even by Japanese standards), being probably around forty-five. Even being European did not necessarily make him unique in the Japanese Buddhist world. By 1902, two decades after the American Theosophist Colonel Olcott had first visited Japan in his quest to unite "Southern" and "Northern" Buddhism, Tokyo was awash with Europeans. The Japanese Buddhists—some of whom, like the august Shimaji Mokurai, were well traveled overseas—had encountered various Euro-American Buddhists, even if not Euro-American Buddhist monastics.

With the untypical exception of Shaku Kozen's one-man campaign to proselytize on behalf of Theravada Buddhism in Japan, the Japanese idea of a modernized, global Buddhism guided by young Buddhist activists from rapidly industrializing Japan (Figure 4.2) did not, in 1902, envisage a turn toward the Theravada ideal of the traditional, barefoot, possessionless, mendicant monastic. Quite the reverse; Japanese priests of all sects after the Meiji restoration were increasingly expected to be married and to make a living from their family-owned temples or from teaching or other productive secular activities. The Shinshu Pure Land sect, which ran Takanawa Buddhist University and was directly sponsoring the IYMBA, had promoted clerical marriage since the thirteenth century.

Hence, Dhammaloka was in some ways an unlikely, and probably unlooked-for, guest speaker. Insofar as he did fill a specific role in the program, it may have been as a representative of the Buddhist revival in other Asian countries. As a stand-in for the absent Anagarika Dharmapala, it probably helped that the names Dhammaloka and Dharmapala sounded not too dissimilar to the Japanese.

After he left Japan, Dhammaloka claimed that he himself was the founder and indeed president of the IYMBA[37] and made a side-claim that he had guided the formulation of some of its financial policies,[38] but these assertions find no support in Japanese records. The *Yomiuri Shimbun* newspaper had announced back in May the launch of the Association by Dharmapala, general secretary of the Maha Bodhi Society, Calcutta, during his third visit to Japan. The paper revealed on May 19, 1902 that

> [t]he International Buddhist Youth Association will have its base at Takanawa Buddhist University. The league will engage Buddhist youths from America, Hawaii, India, Siam, Burma, China, Korea and Ceylon, as well as from all the nations of Europe. The league was launched [*sic*] in the university on 16th [May 1902]. For the present, *Darumabara* [Dharmapala] insists that most effort be directed towards Burma, Siam and Ceylon.

In fact, the launch had not taken place. It was delayed until September, by which time Anagarika Dharmapala had left Japan for America and Dhammaloka had arrived from Burma. Dharmapala already had a long record as an instigator and promoter of pan-Buddhist movements worldwide, whereas Dhammaloka's active involvement in Buddhist organizing was restricted to Burma.

Dhammaloka's claim to be president and founder of the Tokyo IYMBA is also contradicted by the *Takanawa University Gazette's* account of the launch, published on October 5. There is no suggestion that Dhammaloka was offered the presidency and it is indicative that, while only positive things were said about him in the *Gazette* report, little of Dhammaloka's own speech was reported. Shimaji Mokurai's silken suggestion that Dhammaloka was a Euro-American "child" may have reflected Pure Land piety, racial or intellectual condescension, or perhaps all three, given the veteran Shimaji's expertise as a speaker. Although Dhammaloka was one of the speakers at the event and the only foreign monk present, his participation seems from the Japanese point of view to have been largely tokenistic. It is made clear in the *University Gazette* that Shimaji was elected president by acclaim, despite his self-deprecating response. Dhammaloka, as a European Buddhist monk, could be a useful prop in a Japanese Buddhist play, but he was not necessarily seen as a central actor by the senior Asian Buddhist leaders around him.

Return to the Buddhist University

The second public event in Japan featuring Dhammaloka was the "Autumn Student Conference" convened at the same Takanawa Buddhist University in

Tokyo. It was held on October 10, 1902, nearly three weeks after the IYMBA inauguration. Dhammaloka was not asked to speak this time, but he was an invited guest; one of those who took tea beforehand with the university president. The *Takanawa University Gazette*'s report of the "lecture section" of the Student Conference (other activities included all-day tennis and kendo sports tournaments and an evening music concert) included the following:

> The Lecture Section began with a lecture meeting in the auditorium at 1pm. First of all, our own student Fujieda Sensho[39] gave an opening address. Then a member of our staff, Mr Kitamura Kyogon, offered his wholehearted opinion on "The future prospects of Buddhism; my personal outlook" and Mr Uchimura Kanzo,[40] titling his talk "A phase of my religious life" spoke from a personal standpoint about the conflicts in society over the last 25 years. . . . After him an Indian, Mr Puran Singh who had come to this country some time ago in company with Mr Dharmapala[41] and who spoke in English, said amongst other things that he personally had a great deal of sympathy for what Mr Uchimura had said, but that his own belief in the Buddha's teachings was not a question of mere custom. Following on, the Indian Doctor of Philosophy [*sic*], Mr Swami Rama,[42] also speaking in English, said that the misunderstanding of Nirvana among people at large was truly regrettable; Nirvana is great joy and happiness. Speaking with great passion, he said that of all the world's religions— Christianity, Brahmanism, Islam and so on, the truth, rationality and nobility of the Buddha's teachings was the most elevated. Finally, Mr Sensho Murakami[43] delivered a characteristically stern lecture on "Differences and Similarities between Logic and Religion."[44]

This lecture program seems to have been a student-level attempt to hold a mini-parliament of religions, with a rather impressive lineup of speakers representing Buddhist (Kitamura, Puran Singh), "Indian" (Puran Singh, Swami Rama), and Christian (Uchimura) standpoints and concluding with Sensho Murakami, well known for introducing Western scholarship on Buddhism to Japan, comparing religion with (scientific) logic.

It is perhaps not surprising that Dhammaloka was not invited to lecture on Buddhism. Buddhist speakers were the least difficult to find in a Buddhist university, and Dhammaloka could not speak Japanese. Moreover, the Japanese were by now familiar with his educational level and confrontational style and probably regarded him as a potential loose cannon. In his first IYMBA speech at Takanawa on September 23, Dhammaloka had told how "on one occasion he brought back to their original Buddhist faith two hundred converts to Christianity" and we may infer from this that his IYMBA talk was not very much different from the rousing address witnessed by Sara Jeanette Duncan (Mrs. Everard Cotes) the

previous December at Asoka II's novice ordination in Rangoon. On this occasion, Dhammaloka had

> related, with modesty, some of his own exploits in defence of the indigenous
> faith. He had shut up no less than three mission stations, he told us, mainly by
> force of public argument, and he gave us details of one polemical struggle in
> which the missionary was fairly routed in the eyes of the audience because he
> was unable to produce "any sort of proof" for the story of Joshua and the sun.
> He was modest, but he also gloried. "If anyone gives trouble on these subjects"
> said he, "just you refer him to me. I don't think there'll be much more anxiety
> for public controversy so long as I'm around."[45]

Dhammaloka had recently been denounced in the Tokyo press by the Christian
editor of *The Voice*—the wonderfully named Eugenese Snodgrass.[46] Hence,
Dhammaloka might well have used the opportunity of a public speaking event
at Takanawa Buddhist University to respond in kind. But in 1902, nearly ten
years after the Chicago Parliament of Religions, his truculent anti-Christian
rhetoric was not what parliamentarians of religion wished to hear. The Western,
broadly Protestant, understanding of religion as a private matter of "doctrine-
faith-religious experience," to borrow Helen Hardacre's term, was by now widespread in Japan, more than a decade after the 1890 Meiji Constitution had
enshrined the separation of "religions" from the state (albeit a state ruled by a
divine emperor).[47]

A "world religions" approach, based on this privatized and voluntaristic
understanding of religion, is well reflected in the multi-religious program at
Takanawa, which after all was a Buddhist university. Uchimura's Christian
speech was even published in full in the university's magazine. The prevailing
intellectual discourse of the time, which identified "the world's religions" as a
genus of which Buddhism, Christianity, and so on, were different and not necessarily competing species, played an important political role in late Meiji Japan,
where the internationally sensitive question of freedom of religion (primarily for
Christians) had been at issue since before the Meiji Restoration of 1868.[48]

Within Japan, the issue of religious freedom revolved around the relationship between religions based on voluntary individual or family adherence,
such as the many Buddhist and Christian denominations as well as various
new or minority religions recognized as "Shinto sects," and the compul-
sory "supra-religious" or "nondenominational" national cult of reverence
for the divinized emperor; the modern (Meiji-era) form of Shinto.[49] Shimaji
Mokurai, the recently elected president of the IYMBA, had articulated his
view on the difference between "religions" and Shinto as far back as June 1874,
declaring that:

What we know as religions, Buddhism, Christianity, etc., are all universal. These religions talk of the mysteries of the other world in terms of the two realms or the three realms; they explain the laws of cause and effect, known as karma; they offer faith in a truth beyond the reality of experience and knowledge; they lead the believer, by stages, towards good and away from evil. . . . As for the deities venerated in these creeds, sometimes they are monotheistic, sometimes polytheistic; but they are always mysterious and reside in the other realm.[50]

Within such a "religions of the world" model, attacking one religion—Christianity—as a moral and cultural menace and a bar to rationalistic atheism and scientific progress, as Dhammaloka was prone to do, could undermine the case for respecting any religion, including Buddhism. If within the British empire, Dhammaloka could speak for an embattled native religion against colonial Christianity, independent Japan was becoming a Great Power in its own right. Japanese Buddhists sought mutual recognition with Christianity, on the world stage and internally, where Shimaji's position outlined a strategy aimed at securing endorsement of Buddhism by the imperial Japanese state.

A Woman Alone in the Heart of Japan

The *Takanawa University Gazette* identifies among the foreign guests not only Dhammaloka, but also "the editor of the Theosophical Magazine" (unnamed), and Damodar Singh, Puran Singh's fellow scholarship student in the science faculty of Tokyo Imperial University. Dhammaloka brought two further guests; an elderly Irishwoman from Australia, Mrs. Letitia Jephson,[51] whom the *Gazette* describes as the "head of the Theosophical Society" (probably a reference to her long-standing involvement in the Brisbane Society), and a young American travel writer, Gertrude Adams Fisher from New York .

Fisher wrote in her subsequent 1906 book, rather disingenuously titled *A Woman Alone in the Heart of Japan*, of her day at "the Buddhist University." Fisher can have understood little of the talks, all except those by the two Indians being in Japanese. She did note three "earnest" female students in the audience, suggesting that the IYMBA was not entirely male.[52] Fisher was entranced by the romantic figure of Swami Rama Tirtha and equally prejudiced against Dhammaloka and her other fellow Europeans. Her chapter on "The Buddhist University" begins:

The old Irish-Australian lady, advanced theosophist and incipient Buddhist and all-round crank, had in tow an Irish ex-priest, sycophant and parasite, who was ready to embrace any doctrine which meant no work and fruitful returns.

He claimed to have studied, long years, the occult science in India. He had been denounced by an ex-missionary,[53] editor of *The Voice*, in Tokio, and was challenged to an argument. Though the old lady was willing to believe in the Irishman, with limitations, she did not wish him to run on to sure ruin, and offered her advice, when he declared he should answer the challenge. "Sure, you'll do no such thing. You can't answer those arguments. You haven't got the wisdom nor the learning to open your mouth, and you must just keep still." It was difficult to down the Hibernian fakir, but the old lady prevailed, and then we accepted his invitation to the Buddhist University, seat of mystic learning, in a grove outside of Tokio.[54]

Fisher understood very little about Dhammaloka's position as a Buddhist monk. Unaware that Dhammaloka was not expected to handle money, she interpreted his request for Letitia Jephson to pay the tramway fare as presumptuous.

He met us at the station, robed in flaming orange. He looked like a cutthroat playing a saintly role. His two brethren were less conspicuous in gray togas. It would have cost a mite to pass the turnstile with a platform ticket, so they waited just beyond, and their sandals scuffled through the dust as we made our way to the jogging tram. "You will kindly pay our fares," said the Irishman, with calm assurance. "Oh indeed, sure, we will do that, with pleasure." said the old lady.[55]

It appears that Jephson also provided some material support for Dhammaloka and acted as lay donor for part of his time in Japan. Fisher describes how, as well as paying Dhammaloka's fares, Jephson baked for him a "mammoth sponge cake," swearing (untruthfully) that it contained no eggs.[56]

We have evidence of at least one more public event to which Dhammaloka was invited, this time again as a speaker. According to the Shingon Buddhist magazine *Dento* of October 28, 1902, Dhammaloka's former host Oda Tokuno, one of the organizers of the "East Asian Buddhist Association," invited him to speak at a memorial gathering of the Association on October 25, 1902. Other speakers would include the former military officer and statesman Miura Goro, the scholar Sensho Murakami (mentioned earlier), and the lay Buddhist activist Ouchi Seiran. Around two hundred were expected, including luminaries such as Shaku Unsho, the abbot of the temple where Dhammaloka had earlier resided, and Shimaji Mokurai, now president of the IYMBA. We have no record of Dhammaloka's involvement in the event beyond the announcement, but it demonstrates that Dhammaloka was continuing to engage with his Japanese Buddhist counterparts.

Figure 4.2. Modern Japan: Downtown Tokyo around the time of Dhammaloka's visit, with electric trams, telegraph wires, and hand-drawn carts.
Library of Congress/H. C. White Co.

A Transnational Perspective

In December, Dhammaloka was interviewed at length by a reporter from the national *Nipon* newspaper. By this point he was living at a third Tokyo location, in Rekisen, having left Shaku Unsho's temple. In this major interview, published in nine parts between December 14 and 25, 1902, Dhammaloka not only talks about his own Buddhist activities, claiming incidentally that he had been practicing and promoting Buddhism in Burma for ten years and was also very familiar with Ceylon, but also provides a detailed description of Burma with some pride. He could easily have been writing for a Burmese tourism promotion board. He depicts Burma's people, its level of social equality including the high status of women, its fortunate climate, free Buddhist education system, high wages, abundant crops, impressive pagodas, productive industries, and advanced river and rail transport network.

In this, he offers a portrait of Burma as not only particularly modern but also, and in extremely positive terms, as a country that would actively welcome Japanese immigrants—unlike the United States and Australia, which treat Asian incomers so badly, or Ceylon, where people are poor and immigrants cannot find employment. He also makes it pointedly clear that Buddhism is understood by Burmese people to be quite different from "superstitions"—in other words, unlike the Buddhism he has encountered in Japan including, he says, at Shaka Unsho's temple.

Dhammaloka left Japan in January 1903, after a challenging six-month immersion in a rapidly industrializing society very different from that of colonial Burma, and after an extended engagement with forms of Buddhism quite unlike his own. If he had come intending to be part of another World's Parliament of Religions, he had—formally at least—been marginalized to the role of a minor player in Japanese Buddhist efforts at internationalization. The experience seems to have confirmed his view that his own renunciate Burmese Buddhism was superior to "Northern" forms, but at the same time Dhammaloka was evidently enthused and inspired by the energy and the global leadership ambitions of the modernizing Buddhists he encountered in Japan.

As we shall see, Dhammaloka made sincere attempts after leaving Japan to implement in his own fashion some of the aims of the IYMBA. In December 1902 the IYMBA in Tokyo was, according to a later official history of the association, establishing missions in four places—Hong Kong, Canton, Brisbane, and Penang.[57] In reality, this was Dhammaloka's agenda.[58] He left Kobe in February for Hong Kong and very possibly visited Canton, too; in subsequent years he put considerable time and effort into missionizing Penang (see Chapter 5). Brisbane was of course home to Dhammaloka's Irish-Australian Theosophist ally in Tokyo, Letitia Jephson. Dhammaloka intended to visit Australia in 1904 but did not make it there until 1912 (see Chapter 10). As we shall see, in Bangkok in 1903, inspired by events in Tokyo, Dhammaloka planned to build a great international center for Buddhists worldwide and actively sought to bring the different local Siamese Buddhist movements together under the aegis of the IYMBA. In Singapore in 1904 he succeeded in organizing innovative pan-Buddhist New Year celebrations.

In fact, Dhammaloka's globalizing efforts rapidly surpassed those of the IYMBA organizers he left behind in Tokyo. A 1939 history of Ryukoku University, describing the IYMBA's activities in Tokyo from May 1903 onward, says:

on 12 May, a resolution was passed at the second Association meeting for the construction of a conference hall, and on July 6th plans were made at the delegates conference for the raising of funds during the summer vacation. It appears that this was carried out by the Lecture Department during their summer mission work. After this period there was nothing; the university had numerous problems and because the [Takanawa] university closed, the IYMBA had no reality.[59]

Dhammaloka's repeated claim outside Japan to be founder and president of the IYMBA was, to say the least, an exaggeration, but it held a kernel of truth. He was the only European and the only non-Japanese Buddhist monk present at its founding, and he did make an invited speech at the launch alongside several prominent Japanese Buddhist intellectuals. We also know that he was present at the student conference at Takanawa Buddhist University, that he was invited by Oda Tokuno to address the members of the prestigious East Asia Buddhist Society, and that he was interviewed *in extenso* by the national press on matters Buddhist and Burmese. After Japan, he became and remained an energetic activist for Buddhism across Asia. These are not small achievements for an uneducated ex-hobo from Dublin.

5

Multiplying Buddhist Missions— Singapore, Bangkok, Penang

1903–5

Dhammaloka had left Burma for Japan without warning in the summer of 1902. By late February 1903 he was back in Singapore (see Map 5.1). However, rather than return to his Burmese supporters, he now sailed to Bangkok, the capital of independent Siam (Thailand). Why?

The answer lies in Dhammaloka's visit a year earlier to Mandalay's Society for Promoting Buddhism (SPB) and a series of patronage connections that began there. Arriving in Mandalay on December 29, 1901, he missed by a month both Viceroy Lord Curzon's visit and a high-level encounter between the SPB and an influential group of *saophas* (rulers) of the semi-autonomous Shan States, gathered in Mandalay to meet the Viceroy.[1] The Shan States, under British protection, lay in northeastern Burma on the sensitive border with China, French Laos, and independent Siam. Beyond meeting Lord Curzon, the highlight for the Shan visitors was a grand SPB-hosted dinner where the saophas, Dhammaloka learned, had pledged both financial and moral support for the work of promoting Buddhism.[2]

Perhaps Siam held such a pull because Dhammaloka, inspired by the global ambitions of the Tokyo IYMBA, was also hoping to secure support from Buddhist Siam's royal family. The Siamese Crown Prince, Vajiravudh, was due to visit Japan on his way home from an English education and King Edward's coronation.[3] Japanese Buddhist reformers had high hopes for the visit, the Siamese crown having previously supported Anagarika Dharmapala's Maha Bodhi Society. Although Dhammaloka missed both the saophas in Mandalay and the Siamese prince in Tokyo, a confidant of his had met both parties and reported on their movements in relation to Dhammaloka. U Maung Maung, a former Burmese civil servant and SPB correspondent to the *Times of Burma*, met the saophas in Mandalay, then left in January 1902 for Siam.[4] Later that year we find him with Dhammaloka in Japan, and in 1903, now identified as a jewel merchant, assisting Dhammaloka in Bangkok.

The Irish Buddhist. Alicia Turner, Laurence Cox, and Brian Bocking, Oxford University Press (2020)
© Alicia Turner, Laurence Cox and Brian Bocking.
DOI: 10.1093/oso/9780190073084.001.0001

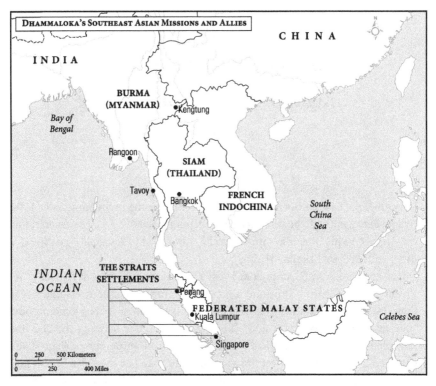

Map 5.1. Dhammaloka's Southeast Asian Missions and Allies.

Maung Maung, like Dhammaloka, tied many worlds together. In Mandalay, he had donated five precious items to the SPB, described as

> 1 Panel size photo of Great Japanese Image of Buddha at Buddha Gya,[5] at present enshrined at King Mindon's Zayat there.
> 1 Panel size photo of the Saranath Stupa at Isipatana, Benares.
> 1 Panel size photo of Lord Elgin and suite at the Bodi-tree, the Mahant worshipping the Viceroy.
> 1 Cabinet size photo of Madame Blavatsky.
> 1 do do [=ditto] of Col Olcott.[6]

This collection, with its intertwined references to archaeology, colonial power, and Theosophy, epitomizes the "globalizing" Buddhism of the period. The first item is a modern photograph brought back to Mandalay of a Japanese image sponsored by the Sinhalese-led Maha Bodhi Society and placed in the Burmese-donated rest house at Bodh Gaya in India. Maung Maung himself seems equally transnational: while writing about an Irish monk in Mandalay, he was about to head off to Siam and then Japan.

When he left Japan in early 1903, Dhammaloka planned to promote, initially in China, the energetic Buddhist ecumenism envisioned by the IYMBA in Tokyo:

> I am to China next month—and I hope to arrive in Pekin about the 1st of February—to call a meeting of the Chief Abbots, and to bring about a better understanding amongst all Buddhist countries. And, after that, I shall cross overland through China to either Siam or Burma. And I expect I shall arrive in Rangoon about the middle of May or the first week of June, and remain there a few weeks before proceeding on my journey to Lhassa in Tibet.[7]

Both this Burma-Lhasa itinerary and an alternative overland one via Peking were announced during Dhammaloka's journey from Tokyo via Kobe to Hong Kong.[8] But then he announced a change of route. He would now proceed to Singapore, then Bangkok, then overland through Siam and Burma to Lhasa.[9] The last-minute diversion to Singapore, it turns out, was prompted by his Siamese and Shan connections.

Intrigue with the Saopha: From Singapore to Bangkok

Dhammaloka returned from Japan a celebrity. Disembarking in February at Singapore, robed temporarily in the black garb of a Japanese "Lord High Abbot,"

> he received a grand welcome, from all the leading Buddhists of this City. . . . The Chinese community of Singapore have been holding feasts in Dhammaloka's honour, as though he were a Royal Prince. . . . All the Chinese Lamas, or Buddhist Priests, of Singapore, came to pay their respects to his Lordship, the Rt Revd U Dhammaloka. He also gave a lecture to some of the Europeans, at the Temperance Club. I see that all the Singapore papers speak very highly of him.[10]

Despite this enthusiastic reception, Dhammaloka cut short his visit to sail for Bangkok, subsequently telling the *Bangkok Times* that he expected to be in Siam for eight to nine months, to wait for the most propitious time to begin the long overland journey to Lhasa. All the more surprising then that he left Singapore so abruptly: "Mr. Dhammaloka was to have addressed a public meeting on Buddhism here, but unfortunately was prevented from so doing on account of his time being limited," ventured the *Straits Times*.[11] In fact, Dhammaloka left to accompany a Shan saopha to Bangkok.

Sao Kawng Kiao Intaleng, the thirty-two-year old Saopha of the Shan State of Kengtung (see Figure 5.1), had met Maung Maung at the grand SPB reception in Mandalay in December 1901.[12] Before Singapore, Intaleng had attended

Figure 5.1. Sao Kawng Kiao Intaleng, the Saopha of Kengtung, at the Delhi Durbar of 1903, from a group portrait of the Shan *saophas* dressed in ceremonial attire.
The British Library Board, December 3, 2019, Image c07765-03.

with the other saophas the great Delhi Durbar of January 1903, held to mark the accession of Edward VII and Queen Alexandra as emperor and empress of India. This event had a formative impact on Intaleng, underlining the glories of colonial power and his subordinate status as an isolated Shan leader. As Andrew Marshall explains,

> The wealth and grandeur of India's native rulers, the immense areas they controlled, the respect they were apparently accorded by the British—all this made him see the Shan chiefs in a new light. "We thought we were great men," Intaleng was heard to remark, "but now we see that we are only monkeys from the jungle."[13]

While the other *saophas* enjoyed a pilgrimage to Bodh Gaya, Intaleng, with a new purpose to establish himself as a leader and patron of Buddhism, traveled via Ceylon to Singapore, arriving on February 16, only a few days after Dhammaloka's triumphal return there from Japan.[14]

On arrival, the Saopha was whisked onto the governor's yacht to discuss affairs of state, and on February 19 Intaleng and Dhammaloka sailed together for Bangkok. Given the short time both had been in Singapore, we can only assume they had already corresponded and the Saopha was eager to sign on as a patron to Dhammaloka as part of his plans to reinvent himself as a modern Buddhist ruler. We don't know what they talked about on the boat, but the two men shared ambition and an unconventional approach, and it seems they fomented a number of plans on the trip.

In Bangkok, the Saopha was to meet Prince Damrong, the Siamese minister of the interior and a powerful modernizing advisor to the king.[15] A border conflict and rebellion involving Shan traders and Siamese forces had been ongoing since July 1902. The Saopha's purported purpose was to negotiate a peaceful settlement to what was potentially an international dispute involving the British, French, and Siamese powers.[16]

The Saopha's closeness to the much-traveled Irish Buddhist raised French suspicions that Dhammaloka was a British agent, sent to hinder Britain's imperial rival, France, from making further inroads with the still-independent Siamese.

> When first [Dhammaloka] went to Siam, it was darkly hinted that he was a British agent in disguise, with a mission to thwart the aims of M Beau and overwhelm Delcassé in a vortex of intrigue.... But U Dhammaloka pursued an even course, undisturbed by inuendoes [*sic*].[17]

This was a time of intrigue and rumors for the Burmese in Bangkok. As well as the Shan conflict, there were rumors of Burmese in Bangkok smuggling cash to a Mingyun prince (a pretender to the Burmese throne) and of intrigues by the Saopha himself around opium sales.[18] Moreover, the Saopha was using the negotiations on the border conflict to hide his own illegal negotiations to sell opium behind the back of his British minders.[19] British intelligence was in fact tracking Intaleng's movements, but hardly likely to send a headstrong working-class Irish Buddhist monk on a mission to infiltrate royalty, especially given the colonial government's deep suspicion of Dhammaloka after the recent Shwedagon shoe controversy (see Chapter 3).

Intaleng and Dhammaloka did have a cunning plan involving Bangkok, but it was not political; rather, it was a scheme to establish both of them as Buddhist leaders in a city where neither was yet known. At the Delhi Durbar, the Saopha had seen himself revealed as a minor character in a grandiose imperial play, and was looking for ways to elevate his importance on the regional stage.[20] He knew from Mandalay that the Burmese were acutely feeling the lack of a royally-sanctioned *thathanabaing* (head of the sangha) as a patron for their Buddhism. The Saopha saw a role for himself as a new kind of Buddhist monarch and patron of international Buddhist reform. Dhammaloka, despite his celebrity in Burma and Singapore and connections with Japan, was also aware of his relative insignificance in larger networks.

The pair arranged a press interview before disembarking at Bangkok, a profile of each appearing in the next day's paper.[21] More publicity would follow. Dhammaloka, always on the lookout for a confrontation in which he could act as hero and guardian of Buddhism, found an opportunity in a burgeoning crisis involving Burmese Buddhists in Bangkok, where enmity between Siam and the Burmese Shan States was causing a religious problem for the many devout Burmese residents of Bangkok:

> *The Siam Free Press* says that during the recent troubles in Northern Siam all the Burmese in Bangkok were denied the right of "korapping" (kowtowing) to the emerald Buddha in the Palace Wat [monastery] in Bangkok and the Burmese residents in Siam are greatly indignant against this insult cast upon them.[22]

With the Saopha's successful negotiation with the Siamese crown over border issues concluded, Dhammaloka (with a large delegation of Burmese residents in tow) requested that the Saopha of Kengtung intercede with the king:

> His Highness the Sawbwa [Saopha] will ask the King not to deny this privilege to Burmese who have a particular right to this emerald Buddha. Our contemporary [newspaper] also says that "his Buddhistic Venerableness Dam-a-looka [*sic*] at the head of 200 Burmese will wait on His Highness the Sawbwa and well-come him, at the same time asking His Highness to use his influence with

the King of Siam to permit them to 'korap' the Emerald Buddha as formerly and not to be angry with them, because of the trouble in the north of Siam as they cannot help it."[23]

Dhammaloka benefited from this arrangement. Both men were elevated in local prestige, and Dhammaloka garnered the support of the Burmese community in Bangkok for his next project.

Lhasa Can Wait: New Projects in Bangkok

Dhammaloka had planned to take a long and difficult overland route with the Saopha through Siam to Kengtung, continuing alone through Burma to Tibet. But again he changed his mind.

> The Irish Buddhist, the Lord Abbot Dhammaloka, who is staying at Wat Beromaniwate [subsequently corrected to Wat Ban Thawai,[24]] now intends to stop in Bangkok for about a year, for the furtherance of his work for the Buddhist Young Men's Society with which he is connected. At one time he intended to go North with the Sawbwa of Keng Tung, who left for his own State on Thursday; but he sees possibilities of useful work here which has made him stay on.[25]

Within six weeks, the newspapers were announcing what would become Dhammaloka's most successful project in Siam, and one of the most enduring legacies of his career.

> U. Dhammaloka, the Irish Buddhist now in Bangkok, has started a school at Wat Ban-ta-wai [Thawai] for the instruction of Siamese and Chinese boys in English. Already a large number of pupils have begun to take advantage of the opportunity afforded them of learning English, some 50 scholars attending daily. The class is held in a new building which was specially erected for the purpose of a schoolroom. No charge is made for attendance at the class.[26]

The school, which remarkably exists to this day in Bangkok, as Phibul Choompolpaisal discovered, was modeled on the Buddhist Anglo-Vernacular schools being opened in Burma.[27] These supplanted the Christian ethos of missionary schools with a Buddhist environment, while offering the Western English-language curriculum that attracted parents anxious for opportunities for their children's advancement.

Dhammaloka had some experience of Buddhist English-language schools. The key organizer of the SPB back in Mandalay, the former school inspector U Kyaw Yan, had opened several such schools in Burma. Dhammaloka, on tour in Burma in 1902, was often hosted by these institutions. Moreover, his own Tavoy monastery in Rangoon was, as he had told a journalist in Tokyo, "the big school of Rangoon." He explained:

> Buddhist monasteries are like schools, in short. Because they go there and learn reading and writing for the first while. Of course they cannot get on in monasteries for long; they cannot possibly stand it there. So they stay for a month or six weeks, and then they leave there, go to schools built by the government, and take regular education there. . . . If on the other hand a boy is from a poor family and cannot afford to pay for himself, he can of course receive education at a monastery indefinitely, and he can receive necessities of life at a monastery, according to the state law. Therefore, the literacy rate in the country is higher than most other places.[28]

As a newcomer to Bangkok, Dhammaloka could start a successful institution along these lines only through his Burmese connections.

> In Burma this European Buddhist was a power in the land but in Bangkok he was unknown. However, as like flies to like, he found several Burmans who had found their lines laid in easy places.[29] When the project of starting a school was mooted to them they immediately responded and immediately a thousand ticals[30] were subscribed. The school building was built and a start made—always under the auspices of the Society for Promoting Buddhism, whose headquarters is in Mandalay. A Committee of management was appointed, consisting of the Principal, U Dhammaloka, Moung Shwe Choung, the cashier of the Bombay Burma Trading Corporation; Moung Bah Yet, chief clerk in the same body; Maung Maung diamond and ruby merchant, and the general corresponding secretary of the Society in Bangkok.[31]

Dhammaloka had seemingly returned to his Burmese roots, laboring on behalf of the Mandalay SPB. In reality, the Bangkok school developed its own distinctive character under his guidance. Initially advertised as a free Buddhist English-language school, the Wat Ban Thawai school became increasingly cosmopolitan and inter-religious. An observer noted:

> A big sign outside the building says in Siamese and English "Buddhist School," but to a certain extent, that, as stated, is a misnomer. At the present time (and it should be borne in mind that the school has been open for only six weeks)

there are sixty pupils—Mahommedans, Eurasians of all creeds, and of course, Buddhists.[32]

The name "Ban Thawai" signals Dhammaloka's connection to Burma. "Thawai" is a Thai pronunciation of Burmese "Dawei," the name of the important trade port which colonial-era English converted to "Tavoy." Tavoy was directly west of Bangkok over the Tenasserim mountains—and Bangkok had long housed a Tavoyan population. Dhammaloka's wat was located in a multicultural area housing foreign embassies, communities of Europeans, and immigrant non-Thai Asian communities. In this latter aspect it was quite similar to the Tavoy monastery in Rangoon. As the *Bangkok Times* explained in June 1903:

> Wat Dawn [the alternative name for Ban Thawai] has found an exceedingly handy place for this school. It is in the centre of a populous district, where a large working-class population congregates, while being built away from the mire and confusion of the streets.[33]

The Wat had a rather wonderful logo, displayed at the school until 2014 (see Figure 5.2). Top right are the English letters A and Z, and top left the first and last letters of the Thai alphabet, *ko* and *ho*, arising from a chalice of knowledge held in cupped hands.

Dhammaloka's offer of an English-language education in a Buddhist temple school challenged the traditional Siamese system, though free education in itself was not new. As the *Bangkok Times* observed:

> [Dhammaloka] seems to be labouring under the misapprehension that free education is something new to Bangkok. . . . The education given at Siamese schools has always been free. . . . All the same anyone who can get more of the youth of Bangkok into school is doing work of the utmost value.[34]

International Buddhist Plans

Dhammaloka had further ambitious projects in mind. On June 7, the *Bangkok Times* reported that a joint meeting would be held eight days hence of three Buddhist societies represented in Siam, "the Society for Promoting Buddhism, the International Young Men's Buddhist Association and the Maha Bodhi Society," with a view to forming an independent "Siam Buddhist Society." The SPB was of course based in Mandalay, the IYMBA in Tokyo, and the Maha Bodhi Society in Calcutta.

Figure 5.2. Symbolizing progress: The logo of the bilingual school founded by Dhammaloka at Wat Ban Thawai, Bangkok.

Graphic © Chad Hubert 2019, from photo by Phibul Choompolpaisal.

Whatever money the Society raises will thus be expended in this country for the purposes of the Society, and not sent abroad. This was the plan adopted in Japan on the advice of U Dhammaloka, who is also the moving spirit here.[35]

And by July, Dhammaloka was describing himself as "the founder and president of the recently formed Siam National Buddhist Association."[36]

On June 10, 1903, *the Bangkok Times* publicized his next scheme, to build a new kind of wat designed specifically to accommodate visiting foreign Buddhists:

Already the success of the scheme is assured; the land has been secured through the generosity of a Buddhist layman; the plans for the building have been prepared and a considerable sum of money has been subscribed towards the erection of the building. It will be an international institution in every sense of the word. It will, as a matter of fact, be more than a Wat. There will be a hall, capable of seating 200 persons, where English lectures on Buddhism will be given; the hall may also be used as a schoolroom, or for any purpose calculated to advance Buddhism. At the rear there will be quarters for a large number of priests besides other rooms which may be used for a variety of purposes. It will be the headquarters of the International Buddhist Association [meaning the IYMBA] in Siam.[37]

Why was this innovative building required in Siam? "In Burma" Dhammaloka explained, "there is no need for it, the monasteries being open to every visitor, be he Buddhist priest in yellow robes or needy European who seeks hospitality."[38] This was certainly the approach of the Tavoy monastery in Rangoon.

A fortnight later, on June 23, Dhammaloka was promoting yet another project which, if successful, would more than justify the new building. The *Bangkok Times* explained:

The Irish Buddhist priest U Dhammaloka is at present sending out circulars announcing that it is proposed to hold an international Buddhist congress at Bangkok in the early part of next year. The congress would be under the auspices of the International Buddhist Association [i.e., the IYMBA], and it is hoped that delegates representing the society will be sent from Ceylon, Burma, China, Japan, America and England. . . . So far there has been no general meeting of the representatives of the International Association but interest in the movement has been stirred by the recent journey of U Dhammaloka to Japan and China. In Japan it was suggested that such a congress might be held, and now it seems that Bangkok is considered the most central situation for the holding of such a gathering. The main business of the congress would, of course, be the consideration of the best methods by which Buddhism could be advanced, and the reconciliation of the tenets held by the northern and southern schools of Buddhist thought. The various centres where the International Association has been established will be asked to send representative men, priests and laymen, and it is believed that some 500 will respond to the call.[39]

In proposing a Bangkok congress, Dhammaloka was aligning himself with the aims of the Japanese-led IYMBA in Tokyo, whose rules

stipulated that the purpose of the Association was to act as a network for all Buddhist believers, and those engaged in Buddhist studies, to which end it would promote, by mutual communication, the true spirit of Buddhism. Its activities would involve 1) communication with Buddhists of all nations, and dissemination of information on the ideas and current situation of Buddhists in every region; 2) sponsoring Japanese Buddhists to go overseas and foreign Buddhists to come to Japan; 3) reporting, in English, news from each region and *the convening in Japan and elsewhere of occasional congresses.*[40]

In retrospect, Dhammaloka's efforts in Bangkok in the IYMBA's name compare favorably with the fading achievements of its Japanese activists in Tokyo.

Meanwhile, his frequent use of "International Buddhist Association" as short-hand for the IYMBA succeeded in ruffling feathers in Burma. "International Buddhist Association" and "International Buddhist Society" were indistinguishable as translations of *Buddhasasana Samagama*, the society established by Ananda Metteyya (Allan Bennett) in Rangoon, who complained to the Bangkok papers;[41] just one example of the ongoing friction developing between the two pioneer European Buddhists of Rangoon (see Chapter 6).

A Chinese Invitation to Singapore

In August 1903, with Dhammaloka's Bangkok projects apparently thriving, the Singapore *Straits Times* revealed that he was leaving:

> The European Buddhist Priest, U. Dhammaloka, was shortly leaving Bangkok for Singapore. He expects to be away from Bangkok for about a month. He has been requested by a Chinese in Singapore to assist in establishing a Buddhist school here.[42]

Dhammaloka had been very warmly received in Singapore seven months earlier. European members of the Temperance Club were impressed by his "elegantly handled" talk, while the Chinese community held feasts in his honor.[43] Moreover:

> During his stay here he has held a conference of the principal Buddhists and discussed matters with them and a capital photograph of the group was taken. A more cosmopolitan assemblage it would be hard to find and it shows how widespread is the cult of Gautama.[44]

Some of Dhammaloka's Singapore contacts had evidently followed his progress in Bangkok, and felt his presence could benefit Singapore.

When, a few months later, Dhammaloka opened a school and Buddhist mission in Singapore, it occupied one of several properties on Havelock Road belonging to a leading Singapore Chinese businessman, Cheang Jim Chuan.[45] Jim Chuan's father, Cheang Hong Lim (1841–1893), a keen philanthropist and educationalist, ran a powerful opium and alcohol operation in the Straits Settlements while serving as a justice of the peace, a member of the legislative council, and head of the Hokkien Chinese community.[46] Hong Lim's eldest son, Cheang Jim Hean, shared his father's interests and in 1892 had established an

"English and Chinese Free School in Havelock Road." The school was a local success, receiving government grant aid, teaching up to forty-five boys to the sixth standard and featuring regularly in the papers for its students' prizes.[47] But when Jim Hean died unexpectedly in May 1901 the school, very much the product of his generosity, closed abruptly "without notice to masters or pupils."[48]

Cheang Jim Chuan (see Figure 5.3), Jim Hean's younger brother, now inherited the family's business, properties, and prestige. In Dhammaloka—an energetic English-speaking organizer who believed in the cause of free education for poor Asian pupils—Jim Chuan saw an opportunity to restore his brother's philanthropic school. The Cheangs had no specific tie to Buddhism—Jim Chuan's father had supported mainly Daoist temples—but there were many Buddhists in the Singapore Chinese community.

Back in Bangkok, the complaint against Dhammaloka from Ananda Metteyya in Burma seems to have rendered English-language newspapers less willing to accept Dhammaloka's press releases at face value, for a more skeptical tone set in. The *Bangkok Times* printed a story from the vernacular press that Dhammaloka had asked the Thai prince for passage to Singapore on the royal yacht the

Figure 5.3. An ambitious philanthropist: Cheang Jim Chuan, sponsor of Dhammaloka's free school and Buddhist mission on Havelock Road, Singapore.
Cornell University Library.

Mahachakkri and received an "unprintable" reply, adding that the sister news-paper "prays for a blessing on U Dhammaloka's work in Singapore, and trusts the fruits will be much greater than in Bangkok. It adds that Bangkok is not likely to see his face again."[49]

The following month, the *Bangkok Times* reproduced four earlier items from the *Times of Burma* which, it said, had been dispatches from the paper's "acting Bangkok correspondent" "Captain Daylight"[50]—who, it revealed, was none other than Dhammaloka. In blowing Captain Daylight's cover, the *Bangkok Times* was choosing to side against Dhammaloka. The first dispatch reported the theft of Dhammaloka's "beautiful marble clock, which was presented to him by some friends at the British Legation to adorn his school-room." The second advised readers that

> [t]he Irish Phongyee, U Dhammaloka, is building a grand kyoung [monastery], and school room. No doubt the Siamese are looking to the future, so that when he is elected as the Archbishop of Siam, he may have a grand residence to sustain the dignity of his office.[51]

The third, like Dhammaloka's earlier temperance speech in Singapore, demonstrates that for Dhammaloka the cause of temperance transcended religious boundaries.

> The Rev. Canon Greenstock and U Dhammaloka are opening a temperance club jointly in Bangkok. I wish them every success in their noble efforts to keep drunken men sober.[52]

Another, and by far the most grandiose, "Captain Daylight" piece had been dispatched from Bangkok on July 24, just after Ananda Metteyya's complaint had arrived. Captain Daylight wished Dhammaloka's sensitive critics in the *Buddhasasana Samagama* to know that

> [t]he Revd Lord Abbott, U Dhammaloka, with a numerous staff, returns to Rangoon about the end of October, and will make a tour throughout Burma. From Burma he goes to Calcutta, where he will probably meet the Viceroy before starting for Lhassa by way of Darjeeling. It is already understood that the Indian Government will place no obstacle in the pilgrim's path, the Chinese Government having already issued, to the Lord Abbott, a special passport to enter the Sacred City of Lhassa. His large number of admiring friends will welcome the return of the Irish Hpoongyi to Burma; and he will be missed from Bangkok, even by the European community with whom he is very popular.[53]

Flag of Truth Unfurled

Dhammaloka's projects in Singapore between 1903 and 1905 met with real success. On October 6, 1903, he restarted the Cheangs' school and launched his own "English Buddhist Mission," both occupying "a comfortable-looking little place perched on a shady hill" on Havelock Road.[54] Under Dhammaloka's tutelage the student body diversified. The *Journal of the Maha-Bodhi Society* in Calcutta carried a report (from the busy pen of Captain Daylight, now suddenly in Singapore) that "the school was located in one of the poorest localities of Singapore, where children of the factories around the locality can get a free English education as well as a religious education in the doctrines of our holy religion."[55] Dhammaloka had resumed the mission of the deceased Cheang Jim Hean's school: to educate "mostly children of very poor people."[56] In addition to the surviving brother Jim Chuan's support, Mr. B. P. de Silva, a Sinhalese immigrant who had arrived in Singapore with a handful of gemstones and built an enduring business as a jeweler, offered a scholarship.[57] Like Dhammaloka's school in Bangkok, the Havelock Road school was soon a success, averaging sixty students and garnering a positive reputation.

The school was only one half of the Havelock Road project. The English Buddhist Mission there announced that "young Straits-born Chinese can attend the evening classes and lectures for the study of the Dharma of our Lord Buddha . . . under the superintendence of the Rev. U Dhammaloka, better known as the Irish Buddhist Phongyee."[58] A Buddhist Sunday School welcomed all comers, there were plans to promote Buddhism more broadly across the Straits Settlements, and a call for a "European Buddhist lady . . . to commence a girls' Buddhist school upon the same lines as our boys' school has been started." By January 1904, "although primarily intended for the Chinese, work [at Havelock Road] is stated to have been so successful that the movement has been widened to embrace all classes."[59] The *Straits Chinese Magazine* likewise judged Dhammaloka "very successful in his work among a certain section of Europeans, and of course among the Singhalese."[60]

The mission also had some international resonance. In January 1904, Dhammaloka had "decided to publish a hymn-book in English, the Buddhist principles in metre being set to well-known English tunes," and one hymn ("Rejoice!") from this book, credited to Dhammaloka, was used by the Japanese-led Buddhist Mission of North America in its San Francisco mission.[61] The words, translated in Paul Carus's *Gospel of Buddha*, had been versified by the English lay Buddhist Major Dawsonne Strong in 1899. Dhammaloka (who in 1902 was distributing Strong's pamphlets free from the Tavoy monastery) seemingly edited Strong's text and put it to music—to the tune of "Ye banks and braes."[62]

The *Straits Times* offers a glimpse of the Havelock Road Mission choir, led by Dhammaloka, singing "a chant of praise in English."

The little Chinese youths showed that they had been well taught and their shrill little voices made the echoes ring with their hymn of praise. The last verse of the chant was as follows:

> Hail to Buddha, Hail the Dharma,
> Tell it to the World,
> Hail to Buddha, Hail the Sangha,
> Flag of Truth Unfurled.[63]

Dhammaloka's Singapore patrons were varied as ever. Arriving in Singapore from Bangkok in August 1903, Dhammaloka stayed first at 65 Sarangoon Road, the Japanese Buddhist Mission established in Singapore in September 1899 by "Rev. Ocha."[64] The Reverend is an enigma. We have found no record of him anywhere beyond his evidently willing involvement in Dhammaloka's projects, including the Buddhist New Year celebrations, a novice ordination (described in the following), and a comment by the German monk Nyanatiloka, who in 1904 stayed in Singapore first with "U Dhammaloka, of dubious repute" and then with "a very friendly, though married Japanese priest."[65] No doubt Ocha figured in the "cosmopolitan assemblage" of "the principal Buddhists of Singapore" photographed with Dhammaloka in February 1903.

Ocha may have been dispatched to Singapore as a Buddhist chaplain to Japanese workers and sailors just as, ten years earlier, Rev. Soryu Kagahi had been sent to Hawaii by the Shin Nishi Honganji main temple in Kyoto to serve Japanese laborers toiling in the sugar cane plantations.[66] However, 1899 was also the date of the first Japanese Buddhist missions to California, and Ocha's arrival coincided with those initiatives. Whether Ocha's bulletins back to Japan mentioned naval shipping movements and other interesting information to be gleaned in Singapore as well as the spiritual welfare of his Japanese flock is unknown, but not unlikely. The idea of Buddhist priests as spies was commonplace, as we saw with suspicions of Dhammaloka and the Saopha, and indeed immortalized in Kipling's *Kim* (1901). Japanese priest Kawaguchi Ekai, disguised as a Chinese monk and herbalist, had trekked into Tibet in 1897 and found that when he came under suspicion, it was of being a British spy.[67]

Dhammaloka had been invited to Singapore by several Chinese sponsors. In a letter to the journal of the Maha Bodhi Society he listed, as well as Cheang Jim Chuan, "Mr. Tan Ban Hau, Mr Cheang Jim Eng, Mr. Cheang Beng Sieuw, Mr Tan Teck Soon and also [the Ceylonese] Mr. B. A. De Silva." On one occasion the *Straits Times* identified the headquarters of Dhammaloka's Buddhist mission as Kling street, "where enquirers will receive every information from the Phongyee [Dhammaloka]."[68] In fact 65 Kling Street was the address of Tan Teck Soon, a Singapore Chinese public intellectual and supporter of Anagarika Dharmapala's Maha Bodhi Society. Tan was a surprising ally for Dhammaloka.[69] In terms of class, education, and religion, the two men could hardly have been more different, Tan being the son of Presbyterian missionaries and a member of the Straits Chinese Christian Association. However, as a subscriber to the Maha Bodhi Society and passionate advocate of a modern revival of Chinese (mainly Confucian) heritage, Tan found common cause with Dhammaloka's modernist Buddhist mission and, along with the Sinhalese gem merchant B. P. de Silva and Cheang Jim Chuan, became one of Dhammaloka's strongest supporters.

Cosmopolitan Buddhism

By January 1904, Dhammaloka was literally flying the flag for Buddhism in Singapore. Above the Havelock Road mission fluttered the multicolored Buddhist flag created by Buddhist reformers in Ceylon in 1885 and redesigned by Col. Olcott and the Maha Bodhi Society.[70] In March, Dhammaloka returned to his propagandist roots and began distributing circulars promoting Buddhism over other religions. Many people, he claimed, were "turning their eyes upon Buddhism as the most rational, philosophical and cosmopolitan religion of the twentieth century" and as such "it is the ideal of the young Buddhists of Singapore to propagate the Gospel of Buddhism over all nations and to inculcate it to all the races on earth."[71] The "Buddhist Young Men's Association" would "try to become the spiritual awakener of the Asiatic people, endeavouring at the same time to diffuse the trust of their religion through the length and breadth of the world."[72]

The finest example of Dhammaloka's ability to mobilize diverse institutions in a common Buddhist cause occurred on April 30, 1904, when for the first time Buddhist New Year festivities in Singapore were jointly celebrated. A remarkable range of festivities and Buddhist generosity was displayed at multiple locations. At Dhammaloka's English Buddhist Mission, a special morning service attracted 300 people. Afterward, "an entertainment in the shape of a feast was given to all of the pupils of the school and also to their parents."[73] Simultaneously, Rev. Ocha officiated at the Japanese Buddhist Mission at Sarangoon Road.[74] The new Chinese Buddhist Temple on Balestier Road hosted day-long celebrations, with the Ceylonese B. P. de Silva providing funds to have the Chinese temple specially decorated and for "three thousand of his poor coreligionists" to enjoy a feast there."[75] Meanwhile, "A generous Chinese

Buddhist provided refreshment and cigars for the European patients in the Tan Tock Seng Hospital and these were distributed by the Rev U Dhammaloka."[76] Finally, all Buddhists, "both European and native," were asked to illuminate their homes for the evening.

Dhammaloka's trans-sectarian Buddhist New Year celebrations presented a positive image of Buddhism that was widely publicized. He evidently set out to highlight Buddhist pan-ethnic solidarity. In the morning an Irish monk offers food and guidance to mainly Chinese pupils and their parents while a service is held at the Japanese Buddhist mission. Next, a rich Sinhalese jeweler offers food to a massive crowd of poor Chinese Buddhists at a new Chinese temple. Finally, a Chinese donor provides refreshments distributed by the Irish Buddhist monk to European patients at a Chinese-sponsored hospital. A newspaper list of wealthy Chinese businessmen and employees supporting the various festivities completed an impressive picture of Buddhist generosity across ethnic lines.[77]

This innovative 1904 New Year's festival epitomizes Dhammaloka's work in Singapore. It reveals diverse interconnections among Buddhist and non-Buddhist communities; communities which, in later nationalist retellings of Buddhist history, were too often portrayed as strictly separated on ethnic or religious lines. Moreover, while Dhammaloka's main concern was to advance Buddhism, others involved had even broader sympathies. There was something in the philosophy and spirit of free education that spoke to the kind of cosmopolitan modernity and developing Asian cultural identity they all envisioned.

New European Buddhist Monks

At the time of the New Year's celebrations there was a hint of the next turn in Dhammaloka's plan—"Singapore European C. Roberts, and a Ceylon Eurasian are to be sent to the Dawai Kyoung [Tavoy monastery] at Rangoon for a course of two years' study preparatory to entering the priesthood."[78] And in June, "Mr Arnold Abraham [actually Abrams], a Jewish gentleman, has left for Rangoon, under the auspices of the Buddhist Mission at Havelock Road, Singapore, to enter the Buddhist Priesthood."[79]

Thus far, Dhammaloka had sent potential monks to Rangoon for novice ordination by Burmese Buddhists, but October 1904 saw a major shift. Dhammaloka began to ordain Europeans himself in Singapore, beginning with M. T. de la Courneuve, a former policeman from the Straits Settlements.[80]

The *Straits Times* published a lengthy account of an unusual ceremony on Sunday last—the ordaining of the first European resident of the Settlement into the Holy Brotherhood of Buddhism. The ceremony took place in the Buddhist Mission Hall and was conducted in the presence of the Lord Abbot, the Right Ven. U. Dhammaloka; the Rev. Ocha, head of the Japanese Mission in Singapore; U. Dhammawanga [Roberts], a novice, and a number of friends, including some Europeans. After a Chinese juvenile choir had chanted praise to the Buddha in English, the European novice to be ordained M. T. Courneuve (until recently a police officer in Pahang) entered the room, knelt down and bowed three times to a small Siamese Buddha. He then prostrated himself before U Dhammaloka and repeated the ordination service in Pali, at the end of which a yellow robe was given to him which he donned in an ante-room. On re-appearing, he was given the priestly name of "Dharmatrata" ("Saviour of the Lord").[81] U Dhammaloka then congratulated the novice on being a "Sumanera" [sic] and announced that he would be sent to Pulo Tikus, in Penang, where he would continue his studies under Burmese priests at the monastery there.[82]

No quorum of monks is prescribed for a novice (samanera) ordination, but most observers would have found it unorthodox to include the Japanese cleric, Rev. Ocha. Nevertheless, the ceremony captured public attention and marked a new phase for Dhammaloka's Straits Young Men's Buddhist Association, so far limited to Bangkok and Singapore. He was now intent on creating a network of European monks like himself to serve Buddhist missions across Asia and even beyond.

This plan was not entirely new. In 1902, Dhammaloka and IYMBA colleagues in Tokyo had listed target areas for IYMBA evangelization as Hong Kong, Canton, Brisbane, and Penang.[83] Now,

[o]wing to the proposed extension of the "Straits Young Men's Buddhist Society" and of the Buddhist Mission in Penang, and Thursday Island, North Australia where new branches are about to be opened up, U Dhammaloka a Buddhist ecclesiastic here, will postpone his visit to Burmah until some future date. U Dipalankara [Roberts], another ecclesiastic together with another Englishman . . . will proceed to Penang very shortly to open a mission there: the latter will also proceed after an interval of a few months to Kuala Lumpur with the same object in view. A Mr. Abrams, formerly a resident of the Straits Settlements, will be recalled from Rangoon to proceed to Australia to open a mission there.[84]

We will return to Dhammaloka's ordinations in Chapter 6. Meanwhile, the proposed trajectories of his new monks—Penang, Kuala Lumpur, and even distant Australia—foreshadowed his own future movements.

Dhammaloka Takes His Well-Earned Leave

In late January 1905, Dhammaloka reappeared in Burma.

> U Dhammaloka returned to Rangoon yesterday, to spend the Chinese holidays,
> his large Mission school in Singapore being closed for a few weeks. He was wel-
> comed by a party of his old followers; and all his old friends have been glad to
> see him again in the best of health.[85]

While the Chinese New Year break may have offered a face-saving excuse for
leaving Singapore, Dhammaloka would be away far longer than a few weeks. An
impassioned tirade against him by Edward Alexander Morphy, the (Irish) editor
of Singapore's *Straits Times*, on January 19 undoubtedly hastened his departure.
The editor of the previously friendly newspaper now declared the Irish monk
"a fraud."[86] Dhammaloka, Morphy fulminated, had (in unspecified ways) committed "blackmail" in Rangoon using Morphy's name, and Morphy, summoning
Dhammaloka to his office, had forced him in the presence of a policeman to
write a confession and apology. Within a lengthy catalogue of Dhammaloka's
faults, Morphy honed in on a recent "open letter" to missionaries entitled "What
is the use of prayer?" submitted by Dhammaloka to the *Straits Times*. "I can confidently assert," wrote Morphy,

> that [Dhammaloka] never wrote the essay on prayer which bears his fantastic
> signature. He may have conceived some of it, but he never wrote it. He could
> not. . . . He is clever, but illiterate, inasmuch as he is not a scholar, and can write
> with difficulty and cannot spell at all. Samples of his handwriting are difficult
> to obtain, because he almost invariably corresponds by means of a typewriter
> using an amanuensis who understands the principles of orthography. The only
> biographic document we have ever seen bearing his name and being purely
> in his own handwriting is another open letter similar to this exhortation to
> Christian Workers in the Vineyard. . . . It bears the earmarks of the illiterate. The
> handwriting is stiff, slow, laboured and bad, like that of a child on a slate; the
> spelling and syntax are alike infantile.[87]

Evidently Dhammaloka had not done very well at school in Booterstown; or he
may have been in some respect dyslexic. It is all the more remarkable that he was
now successfully opening schools of his own.

Dhammaloka of course had interests beyond Singapore. In October 1904
he had discussed visiting his new missions, and on December 17 the *Torres
Straits Pilot*, in the far northeast of Australia, published a letter from Singapore
saying that Dhammaloka (not Abrams) was expected shortly at Thursday

Island.[88] However, Dhammaloka headed not to distant Australia, but to neighboring India.

Into India, from Amritsar and Assam to Bengal and Chittagong

Two conflicting accounts have survived of Dhammaloka's travels during the spring of 1905. The *Times of Burma* in June published what is probably Dhammaloka's own account (remarkably, most of it reprinted in a Catholic newspaper in Wichita, Kansas).[89] And in May, Harry Franck had interviewed Dhammaloka on a Ganges ferry and heard a very different story.[90] Here is the *Times of Burma*'s version of events:

> [Dhammaloka] left Rangoon about the middle of March for Calcutta and upper India, whither he went visiting the sacred shrines of the Buddhists. He went through Bengal, the United Provinces and the Punjab, as far as Amritsar, where he inspected the Golden Temple and the other sacred edifices. Returning to Calcutta, U Dhammaloka travelled into Assam as far as Shilling, whence he journeyed overland through the Hill Tippers, the rajah of which independent state entertained the traveller in regal style for ten days; and when the guest departed he was provided with elephants, servants, and an escort over the frontier as far as Comilla the terminus of the Eastern Bengal State Railway, where special saloon accommodation was reserved for him on the mail train to Chittagong.
>
> While in Calcutta the Bengalis took unusual interest in the European Buddhist priest as soon as they heard he came from Japan. Every afternoon crowds of babus [educated men] sought to be introduced to the Lord Abbot who was loaded with offerings.[91]

Franck's account tells instead of meeting Dhammaloka in Calcutta on Friday May 11,[92] far across the Ganges from the Hill Tippers-Comilla itinerary, and of Dhammaloka traveling second class[93] from Calcutta to the ferry at Goalando for Chittagong. Dhammaloka makes no mention of Amritsar or Bengal, instead telling Franck, "I'm coming back now from three months with the prince of Nepal, teaching his priests, him giving me the ticket to Chittagong."[94]

Two months earlier in Colombo, Ceylon, the Irish beachcomber "John Askins" had told Franck, à propos of European Buddhists, that "[a]n old pal of mine wears the yellow up in Nepal."[95] Dhammaloka was almost certainly this "old pal." However, we have found no evidence that Dhammaloka actually went to Nepal, and in this period reformist Buddhists, of any nationality, were extremely unwelcome there.[96]

Dhammaloka's next destination, the Chittagong Hill Tracts, housed a large Buddhist population. In the 1900s, they were reviving old connections with the sangha in Arakan, just across the Burmese border, and helping to build new organizations further afield.[97] The Chittagong diaspora in Calcutta supported Maha Bodhi and other Buddhist activities. Franck shows us a Dhammaloka well-connected to Chittagong Buddhism:

> When we come to Chittagong you can stop with me. Then I'll give you a chit to the Tavoy in Rangoon and you can stay there as long as ever you like.[98]

Franck and his two traveling companions spent 13th–15th May in Chittagong after reuniting there with Dhammaloka. Three days afterwards:

> A public meeting was held in the premises of Anath Bazaar Monastery, Chittagong, on Thursday the 18th May, the Anniversary Parinivabana [sic] day of the Lord Buddha at 5:30 p.m. when the Revd U Dhammaloka, the Irish Buddhist priest, delivered a lecture on Buddhism. The attendance was large, and included the Commissioner, the D. C. [Deputy Commissioner] and a number of Europeans.[99]

On May 25, a year after the splendid Singapore celebrations, Dhammaloka spent the 1905 Buddhist New Year in Akyab, Arakan—site of his own tours of five years before, of Asoka's earlier tours in 1900, and of Ananda Metteyya's 1902 ordination. From Akyab, Dhammaloka sailed to Rangoon via the port of Kyoukpyu, where the assembled crowds "were disappointed at his not landing; and several of the leading European residents of the place were unable to get him to break his journey for a week."[100] By June 3 he was back in Rangoon. However, this would be a short stop.

A Multi-Religious Mission to Penang

Dhammaloka's scheme to found new missions staffed with his own ordained European Buddhists had made some headway in his absence. In Rangoon, he arranged with another European monk, U Vara (Richard Laffère, a former Dublin surveyor who had worked in Siam, the Straits Settlements, and India), to found a Buddhist Mission in Penang—the island in the Straits Settlements halfway between Rangoon and Singapore housing the colonial port of Georgetown.[101] Dhammaloka had visited Penang in 1903 during his return from Japan.[102]

Dharmatrata (Courneuve), ordained by Dhammaloka in Singapore in the spring of 1904, had originally been destined for "Pulo Tikus, in Penang to continue his studies under Burmese monks there."[103] Dharmatrata and Dipalamkara (Roberts) were to start a Buddhist mission there, but seemingly did not, if Dhammaloka needed to come a year later with Vara to establish the mission himself. However, sending newly ordained monks to Pulao Tikus, then a fishing and sailing village in the middle of Penang island, had been a logical move.[104] In 1803, a wealthy Burmese woman had established the Dhammikarama Burmese monastery, still there today. It was an important center, housing the only drinking water well for the sailors, petty traders, and fishermen in that part of the island.[105] Not only was its monastic lineage Burmese, but local historians claim that the Burmese community of the early nineteenth century was largely from the Tavoy area. For Dhammaloka, then, the Dhammikarama monastery was part of a network that included the Rangoon Tavoy monastery and Bangkok's Wat Ban Thawai.

Reaching Penang, the two Dublin Buddhists approached various organizations well beyond the Burmese and Buddhist communities for support. Penang had a thriving multiethnic Asian civil society, well known for its educational and progressive enterprises. On July 5, lecturing at the "Penang Mutual Improvement Association," Dhammaloka, introduced as "Head of the Buddhist Mission of Eastern Asia,"

> dwelt on the causes which had brought about the stagnation of Buddhism in the East at the present time, and alluded to the fact that, the worship of images, the burning of joss papers and the general belief in charms were totally opposed to the teaching of Buddha. The mission of Gautama was not to collect large sums of money from the people and expend these in gorgeous temples, but to teach them in the right way of living in their natural lives, and to adapt themselves by education to the proper needs of their times. Hence Buddhism was distinctly a progressive religion and did not rely upon ignorance and superstition for its success.[106]

Education as part of religious and social reform, a favorite topic for Dhammaloka, appealed to Penang's education-minded Chinese population. The talk won Dhammaloka an invitation to lecture (with Chinese translation) at the Chinese Town Hall two nights later.

> A very interesting and instructive lecture upon Buddhism was given . . . by the Rev U Dhammaloka the Irish Buddhist priest who has come to Penang to encourage the revival of Buddhism. There was a very large attendance including a number of the leading Chinese of Penang.[107]

Dhammaloka declared that, through his mission,

> [t]he people were taking a greater interest in the religion—he did not mean
> they were lavishing money on extravagant buildings, as in the past, but that
> they were establishing schools. That is what we want here in Penang, said the
> Rev U Dhammaloka, amid applause. He had already told the Chinese that they
> lavished too much money over that big temple at Aier Etam: "if that money
> was spent on schools, what a beautiful thing it would be for Penang." (fur-
> ther applause). And how it would raise the moral status of the people! Said
> Dhammaloka. . . . [H]is most important point was to urge upon those present
> the necessity for infusing more activity in the religion and generally taking
> an active part in improving the status of Buddhism in Penang. Large sums of
> money were then subscribed.[108]

Dhammaloka's host and sponsor for the talk was Dr. Gnoh Lean Tuck, a.k.a.
Wu Lien Teh, a Cambridge-educated medical doctor and one of the most vocal
advocates of the anti-opium movement in Asia. Like Singapore's Tan Teck Soon,
Dr. Wu promoted Chinese culture and modernity rather than Buddhism.[109] He
was evidently drawn to Dhammaloka's humanist emphasis on fostering education and ethics in place of temple-building, and his anti-opium position sat well
with Dhammaloka's temperance campaigns.[110]

In late July, Dhammaloka delivered a lecture at the Penang Hindu Association
on "the realities of the inner life." He argued for the superiority of Hinduism and
its "sister religion" Buddhism over Western Christianity and the materialism
of the modern world, "exhorting the Hindus to do their best for this cause of
religion."[111]

Buoyed by encouraging responses from different quarters, Dhammaloka
launched a Penang YMBA with Chinese, Indian, and Sinhalese support (thus
achieving another objective of the now-defunct Tokyo IYMBA):

> A meeting convened by the Lord Abbot U Dhammaloka, was held in the
> Chinese Town Hall on Saturday night, the 5th instant [August] at 8 pm for the
> purpose of establishing a Penang branch of the Straits Young Men's Buddhist
> Association. There was a fairly large attendance about eighty Chinese, Indian
> and Sinhalese gentlemen of wealth and position being present. . . .
>
> Revd U Dhammaloka explained to those present the necessity of forming
> such an association in Penang. In a place like Penang where there is such a large
> Chinese population, it was a pity to see that nothing was given to the rising gen-
> eration in the way of religious instruction. If any Chinese youth here were asked
> what his religion was, the reply would most probably be "I don't know." It is the
> subject of the proposed Association to make the Straits Chinese and Hindus

more acquainted with their religion. With the Association he also proposed to establish a Buddhist School, where poor children can be taught Buddhism free. Forty-two members were registered, and a Committee was formed to frame the by-laws.[112]

We have no further news of the Buddhist school project, but Dhammaloka's work continued. In September 1905, in Ipoh, second city of the Federated Malay States, he was "delivering lectures on Buddhism in Kinta District before larger and appreciative audiences . . . of Chinese and Singhalese."[113] By October he was heading via Taiping in Perak to the capital, Kuala Lumpur, in some style:

> U Dhammaloka (the Irish hpoongyi) is touring through the Malay States, a very wealthy Chinese gentleman having provided "his reverence" with a handsome motor car for his journeyings.[114]

This is the last we see of Dhammaloka for over 18 months, probably due to the paucity of surviving printed materials for the period.

The Smell of the Sea

As distinct as Penang, Singapore, Bangkok, and Rangoon were, there is a similar feel to each of Dhammaloka's homes and their communities. All are close to the water, with active shipping and sailors, and thus to multiethnic interactions. The Tavoy monastery was located just up Godwin Road from the busiest public wharf in Rangoon. Adjacent to Chinatown and the haunts of travelers from throughout lower Burma, the monastery was known to welcome sailors of all stripes. In Bangkok, Wat Ban Thawai, located in a multiethnic working-class area near the busy river running through the heart of the city, was close to centers of commerce and foreign embassies. In Penang, the Dhammikarama monastery in Pulao Tikus, Dhammaloka's base, was central to the island's fishing and sailing community and the local ethnic Burmese and Thai communities. Located two blocks from the sea and hosting the only well, it was a meeting point for people from all over. Shrines at the monastery were created for contingents of seamen— clearly the key constituency, and a source of pride for this fast-growing, multi-ethnic part of Penang. The Havelock Road Buddhist mission was situated some way inland, but in Singapore the sea with its trade and transit is never far away, and we have seen how Dhammaloka's educational and Buddhist reform activities attracted Chinese, Sinhala, Japanese, and European participants.

Moreover, Dhammaloka's bases in Rangoon, Penang, and Bangkok were all connected with the port city of Tavoy. The Rangoon Tavoy monastery was built to house monks and travelers from Tavoy, while Wat Ban Thawai, in "the Tavoy village" (today's Ban Yan Nawa), served Tavoyans in Bangkok. Dhammikarama monastery in Penang, still known as the "Burmese" monastery, has strong ties to Tavoy and other ports up the Andaman Coast. The two longest-presiding abbots of the monastery during the twentieth century were Tavoyans and spent time in the Tavoy-affiliated monastery in Bangkok before coming to Dhammikarama.[115]

It was this Tavoyan network that facilitated Dhammaloka's missionary efforts in Bangkok, Penang, and Rangoon. Dhammaloka, a former sailor, no doubt knew Tavoy and its people well. The river, the sea, boats, and a sense of movement and people in transit are ever present there, from the docks to the well-worn statue of the earth goddess, protector of seafarers, at its central pagoda.

Tavoy's location had long made it an ethnic and cultural meeting point. It had landward links to Karen, Mon, Siamese, and central Burman communities, and increasing numbers of Chinese and Indian migrants arrived after the British takeover in 1826. A growing tin mining industry and the town's maritime connections made Tavoy an ethnic crossroads, with a reputation for being culturally inclusive.

There is something of the Tavoyan attitude in each of the places Dhammaloka called home during those years. In fact it is not only Tavoyans who would have felt at home in the Rangoon Tavoy monastery, in the Tavoy village in Bangkok, or the Dhammikarama monastery in Penang; Dhammaloka would have felt at home as well. Walking the streets of contemporary Tavoy, Pulao Tikus, or the neighborhood near Wat Ban Thawai, Bangkok is not so different from a walk from Booterstown Avenue, where Laurence Carroll was born in 1856, to the docks. Booterstown, too, on the new railway line between the mail port of Kingstown and the Dublin cargo docks, was a village that was becoming absorbed into a colonial port city.

A Plebeian Cosmopolitanism

There is another aspect of Tavoyan experience that connects with Dhammaloka's experiences. Most writing on cosmopolitan colonial port cities in Southeast Asia has focused on the culture of elites, and on centralized identities and political connections.[116] By contrast, Dhammaloka's missions across Southeast Asia were deeply embedded in poor local Asian communities, in locales with an abundant, and much more plebeian, cosmopolitanism. The publicity for Dhammaloka's schools in Bangkok and Singapore emphasized the advantages of free Buddhist English-language education for the poor of the neighborhood.

In Siam, the objection that (Buddhist) education was already free only underlined the fact that Dhammaloka's English-medium school was a different

project, aimed not at the middle classes who sought out private English education, but at plebeian and poor boys excluded from colonial prosperity and modernity. Havelock Road in Singapore is similarly described as a district of poor
Chinese migrants and laborers. While Cheang Jim Chuan exercised arm's-length
philanthropy, under Dhammaloka's leadership the students, and their parents,
seem to have been actively engaged as constituents, participating in the rituals
and extracurricular work of the mission.

In Bangkok, the community surrounding Wat Ban Thawai, originally Tavoyan,
grew into a multiethnic intersection of cultures with "a large working-class population."[117] In Rangoon, the Tavoy monastery was close to poor working-class
communities not well served by the elite colonial educational institutions nearby.
While Dhammaloka forged connections with elite patrons, the community he
engaged with daily at each of these sites was distinctly plebeian.

Dhammaloka also held, as Tavoyans did, an ambiguous relationship to the
center of power, and to centralizing religious and political groups. Tavoyans
had long claimed Burmese identity, but maintained its distance from Burmese
culture and Buddhist authority. Without threatening the center, they used their
marginal position to assert local autonomy and make space for religious and cultural innovation and interaction. The Tavoy monastery in Rangoon reflected a
similar sensibility. Situated in the heart of the city, safe in its respected position
as a Buddhist institution, it was persistently unruly, marginal, and disruptive to
Burmese elites and hegemonic Buddhist institutions.

Likewise, Wat Ban Thawai in Bangkok was a Buddhist institution in an international district, but its monks had long been engaged in the defense of non-
Siamese and non-state-affiliated Buddhist identities in Bangkok, seeking to avoid
monastic reforms by the dominant royal Siamese sangha designed to increase
central control.[118] Dhammikarama monastery in Pulao Tikus welcomed all
Asian ethnicities, maintaining a space separate from elite colonial Georgetown.
A Tavoyan spirit can thus be discerned in each of these centers, playing with the
ambiguous advantages of marginality—pushing just enough not to provoke the
ire or the regulating impulses of those in power, but sufficient to assert space for
autonomy, mobility, and invention.

A striking example of such disruption was the extent to which Dhammaloka
rendered boundaries of race and religion irrelevant in promoting a Buddhism
for the modern age. For the colonial state, race and religious identity were key
to regulation. With its reliance on the technology of the census, the colonial
state's very mode of being required the construction of strict divisions between ethnic and religious communities. Cities were designed with distinct
quarters for Chinese, Indians, Malays, Siamese, Burmese, and so on, and the
law was applied according to religious identity, based on the idea that British
rule enacted religious tolerance by enforcing a community's own religious

customary law.[119] In fact, much of this customary law was articulated and codified only to reinforce the divisions that the British were producing.[120] Vast amounts of physical and intellectual labor thus went into constructing and identifying differences.

And yet Dhammaloka and his associates seem to have been largely indifferent to them. At a moment when *both* the colonial state *and* emergent nationalist discourses were struggling to make Chinese, Burmese, Indian, Irish, and Sinhalese see others as radically distinct identities, connections across ethnic lines were not merely normal in the Rangoon Tavoy monastery, Wat Ban Thawai, the Havelock Road Mission, and Dhammikarama, they were essential for the survival of these institutions and central to their mission.

Ethnic and religious intermixing were in fact the most commented-upon aspects of Dhammaloka's projects in this period. His Bangkok school took not just poor Siamese and Chinese boys as initially reported. Instead,

> the children of Malays, Siamese, Chinese and Hindus were taught English and the three "R"s without fee. It mattered not whether the pupils were Mahommedans, Christians or Latter-Day Apostles—they were received at Wat Dawn [Ban Thawai] school.[121]

Complaints of ethnic or religious interaction were leveled at the Thayettaw monastic complex housing the Tavoy monastery in Rangoon—elite Burmese were shocked to find it full of Indians and Chinese during Buddhist rituals. And despite Dhammaloka's unswerving faith in Buddhism as the answer to the ills of colonialism and moral laxity, he found no contradiction in engaging with non-Buddhist traditions. He encouraged the Hindu association in Penang to learn more of their religion (*inter alia* dismissing the erroneous idea that Buddhists are atheists!), and collaborated with Theosophists, Daoists, and Confucian revivalists. Missionary Christianity—except where it embraced temperance—stands alone as the totemic colonial enemy and common threat to Asian culture and well-being.

Dhammaloka did, of course, engage with elites and with centralizing and nationalist reformist discourses if he found support for his own projects. Despite his plebeian background and loyalties, he convinced several prominent reformers that he was in common cause with their diverse religious, political, and philosophical goals. The Saopha of Kengtung attempted to re-envision modern Buddhist kingship. Cheang Jim Chuan's family empire in Singapore was close to the center of power. Tan Teck Soon's Presbyterian-Confucian philosophical project to produce a modern Straits Chinese identity was an elite discourse. In Penang, Dr. Wu was an important Chinese intellectual and reformer whose vision of modernity hardly meshed with Dhammaloka's Buddhism.

Visions of a Rainbow Future

To understand Dhammaloka's appeal beyond Buddhism, we should perhaps re-call that the future as it actually turned out in the twentieth century—an Asia constituted primarily of ethnically defined nation-states—was not at all an ob-vious outcome in Dhammaloka's day. Many among the Asian elites shared with Tavoyans an interest in exploring a future not limited by national-territorial definitions, but instead fostering trans-border, cross-cultural collaborations, connections, and alliances as a source of strength. Was Dhammaloka, through Buddhism, asserting the broad and tantalizing prospect of such an autono-mous Asian modernity, freed from divisive European interests? The Mandalay Buddhist elite clearly saw this in Dhammaloka, but his wide range of non-Buddhist sponsors and allies shows how effectively Dhammaloka's projects defied the assumed boundaries of religion—exposing the myth of clear divisions between religions and ethnicities as a colonial fallacy.

As we saw in Chapter 1, long before arriving in Asia the future Dhammaloka was repeatedly confronted with conflicts where he could choose to identify in ethnic terms or not: Protestant and Catholic in Liverpool, black and white among hoboes, Chinese and Irish in California, whites and Chinese on the Pacific liners. His ability to "go native" in colonial Asia probably had long roots in his own past behavior.

Dhammaloka the monk never renounced his "Irish" label, but he refused to let ethnicity define his behavior, starting with his ordination as an Irish monk with a Chinese sponsor in a Burmese lineage. His missionary work across Southeast Asia took this to another level. The networks of sailors, traders, merchants, monks, and schoolboys that supported him reflected an exception-ally robust plebeian cosmopolitanism in the colonial port cities. Transit, petty commerce, and sheer survival in these conditions relied on strong connections across boundaries—to the extent that regularly ignoring ethnic and religious divisions in the course of everyday life would have been normal for those in Dhammaloka's circle.

Life for migrants, petty traders, laborers, and mariners of all ethnicities and religions in the rapidly changing colonial world relied on more than the new connective technologies of telegraphs, railroads, and steamers; they depended upon a set of local relationships among people at the bottom of society en-gaged in day-to-day interactions rarely visible from elite vantage points. The movements of workers, migrants, and pilgrims were facilitated by networks of fellow travelers and connections of knowledge, trust, and transactions. Newcomers to the port cities often sought out those from their own home re-gion, but the realities of plebeian life meant also substantial interaction and intermixing.

By Dhammaloka's time, being accepted as "one of us" at the Rangoon Tavoy monastery meant less that you came from Tavoy, and more that you shared certain experiences, expectations, and hardships, or a vision or goal. In this spirit the Tavoy monastery offered succor to all ethnicities—as did the Tavoyan communities in Bangkok and Penang and Dhammaloka's mission in Singapore.

Dhammaloka was contributing to a larger project carried out by other monasteries and Buddhist associations in this period. His projects as a radical monk were unique, but only possible because thousands of sailors, monks, merchants, and migrants had participated in the connections and flows facilitated by Buddhism in the past. Uncovering Dhammaloka's activities offers us a remarkable window into these cosmopolitan connections—among Tavoyan monks, Shan saophas, central Burman gem merchants, poor Chinese, Muslim, or Eurasian schoolboys, and many others. Most of these connections were invisible from the official, colonial, and nationalist perspectives of the time that would ultimately inform the dominant histories. But networks like these, which underpinned much of the day-to-day toil of the colonial period in Asia, made the modern Buddhist revival possible.

6

Interlude

Who Was the First Western Buddhist Monk?

In the early 1900s, there was significant competition around the claim to be "the first European (i.e., Western) Buddhist monk." However much Dhammaloka and his contemporaries were embedded in networks of Asian actors, the claim to be the first European ordained brought both prestige and notoriety. And yet such claims reflected a false binary distinction between West and East, mirroring high imperial-era preoccupations with difference based on color, race, and geography. Such distinctions were underpinned by Western ideas of superior and inferior races, civilizations, and religions, and were enforced by law and behavior. The colonial perspective saw the conversion of Asians to Christianity as a sign of progress. By contrast, as we have seen, Europeans becoming Buddhist transgressed many cultural boundaries.

Throughout the twentieth century, virtually every history of modern Buddhism repeated the claim that the first Western monk was an Englishman named Allan Bennett, ordained in Burma as Ananda Metteyya in the early years of the twentieth century.[1] Arriving in London in 1908, Bennett has also been seen as the first Buddhist missionary to the West. This all makes for a simple story, but it is hardly true. Our research over the last decade has uncovered not just the figure of U Dhammaloka (ordained well before Ananda Metteyya) but *dozens* of early Western Buddhist monks, named or unnamed, from the period around 1900.[2] Nor was Ananda Metteyya the first Buddhist missionary in Europe; that honor currently belongs to another Irishman, Charles Pfoundes.[3]

There are undoubtedly more "first" Western Buddhists to find. While finishing this book we came across a photograph of a previously unknown "eminent British officer" who "used to wear the monks' yellow robe" in monasteries near Moulmein in Burma.[4] The image, of a now-elderly man displaying his bhikkhu's robes (see Figure 6.1), was taken in a London studio and appeared in the *Sketch* magazine during the 1895 "Empire of India" exhibition at Earl's Court. Moulmein was a substantial Burmese colonial port; an "eminent" officer (civil service or military) donning Buddhist robes in the late 1880s could not have passed unnoticed, but he has never appeared in histories of Buddhism.

The Irish Buddhist. Alicia Turner, Laurence Cox, and Brian Bocking, Oxford University Press (2020)
© Alicia Turner, Laurence Cox and Brian Bocking.
DOI: 10.1093/oso/9780190073084.001.0001

Figure 6.1. The "eminent British officer" who frequented Buddhist monasteries around Moulmein in the 1880s–1890s.

© Illustrated London News Ltd./Mary Evans.

The matter was simply not worthy of enough comment to have survived to our day, except for this later chance event in London.

We will never know who was the first Western Buddhist monk. Buddhism, like Christianity and Islam, welcomes recruits from any background. Ever since Buddhism began in India, Europeans finding themselves in Asia have had the opportunity to join the Buddhist sangha. Those who become Buddhist monastics renounce their previous name and make a virtue of uniformity after ordination; there is no reason for such conversions to make it into the history books. Even a high-profile convert like Dhammaloka was quickly forgotten.

This said, if we restrict ourselves to the height of Western imperial incursion into Asia, a number of early Western monks appear. The French journal *Annales de l'Extrême Orient* recorded in 1879 that an unnamed "Austrian," mockingly nicknamed "Phr'a Kow-Tow," had been ordained as a monk in September 1878 and was serving the Siamese king.[5] An unnamed destitute Russian was reportedly ordained in Siam even earlier in the 1870s.[6] Our "eminent British officer" in Moulmein, Burma, must have taken the robes before 1890. A Mr. MacMillan sought ordination in Ceylon in 1892.[7]

Boundary Crossing in High Imperialism

These earlier ordinations attracted little attention, but by 1900 the mood had changed, and Westerners in Buddhist robes began to stand out. From the colonial side, the attempt to maintain the racial status order meant stricter dress codes—with Europeans avoiding native clothes and insisting on Western-style shoes and hats—and sharper religious distinctions between Christians and others. For a European to become a barefoot, shaven-headed, Buddhist monk undermined both sartorial and religious hierarchies. In this context, a Westerner's Buddhist ordination was increasingly significant because it marked the formal incorporation of a European into an *Asian* organization. At this highpoint of colonialism, matters were supposed to be going the other way, with colonial subjects seeking Western-style education and employment and the privilege of membership in clubs, fraternal organizations, scientific societies, and so forth.

From the Buddhist side, too, there was increasing focus on reformist monastic lineages and affiliations between Buddhism and emerging national identities. In this period the role of a Buddhist monk was in flux in many Asian countries. Reformers were questioning the orthodoxy of established lineages, and were reordaining monks in their own orders. In the Buddhist monastic orders of South and Southeast Asia, what a monk should be and do was the topic of intense discussion and practical initiatives: preaching was changing from Pali recitation to vernacular sermons; traditional monastery seminaries were declining; the "political monk" was emerging as a leader of movements (even uprisings) among the laity. European converts may have been formally subordinated to Asian superiors, but at the same time, simply by being white, they retained a certain prestige in colonial society. This ambivalence allowed European converts such as Dhammaloka to experiment with what could be done in the role of monk, making them potentially useful adjuncts to Asian Buddhist movements.

Exploring these first documented Western bhikkhu ordinations thus opens a window into a far wider world of intercultural encounters that challenged high imperialism's racial and religious boundaries and gave impetus to the many competing programs for Buddhist reform. Western bhikkhu ordination belongs among other ritual events of this nature across Asia which together map out a multiplicity of encounters beyond those recovered in this book: Anagarika Dharmapala's triumph at the Chicago World's Parliament of Religions in 1893 and his attempt (1897–98) to found a new lay Anagarika Buddhist order;[8] the conversion ceremonies held by Ceylon's Buddhist Theosophical Society between 1886 and 1907;[9] Sister Sanghamitta (Countess Canavarro) and her ten-precept nuns' order, the Sanghamitta Upasikaramaya (1898–9);[10] Shaku Kozen in 1886 and Shaku Soen in 1887, the first known Japanese to take Sinhalese bhikkhu ordination as part of rapidly industrializing Japan's quest for "original" Buddhism;[11] the various initiations of Japanophile Irishman Charles Pfoundes in 1890s Japan;[12] and the later 1915 ordinations of William McGovern and Mortimer Kirby as Japanese Buddhist priests taking bodhisattva vows.[13]

In this wider context, bhikkhu ordinations around 1900 are a particularly useful point of departure for transnational research. Because of the central role of the bhikkhu sangha (the Buddhist monastic order), the issue of whether and how to ordain Europeans was faced in most Southeast Asian countries, not confined to a single location. The apparently straightforward meaning of such events (and, for the colonial press, the sheer visibility of a Westerner in saffron robes) means that there is a relatively wide range of documentation, so that we can compare at least fragmentary information on many kinds of early Western Buddhist monks, not simply those who were well known or linked with organizations whose internal records have survived. Indeed, many converts came from the scattered and largely undocumented ranks of "beachcombers"—Europeans who were scratching a living on the margins of empire.

Beachcomber Bhikkhus

The beachcomber bhikkhu—or rather, the poor white, going native by becoming a Buddhist monk—was becoming a recognized figure in the Asia of the 1900s.[14] We can research these converts partly because their lowly status attracted polemic from Christian missionaries and mockery from the colonial press. Newspapers in Rangoon and Singapore referenced "European loafers as Buddhist priests,"[15] and others referred to Dhammaloka as "on the graft," implying that collecting alms was a form of deception and embezzlement. Another account identified two European ex-bhikkhus associated with Ananda Metteyya as residents of the Calcutta workhouse and a third as deported.[16] Less judgmentally, beachcomber John Askins commented in Ceylon in 1905 that "[t]here's a bunch of one-time beachcombers scattered among the Burmese monasteries,"[17] and American author Louis Brownlow met two American beachcomber bhikkhus.[18]

Many were sailors, including an exotically tattooed sailor-monk seen at the Tavoy monastery (Chapter 7) and the news that "[q]uite recently two stokers from one of the steamers arriving in Burma found their way to a Buddhist monastery, and professing themselves converts were made honoured monks."[19] The Ceylon *Catholic Messenger*'s Burma correspondent described "the Europeans who have lately put on the yellow robe. There are about half-a-dozen of these, most of them old sailors";[20] and there was "Kelly," an Irish monk (seemingly Dhammaloka), who told Sir Thomas Lipton in Mandalay that he had started as a "shipwrecked sailor."[21]

We also see a constant stress on the difficulties of staying the course: many disrobed after a short time. Drink also looms large in their stories. The *Burma Echo* mockingly reported one sad tale:

> For the 2nd time Mr. Solomon embraced Buddhism, the calling of a novice to that priesthood, and a Yellow Robe. He looked very gaudy. A few nights later he called on some of his old friends, still unconverted, and he joined them in quaffing the convivial glass of alleged whiskey and soda, which ceremony lasted until the daylight next morning was about to appear. On Thursday the novice retired from the order, his name being erased from its rolls, this aspect being gaudyless.[22]

Colonial detractors used allegations of alcohol problems to criticize Western monks, often playing on stereotypes of the Irish. The charge that assuming a life of poverty was a cynical way of evading debt was another favorite theme for European critics who felt their racial and religious identity threatened by the early Western Buddhists. M. T. de la Courneuve, ordained in Singapore in 1904, was pursued by allegations of outstanding debts,[23] as Gordon Douglas had been in Ceylon.[24]

Not every European monk was a beachcomber, ex-sailor, alcoholic, or otherwise in trouble; but many of them (and most of those featured in the colonial press) seem to have been one or more of these. This was fuel for polemic by their opponents (Christian, colonial, or, in the case of Dhammaloka and Ananda Metteyya, competing Western Buddhists), but it can perhaps now be seen differently. True, there were many poor whites in Asia, going native to a greater or lesser degree. Yet ordination as a response to personal problems or social failure was hardly unknown in Asia. Not every monk had a deep religious vocation overriding a plethora of alternative possible careers. These ordinations might better be considered as a plebeian level of intercultural encounter that challenged the racial and status hierarchies that maintained empire.

Three Contenders for the Title

At the turn of the twentieth century, three now well-documented candidates in Southeast Asia vied publicly for the role of "first Western Buddhist monk": Bhikkhu Asoka (Gordon Douglas), ordained in 1899 and dead by April 1901; our Irish Buddhist, U Dhammaloka, ordained in July 1900; and Ananda Metteyya (Allan Bennett [MacGregor]), ordained in 1902. The three followed very similar orthodox ordinations and career trajectories, and had substantial agendas and egos, but far from their stories being the outcome of their own initiative or agency, their ordinations were the result of wider Asian Buddhist competition. Of these, only Dhammaloka could truly be classed a beachcomber: he undoubtedly came from a working-class life and this class status was repeatedly invoked to question his legitimacy. It might seem obvious that Gordon Douglas, ordained as Asoka in 1899, was first in line before Dhammaloka (1900) and Bennett (1902), but things are not that simple.

A Buddhist monk is first ordained as a novice (*samanera*), then receives full (*upasampada*) ordination, usually after living the renunciant life for a trial period. Traditionally, boys in Southeast Asia would ordain as novices for some period as a child. Adult Westerners seeking to become lifelong monks with no childhood novitiate were therefore in an anomalous position. The Buddhist monastic rules (*vinaya*) do not prevent both novice and full ordination occurring on the same day, which happened in Asoka's case in Ceylon. Ananda Metteyya, by contrast, received novice ordination in Burma in December 1901 and was not fully ordained until May 1902.[25] Dhammaloka received full ordination in July 1900, but we do not know when he received his novice ordination. It could have happened on the same day, but it is perfectly possible that Dhammaloka was ordained years, even decades, earlier, perhaps in the 1880s.[26]

Bhikkhu Asoka (Gordon Douglas)

Gordon Douglas's background before arriving in Ceylon remains obscure. He was well educated, rumored to be from an aristocratic family, and had leftist political leanings.[27] Before his ordination, Douglas was successively overseer of a tea plantation, taught at St. Thomas's (Anglican) College, Colombo, joined the Buddhist Theosophical Society, and was hired as principal of its Mahinda College in Galle.[28] It is unclear what drew him to Ceylon, and then to Buddhism. However, his personal motivation was only part of the story.

Douglas's ordination reveals how the earliest Western Buddhist monks could be instruments in longer standing local projects. He was ordained in Ceylon, but not by Sinhalese monks. Instead, U Vajirarama, a visiting dignitary of the royally sanctioned Burmese Thudhamma lineage, officiated. Vajirarama's presence in Ceylon was linked to internal Burmese monastic rivalries that came to involve Sinhalese, and now Western, monks.

In the mid-nineteenth century, after the British annexed Lower Burma, public concern grew that Burmese Buddhist monks were becoming lax, neglecting the vinaya rules. This prompted the creation of breakaway monastic reform sects that challenged the Thudhamma lineage's orthodoxy by claiming superior asceticism and fidelity to the rules.[29] These schisms led to public disputes in the 1860s–80s about orthodoxy in Burma, and the contest spilled abroad. The heads of both of the breakaway monastic sects engaged in missions to largely Buddhist Ceylon and, in bids to reinforce the authority and legitimacy of their respective sects, re-ordained groups of Sinhalese monks into their own Burmese lineages.[30]

The Thudhamma response in Burma was to dispatch its own missionary monks to bring errant Burmese reformist Buddhists back into the orthodox fold, and to send parallel missions to Ceylon to compete for prestige abroad.[31] The most famous Thudhamma missionary was Thingaza Sayadaw (1815–86), whose chief disciple, U Vajirarama (1830–1909), became his successor.[32] Vajirarama thus saw himself as in the vanguard of Burmese orthodoxy, ready to take extreme steps to preserve Thudhamma authority. Not to be outdone by the reformists, he made two missions to Ceylon to re-ordain Sinhalese monks in the Burmese royal Thudhamma lineage. On his second visit, in January 1899, as part of this project, Vajirarama convinced the local Sinhalese Buddhist authorities to allow him to donate a jewel-encrusted gold casket to encase a precious tooth relic of the Buddha, and to host a procession and viewing of the relic.[33]

It was during the preparations for this ritual that U Vajirarama came to ordain Gordon Douglas. Douglas had previously approached the senior Sinhalese cleric Hikkaduve Sumangala, who refused to ordain him in his Sinhalese lineage.[34] Hence the ordination of this "first" Western Buddhist monk did not happen simply because a European wanted to convert to Buddhism. His novice and full ordinations, completed within a day, were tied up with an internal Burmese Buddhist competition played out on a Sinhalese stage.

Douglas was ordained as "Bhikkhu Asoka" at the Jayasekera Ramaya Temple, Colombo, on January 20, 1899, in the presence of "a hundred Burmese pilgrims" (i.e., the royal tooth relic delegation).[35] His ordination, widely reported in Ceylon and India, was part of Vajirarama's show of strength in Ceylon, one of many events intended to display Burmese and Thudhamma piety. Asoka was only a minor character—an oddity who added heft, but with no speaking role. During the pinnacle ritual of Vajirarama's trip—a display of the tooth relic in its new Burmese casket—Asoka was relegated to a second-class rail carriage, while the relic and Vajirarama rode first class. St. Thomas's College in Ceylon, where Douglas had once taught, publicly branded him a fraud.[36]

The newly ordained Asoka returned to Burma with U Vajirarama, stayed for a while in a Rangoon monastery and then traveled west to Akyab in Arakan and Bassein in the Irrawaddy river delta, where he was met by adoring crowds.[37] Yet almost immediately, Asoka was eager to travel further afield. Burma was not, it seems, his preferred mission field. By July he was seeking donors to fund his way by steamship to Siam and threatening that if sufficient donations did not come through he would go there alone, overland.[38] This was shocking behavior for a monk, not just because the monsoon season made travel perilous but because monks are forbidden to travel during this time.

However, after a visit to his sponsor U Vajirarama in Mandalay, where Asoka was again met with crowds spreading silk garments for him to walk upon, he was persuaded instead to visit India to report on some recently discovered Buddhist relics.[39] He traveled in India for a few months, wandering barefoot to sacred sites including Benares.[40] Returning to Burma and another warm welcome in Akyab, his visit was cut short when he died suddenly of cholera during a trip to Bassein in mid-April 1900.[41] His career as a monk had lasted just over a year. Competition for the prestige of being affiliated with a "white monk" persisted after his death, with Asoka's devotees in Akyab and Bassein fighting over the right to inherit his legacy, including his books.[42] Still mourning Asoka, the local Buddhists offered Dhammaloka a heartfelt welcome when he visited Bassein in 1901 (see Chapter 2).[43]

Dhammaloka

Dhammaloka, identified in Burma as William Colvin, received full ordination in Rangoon on July 8, 1900. His monastic preceptor for the ordination was Myataung Sayadaw from Mandalay who, like Vajirarama, was a disciple of Thingaza Sayadaw and stalwart of the royal Thudhamma revival.[44] Dhammaloka's ordination could thus be seen as part of the same Thudhamma project carried out by Vajirarama in Ceylon and now transplanted to Rangoon.

The list of abbots who oversaw the recitation at Dhammaloka's ordination is telling. They are evenly split between the heads of monasteries in the Bahan area of Rangoon—the monasteries encircling the Shwedagon Pagoda, an ancient and important pilgrimage site—and the heads of monasteries, including the Tavoy monastery where Dhammaloka lived and where he would base his illustrious career, located in the Thayettaw Kyaung Taik, the monastery complex on Godwin Road in downtown Rangoon near the port.

Like Asoka (Douglas) before him, Dhammaloka set his sights beyond Burma and undertook ambitious travels and missions from Burma to Japan, Siam, Singapore, and Ceylon, aimed at Asians, largely Buddhists, who Dhammaloka felt were besieged by colonial values and in danger of losing their religion and their culture. In this way he fulfilled the hopes of many Burmese who initially saw him as filling the role left by Asoka. Both Europeans underwent highly orthodox ordinations by high-ranking Burmese monks and carried with them the prestige of the Burmese project of Buddhist revival.

Ananda Metteyya

Ananda Metteyya (Allan Bennett) developed an interest in Buddhism through English occultism, participating in the Order of the Golden Dawn in London with his friend Aleister Crowley. Arriving in Ceylon with Crowley in 1900, Bennett gave a very well-received public lecture on the Buddha's four noble truths.[45] While there, he met a Burmese modernist intellectual and supporter of the Maha Bodhi Society, Dr. Tha Nu, of Akyab in the Arakan region of Burma. Tha Nu offered to bring Bennett to Arakan, where he received novice ordination on December 8, 1901. This gesture reflected long-standing Arakanese support for international Buddhist organizing efforts. Arakanese elders had sought out Colonel Olcott in 1891.[46] Ananda Metteyya lived in Arakan until his full ordination in Akyab on May 21, 1902.[47]

Ananda Metteyya's full ordination was again a popular affair. But while we know of Asoka's and Dhammaloka's ordinations from others, Ananda Metteyya published his own account of both his ordination and the lecture he gave afterward.[48] A Buddhist ordination must take place in a *sima*, a location reserved for that purpose. Bennett's Akyab ordination took place not in a typical sima, an ordination hall on dry land, but on a boat in the middle of the river. Monastic schisms and disputes in Southeast Asia had long centered around the consecration and maintenance of sima ordination halls, because the discovery that a sima had been improperly constituted would invalidate all ordinations conducted there—and thus any subsequent ordination overseen by those monks— potentially undermining an entire Buddhist lineage. A vinaya-sanctioned option was to constitute a sima over water. While temporary, it would be unquestionably orthodox and valid. The Arakan Flotilla Company duly donated their launches for the event. Despite these careful preparations, Ananda Metteyya later chose to be re-ordained in Mandalay, in the Thudhamma monastic lineage, by the Engan Sayadaw.[49]

Though with limited means and often in poor health, Ananda Metteyya (see Figure 6.2) was a well-educated middle-class Englishman. His Buddhist missionary message was couched in scholarly terms and directed primarily toward his peers in Europe. Once fully ordained, he began his project to bring Buddhism to the West.[50] With the support of Daw Mya May, a wealthy Burmese woman who patronised Buddhist reform activities, he founded the *Buddhasasana Samagama* (International Buddhist Society) in Mandalay in July 1902.[51] He also launched a journal, *Buddhism: An Illustrated Quarterly Review*, intended for subscribers and libraries worldwide, insisting that it should feature the highest-quality photographs that publishing technology allowed. The result was a beautiful, but very costly, publication.[52] Ananda Metteyya anticipated a European and American audience for his journal and expected numerous converts from Europe. He was repeatedly disappointed when subscribers turned out to be mainly Burmese Buddhists. It was when his plan to create a lineage of European Buddhist missionaries to the West failed to materialize in Burma that he organized the 1908 mission to London to deliver his message there in person.

Bennett's return to London as Ananda Metteyya in 1908 prompted, in advance of his visit, the founding of "The Buddhist Society of Great Britain and Ireland."[53] As a founder of an august and surviving Buddhist association in Europe, he was for a century thereafter routinely hailed as the first Western Buddhist monk, carrying out the first Buddhist mission to Europe.[54] Until we discovered Dhammaloka, the figure of Ananda Metteyya had completely obscured from view not just Dhammaloka but all the other Western Buddhist monks ordained before Ananda Metteyya.[55]

Ananda Metteyya vs. Dhammaloka

Rangoon, it appears, was not big enough to hold both Dhammaloka and Ananda Metteyya. The two European monks seldom if ever met face to face, but they clashed repeatedly with each other at a distance, wrangling in public through the press.[56]

In July 1903, when Dhammaloka had been away from Burma for a year, the *Rangoon Times* ran an article praising Ananda Metteyya, as

> without a doubt, a decided improvement on his predecessor U Dhammaloka, for the simple reason that he is more intellectual and has bright ideas of the religion he professes. He is a man of culture as his works go to prove.[57]

Figure 6.2. "U Ananda Mitria" (Ananda Metteyya). Colored postcard by D. A. Ahuja, Rangoon, ca. 1902.

© Collection of Sharman Minus.

Dhammaloka, then in Bangkok, took offense, as was clearly intended, and fired off a retort. He was upset that Ananda Metteyya's *Buddhasasana Samagama*, dubbed in English the "International Buddhist Society," seemed to plagiarize his work in promoting the Society for Promoting Buddhism (SPB) in Mandalay, cofounding the International Young Men's Buddhist Association (IYMBA) in Tokyo, and now launching the Siam National Buddhist Association. He did not want to be confused with Ananda Metteyya, whose work he distrusted. Dhammaloka's assistant Maung Maung presented the *Bangkok Times* office with photographic proof of Dhammaloka's role in both the IYMBA and the SPB, showing that Dhammaloka was in no way associated with Ananda Metteyya, nor wished to be.[58]

Ananda Metteyya was certainly more interested in Buddhist ideas, particularly modernist interpretations of Buddhist doctrine found in European works. Dhammaloka, by contrast, left expositions of Buddhist doctrine to Burmese monks; his special mission was to galvanize Buddhists to protect their religion from the European values and attitudes exemplified by missionary Christianity and strong drink. Nonetheless, each was proud of his organizational acumen, as this public spat over who had founded the earliest, best, or most Buddhist societies revealed.

The *Bangkok Times* highlighted a further difference between the two, saying of Ananda Metteyya that "he has not yet accustomed himself to the Burmese mode of living, although he eventually intends doing so."[59] He reputedly had a separate monastery built for himself and his later European monks. Not so Dhammaloka, who lived as a Burmese in the busy Tavoy monastery and whose legitimacy in the eyes of the audiences on his preaching tours derived from his ability to perfectly embody Burmese monastic culture. Dhammaloka ate, breathed, and slept as his plebeian Burmese friends did. This was never true of Ananda Metteyya.

Respect for Burma's traditional Buddhist culture remained a bone of contention between the two. In a 1907 broadside delivered via the *Burma Echo*, Dhammaloka wrote that the "dubious character" Ananda Metteyya

was alleged to be the author of certain Articles on the "Philosophy of Buddhism" which few who read them will forget in a hurry.

In those articles Ananda Metteyya had encouraged Burmese to preserve their religion or culture. "Yet," wrote Dhammaloka:

on the 26th instant, he in this evening paper, now pens a paragraph condemning the Burmese Buddhists for not changing their customs and

religious ideas. He condemns "pwes" [Buddhist festivals that included theatrical performances], and he calls the cremation of hpoongyi (Buddhist priests)
gruesome affairs. Yet, a couple of years ago, in his "Buddhism" he described
hpoongyi-byans [cremations] as being "the most philosophical as well as the
most scientific way of disposing of the dead." He wonders why Burmese do not
continue to support his literature, in these days; and possibly his previous phe-
nomenal success may explain this circumstance. Nobody better than himself
should be able to explain this thing.[60]

To Dhammaloka, Ananda Metteyya was a hypocrite who neither understood nor approved of the real Buddhism lived by the Burmese people—the
very Buddhism Dhammaloka was fighting to defend. Ananda Metteyya,
Dhammaloka suggested, recognized only the "Buddhism" created in European
texts. He thus proved himself a threat to living Burmese culture.

In 1908, Dhammaloka again challenged his rival's legitimacy, this time in the
London investigative weekly *Truth*. Contradicting press reports that Ananda
Metteyya was the first ordained Buddhist to visit Europe, Dhammaloka pointed
to visits by others, including U Vimala from the Tavoy monastery who had
studied English "twelve years ago," two or three Sinhalese monks who "resided
several years in England," and the Japanese scholar-priest Dr. Buniyo Nanjio,
"who was seven years at Oxford."[61]

The press's error enabled Dhammaloka to go to town on the question of his
opponent's monastic legitimacy. "Ananda Mittriya," he wrote, "is not generally
recognised here [in Burma] as a properly ordained mendicant, and has been
turned out from three monasteries in this province—one in Akyab and two in
Rangoon." He listed financial irregularities and criticized Ananda Metteyya
for reportedly turning his back on his own sister, calling this unprecedented
"[a]ccording to the tenets of Buddhism in Burma." Finally, he quoted a scriptural
rule that a monk must be free of asthma for ordination.[62]

In his response, Ananda Metteyya said he had been ordained not once but
twice, and that the high status of the presiding monk Engan Sayadaw at the
second ritual in Mandalay guaranteed him legitimacy in the eyes of "any educated
Burman." He had not been "turned out" from any monastery, nor even met his
sister in England, and he disputed Dhammaloka's financial claims. Questioning
whether asthma was included in the ordination rules, he says that in any case he
had believed himself cured at the time of his ordination.[63]

The tone of this debate in the pages of a London journal was surprisingly
Burmese and Buddhist, hinging on specific and technical violations of vinaya
rules. The question of "authentic" Buddhism had long been the subject of controversy in London and elsewhere, but this is the first known case of the Western

press debating the legitimacy of Buddhist ordinations. The editor, however, shifted the debate to the question of which man would be considered more respectable by London society, commenting:

> I am not in a position to decide between them, but I may say that an English journalist who knew "Dhammaloka" in Siam a few years ago, and incidentally mentions that he is a Buddhist from Dublin, describes him as an adept in the art of self-advertisement.[64]

Building and Breaching Barriers

It would be tempting to depict the achievements of Asoka, Dhammaloka, and Ananda Metteyya as the purposeful acts of pioneering, strong-willed individuals; great and even holy men heroically breaching the barrier between East and West and building new connections between Europeans and Asians, through the strength of their personalities and the clarity of their visions. Indeed, this is how Ananda Metteyya's story has been presented for almost a century. The far more interesting reality is that a Westerner's entry to the sangha was entirely dependent on Asian ordination sponsors, lay and monastic, and subject to their purposes. In each case, those sponsors saw the ordination of a European as assisting a much larger strategy aimed at specific Burmese goals.

This truth becomes all the more essential in the context of colonial history, where too often the emphasis is put on European agency and initiatives. While Gordon Douglas, Allan Bennett, and "William Colvin" undoubtedly breached an ethnic boundary by entering the Buddhist monastic fold as Europeans, they were simultaneously being used to reinforce the boundaries of a local community that felt itself under serious threat—Thudhamma orthodoxy in the case of Asoka and Dhammaloka, and the Arakanese modernists in the case of Ananda Metteyya. Far from weakening these boundaries, the Europeans' inclusion through ordination reinforced the defenses of Burmese Buddhist orthodoxy and legitimacy. Thus they were in many ways the objects of Asian agency, rather than agents of their own destiny.

While each man clearly sought refuge from his own culture, and in doing so rebelled against colonial and Christian institutions, ordination meant submitting to Burmese monastic rules. Emphasizing the orthodoxy of the ordination rituals demonstrated the total subjection of these Europeans to Buddhist, rather than British, laws, a particularly striking colonial reversal. The length of time a monk had spent in robes determined status in all things, so as relatively recent ordinands all three men lost much of their usual European privilege. Asoka and Ananda Metteyya in particular chafed at the restrictions they had adopted, Asoka attempting to travel during his very first rains retreat, and Ananda Metteyya denigrating local Buddhist culture and customs. Dhammaloka, who may have been ordained far longer, was more adjusted to Burmese life, but certainly bent the rules, as in his claiming (mainly outside Burma) to be a Japanese-style "Lord High Abbot" and in his often feisty and un-monk-like public persona.

As publicly recognized monastics, each of these three invented the role of "European Buddhist monk" through his own practice. Asoka's brief career as a monk was soon forgotten, but Ananda Metteyya (albeit through his early associate Nyanatiloka) and Dhammaloka both fostered their own lineages. Yet the very public conflicts between Dhammaloka and Ananda Metteyya demonstrate how the meaning of "Western Buddhist monk" was contested from the start. The two had very different ideas about appropriate behavior and about the vision of Buddhism that each sought to promote. The contrast between Ananda Metteyya's intellectual and Western-oriented style and Dhammaloka's more localized and grounded approach reflects a tension in understandings of Buddhism—as a universal philosophy or a locally embedded way of life—that is still being played out today.

Ordaining Others: Creating Lineages

Both Dhammaloka and Ananda Metteyya aspired to bring more Europeans (and in Dhammaloka's case, Eurasians) into the sangha, setting out to create a lineage of monks. These lineages highlight their conflicting approaches, but more than this, they show the difficulties of creating legitimacy and respectability for those who were simultaneously Buddhist and Western.

Ananda Metteyya at his own higher ordination had called for the creation of an order of European bhikkhus.[65] He claimed to have corresponded with "eminent Buddhists in England, Germany and America" about potential recruits.[66] In 1904 one European novice writes of Ananda Metteyya as the leader of a growing body of Western monks. In 1905 we find references to "Mr B," "M. the Canadian Phoongyee" and "Mr X," all implicitly connected to Ananda Metteyya.[67] A 1902 report states, "He proposes to stop in Rangoon for three months to recruit."[68] The two most famous Western monks affiliated with Ananda Metteyya are the German Anton Gueth, ordained as Nyanatiloka, and J. F. McKechnie, a Scottish supporter from Rangoon, who became Silacara.[69]

While Silacara became a key supporter of Ananda Metteyya's work in the *Buddhasasana Samagama* and the journal, and later wrote a number of key articles, Nyanatiloka went on to become one of the most famous Western Buddhists of the twentieth century, founding a lineage which continues to this day. Both were part of Ananda Metteyya's early vision of a "Sangha of the West."

Nyanatiloka had contacted Ananda Metteyya before his ordination in 1904, and Silacara's ordination was sponsored by Ananda Metteyya's patron. The enduring lineage directly connected to Nyanatiloka includes four monks Nyanatiloka ordained between 1905 and 1907 and another twelve novices ordained before 1914. Nine of these soon disrobed; a propensity for monks to leave the order happened, and still happens, across all ethnicities and lineages.[70]

What, then, of Dhammaloka's lineage? In 1905 we hear that: [It was] "seven years ago [*sic*] when the Revd Dhammaloka entered the Buddhist priesthood. Since the establishment of the society in Burma, fifteen Europeans had joined the priesthood."[71] When Dhammaloka was in Ceylon in 1909, the hostile *Catholic Messenger* wrote of "thirteen white bonzes [monks] he left behind in Burma."[72]

We can put names to several people ordained by, or on behalf of, Dhammaloka:

- The second Asoka, Asoka II, likely James Butement or Butemen (see Chapter 2);[73]
- Theeyedaza, Mr. Warwick, ordained in the spring of 1902;[74]
- Arnold or Aaron Abrams (sometimes given as Abraham);[75] he may have disrobed in 1905 but continued supporting Dhammaloka's projects in Penang;[76]
- Dharmatrata, M. T. de la Courneuve (see Chapter 5 and discussion in the following);[77]
- Dipalamkara/Dipalankara (sometimes given as Dhammawanga or Dharmawanga), C. A. Roberts (see Chapter 5 and the following);[78]
- An unnamed "Ceylon Eurasian," sent to the Tavoy monastery in Rangoon with Roberts (Chapter 5);[79]
- U Vara, Richard Laffère, b. 1867, died in Persia in 1909;[80]
- We can probably add the tattooed American monk encountered at the Tavoy monastery in 1905,[81] Dharmakeeta (Mr. Hardy),[82] and perhaps the Irish activist U Visuddha in South India.[83]

Thus we have seven to ten possible names. The "European novices" collecting money for a library in Rangoon in late 1904 may be additional to this list, and Mr. Solomon's short-lived ordination might be an example of Dhammaloka seeking to save a man from drink.[84]

In 1901–2 Dhammaloka participated in Asoka II's novice and upasampada ordinations, stating at the novice ceremony that "two other Europeans would become hpoongyis within the next few months."[85] In 1902, for Theeyedaza's up-coming full ordination, the *Times of Burma* anticipated seeing "[t]he officiating high-priests, about twenty in number, headed by U Dhammaloka. . . ."[86] This would be unusual, given that Dhammaloka had not been ordained the requisite ten years. Maybe (as with Asoka II) a senior monk presided at the ceremony and

Dhammaloka gave a speech. This might explain how in 1902 he could tell the *Times of Burma* that

> [a]t present I have five European novices, and expect to have this number doubled in a couple of years.[87]

Theeyedaza in Letpadan and Dharmakeeta (Mr. Hardy), a Eurasian man from Bangkok, in Moulmein may well have fit within this approach.[88]

A January 1903 report from Japan said that

> U Dhammaloka, next week, will ordain two young Japanese novices, who intend entering the priest-hood, and going to Burma. This ceremony will take place at the Japanese Indian Club.[89]

The report was from the club's secretary, suggesting the plans were reasonably concrete. These may be the two Japanese Buddhists whom Dhammaloka claimed, in Hong Kong shortly afterward, would accompany him to Tibet, but we hear nothing further of them.[90]

There is no indication that Dhammaloka ordained anyone in Bangkok during 1903, but in 1904, having established his Singapore Buddhist mission and school, the ordinations began anew. First, he sent Roberts, the unnamed Eurasian, and Abrams to Rangoon for ordination, in April and June.[91] By October, however, he was handling matters himself. He disrobed Dipalamkara, ordained Dharmatrata (sending him to Penang to study at the Burmese monastery there), ordained a second, unnamed Englishman, and announced plans for further missions. Abrams was initially assigned to Thursday Island in Australia, Dipalamkara to Penang, and the Englishman to Kuala Lumpur.[92] It appears the plan was for English-speaking bhikkhus to run schools as the basis for missions (as in Singapore and Bangkok).[93] In February 1905 we read that

> [Dhammaloka] proposes to establish a school at Penang on the same lines as the one at Singapore where he was greatly helped by all classes of the Buddhist community, including Chinese, Singhalese and Japanese.[94]

In July 1905, we see Vara traveling to Penang from Rangoon in preparation for Dhammaloka's visit to found a new Buddhist mission.[95] Abrams, however, did not go to Australia. In June 1905 he was said to have gone to "Bombay, Calcutta, and other places in India, fasted, clothed himself and prayed as a Bhuddhist [*sic*] priest but has now decided to revert to Judaism."[96] More likely he simply disrobed, since in August he was on the founding committee for the Penang branch of Dhammaloka's Straits Young Men's Buddhist Association as "M[r?]. Abraham."[97]

Our information is patchy, but the general picture is one of experimentation: first Dhammaloka's instigation of and involvement in ordinations in Burma,
then dispatching aspirants from Singapore to Burma for ordination and study;
then his own ordinations in Singapore and efforts to start new missions on this
basis. Reports of Dhammaloka ordaining people vanish from the record after
1905. If the 1909 claim of thirteen monks in his lineage was accurate, he must have
carried out more ordinations, but perhaps did not expect so much from them.

Ananda Metteyya had also set out after his own ordination in 1902 to gather
and ordain a group of Europeans. Dhammaloka's success in contrast to the few
ordained in direct association with Ananda Metteyya is notable, especially since
this was only part of Dhammaloka's extensive repertoire of pan-Asian touring,
preaching, temperance campaigning, publishing, and building schools and
missions. Of course, Ananda Metteyya targeted only Europeans in Europe, while
Dhammaloka was happy to recruit those already living in Asia. However, it is
also relevant that Ananda Metteyya appealed to a more middle-class and literate
audience, primarily through publications and communication with European
Buddhist sympathizers. Those who were ordained through Dhammaloka seem
to have had more plebeian backgrounds.

Liturgy and Legitimacy

As might be expected in this period of experimentation, widely different
approaches were adopted to the ordination of Westerners. Sometimes, great
pains were taken to establish the legitimacy of particular events, but not always. Thus we read of the distinctly unorthodox novice ordination of Ananda
Metteyya's associate J. F. McKechnie (Silacara) in 1907:

A very interesting ceremony took place at the Buddhist Girls' School, in
Pagoda Road. Mr. McKechnie, a Scotch gentleman who has been some time in
Rangoon, was ordained as a Novice of the Hpoongyi Order on Tuesday 22nd
instant. The ceremony was most interesting by the fact that it was performed
by Mrs. H. Oung (Mah Mya May). The ceremony was kept as select as possible, only a few Europeans being let in to witness it. Since Tuesday the Buddhist
priesthood of Rangoon has been exercised as to the legality, or otherwise, of
this ceremony for the performance of which there is apparently no provision
made in the Vinaya or Sacred Buddhist Rituals.[98]

A broader sketch of the ordinations of three of the monks in Dhammaloka's
lineage—Asoka II, Dharmatrata (Courneuve), and Dipalamkara (C.
A. Roberts)—shows not only the difficulties and novelties of ordination rituals

and the creation of new lineages of Western monks, but also the problems of remaining a monk in these contexts.

Ordination at the Tavoy Monastery:
December 1901/May 1902

Asoka II's novice ordination took place on December 15, 1901, at the Tavoy monastery in Rangoon. The newspapers were unsure of Asoka II's previous identity. A Mr. Butement had been ordained, presumably as a novice, some time before January 22, 1902, "under the guidance of the Sayadaw U Sanda in Thayettaw Monastery (the compound containing the Tavoy monastery) and under the titled Thanyok Sayadaw of Gya Tawya Monastery."[99] There were also reports of preparations for Asoka II's higher ordination in the town of Zigon,[100] though ultimately the event took place in Rangoon on May 21, 1902.

Sara Jeanette Duncan, writing as Mrs. Everard Cotes, published a lengthy article, "The Ordination of Asoka," that provides not only one of the fullest interviews with Dhammaloka we have (and one of only two surviving photographs—see Figure 2.1 in Chapter 2), but also a detailed account of the December novice ordination ceremony.[101] At Dhammaloka's invitation, Cotes observed what she understood to be "the second induction of a European into the Buddhist priesthood." Arriving at 9 a.m., she was asked to wait while the candidate's head was shaved; "two comely Burmese maidens" brought them chairs, a table, cakes and tea, and at ten, Dhammaloka invited them into the monastery building:

> Most of the assemblage had drawn to one side of the room, and there it crouched on the floor upon its heels. On a mat before the people sat the old *Sadaw*, the abbot. . . . A younger priest hovered about him, others huddled in the background. There was not a semblance of order; quite as many Burmans, men and women, were walking about and talking as were sitting in rows on the floor. The women especially bustled and laughed at the other side of the room, bending over baskets of eatables, not in any way humbled by the occasion, rather in their way mistresses of it. . . . A few Chinamen mingled with the Burmans, and many in whom the races were plainly blended.[102]

Dhammaloka called the room to order, and the candidate, "a bent old man," entered in white robes and knelt before the officiating priest and the abbot. Cotes struggles to describe the scene and the emotions it produced:

> The candidate kneeling lifted his head and looked up at them, with affection and confidence and docility and submission, between man and man and indeed a

curious regard—across this gulf of race and tradition . . . how is one to write of the strange pang it brought?[103]

The candidate requested admission to the order in Pali and retired to change into saffron robes. Returning, he repeated the refuges and precepts after the priest:

> He stumbled over some of the words—there was pathos here—and the cadence he gave to some did not satisfy the priest, so that, looking up like a child, he was obliged to say them several times. The words of the precepts were harder still— that by which he vowed to abstain from beautifying his person with garlands contained twenty syllables—and here the candidate often broke down, shaking a discouraged head.[104]

The candidate then accepted the name "Asoka" from various suggestions from the monks and congregation. After a typically energetic speech by Dhammaloka "through an interpreter," the new bhikkhu was given a begging-bowl and

> sent among the women at the other side of the room. They heaped it heartily, one after another, with good things, rice and cakes fried in butter and condiments, putting in their packages with many jokes among themselves. Only Asoka, who moved gravely upon his quest, looked a little dazed at the laughter.[105]

Cotes writes, "I think they scamped the service; we were in Lower Burma, where orthodoxy of late years, has suffered some dilution." The liturgy and vinaya quorum were adhered to nonetheless, and the new bhikkhu would be regarded as legitimately ordained in Burma.

Dharmatrata Ordained in Singapore: October 1904

We know something about Dhammaloka's ordination of Dharmatrata (Courneuve) and his disrobing of Dipalamkara (Roberts) in Singapore, not least because of the controversy surrounding them. The *Perak Pioneer* commented on Dharmatrata's ordination that

> [his] services were dispensed with by Government so recently as the 1st ultimo. His hurried departure from Taiping consequent on the ardent desire to embrace the new Faith had afforded him no leisure to call on sundry creditors to settle his worldly accounts with them.[106]

A few days later Dhammaloka came to the *Straits Times* offices in Singapore, stating that Dharmatrata, when requesting novice ordination, had produced a letter from the Singapore Chief of Police stating that he "was leaving the Police Force of his own free will, and had nothing against him." Dhammaloka had also been assured that there were no outstanding debts to disqualify the applicant.[107] However, the newspapers were not questioning the legitimacy of Dharmatrata's Buddhist ordination, but highlighting the overlap between values of the vinaya and colonial capitalism. The *Perak Pioneer* opined: "It is to be hoped that it is one of the fundamental tenets of Buddhism that the discharge of one's lawful debts is an indispensable preliminary to salvation."[108]

We have two detailed reports of Dharmatrata's ordination ceremony.[109] According to the *Straits Times,*

> When everyone had been seated, including about one hundred little Chinese boys belonging to the School attached to the Mission, the Lord Abbot the Right Rev. U. Dhammaloka took his seat opposite the audience. The Rev. Otha [Ocha], head of the Japanese mission in Singapore . . . sat on the Abbot's right hand, being the next senior priest. U Dhammawanga, a novice (Samenera), who is a Welshman by birth, sat on the left of U Dhammaloka. Dead silence prevailed for a few moments and the choir of the Buddhist Mission, led by the Abbot, then sang a song of praise in English.

When the novice entered he was

> a short, well built young man of good appearance and was neatly dressed in a black suit of European cut. If it were not for the fact that his head had been shaved as bald as a trout, he might easily have been mistaken for one of the European guests.

The candidate then bowed three times to a statue of the Buddha:

> It was indeed a strange sight to behold a European bowing down to a graven image, and a thrill of astonishment passed through the Europeans present, who had never dreamed such a thing possible. The candidate then prostrated himself before U Dhammaloka and repeated after him in Pali the ordination service. This lasted about half an hour and a yellow robe was then handed to him. He retired to an inner recess to don his robes while the choir sang another chant of praise.[110]

On return, Courneuve received the name Dharmatrata. Dhammaloka congratulated him, announcing that he would be sent to Penang. Dipalamkara (Roberts, here given as Dhammawanga) then explained Buddhist beliefs in English and was disrobed (see the following section). The event concluded with light refreshments and a photograph—and three days' holiday for the pupils of the Buddhist Mission School.

This ceremony, manifestly more innovative than the ordination of Asoka II, appears to be the first ordination carried out by Dhammaloka himself. It was nearly five years since his own 1900 upasampada ordination and perhaps he felt this gave him sufficient seniority. The presence of Rev. Ocha, head of the Singapore Japanese Buddhist mission, showed Dhammaloka's friendly relations with the Buddhists of Singapore but hardly added to the orthodoxy of the event.[111] Of course, Dhammaloka's main audience at Havelock Road comprised Chinese and Europeans, neither community being in position to question the legitimacy of a supposedly Burmese-style ordination.

The Ordination and Disrobing of C. A. Roberts: April/October 1904

Six months earlier, U Dipalamkara, then C. A. Roberts, had been sent by Dhammaloka's Buddhist Mission in Singapore to the Tavoy monastery in Rangoon for novice ordination and "a course of two years' study preparatory to entering the priesthood."[112] Evidently he soon connected with Ananda Metteyya, for he "accompanied the Secretary General of the International Buddhist Society on his recent tour as far as Sagaing, and was there ordained a Samanera, or Novice, by the Ven. Rajinda Thera."[113] In June, we find Dipalamkara in the central Burmese town of Kyoukse, receiving a visit from the Deputy Commissioner to the Ratana Biman Anglo-Vernacular Buddhist Boy's School and announcing, like Dhammaloka in Singapore, that a girl's school would be established as soon as funds permitted.

Dipalamkara had earlier given a lecture at the school on a "Buddhist temple in Canton," describing being carried in a chair to this temple in China. In his conclusion he "pointed out the difference between the Christian Idea and that of the Great Teacher Gautama," saying that Burmans "hail with satisfaction the recent arrival of several European Bhikkhus who have taken the yellow robe, and are now preaching throughout the country."[114] It is unclear whether the Kyoukse work was connected with Ananda Metteyya or not, but in October we find Roberts with Dhammaloka at the ordination of Dharmatrata in Singapore and being disrobed at the same event, where Roberts announced that after five months as a novice he must leave the order because he had accepted a remittance from his parents. Dhammaloka reportedly said that Dipalamkara was being disrobed for traveling during the rainy season.[115]

A few days later, Roberts wrote to the *Straits Times* (as Roberts and also still "Rev. U Dipalamkara") contesting this version of events. "Buddhism as enacted in Singapore and Buddhism as a system of morals, precepts and philosophy" he wrote, "are widely apart." He went on to defend "those Europeans who have voluntarily renounced the world and taken the Yellow Robe in Burma just now and of whom the Rev. Ananda Maitriya is the head" from charges of being motivated by material gain.[116] The picture is unclear, but suggests someone with a longer-term interest in Buddhism who perhaps hoped not to have to choose between Dhammaloka and Ananda Metteyya.

Legitimacy and Boundaries

In Rangoon, on May 21, 1902, the same auspicious day as Asoka II's full ordination, Ananda Metteyya received ordination and published *The Foundation of the Sangha of the West: Being an Account of the Upasampada Ordination of Bhikkhu Ananda Maitriya (Allan Bennett MacGregor)*. This grandiose title underlines the significance that could be read into the ordination of Westerners. What made his ordination "the Foundation of the Sangha of the West" was not his own status as European—he was aware of other Western Buddhist monks, including Dhammaloka and the deceased Asoka (Gordon Douglas). It was the intention to ordain others in the West; that is, to found an ordination lineage.

Given this lofty goal, it is something of a surprise to find little or no contention around the legitimacy of ordinations done *by* Europeans. In Buddhist history, precisely because sangha hierarchy and legitimacy are so vital, ordinations—and new departures in ordinations—are frequently the locus of controversy, raising fervor around subjects such as the ordination status of the monks performing the ordination or the correct way to construct an ordination boundary (sima). Yet ordinations of—and by—Westerners seem to have provoked hardly any debate. Dhammaloka's creative novice ordination of Courneuve in Singapore in the presence only of himself, a European Buddhist novice, and a Japanese priest excited no controversy.

There were a few indications of controversy around the Burmese ordination of Europeans. McKechnie's was questioned, as was Ananda Metteyya's, albeit in the pages of the London periodical *Truth*, where in 1908 Dhammaloka disputed Ananda Metteyya's claim to be a monk. There were no known reverberations within the Burmese sangha hierarchy or among Buddhists in the West. A second, and recurring, theme within the colonial press in Burma and across Buddhist Asia was mockery of the alcoholic backsliding of newly ordained European bhikkhus and the suggestion that they ordained to escape debts or secure food and shelter. This was not an issue for the sangha hierarchy, and indeed such reports often relate to routine disrobings.

The impressive array of senior monks involved in Dhammaloka's own upasampada ceremony in Rangoon (Chapter 2) might indicate a concern within the sangha hierarchy to preempt any challenge to the legitimacy of the ordination. In fact, the Burmese Buddhist authorities made every effort to render the conversions and ordinations of Asoka (Douglas), Dhammaloka, and Ananda Metteyya unquestionable. The vinaya-based orthodoxy of all three ceremonies is notable, especially when contrasted with the innovative lay conversion ceremonies being held in Ceylon or the United States at the time.[117]

In Ceylon, High Priest Hikkaduve Sumangala was evidently reluctant to ordain Europeans. Gordon Douglas applied to be admitted into the ranks of the Buddhist monks, but the High Priest declined.[118] Yet Sumangala's seems the only case of sangha objections to the ordination of Europeans—and it looks as though Douglas and Bennett were helped to make contact with Burmese monks willing to ordain them, so it is hard to discern any objection of principle. It seems that the ordination of Westerners mattered only as it related to internal local sangha prestige and projects—advancing the Thudhamma reform project in the case of Bhikkhu Asoka and Dhammaloka, and avoiding controversy and undue entanglements in the case of Sumangala's resistance. Perhaps Western monks were enough of an oddity that their ordinations did not raise concerns for the Burmese and Sinhalese sanghas unless they impinged on internal politics.

In the light of Buddhist history, even up to today, the relative absence of polemic about ordinations of Westerners stands out. Presumably, the feeling was that the usual strict standards did not apply to Westerners, or perhaps to any foreigners. In this period there were relatively few such ordinations and yet—in a period of Buddhist globalization—the relatively high profile of figures such as Dhammaloka, Ananda Metteyya, or Nyanatiloka, each of whom worked to create a lineage, marks these ordinations as significant.

What this lack of concern likely reflects is the embedded weight of indigenous sangha sects and lineages as against the comparatively flimsy structures erected by Western Buddhists in this period. Up until 1914, it could hardly be argued that Ananda Metteyya, Dhammaloka, or Nyanatiloka had created a lasting lineage of a kind that would pose any real challenge to existing Asian sanghas. Only Nyanatiloka's lineage survived to become a long-standing fixture on the stage of global Buddhism. These were still liminal figures and experimental spaces.

Yet these early attempts at ordaining and creating lineages of Western monks in Asia tell us something about the ways in which both the local sangha structures and the problems and priorities of Europeans in Asia were being reconfigured in this era. The projects that Dhammaloka and Ananda Metteyya furthered did not fit entirely with Asian agendas for monasticism in this period, but neither were

they seen as a threat. The Europeans they drew to ordination were marginal figures, drawn from a class of white men on the periphery of the colonial world—
beachcombers, sailors, and low-level migrants. They show us a transitory era, in
which European bhikkhus were visible because of hardening racial attitudes in
empire and centralizing sangha agendas. They were thus able to play a role in the
multiethnic and transnational networking processes that globalized Buddhism
within Asia, prior to its globalization beyond.

7

The Vagabond Traveler's Account

1905

Hoboing around the World

The liveliest firsthand description of Dhammaloka is found in a best-selling 1910 travel book entitled *A Vagabond Journey Around the World: A Narrative of Personal Experience*.[1] Its author, an intrepid and articulate young American named Harry Alverson Franck, was born in Munger, Michigan, and graduated from the University of Michigan in 1903 with a degree in modern European languages. The son of a blacksmith and well used to manual labor, Franck paid his own way through university by the sweat of his brow. During five college summer vacations he worked, "with pick and shovel, or in the harvest fields of the Northwest, and, having sent back the tuition thus earned, 'hoboed' back to the college town."[2] On occasion he went farther afield; to Liverpool in the United Kingdom, where he ended up with only four cents to his name ten days before college was to begin but somehow still managed to earn his college fees in time to join classes, and to mainland Europe, working on a cattle boat.[3] By the time he graduated, Franck had become a seasoned and resourceful traveler, who could take care of himself in the roughest company.

In his final year of university, during a debate with fellow students about how many thousand dollars would be needed for a trip around the world, Franck boldly asserted that it could be done for nothing. The following year, 1904, he set out to prove it. Aged twenty-two, and with $104 saved from a spell of high school teaching, he left Detroit on June 18 to travel around the world on his wits. He landed back in Seattle—disembarking from one of the last surviving sailing ships on the trans-Pacific route from Japan—in September 1905. He had $113 in his pocket and an astonishing story of travels, largely on foot, among the lowest strata of society in Europe, the Middle East, and Asia. When the story of this adventure was published in 1910 as *A Vagabond Journey Around the World* it attracted a worldwide readership.[4]

Hailed at the time as "unique," *A Vagabond Journey* remains so for the sociological light it sheds on life among the poor, mainly European, beggars, tramps,

The Irish Buddhist. Alicia Turner, Laurence Cox, and Brian Bocking, Oxford University Press (2020)
DOI: 10.1093/oso/9780190073084.001.0001

itinerant seamen, confidence tricksters, invalids, and ex-prisoners (collectively known as ' "beachcombers") whose lives Franck shared during the fifteen months of his travels. The book also offered an unprecedented view from below of the local inhabitants, ranging from impoverished villagers to high-up local gentry and colonial officials, whom Franck encountered in the many countries he traversed.

Franck's own working-class background and experience from his working holidays gave him a real advantage in his "participant observation" approach to the journey. Traveling usually alone, with no financial reserves or official backing, he shared with others like him across the world the daily struggle to find food and shelter. He had the advantage of being a white man, but traveled as a "poor white," never, so far as we can tell, revealing his college-educated status to impress the colonial authorities. Being American offered him little advantage; in British-ruled Ceylon he was offered work as a policeman, only to lose the opportunity when he revealed his nationality. Perhaps the only features that distinguished him from his fellow beachcombers were his plan to travel around the world, and the fact that he was documenting his experiences.[5]

Not that a college degree or any other sign of a cultured upbringing would necessarily save a man from destitution. While Franck observed much that would confirm popular stereotypes of the poor white beachcomber as barely educated, workshy, and unreliable, he could often enlighten and surprise his reader, as in his account of an evening concert held in a Christian mission hall for vagrant seamen in Calcutta. Some of the ballads volunteered by the sailors proved unsuitable for the ears of the ladies present, and the proceedings were brought to a temporary halt, until

a tow-headed beachcomber—a Swede by all seeming—was forced to his feet and advanced self-consciously up the aisle. He was the sorriest-looking "vag" in the gathering. His garb was a strange collection of tatters, through which his sunburned skin peeped out here and there; and his hands, calloused evidences of self-supporting days, hung heavily at his sides. The noises thus far produced would have been prohibited by law in a civilized country, and I settled back in my seat prepared to endure some new auditory atrocity. The Swede, ignoring the stairs by which more conventional mortals mounted, stepped from the floor to the rostrum, and strode to the piano. The audience, grinning nervously, waited for him to turn and bellow forth some halyard chantie. He squatted instead on the recently vacated stool and, running his stumpy fingers over the keys, fell to playing with unusual skill—Mendelssohn's "Frühlingslied." Such surprises befall, now and then, in the vagabond world. Its denizens are not always the unseeing, unknowing louts that those of a more laundered realm imagine.[6]

During his travels Franck was welcomed and helped by many people, and his account highlights numerous examples of extraordinary camaraderie, sociability, and enterprise among his fellow homeless wanderers. However, his odyssey was also fraught with danger. Strangers, especially destitute strangers, were often treated with suspicion or outright hostility, and Franck was in peril of his life on several occasions.

Franck Encounters Buddhism

A Vagabond Journey remains an enthralling and informative read today, though the modern reader's sensibilities will be jolted by the casual racism of the period, reflected in the vocabulary and actions of some of Franck's associates. Franck himself was sensitive to different cultural norms and values, as illustrated in his account of a visit to the Buddhist "Temple of the Tooth" in Kandy, Ceylon. Franck was taken to the temple by a local Sinhalese boy who knew English. The two were shown around by the head monk, the boy translating the monk's explanations about various precious items, including the tooth relic of the Buddha housed in its nest of elaborate caskets (see Figure 7.1).

Figure 7.1. The golden casket presented by U Vajirarama to the Temple of the Tooth, Kandy, Ceylon, and shown to Harry A. Franck in 1905.
Photo by Andrée, Colombo, 1907. From the New York Public Library, digitalcollections.nypl.org.

In an aside to the reader, Franck confesses that it seemed clear to him the tooth never came from any human mouth, but to his guide at the time he showed only politeness and respect. At the end of the tour, the head monk— in faultless English—invited Franck to think seriously about becoming a Buddhist monk:

> "White men," ran his speech, "often join the true religion. There are many who are priests of Buddha in Burma, and some in Ceylon. They are much honored."[7]

Franck was astonished to find that the head monk spoke English, but the boy explained that most European visitors to the monastery were rude and dismissive of Buddhism, so the monk had waited to see how Franck would behave. Evidently Franck had passed the test, for over the next few days a constant stream of monks and lay Buddhists approached him to encourage and congratulate the prospective convert.

Escaping to Colombo, Franck met up again with the Dublin university-educated beachcomber "John Askins."[8] Franck told Askins of his near-conversion.

> "It's an old game out here," mused Askins. "In the good old days, whenever one of the boys went broke, it was get converted. Not all played out yet either."[9]

The Vagabond Traveler and the Beachcomber *Bhikkhu*

Franck's journey is fascinating in itself. However, we are primarily interested in his tale because in early May 1905 he encountered Dhammaloka boarding a railway train in Calcutta. Over the following days, Franck spent a good deal of time in Dhammaloka's company, interviewing him and observing him in action. Franck found Dhammaloka intriguing, and Dhammaloka gave Franck plenty to write about; the account of the Irish Buddhist "Bishop of Rangoon" spans nine pages of *A Vagabond Journey*. Although Dhammaloka probably never knew it, Franck would spread Dhammaloka's name worldwide—or at least the name "Oo Dama-laku," which is how Franck rendered it.

Franck had been traveling for eleven months when he met Dhammaloka in Calcutta. In that time, he had walked through Europe and the Middle East and stowed away at Port Said to make the sea crossing to Asia on the SS *Worcestershire*, heading for the Suez Canal on its way from London to Rangoon. He was thrown off the ship at its next stop, Colombo (Ceylon). After various adventures in Ceylon, and buoyed financially from a stint as a circus hand, Franck sailed for India on April 4. Within India, he traveled mainly by rail,[10] visiting Madras, Puri,

Benares, Agra, Delhi, and other places before finding himself, on the evening of Thursday, May 11, 1905, at Calcutta's Howrah railway station.

Dhammaloka was there, too, waiting to board the overnight train to Goalando, a small ferry quay on the west bank of the Ganges. Franck was traveling with another American drifter called Clarence Rice and an Australian, Gerald James. They planned to take the cross-Ganges ferry to the seaport of Chittagong (in present-day Bangladesh), traveling thence to Mandalay in Burma and on to the river port of Rangoon for the best chance of a ship to Hong Kong. Franck and his colleagues were being sneaked ticketless onto the train by a friendly Australian policeman when Franck first caught sight of Dhammaloka:

> The platform was swarming with a cosmopolitan humanity. Afghans, Sikhs, Bengalis, Tamils, and Mohammedans strolled back and forth or took garrulous leave of their departing friends through the train windows. Suddenly my attention was drawn to a priest of Buddha pushing his way through the throng. The yellow robe is rare in northern India, yet it was something more than the garment that led me to poke the policeman in the ribs. For the arms and shoulder of its wearer were white and the face that grinned beneath the shaven poll could have been designed in no other spot on earth than the Emerald Isle!

The policeman and Dhammaloka recognized each other from earlier days in Singapore. "Blow me," cried the officer, "if it ain't the Irish Buddhist, the bishop of Rangoon! I met 'im once in Singapore. Everybody in Burma knows 'im"; and he told Dhammaloka of Franck's plans to travel to Chittagong.

> "Fine!" cried the Irishman. "I'm bound the same way. I'm in second class but I'll see you on the boat tomorrow."[11]

The following morning, the three beachcombers found Dhammaloka washing his legs in the river at Goalando. Waiting on the deck of the tiny steamer for its noon departure, Dhammaloka struck a bargain with the youthful travelers. He would give them his "yarn," if they would listen to a talk about Buddhism. Franck's record of this encounter includes not only the fullest and most colorful version of Dhammaloka's own life-story, including his epic (if entirely fictional) journey to Lhasa, but also Franck's independent firsthand account of the Irish Buddhist's humiliation of an Indian Christian evangelist. Unlike Franck, we have some reason to doubt Dhammaloka's life-story, but there is no reason to question Franck's description of the debate with the evangelist. Both narratives seized the imagination of readers and reviewers worldwide after the book was published five years later.[12]

Dhammaloka Spins His Yarn

Franck was inclined to believe what Dhammaloka told him, not least because, by a remarkable coincidence, their stories intersected on the Sacramento river in California. As a young man, wrote Franck, Dhammaloka

> had emigrated to America, and, turning "hobo," had traveled through every state in the Union, working here and there. He was not long in convincing both Rice and me that he knew the secrets of the "blind baggage"[13] and the ways of railroad "bulls."[14] More than once he growled out the name of some junction where we, too, had been ditched, and told of running the police gauntlet in cities that rank even to-day as "bad towns."
>
> "Two years after landing in the States," he continued, "I hit California and took a job trucking[15] on a blessed fruit-boat in the Sacramento river, the Acme —"
>
> "What!" I gasped, "The Acme? I was truckman on her in 1902."
>
> "Bless my eyes, were you now?" cried the Irishman. 'Tis a blessed small world. Well, 'twas on the Acme that I picked up with a blessed old sea dog of the name of Blodgett, and we shipped out of Frisco for Japan. Blodgett, poor boy, died on the voyage, and after paying off I went on alone, fetching up at last in Rangoon. The English were not holding Burma then, and white men were as rare as Siamese twins.[16] Bless you, but the natives were glad to see me, and I lived fine. But best of all, I found the true religion, as you would call it, or philosophy as it should be called. When I was sure 'twas right I took [holy] orders among them, being the first blessed white man to turn Buddhist priest."
>
> "Good graft,"[17] grinned Rice.
>
> "The remark shows your ignorance," retorted the son of Erin. "Listen. Up to the day of my confirmation I was drawing a hundred rupees a month. I quit my job. I gave every blessed thing I owned to a friend of mine, even my socks. . . . If I'd put on European clothes again, for even one day, I'd be expelled. I cut off my hair and as fine a moustache as ever you saw. If I'd let them grow again I'd be expelled. If I'd put on a hat or shoes I'd be expelled. So would I if I owned a farthing of money, if I should kill so much as a flea, if I'd drink a glass of arrack, if I touched the oldest hag in the market place with so much as my finger."[18]

Dhammaloka went on to describe the daily monastic routine of begging for food, which, he said, he had followed for five years after first taking the robe (of a novice) "twenty years ago" (implying 1885).

> 'Twas hard, the first months, eating nothing but curry and rice. Now, bless you, I'd not eat European food if 'twas set down before me. Every blessed afternoon

I studied the history of Buddha and Burmese with the old priests. 'Twas a fine thing for me. Before I found the true faith I was that blessed ignorant I could hardly read my own tongue. To-day, bless you, I know eight languages and the ins and outs of every religion on the footstall.[19] I was a vile curser when I was hoboing in the States, and 'twas hard to quit it. But every time I started to say a cuss-word I thought of the revered Gautama and said 'blessed' instead, and I'm master of my own tongue, now."

"Then you really worship the Buddhist god," put in James.

"There again," cried the Irishman, "is the ignorance of them that follows that champion faker, Jesus, the son of Mary and a drunken Roman soldier. The Buddhists worship no one. We revere Buddha, the finest man that ever lived, because he showed us the way to attain Nirvana, which is to say heaven. He was no god, but a man like the rest of us."[20]

After five years, said Dhammaloka, he received (full) ordination (implying 1890), then spent five years "teaching the other novices and the children, the Tavoy monastery being the big school of Rangoon" and was made an elder (1895). Then he became the abbot and finally, after fifteen years, "the bishop, as you would call it, of Rangoon." Although the five-year periods (and clerical titles) as recorded by Franck are confusing, Dhammaloka tells Franck he has been "bishop" for six years, loosely suggesting the period since his independently documented full ordination in 1900.

"'Tis the bishop's place to travel," he went on,
"and in these six years gone I've visited every blessed Buddhist kingdom in Asia, from Japan to Ceylon; and I was in Lhasa talking with the Dalai Lama long before Younghusband would have dared to show his face there.[21] There's not a Buddhist king nor prince that hasn't treated me like one of them, though they'd have cut the throats of any other European. I'm coming back now from three months with the prince of Nepal, teaching his priests, him giving me the ticket to Chittagong."[22]

Dhammaloka then invited the young travelers to stay with him in Chittagong, where he would give them a chit for the Tavoy monastery in Rangoon. "If ever you have no place to put up in a Buddhist town," advised Dhammaloka, "go to the monastery. And if you tell them you know me, see how fine you'll be treated."

"Aye, but we'd have to know your name," I suggested.
"As I was going to tell ye, it's U (OO) Damalaku."
"Don't sound Irish," I remarked.

"No, indeed," laughed the priest, "that's my Buddhist name. The old one was Larry O'Rourke."

"You call that graft, you and your likes," he concluded, turning to Rice, "giving up your name and your hair and a fine moustache, and your clothes, and owning not an anna, and having your own ignorant race laughing at you, and having your body burned by the priests when you're born again in another one! But it's the true philosophy, bless you, and the right way to live. Why is it the white men that come out here die in ten years? Do you think it's the climate? Bless you, no, indeed, it's the strong drink and the women. Look at me. Would you think I was fifty-five if I hadn't told you?"

He was, certainly, the picture of health; deeply tanned, but with the clear eye and youthful poise of a man twenty years younger. Only one hardship, apparently, had he suffered during two decades of the yellow robe. His feet were broad and stumpy to the point of deformity, heavily calloused, and deeply scarred from years of travel over many a rough and stony highway.[23]

When James expressed skepticism about Dhammaloka's claims, Dhammaloka pulled out a "small, fat book" containing more than a hundred newspaper clippings "bearing witness to the truth of nearly every assertion he had made." Thanks to the recent digitization of historic newspapers as well as preservation of paper archives, we have been able to assemble many of these clippings that Dhammaloka evidently carried around, chronicling his time in Burma, Japan, Bangkok, and elsewhere, and offered as "proof" of his bona fides. In reality, Franck was reading reports from 1903 of Dhammaloka's *planned* trip to Lhasa, and perhaps reports of his intention to visit Nepal earlier in 1905. "The general trend of all," wrote Franck,

> may be gleaned from one article, dated four years earlier. In it the reader was invited to compare the receptions tendered Lord Curzon and the Irish Buddhist in Mandalay. The viceroy, in spite of months of preparation for his visit, had been received coldly by all but the government officials. Damalaku had been welcomed by the entire population, and had walked from the landing stage to the monastery, nearly a half-mile distant, on a roadway carpeted with the hair of the female inhabitants, who knelt in two rows, foreheads to the ground, on either side of the route, with their tresses spread out over it.[24]

This event, as imagined by an American newspaper illustrator (see Figure 7.2), appeared in 1911 in a story about Dhammaloka based on Franck's *Vagabond Journey Around the World*.[25]

"A double row of dark-haired maidens extended for nearly a mile along the dusty road and the American Buddhist strode over their flowing hair."

Figure 7.2. Orientalist vision of an Irish monk in Burma: Dhammaloka's reception in Mandalay, walking on the hair of female devotees—as imagined by an American newspaper illustrator in 1911.

San Francisco Examiner.

"*All* Sahibs are Christians!"

The ferry at Goalando was still filling up with passengers for the afternoon sailing as Dhammaloka wound up the story of his life and began his promised sermon on Buddhism. Franck was then witness to a remarkable encounter between Dhammaloka and an earnest Indian peddler of Christian tracts; the unfortunate Christian found himself drawn unawares into a debate on the truth of Christianity with Burma's sternest critic of that faith. Franck's description of this encounter was reproduced in numerous reviews of his book: here was an unprecedented inversion of religious and racial stereotypes: the Irish Buddhist challenging the Hindu Christian to debate, and roundly vanquishing the native representative of the imperialists' creed.

As the afternoon wore on a diminutive Hindu, of meek and childlike countenance, appeared on board, and, hobbling in and out through the alleyways on a clumsily-fitted wooden leg, fell to distributing the pamphlets that he carried under one arm. His dress stamped him as a native Christian missionary. Suddenly, his eye fell on Damalaku, and he stumped forward open-mouthed.

"What are you, sahib?" he murmured in a wondering tone of voice.

"As you see," replied the Irishman, "I am a Buddhist priest."

"Bu—but what country do you come from?"

"I am from Ireland."

Over the face of the native spread an expression of suffering, as if the awful suspicion that the missionaries to whom he owed his conversion had deceived him, were clutching at his heartstrings.

"Ireland?" he cried, tremulously, "Then you are not a Buddhist! Irishmen are Christians. All sahibs are Christians," and he glanced nervously at the grinning Burmese about us.

"Yah! That's what the Christian fakers tell you," snapped the Irishman. "What's that you've got ?"

The Hindu turned over several of the tracts. They were separate books of the Bible, printed in English and Hindustanee.

"Bah!" said Damalaku, "It's bad enough to see white Christians. But the man who swallows all the rot the sahib missionaries dish up for him, when the true faith lies not a day's distance, is disgusting. You should be ashamed of yourself."

"It's a nice religion," murmured the convert.

"Prove it," snapped the Irishman.

The Hindu accepted the challenge, and for the ensuing half-hour we were witnesses of the novel spectacle of a sahib stoutly defending the faith of the East against a native champion of the religion of the West. Unfortunately, he of the wooden leg was no match for the learned bishop. He began with a parrot-like repetition of Christian catechisms and, having spoken his piece, stood helpless before his adversary. A school boy would have presented the case more convincingly. The Irishman, who knew the Bible by heart, evidently, from Genesis to Revelations, quoted liberally from the Scriptures in support of his arguments, and, when the Hindu questioned a passage, caught up one of the pamphlets and turned without the slightest hesitation to the page on which it was set forth.

Entangled in a net-work of texts and his own ignorance, the native soon became the laughing-stock of the assembled Burmese. He attempted to withdraw from the controversy by asserting that he spoke no English. Damalaku addressed him in Hindustanee. He pretended even to have forgotten his mother tongue, and snatched childishly at the pamphlets in the hands of the priest. When all other means failed, he fell back on the final subterfuge of the Hindu—and began to weep. Amid roars of laughter he clutched the tracts that the Irishman held out to him and, with tears coursing down his cheeks, hobbled away, looking neither to the right nor left until he had disappeared in the mud village.[26]

Franck Puts Up at the Tavoy

The three young travelers disembarked, eventually found their way to Dhammaloka's monastery in Chittagong, and a few days later set off for Rangoon. The promised chit from Dhammaloka did indeed assure their warm welcome at his home, the Tavoy monastery. Harry Franck describes his impressions on arrival there:

> The far-famed institution occupied an extensive estate flanking Godwin Road, a broad, shaded thoroughfare leading to the Shwe Dagon [Pagoda]. Its grounds were surrounded by a crumbling wall and a shallow, weed-choked ditch that could not be styled moat for lack of water. Three badly-warped planks, nailed together into a drawbridge that would not draw, led through a breach in the western wall, the main entrance, evidently, for many a year.
>
> Inside was a teeming village of light, two-story dwellings, with deep verandas above and below, scattered pell-mell about the enclosure as if they had been constructed in some gigantic carpenter-shop, shipped to their destination, and left where the expressman had thrown them off. The surrounding town was no more densely populated than the monastery village. Beside a small army of servants, male and female, in layman garb, there were yellow-robed figures everywhere. Wrinkled, sear-faced seekers after Nirvana squatted in groups on the verandas, poring over texts in the weak light of the dying day. More sprightly priests, holding a fold of their gowns over an arm, strolled back and forth across

the barren grounds. Scores of novices, small boys and youths, saffron-clad and hairless like their elders, flitted in and out among the buildings, shouting glee-fully at their games.[27]

Other foreign travelers, too, were seeking shelter that evening:

A burly negro, dressed in an old sweater of the White Star line and the rags and tatters of what had once been overalls and jumper, stepped into the inclosure. Anxious to make a favourable impression at the outset, he had halted in the street to remove his shoes, and, carrying them in one hand, he shuffled through the sand in his bare feet, about the ankles of which clung the remnants of a bright red pair of socks.[28]

In a room housing a life-sized statue of the Buddha, among a score of Burmese monks seated around the walls, was an American beachcomber monk.

He was tall and thin of figure, yet sinewy, with a suggestion of hidden strength. His face, gaunt and lantern-jawed, was seared and weather-beaten and marked with the unmistakable lines of hardship and dissipation. It was easy to see that he was a recruit from the ranks of labor.... But it was none of these points in his physical make-up that caused James [Franck's traveling companion] to choke with suppressed mirth. A Buddhist priest, be it remembered, must ever keep aloof from things feminine. The American had been a sailor, and his bare arms were tattooed from wrist to shoulder with female figures that would have out-done those on the raciest posters of a burlesque show![29]

After a week in Rangoon, Franck left for Moulmein, from there setting out on foot across the Malay peninsula, never to see Dhammaloka again. Five years later, the publication of Franck's account of his extraordinary vagabond journey around the world would make the name of "Oo Damalaku" truly famous. Newspapers in the United States and Ireland in particular reveled in the news that humble "Larry O'Rourke" from Dublin had become "the Irish Buddhist," had traveled to the intriguing and forbidden city of Lhasa, and had there personally instructed the young Dalai Lama in the ways of Europeans.

To his credit, Franck, the covert researcher, had not taken Dhammaloka's stories entirely at face value. He had initially doubted Dhammaloka's claim to be an ex-hobo but was convinced by his knowledge of the hobo life. Like a good scholar, he had checked Dhammaloka's accounts of his travels to Lhasa and adventures in Mandalay and elsewhere against the written evidence—that "small, fat book." Maybe a more leisurely reading of the press clippings would have given Franck pause for thought on some points. But he could testify at first hand that Dhammaloka was both Irish and a seasoned and sincere Buddhist monk, an atheist who knew his Bible backwards, and a verbal combatant who could defeat a native Christian missionary in multilingual debate. As so often with Dhammaloka, the truth was at least as strange as the fiction. Franck's account gives us a unique worm's-eye view of Dhammaloka as seen by his "poor white" peers.

8

A Print Revolution

1907–8

While the publication of Harry Franck's book spread Dhammaloka's story far and wide, Dhammaloka himself was a savvy publicist, using newspapers and the burgeoning publishing industry to spread his own message. Publication—from handbills to social media—is integral to how social movements "agitate, educate, organize," to use the nineteenth-century phrase. In late colonial Asia, the combination of cheap print and railway-assisted post made periodicals a central part of cross-ethnic and transnational organizations, from writing, production, and distribution to the impact of their contentious substance. From 1907, Dhammaloka's Buddhist Tract Society saw Western radical arguments used to develop a complex, contentious, and multiethnic network.

A Gap in the Records

In October 1905, as we saw, Dhammaloka was touring the Malay States in a Chinese magnate's handsome motor car and planning a Buddhist school in Kuala Lumpur.[1] However, our next sighting is not until a year and a half later when, in May 1907, we find Dhammaloka living an uncharacteristically settled life at the Tavoy monastery and participating in the social institutions of Rangoon. During May and June 1907 he chaired the "Debating Society of Young and Elderly Men" and the "Rangoon Debating Society," presiding over discussions of two of his favorite themes: alcohol and education.[2] In early July, he led the opening ceremony for a new Anglo-Vernacular Tamil School in Rangoon.[3]

We know that he had been sick for several months. In September 1907 the Rangoon *Burma Echo* published this communication from Dhammaloka:

> I was ill in the General Hospital, Rangoon, for three months and a half; and was finally discharged with a report that I was incurable and suffering from elephantiasis. I went to Dr Pearce's British Pharmacy, in the Sule Pagoda Road, where I was treated "free of charge," and I was similarly treated at Messrs Allen

The Irish Buddhist. Alicia Turner, Laurence Cox, and Brian Bocking, Oxford University Press (2020)
© Alicia Turner, Laurence Cox and Brian Bocking.
DOI: 10.1093/oso/9780190073084.001.0001

& Co, Fytche Square where Dr Rodrigues confirmed the diagnosis of the British Pharmacy which was that I had no elephantiasis, had never had it, and was un-likely to contract it, even if I tried. A few doses of medicine, in three weeks, completely restored me to health. The General Hospital had very little to do with my recovery.[4]

However, this still leaves over a year unaccounted for. Perhaps sources yet to be discovered will supply the missing information.

Temperance, Tracts, and Tours

The year 1907 saw a new phase in Dhammaloka's career. He was greeted as a returning hero as he resumed his preaching tours in Burma, but his most signif-icant innovation was founding a new organization: the Buddhist Tract Society.

Dhammaloka's activities in the early summer of 1907 seem modest com-pared with his hectic activities in earlier years. In July the *Rangoon Times*, calling Dhammaloka "the only Irish hpoongyi in the world," reports him as saying, "My work at present lies solely in the temperance movement. We have seven Good Templar [IOGT] lodges in Rangoon and after the rains we intend to carry on a temperance crusade on a large scale throughout the whole of Burma." But "does not the Buddhist faith prohibit the use of intoxicants?" asks the interviewer? "Yes," Dhammaloka responds, "but unfortunately the Burmans are falling away from their beliefs in this regard and it is necessary for firm steps to be taken. At the end of the rains I am going to tour the province solely in connection with these two questions."[5]

But even this was disingenuous: Dhammaloka was embarking on a new phase as a publisher. In September 1907 he sprang into renewed action, founding an entirely new institution, the Buddhist Tract Society (BTS), which would shape his mission henceforward. Its initial ambitious goal was by the end of that year, 1907, to publish and distribute throughout Burma a million tracts, in the form of ten thousand free copies of a hundred different works.[6] The BTS crucially ex-panded his communications from preaching tours into print form. From then on, Dhammaloka described himself first and foremost as "President, Buddhist Tract Society."

In October, after the rains, Dhammaloka did undertake a new preaching tour, reviving memories of his earlier successes in 1901 and 1902. The schedule took him to Mandalay, Hsipaw in the northern Shan States, and finally northernmost Bhamo (see Map 8.1). He received once again an ecstatic welcome in Mandalay in November:

Map 8.1. Dhammaloka's 1907–8 Burma Tours.

He was met on the platform by the President of the Society for Promoting Buddhism, . . . as well as a big crowd of other Buddhists who gave him a great reception. It is six years ago since he was in Mandalay; and his reputation as well as his popularity seems to be greater than ever.[7]

Dhammaloka was treated as a dignitary during his stay of more than a month in the former royal capital:

One of the wealthiest Burmese ladies in Mandalay, the wife of one of the late Ministers of State to the ex-King, by name Mah Kin is about to give a grand reception as well as a sumptuous breakfast on Sunday 29th instant in honour of U Dhammaloka, the Irish hpoongyi, to which some hundreds of hpoongyis from far and near have been invited; and it is likely that the Irish hpoongyi (Buddhist Priest) will lecture upon the work of the Buddhist Tract Society.[8]

Clearly, Dhammaloka was not confining his remarks to temperance. In 1902 some of the most respected monastic authorities had greeted him. Now, he met the new British-recognized Thathanabaing, who "received U Dhammaloka in his monastery and expressed thanks to the Irish hpoongyee on account of the work he is doing for Buddhism."[9] In January 1908, Dhammaloka disrupted the annual gathering of American Baptists in Mandalay.[10] The work of the Buddhist Tract Society was well under way.

By February 1908, Dhammaloka was touring the Upper Burma heartland, again reprising his earlier tours and taking trains and riverboat steamers up the Irrawaddy to Meiktila, Myingyan, Pakokku, Pagan, and Minbu. At each stop there were elaborate preparations for his arrival and mass gatherings to hear him speak. In Myingyan, the railway station and road to his accommodation were illuminated and

> thousands of men, women and children lined the roads to get a glimpse of him. His reception was far grander than six years ago, and his popularity seems far greater than it was. U Dhammaloka, it seems, is not yet forgotten by the people of this province.[11]

In Henzada, where "he was met at the steamer landing by thousands of people with golden umbrellas and a Burmese string band," the huge throngs "taxed the capacity of the railway to convey the mass of people across from Henzada shore to Henzada [town]."[12] There he was met by "another Burmese brass band, as well as thousands of people who followed him to his zayat."[13] Even the pilgrimage center of Minbu, well used to Buddhist travelers, saw large crowds waiting hours at the jetty for Dhammaloka's arrival.[14] His popularity among the Burmese never waned. He was able to draw huge audiences in towns and cities across Burma for as long as he continued to tour.

The promise of a talk by the Irish monk drew crowds of thousands, even in very small towns. "Dhammaloka," said a *Burma Echo* report from Pakokku, "is preaching each night to bigger crowds."[15] In Mingyan, the venue was overwhelmed as "big crowds assemble nightly to hear him preach."[16] In Henzada, "the building is far too small to hold the thousands of people who come to hear him; and if one judges his meetings, then he is the most popular hpoongyi that has come to Henzada."[17] While touring, Dhammaloka inspected the work of local Buddhist associations and schools and founded new branches of the Buddhist Tract Society. The headmaster and pupils of the Buddhist Boys' School in Myingyan held a reception:

> The building was beautifully decorated and across the street was a triumphal arch with the following inscription in English and Burmese—"Welcome to

Rahanda U Dhammaloka by the Buddhist Boys' School." The word "Rahanda" means "saintship" or one who is about to enter Nirvana.[18]

The same boys formed a "bodyguard of honour" for Dhammaloka when he left town.[19] In Pakokku he was elected patron of the local Buddhist association, which promptly voted to recommend that all members subscribe to the *Burma Echo*, no doubt encouraging further favorable coverage.[20]

The reports seem genuine enough. True, Dhammaloka was skilled in using the press for self-promotion, the *Burma Echo* was sympathetic, and elsewhere we have traced favorable newspaper coverage to letters or reports sent by Dhammaloka himself, sometimes under a pseudonym, or anonymously. However, the descriptions of these Burmese tours do seem to come from resident local correspondents of the *Burma Echo*, with accounts of Dhammaloka's activities included among minute details of other local events, all reported in the same style.

The Politics of Publishing

Modernist Buddhist organizations in the early 1900s advanced their cause in part by publishing periodicals and books, most of which have been lost to history, with only records of their titles occasionally surviving in published catalogs or advertisements. Our information about these publishing ventures instead often relates to the collection of funds to support publication. The charge that money collected had been misused was routine in inter-Buddhist polemic and surfaced in court proceedings.

For example, in 1902, "During his recent visit to Shwegyin, U Damaloka [*sic*], the Irish hpoongyi, collected a substantial sum of money for the purpose of publishing a book, but unfortunately, one of his followers stole the whole of it at night."[21] It later transpired that the money was not stolen "but simply sent by post to the treasurer in Rangoon," though the suspicion lingered that something untoward was going on.[22] In 1905, the *Rangoon Times* criticized "some European novices, going around the houses of the faithful Buddhists, gathering hundreds of rupees, under the pretence of founding a library." A reference to "Hibernian bravado" suggests that Dhammaloka and his acolytes were being accused.[23] Another example from 1910 concerns "U Wayama, an ex *phoongyi*, and lately first director of the Buddhist Propaganda Society, Rangoon." He was arrested on charges of breach of trust, nearly 2,500 rupees having been collected for a new printing press, but the complainant offered no evidence and the case was dismissed.[24]

Yet some money collected was evidently put to good effect. In 1905, a Singapore correspondent described Dhammaloka as "the head of the only Buddhist mission that keeps a free library." Moreover, "[t]he [Singapore] society or mission is the only one of its kind that does not appeal for public support," presumably indicating a donor satisfied with how the money was being spent.[25]

Such episodes demonstrate that the large-scale production, distribution, and consumption of texts was a central part of Buddhist projects of the period, as of other subaltern worlds. With the "Workers' University" and hobo bookshops, European and American migrant workers also read widely and well (see Chapter 1); Dhammaloka probably consumed such texts for a long period before publishing them himself.

The launch of his Rangoon BTS enabled Dhammaloka to expand the production of texts and extend his influence. His 1900 open letter "Buddhists of Burmah!" had by now reached Frankfurt, Boston, Chicago, and Salt Lake City (see Chapter 2). Over a ten-year publishing career, Dhammaloka became widely known in Asia and to some extent in America as correspondent, author, and publisher. He relied mainly on newspapers to spread his message, especially correspondents' reports. These were often unsigned or pseudonymous, like the letters from "Captain Daylight" appearing in Burma, Siam, and Singapore, while the items he sent to American periodicals usually carried his name. In addition, he penned some "open letters" and, from 1907 onward, BTS tracts.

We cannot recover a complete publication history for Dhammaloka, before or after the launch of the BTS. Many texts are known to us by name only, including two 1901 tracts, "Unity Is Strength" and "Revival of Buddhism"—the latter by a Scottish Maha Bodhi representative—published by Dhammaloka through the "Chinese Cycling Society."[26] A "Declaration" appeared in the Singapore *Straits Times* in 1904, while an open letter "What is the use of prayer?" submitted to the same paper in 1905 went unpublished, the editor having turned against Dhammaloka.[27] An anti-missionary article reportedly appeared in the *United Burma* newspaper of June 1907.[28]

Building the Buddhist Tract Society

In 1907 Dhammaloka changed his publishing strategy in two ways. First, although newspapers remained an important vehicle for publicity and polemic, the BTS began to publish more tracts. Second, Dhammaloka scaled down his own writing and increasingly republished or translated other authors, particularly European freethinkers (atheists). Like most journalists of the period, Dhammaloka had a "cut-and-paste" approach and was not above what would now be condemned as plagiarism. Even when authored by others, BTS tracts included interpolations by Dhammaloka himself—shorter pieces of his own composition, his letters, and advertisements.

Organizationally, the BTS launch marked a significant change. Previously Dhammaloka had relied on friendly newspaper editors publishing his contributions. Falling foul of *Straits Times* editor Morphy (see Chapter 5) may have caused Dhammaloka to rethink his strategy. The launch of the BTS suggests steady sponsors, reliable advertisers, or a good strategy for collecting public funds. It also involved a long-term relationship with a printer, effective distribution networks, and at least one translator.

From late 1907 until 1910 the BTS was publishing from the Tavoy monastery. The BTS logo (see Figure 8.1) features a peacock, traditional symbol of the last Burmese royal dynasty, with its tail closed, which in coming decades would become the symbol of the Burmese anti-colonial nationalist movement.

Figure 8.1. The logo of Dhammaloka's Buddhist Tract Society, 1907–10.
Authors' collection.

The character of the BTS tracts recalls the London-based Rationalist Press Association's later *Thinker's Library*—mostly cheap reprints of rationalist texts, in a standard six-inch format with between thirty-two and sixty-four pages, designed for mass distribution. Figure 8.2 shows an example of a BTS tract from 1909. Shorter, even one-page, tracts may have existed, but we have not discovered any surviving examples.

The BTS used the *Burma Echo* as both printer and co-publisher, which helps explain the *Echo's* interest in its doings. The *Echo* carried articles, often by Dhammaloka himself, offering insights into the workings of the BTS. In early September 1907 we read that

[t]he Buddhist Tract Society, lately founded in Rangoon, holds a special meeting at its head office, at Tavoy Monastery, Godwin Road, Rangoon at 6-30 am tomorrow (Sunday) morning. All members are requested to attend punctually.[29]

The *Echo* soon reported the outcome: "it was resolved to publish and distribute broadcast throughout Burma one hundred tracts (ten thousand copies of each) to be sent out free by the end of the year."[30]

The ambitious prospect of publishing one million tracts in four months set the tone for the coming years. Buddhist Tract Societies in China and Ceylon, operating since the 1880s and 1890s respectively, printed at least 8,000 copies of their material, distributing tracts through their own shops and via monks and lay leafleters.[31] Dhammaloka sought to do more. In 1909 he claimed to have sold more than 10,000 copies of the works of Thomas Paine.[32] These figures have to take into account the low prices (e.g., one anna) and the centrality of *dana* (donations) in publishing activity. Most Burmese Buddhists of the period would have felt it meritorious to have Buddhist books in the house, whether read or not, so buying or receiving Buddhist publications would require little persuasion. Moreover, the BTS was bilingual; it published at least two works in Burmese, possibly many more. Dhammaloka evidently had competent translators serving the society.

Publishing on this scale required substantial means of distribution. At first the BTS built on events involving mass gatherings of Buddhists. At the annual Shwedagon Pagoda festival in October 1907, "the Buddhist Tract Society intend distributing on each of these three days, 25,000 copies of their tracts, or 75,000 copies in all."[33]

Dhammaloka's continued clashes with the Christian missionaries became opportunities to distribute more tracts:

The American Baptists were holding the yearly gathering of their Upper Burma flock at Mandalay, the other day when U Dhammaloka (the Irish hpoongyi)

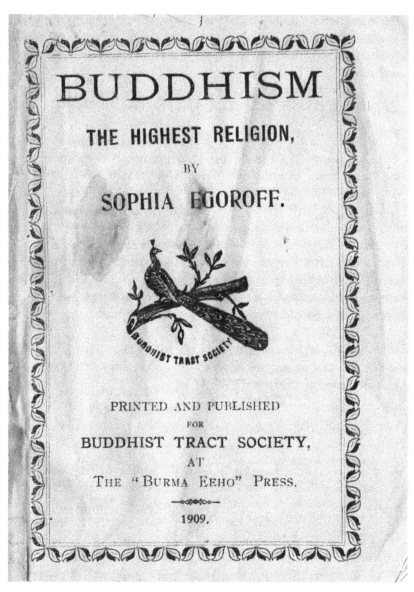

BUDDHISM

THE HIGHEST RELIGION,

BY

SOPHIA EGOROFF.

PRINTED AND PUBLISHED

FOR

BUDDHIST TRACT SOCIETY,

AT

THE "BURMA EEHO" PRESS.

1909.

Figure 8.2. A typical BTS tract, containing Sophia Egoroff's article on the topic of Buddha Sakyamuni as a "divine socialist", an essay about King Asoka's Buddhist empire, letters and comments by Dhammaloka on the shortcomings of Christianity, and of other Buddhist societies and temperance lodges in Rangoon, and adverts for freethinking publications.

University of Nebraska Omaha: Dr C. C. & Mabel L. Criss Library.

representative of the Buddhist Tract Society accompanied by two stalwart Punjabees proceeded to the place of the meeting; and there distributed some thousands of pamphlets among the American Baptist Mission's flock of both sexes.

These pamphlets are being distributed on the main roads and on the platform of pagodas in Mandalay causing some stir in religious circles.[34]

For distribution further afield, the BTS opened new branches and sponsored tours. A Myingyan BTS branch opened in February 1908, joining the existing Rangoon and Mandalay branches. In Myingyan, "their tracts have been widely circulated amongst all classes of the community."[35] In Henzada, during Dhammaloka's visit in May 1908, "[t]he Buddhist Tract Society flooded the town with their anti-Christian tracts."[36]

By 1910, Christian missionary Francis Clark was noting in Burma that "[a] 'Buddist [sic] Tract Society' is sending out its books and leaflets by the million." These were distributed by post, by BTS peddlers, on bookstalls, and from at least one permanent location.[37] Of the stairs leading to the Shwedagon Pagoda in Rangoon (see Figure 3.2 in Chapter 3), Clark commented that

[t]his busy combination of mart and temple the Buddhist Tract Society has chosen as a rare strategic spot from which to disseminate its doctrines, and here is a stall filled with its literature.[38]

Links with International Freethought

Our first evidence of the international reach of Dhammaloka's BTS publications was the BTS logo (see Figure 8.1) stamped on an envelope (Figure I.3 in the Introduction) addressed to A. V. White in Toronto, Canada, British North America.[39] It then emerged that between 1908 and 1911 Dhammaloka corresponded as BTS president with at least three leading US freethinking periodicals: the New York *Truth Seeker*, the Los Angeles *Humanitarian Review*, and the Lexington, Kentucky, *Blue-grass Blade*. The *Blade*, whose founder Charles Moore was twice jailed for blasphemy, had sent Dhammaloka a copy on spec, and Dhammaloka responded with a subscription, commenting,

I was wondering how you got my address, as I did not think that we "heathens" in Burma should attract attention from any person of intelligence, except the "holy and sanctified" Christian missionary . . . I like the motto of your paper. I trust that you will always carry it out in spirit as well as in letter. With best wishes and long life to every champion of Freethought.[40]

The *Blade*'s motto was "We aim to cut down error and establish truth." In the same issue was another letter Dhammaloka sent to the secretary of the Paine Memorial and Historical Association, James Elliott:

> You ask if there are 2,000 admirers of Thomas Paine in Burma. Yes, and double as many. There were sold in Burma over 10,000 copies of the "Age of Reason" last year, as well as some copies of the "Rights of Man."
>
> I trust this year that we shall do better than last year. You will convey the greetings of ten millions of Buddhists of this province to your Association on the occasion of the great celebration of that grand Hero of Freethought. I am making the necessary arrangements to celebrate the occasion on a grand scale....
>
> We have not translated any parts of the "Age of Reason" as yet, but our Society intends to do this work next year, and you shall receive a copy of the same....
>
> I am sure that every friend of Truth will agree with me that it is time that we should show the bigots and the ministers of every church that Thomas Paine was the real friend of man—in fact, we can call him a Humanitarian of the loftiest type.[41]

The New York *Truth Seeker*'s June 27, 1908, issue included an article entitled "Buddhism Misrepresented by Christian Missionaries by Rev. U. Dhammaloka." The same paper reported his trial for "blasphemy" in 1911.[42] Dhammaloka was a frequent correspondent to the Los Angeles *Humanitarian Review* between 1909 and 1911, sending subscriptions, ordering their publications, commending the editor, updating them on his trial, and wishing that "you be spared many years to carry on the work of freeing the minds of the orthodox."[43]

Dhammaloka's freethinker connections spanned the globe. The BTS tract *Buddhism: The Highest Religion* by Sophia Egoroff included advertisements for the *Truth Seeker* as well as the New Zealand–based *Examiner* ("An advocate of rational thought and philosophy, science and religion") and G. W. Foote's *Freethinker*, based in Newcastle, England.[44] Between 1908 and 1911 there was an active two-way relationship between Dhammaloka and Western freethinking journals.

Organizing the BTS: Writing, Publishing, Distributing

Dhammaloka's friends and foes alike agreed that the BTS was a substantial and well-funded operation. The BTS had sizable print runs for multiple titles—anywhere between the eight titles definitely known to us and the hundred titles envisaged at the 1907 launch—with enough supporters to ensure extensive distribution. Dhammaloka's BTS attracted allies and supporters—the "stalwart Punjabees" who helped with leafleting and perhaps also staffed the bookstalls, the volunteers who interpreted speeches or wrote and translated texts for the Society, a cooperative printer (simultaneously a sympathetic newspaper editor), financial sponsors, a treasurer, and others. Keeping this machine running—in the midst of traveling, preaching, and founding other organizations—implies considerable and continuing effort.

This visible effort may also have been part of the point. Both Dhammaloka and his Christian opponents saw his polemic as geared toward returning apostate Burmese to Buddhism. Yet conversion in either direction, though highlighted in periodicals from both sides, was a very small part of the real picture. What publishing BTS texts *did* do was enable lay Burmese (and Punjabis, Chinese lay Buddhists, European novices, and many others) to engage publicly and enthusiastically in the project of visibly agitating for Buddhism. Such action costs the individual time and energy and involves working with other like-minded people—which all builds commitment. Even if many of those who accepted BTS texts in English could not read the language and simply displayed them on a shelf as religious texts, participating in the publication and distribution process identified the author, reader, distributor, or sponsor as an active part of what they referred to as the Buddhist revival—while being "President of the Buddhist Tract Society," of course, did Dhammaloka's prestige no harm at all.

Known BTS Publications

We have reliable information on just eight BTS tracts. "Gray literature" like this seldom makes it into archives and is regularly lost to history. Complete copies of at least three of Dhammaloka's publications have survived. These are *Buddhism: The Highest Religion; The Teachings of Jesus Not Adapted to Modern Civilization;* and *Bible Atrocities and Immoralities.* Another five at least remain to be discovered, but can be described with reasonable confidence.

Thomas Paine, *The Rights of Man* and *The Age of Reason* (BTS, 1908–9)

In 1908 Dhammaloka claimed the BTS had distributed Paine's the *Rights of Man* and *The Age of Reason*, with a three-part Burmese translation of the latter under way. Paine was a classic reference, particularly for radical freethinkers, attractive to deists, anticlericals, and atheists alike, and his influence was global. In 1909, the BTS reportedly distributed 10,000 copies of Paine's *Rights of*

Man—Dhammaloka paints a picture of large-scale gatherings in honor of Paine where the BTS editions no doubt sold like hot cakes after a rousing endorsement of Paine by the famous Irish Buddhist.

> The Buddhist Tract Society of Burmah observed the one hundredth anniversary of the death of Thomas Paine. We had large audiences. I myself spoke to an audience of about five thousand at a town in Upper Burmah.[45]

Anonymous, *Bible Atrocities and Immoralities* (BTS, 1909)

In 1909 the BTS brought out *Bible Atrocities and Immoralities* in Burmese (but with an English title). It resembled many published freethinking collections highlighting heinous elements in biblical narratives. This genre suited freethinkers in Protestant countries, where the main target was the Bible's content, rather than the (mis)behavior of priests.

Sophia Egoroff, *Buddhism: The Highest Religion* (BTS, 1909)

Egoroff, a Russian artist whose paintings of the Buddha were exhibited at the Musée Guimet in Paris around 1908, had in 1906 or 1907 published a life of the Buddha in French. A 1910 English translation, *Buddha-Sakya-Muni*, was subtitled *The Divine Socialist.*[46]

Egoroff is a fascinating character in the history of Buddhist movements of the period, and deserves her own biography. In 1908 she traveled to India with her mother and in January 1909 Anagarika Dharmapala in Calcutta invited her to give a "lecture on the 'Life of Buddha' . . . at the Vidyodaya College" in Ceylon.[47] Egoroff seemingly took this as a commitment to provide for her and her mother in Ceylon, and the matter eventually went to court.[48] Dharmapala, on behalf of the Maha Bodhi Society, denounced her as "neither an artist, nor historian, nor Missionary, nor lecturer, and denied they were liable in any way."[49]

In the meantime, Egoroff and her work had come to Dhammaloka's attention. Dhammaloka, touring Ceylon with Dharmapala (see Chapter 9), was presumably impressed with her and solicited her manuscript for the BTS (see Figure 8.2). Egoroff, like Dhammaloka, linked Buddhism closely with freethought, writing:

> Buddhism preaches that we must make all possible effort towards knowledge, to look at ignorance as an enemy, and to fight it always and everywhere with the weapon of science and Freethought.

Egalitarianism, too, informed her perspective. The book's dedication reads:

> Long live humanity pushed forward by a new torrent of social ideas towards
> peace, fraternity, equality and civilization. Let Buddha Sakya Muni be remem-
> bered and honoured as divine socialist . . .

Egoroff also offers a gender perspective otherwise absent in BTS publications,
listing the "highest men" who have "shown respect to women," including:

> Buddha, Thomas Paine, Robert G. Ingersoll, Charles Bradlaugh, Leonardo da
> Vinci, Berthelot, the French scientist, and other scientists and artists.

The first four tally neatly with Dhammaloka's own favorites. Alongside
freethought, science, and respect for women and children, Egoroff's tract also
highlights temperance, and the BTS's "preaching against Opium, Alcoholic
drink, Morphia, Ganga and Cocaine"—suggesting some editing of the text by
Dhammaloka.[50]

George W. Brown, *The Teachings of Jesus Not Adapted to Modern Civilisation* (BTS, 1910)

Brown's 1891 freethought book, self-published in Rockford, Illinois, was
subtitled "with the true character of Mary Magdalene."[51] The BTS tract includes
themes uncharacteristic of Dhammaloka, including an attack on Christianity's
approval of begging and dependence on the community (a strange target for an
ex-hobo and Buddhist monk), as well as criticism of wealth. Brown represented
middle-class, liberal, and "Protestant" tendencies in freethought—very different
from Egoroff's *Divine Socialism*.

The BTS version includes elements appended by Dhammaloka, including a satirical "hymn" entitled "The Christian Life: Pardon for Rangoon
Parsons," sung to the tune of *Auld Lang Syne*, seemingly prompted by newspaper reports of "Temple Emanuel Baptist Church" in Chicago setting up
a Sunday "kissing booth" with "25 buxom young ladies" to raise funds by
selling kisses, a practice Dhammaloka roundly attacks in a later section of
the tract.[52]

> Speak no more of priestly foible,
> Publish not the Parson's Crime;
> For on Sunday hard we labour,
> Lead a Christian life sublime.

Though we kiss the maid and matron,
Warm embrace them every day,
God will know the sore temptation,
And will wash our sins away!
Tell it not we lie and slander,
Vilify and base defame;
For we serve the Lord Jehovah,
Do it all in Jesus' name.
Though in lies and lust we revel,
Yet we solemn preach and pray;
So the blood of Christ, the Saviour,
Washeth all our guilt away!
Call us not a gang of Humbugs,
Whom the money-lords can buy;
For we safe and sanely pilot
Souls to heaven in the sky.
So laborious our profession,
Now and then we must be gay;
But the Lord will freely pardon
Washing all our sins away!

There are echoes here of Robert Burns's "Holy Willie's Prayer (Address to the Unco Guid),"[53] and other working-class attacks on religious hypocrisy.

Several purported "letters to the editor" appended to the tract criticize various Rangoon Good Templar lodges. One is on "Other Men's Wives"; another, "Good Templary in Rangoon," accuses "a notorious Deputy Grand of the I.O.G.T. order . . . who is also a police officer" of being involved in the "kidnapping of a Japanese girl" (here meaning prostitute). This was a bold accusation, reminiscent of Dhammaloka's actions against a bribe-taking civil servant in Singapore and of his other challenges to corrupt power-holders.[54]

The final appendix is "A Wicked Proclamation to His Fellow Beings from the Sinner in Charge of the Buddhist Tract Society." Here Dhammaloka writes:

Most Societies, like the Y.M.B.A.,[55] and the late International Buddhist Society[56] are loaded to the guards with high sounding titles, principles, platforms and politics. But the Buddhist Tract Society by heaving most of these over-board, is enabled to teach,

Goodness without a God,
Happiness without a heaven,
Salvation without a Saviour,
And redemption without a Redeemer.

It is thus the only Society in the great East that is able to run without a "God" or "Devil" or "Ghost." The Buddhist Tract Society is full of human sympathies; but as none of these are wasted upon the "Saviours" and "Gods." [*sic*] It has an abundance for the beings of earth. . . .

The Buddhist Tract Society fails to see the necessity of a vast host of able-bodied, well-fed Sky-pilots[57] managers of matters between men and the big Papa in the clouds, and it holds that if a man's soul is to [be] saved by man's work, the man that has the soul has got to do the work.

Anonymous, *The Famous Decree* (1910)

The endpapers of *The Teachings of Jesus* . . . advertise the next BTS tract as follows:

The Famous Decree. Famous and infamous decree of the Roman Catholic Council passed at the Lateran, Rome, A.D. 1215, in the original Latin with translation in parallel columns, and with full explanation of its meaning and its results in Europe and Asia. The foundation of the Holy Inquisition.[58]

The 1215 Lateran canons helped form the Inquisition. Unlike other BTS texts such as *Bible Atrocities and Immoralities*, this one specifically targets Catholicism. Dhammaloka certainly did not know medieval Latin, and we have not been able to identify the source of this text.

Wm Emmette Coleman, *The Bible God Disproved by Nature* (by 1910)

Francis Clark, missionary to Burma, ascribed this tract entirely to Dhammaloka, writing:

The Bible God Disproved by Nature is the title of one of [the BTS] tracts, which may serve as a sample of all its literature. It is a booklet of forty-eight pages bound in pink paper and sold for only one anna, or 3 cents, and is printed in English, evidently to counteract the baleful teaching of the missionaries from America and Great Britain.

As in *The Teachings of Jesus* . . .

he "drops into poetry" at times, and turns his rhythmical guns against the "sky pilots," as he facetiously calls the missionaries.

Alas, these verses by Dhammaloka (unless the same as those noted earlier), remain undiscovered.

Clark quotes the tract as saying:

> Of all the cruel, bloodthirsty, sanguinary, malignant, ferocious, diabolical, and infernal fiends and monsters of which the human mind ever conceived, the Bible God is the most devilish and diabolical. . . . Were it possible for such a despicable fiend to exist, no language would be capable of depicting the utter loathing and contempt such a wretch would necessarily inspire in all men and women of kindly sympathies and generous impulses.

Clark concluded that this "outbreak"

> shows that education is not always an ally of Christianity in missionary lands. Mr. Dhammaloka's excellent English education has only made it possible for him to be more vituperative in his abuse of Christ and Christianity, for I have not quoted his most blasphemous words about Christ Himself.[59]

The "excellent English education" was not Dhammaloka's but that of William Emmette Coleman, member of the American Oriental Society, freethinking spiritualist opponent of Theosophy, and author of the thirty-nine-page tract *The Bible God Disproved by Nature*, published in New York in 1875.[60]

Robert Blatchford (pre-1914)

William Purser, Anglican missionary in Rangoon, noted, "He [Dhammaloka] has epitomized some of Mr Blatchford's anti-Christian literature and has had it translated into Burmese."[61] Blatchford, British socialist and founder of the radical *Clarion* newspaper, wrote widely circulated freethinking works, including *Christians and Infidels* and *God and My Neighbour*, both published in 1907.

John Remsburg (no date)

Dhammaloka wrote, "I have asked a bookseller to order twenty copies of Remsburg's work."[62] This may have led to republication. Remsburg, widely read US secularist writer and indefatigable traveling speaker—he reportedly delivered 3,000 lectures—was a man after Dhammaloka's own heart.[63] His many books included *Life of Thomas Paine* (1880), *The Image Breaker* (1882), *False Claims* (1883), *Bible Morals* (1884), *Sabbath Breaking* (1885), and *The Bible* (1903).

An Eclectic Series

The titles mentioned in the preceding, which must be only a snapshot of the BTS's publications, show the eclectic range of authors and perspectives available to Dhammaloka. They vary from "divine socialism" to the defense of capital accumulation, from attacks on the Protestants' Bible to critiques of historical Catholicism. Their arguments invoke science, common sense, economic utility, political implications, textual criticism, and morality. BTS authors are American, British, and Russian (at least), addressing scholarly and plebeian audiences. The tracts are commissioned, republished with interpolations, or sometimes just summarized. This very eclecticism suggests that the works we know are only a sample of BTS publications. Nor were all of these authors "big names"; Dhammaloka evidently read very widely. He ordered pamphlets and subscribed to freethinking magazines; he could also draw on classic authors (Thomas Paine) and visiting authors (Egoroff).

Sources of Dhammaloka's Freethinking

Having found the BTS, we initially hoped to discover exactly what influences had molded Dhammaloka's thinking—what books he had read, what political or social movements he had been involved in—and thereby unveil his pre-Buddhist career. But after extensive research, we had to accept that Dhammaloka's intellectual formation up to 1900 remains as tantalizingly elusive as the rest of his pre-Buddhist life. Was he already a full-fledged freethinker, perhaps anarchist or socialist? Had he once been a Christian, even a Salvation Army officer? So far, we don't know.

What is clear is that the BTS's eclecticism was by choice, not a product of scarcity. Dhammaloka felt no need to represent only one type of freethought. This suggests that his own intellectual culture did not derive from one position; self-educated, he was not beholden to any specific strand of freethought.[64]

We can, however, identify several different traditions of working class freethought—in Ireland, Britain, the United States, and Asia—to underline how *ordinary* this type of intellectual activity was for working men of the period. This was despite legal threats, including the UK Blasphemy Act (in force until 1921) and other laws aimed at suppressing dissident movements. The publishers of the freethinking *Blue Grass Blade* and *Truth Seeker* newspapers were both imprisoned for blasphemy in the United States, and in British Burma, Dhammaloka faced sedition charges for his criticisms of Christianity.

Irish Anticlericalism

On the continent of Europe, not to be a Catholic was to be a freethinker, but in Ireland, not to be a Catholic was to be a Protestant. . . . There was no room for freethought in Ireland.[65]

In Ireland in the second half of the nineteenth century, agitation for Home Rule was at its height. The Land War and subsequent Land Acts saw the dissolution of the largely Protestant aristocracy in favor of the largely Catholic tenantry. The Anglican Church of Ireland was disestablished and the education of Catholic children was handed to the Catholic Church.

Catholic-Protestant sectarianism in Ireland was bound up with ethnic and political identities, as well as with community affiliations and access to social services. Thoughtful, politically conscious working-class men usually drawn to freethinking elsewhere could not, in Ireland, allow hostility to the clergy to express itself in leaving "their" church.[66]

Irish atheism meant anticlericalism. Until very recently, one could be a good Irish republican, a good socialist, and a good Catholic without much practical contradiction. There was nevertheless dissemination of more rationalist ideas. Paine's *Rights of Man* and other works, key reference points for Catholic-born anticlericals, were circulated widely from the 1790s onward.[67] In this context, ideas verging on freethought could be absorbed, even if not expressed openly.

It is entirely plausible that Dhammaloka grew up with an anticlerical attitude and knew Paine's revolutionary writings. Many of Dhammaloka's self-penned attacks on Christianity are attacks on Christian *clergy*, tinged with a class hostility readily understandable to anyone who has seen the nineteenth-century Irish streets of poor terraced houses overshadowed (like Laurence Carroll's home in Booterstown) by opulent Church buildings. An Irish class-based anticlericalism could, in Burma, easily translate into anti-colonial hostility to missionaries.

Freethought and Working-Class Britain

In Britain, unlike Ireland, freethought was widespread and openly expressed.[68] In Dhammaloka's time, all of Ireland was part of the United Kingdom. Irish working-class migration to British cities was routine, and secularist publications had local Irish audiences. Dhammaloka's polemical activity in Burma drew on British as well as American freethinking literature.

Urban Britain in this period was far more secular than either Ireland or America; freethought, no longer a novelty, was all-pervasive. The physical location for secularist discussions was the world of mid-Victorian working-class clubs, particularly in London: a cosmopolis of the self-taught, with earnest reading and intense debate at the sharp edge of working-class politics. Such radicalism frequently also meant opposition to British policy in Ireland; the Star Radical Club of Herne Hill for 1888, for example, had the following program:

(1) Home Rule for Ireland; (2) manhood suffrage; (3) women's suffrage; (4) abolition of present House of Lords; (5) disestablishment of the Church.[69]

Placing Home Rule first was no coincidence: London, like Manchester, Liverpool, or Glasgow, was in significant part an Irish city. Working-class radicalism had involved Irish migrants since at least the 1830s. Support for anti-imperial struggles was widespread: the 1860s saw mass demonstrations against the repression of Jamaican protest and for Irish nationalism. In 1872, atheist Charles Bradlaugh was the main speaker at a meeting organized by the radical London Patriotic Club in support of Irish Fenian (nationalist) speakers.[70]

Into the late 1880s, an alliance between secularist, atheist working-class republicans and nationalist, Catholic Irish laborers in London was central to the politics of the same club. Its support for Home Rule and opposition to repression in Ireland extended to anti-colonial struggles worldwide: for Balkan revolts against Turkey in the 1870s, against the British invasions of Egypt and the Sudan in the 1880s, and for Indian nationalism in the 1890s.[71] Dhammaloka's Irish, atheist anti-colonialism fits well in this context.

Of the many working-class clubs in the London of the 1870s and 1880s:

Some were proclaimedly Radical, some Freethought and Secularist, some expressly educational, some more inclined to be free and easy [i.e., focused on entertainment]: but they often combined all these features and more besides.[72]

Anticlericalism and the clash between science and religion were long-standing features. By the 1870s, an observer at a radical London club saw how "science and religion—the clergy and the scientific teachers—were deadly foes, and [the lecture] was full of sly drives at the clergy, chiefly those of the Church of England, which were highly appreciated by the audience."[73]

The London secularist movement was determinedly working-class; the London "Hall of Science" (to its enemies the "School of Blasphemy, Political Vandalism and Social Retrogression") was full of tradesmen, artisans, sailors, laborers, and navvies in working clothes. Of the many participants at the crowded Hackney Secular Association, a critic sneered that "the close connexion of cleanliness with godliness had been so practically recognized, that they abjured the former with the latter."[74]

By the 1880s, with Dhammaloka perhaps already in Asia, the rhetoric of secular atheism was increasingly stale, and turning to socialism. But if by 1900 secularism was no longer at the cutting edge of London working-class thought, hostility to organized religion was deeply entrenched among the thoughtful working classes. Political radicalism at home, opposition to imperialism abroad, self-confident working-class identities, and freethought were all common features of this milieu.

Did Dhammaloka have a direct connection with London plebeian radicalism? At least one French report suggests that Dhammaloka, passing incognito, could have been in London shortly before 1900.[75] In London, we get a clear glimpse of a world recognizably close to Dhammaloka's in terms of its ideas, experiences, and politics: a world of confident, self-educated working men, conscious of class antagonisms and nationalist opposition to the empires of the day, enriched by the experiences of labor migrants, exiles, and survivors from revolutions and uprisings, hostile to established religion and fond of a good argument. Many poor whites in Asia came from such a background.

Hobo Readers in America

The "Modern School" freethinking movement in the United States reflects a similar world, strongly influenced by European immigrants like the early vagrant and seafaring Dhammaloka.[76] More generally, migrant labor—"hoboing"—was no obstacle to working-class intellectual activity. Hoboes could be voracious readers. Josiah Flynt noted in 1900:

> the keen interest of tramps in all kinds of reading material, especially dime novels and books on political and economic topics. They would use the latter at their "hang out conferences," where they competed to offer the most compelling social analysis. According to Flynt, they liked "any book . . . which 'shows up' what the tramps consider the unreasonable inequalities in our social conditions."[77]

Laborers, frequently unemployed, had time to read and talk. The Chicago hobo bookstore owner Daniel Horsely guessed that at least half of the migrant workers were avid readers, generally favoring "liberal, freethought and radical" magazines, scientific works, and realistic fiction, in addition to newspapers and whatever they could acquire with their limited means.[78]

Such people would become key organizers for the Industrial Workers of the World union and, later, the Communist Party—choices involving the risk of

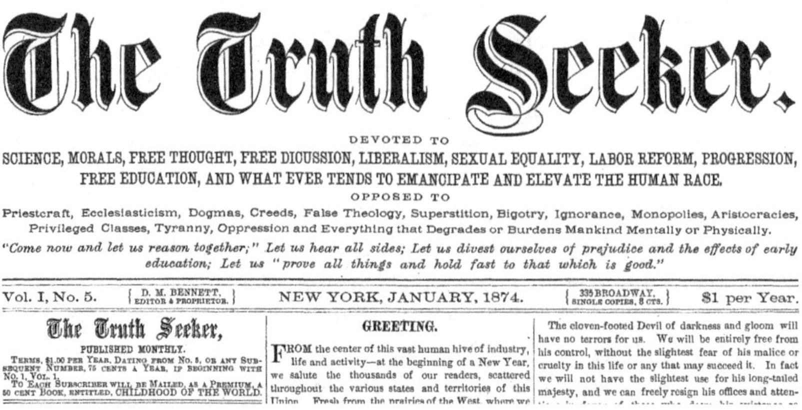

The Truth Seeker.

DEVOTED TO

SCIENCE, MORALS, FREE THOUGHT, FREE DICUSSION, LIBERALISM, SEXUAL EQUALITY, LABOR REFORM, PROGRESSION, FREE EDUCATION, AND WHAT EVER TENDS TO EMANCIPATE AND ELEVATE THE HUMAN RACE.

OPPOSED TO

Priestcraft, Ecclesiasticism, Dogmas, Creeds, False Theology, Superstition, Bigotry, Ignorance, Monopolies, Aristocracies, Privileged Classes, Tyranny, Oppression and Everything that Degrades or Burdens Mankind Mentally or Physically.

"Come now and let us reason together;" Let us hear all sides; Let us divest ourselves of prejudice and the effects of early education; Let us "prove all things and hold fast to that which is good."

Vol. I, No. 5.   D. M. BENNETT, EDITOR & PROPRIETOR.   NEW YORK, JANUARY, 1874.   335 BROADWAY, SINGLE COPIES, 8 CTS. $1 per Year.

Figure 8.3. Plebeian intellectualism: Masthead of the *Truth Seeker* from the young Dhammaloka's time in the United States, showing the range of freethinking causes it supported. Dhammaloka advertised the *Truth Seeker* in his Rangoon BTS publications up to at least 1910.
Image courtesy Marc Demarest/www.iapsop.com.

being sacked and having to travel. The freethought well represented in this culture is recognizably related to Dhammaloka's:

With deep roots in continental Europe, anticlerical ideology based on Enlightenment rationalism was best represented by Tom Paine's famous tract *The Age of Reason*, which enjoyed great popularity among radical workers in the United States in the late nineteenth and into the twentieth century.[79]

On its front page, the secularist *Truth Seeker* newspaper stated exactly what it was for and against, as Figure 8.3 shows.[80]

A combination of freethought and social and political radicalism was thus widely available to European migrant workers in the United States.[81] It is entirely possible that Dhammaloka encountered freethought in this context.

Freethought in Asia

This working-class reading and debating culture traveled with American and European migrant workers to Asia. Harry Franck noted of the Sailors' Home in Chittagong:

Had we rented by cable some private estate we could not have been more comfortably domiciled. . . . The library numbered fully a thousand volumes—by no means confined to the output of mission publishing houses—in one corner were ranged the latest English and American magazines, their leaves still uncut.[82]

Like American hoboes, European sailors in Asia were not devoid of intellectual stimulus; the benefactors who provided sailors' rest homes in distant ports expected them to read voraciously.[83]

Freethought had found an echo in Asia for decades. The London radical and secularist weekly *National Reformer* (1864–93) had tied freethought to anti-colonial and anti-missionary activity, using rhetoric close to Dhammaloka's. Promoting women's rights, socialism, and other causes, it found Buddhism, Theosophy, and Unitarianism more acceptable than establishment Christianity.[84]

Charles Bradlaugh, the paper's editor from 1867 to 1890, would act as an unofficial "MP for India" after his 1880 election as a Member of Parliament (and six-year battle to sit in Parliament as an atheist). Visiting India in 1890, he met twenty Bombay secularists and received an address, signed by "a large number of names . . . from persons in all parts of India and Burma," declaring that "[t]he names of Charles Bradlaugh, Mrs. Annie Besant, Colonel R. Ingersoll and G. W. Foote are, we are proud to say, familiar to thousands of students in all parts of this vast country."[85] Bradlaugh, Ingersoll, and Foote were, as we have seen, points of reference for the BTS, while Besant by this point was a Theosophist.

By Dhammaloka's day, radicals arriving in Asia could find freethought combined with Buddhism. James Peebles in Ceylon republished a tract by Dhammaloka entitled *Buddhism and Christianity* side by side with *A Historical Criticism of the New Testament*, suggesting a combination much like Dhammaloka's own,[86] while the Buddhist Tract Society in Ceylon in the 1880s had published "mostly reruns of Bradlaugh."[87] A contemporary *Who's Who* listing for US freethinker Remsburg noted that "[p]ortions of his writings have been translated into French, Italian, German, Dutch, Swedish, Norwegian, Bohemian, Bengali, Singalese and Japanese."[88] In both Ceylon and Japan, someone was busily importing and translating freethought texts—presumably as weapons against Christian missionaries. Ananda Metteyya announced in 1904 his society's intention to send a representative of Buddhism to "the first International Freethought Congress,"[89] while Dhammaloka in *Teachings of Jesus* warned against Christian missionary expertise "in converting Buddhists and Free-Thinkers to the faith."

The *Burma Echo* in October 1907 published this notice:

It will, perhaps, come as a surprise to many people to learn that, in Rangoon there are considerably more than 300 European and Eurasian Free-thinkers, many of whom subscribe to English and American Journals of Free-thought. These people are all avowed Free-thinkers and never enter a Christian church.[90]

While scholarly types argued the scientific and rational nature of Buddhism from Buddhist texts, Dhammaloka's stance was to *assume* Buddhism's compatibility with secular rationalism, and then defend rational Buddhism—or attack Christianity—on the basis of English and American freethought journals.

His use of secularist rhetoric in Burma, condemning Christianity and its missionaries as a device to promote Burmese culture over British imperialism, was innovative. His ability to be determinedly Irish and anti-colonial, while as a Buddhist completely rejecting any vestige of Christian identity, depended on his being outside Ireland, where Catholic nationalism was central to Irish politics. Buddhism also provided a ready-made atheist critique, enabling Dhammaloka to deploy freethought rhetoric in support of his own religious identity.

Dhammaloka as Plebeian Intellectual

We do not know where Dhammaloka became an atheist; freethought was available to the working classes and radicals in Europe, America, and Asia alike. He may have become a freethinker in the West, subsequently finding Buddhism a suitable means of expression. Or he may have encountered freethinking along with Buddhism in a seaman's home, or in discussion with fellow sailors and beachcombers. Dhammaloka's conversion to *Buddhism* aroused curiosity, yet no one regarded his allegiance to *freethought* as incongruous for a thoughtful migrant worker.

This is not surprising, for the "Workers' University" was international.[91] Similar ideas could be encountered in plebeian anticlericalist conversations in Dublin, in a working-man's club in London, in a hobo bookshop in Chicago, in a sailors' home in Chittagong, or in the pages of battered copies of self-published tracts passed from hand to hand. Dhammaloka favored the pamphlet over the monograph, polemic over exposition, and the implications of specific facts over complex arguments. In this he reflected the intellectual practices of the sociable working-class culture that had formed his outlook, rather than the literary culture of the official universities or churches. Moreover, the work of the BTS reflected and built upon not just Dhammaloka's connections with freethinkers in Europe or the United States, but his vital multiethnic networks stretching across Asia. His connections with plebian Asian Buddhists from Penang to Bangkok to Tavoy demonstrated the vital importance of the freethought critique not just for those in Europe, but for those facing the brunt of European colonial power.

This picture of Dhammaloka as Buddhist revivalist *and* plebeian freethinker *and* Irish supporter of Burmese anti-colonialism is borne out by his enemies. Hostile comments in missionary reports or colonial English-language newspapers accuse him of all these things, as interrelated charges. Dhammaloka was bad news *because* his Buddhism was for Asians rather than Westerners, *because* he attacked Christianity, *because* he was no gentleman, *because* he was Irish—and *because* he was successful.

His enemies routinely contrasted Dhammaloka with "good" European Buddhists like Ananda Metteyya, typically portrayed as a gentleman scholar who understood Buddhism as philosophy, not politics, sought to introduce it to educated people in the West rather than use it to mobilize Burmese against empire, and wanted to see Buddhism recognized as another great world religion, rather than challenge Christianity.

Criticisms of Dhammaloka as uneducated, illiterate, unpolished, and so on, recur constantly—despite his ability to defeat missionaries in debate, deliver short, powerful speeches, and publish influential pamphlets. To the guardians of empire, orthodoxy, and colonial privilege, Dhammaloka was not "one of us." He was lampooned for his working-class Irish accent and unrefined behavior, and for being an uneducated upstart who had so far forgotten his racial duty as to wear native dress and bow down to "idols," utter libels on the eternal verities of Christianity, and question the probity of missionaries. Most alarming of all, he could "stir up the natives."

We might assume that accomplishments alien to Dhammaloka—correct speech, sophisticated arguments, a literary repertoire derived from a formal education, impressive publications, and so on—would have been the most effective means of persuading others. But it was not just on the Ganges ferry with an Indian evangelist that Dhammaloka could win arguments. By repeatedly sharply contrasting Burmese Buddhist culture and Western values, and identifying Burmese Buddhism as superior, he helped form the vanguard of an anti-colonial movement that in a few decades would see the British leave Burma for good.

The Buddhist Tract Society was far more than its modest-sounding name suggests. Dhammaloka's literary output earned no academic plaudits, but as BTS president he had a consistent message and was effective in spreading it across Burma. He succeeded because, behind the pamphlets and leaflets, the polemics and plagiarism, lay a world of purposive and organized activities: collecting funds, printing and distributing dissident texts, and engaging in preaching tours that attracted and enthralled audiences of tens of thousands. In 1909 this same activity would plunge him into the heart of anti-colonial Buddhism in Ceylon.

9

A Controversial Tour of Ceylon

1909

Between August and November 1909, Dhammaloka traveled extensively in Ceylon (now Sri Lanka), on a lecture tour organized and funded by the renowned Sinhalese Buddhist activist and leader of the Maha Bodhi Society, Anagarika Dharmapala (see Figure 9.1).[1] Dhammaloka had been in correspondence with Dharmapala since at least December 1900 and had met him prior to that.[2] Dhammaloka's criticisms of Christianity and colonial rule, elaborated in his Buddhist Tract Society publications, meshed well with Dharmapala's vision for a more aggressive defense of Buddhism by the Maha Bodhi Society.

Dhammaloka's intentionally confrontational tour of Ceylon offers a fascinating insight into the workings of contentious Buddhism in this period, partly because many competing accounts of the events survive. These include transcripts of Dhammaloka's speeches and other material in Dharmapala's weekly paper *Sinhala Bauddhaya*, Dharmapala's diaries (often commenting on the difficulties of working with Dhammaloka), hostile commentary from the colonial and missionary press, statements distancing other Buddhist organizations from the tour, and records of police and intelligence involvement. The variety of sources—read critically—enables us to see this dramatic episode in unusual depth.

British colonies in South and Southeast Asia were deeply interconnected in this period. From 1862 until 1937 Burma was part of British India. Ceylon, a Crown Colony separate from India, was closely tied through shipping, pilgrimage, and migrant links to India and Burma. Expanding rail and steamship networks meant that key ports of India and Ceylon were readily accessible from Dhammaloka's bases in Rangoon, the Straits Settlements, and Bangkok. All the evidence suggests that Dhammaloka had a long relationship with both India and Ceylon. Dhammaloka repeatedly mentioned having traveled to Ceylon before his rise to fame in Burma. In Tokyo in 1902, he said, "I have travelled to most places in Ceylon," and Sarah Jeanette Duncan (Mrs. Everard Cotes) in Rangoon heard rumors that he had been a pearl-diver in Ceylon prior to his ordination.[3] The *Englishman* in 1912 described the tour as "one of his periodical visits to Ceylon."[4]

The Irish Buddhist. Alicia Turner, Laurence Cox, and Brian Bocking, Oxford University Press (2020)
© Alicia Turner, Laurence Cox and Brian Bocking.
DOI: 10.1093/oso/9780190073084.001.0001

Figure 9.1. A saintly campaigner: Anagarika H. Dharmapala, pictured on a fundraising visit to San Francisco in 1902.

San Francisco Examiner.

The 1909 Tour

Traveling from Burma via Madras, Dhammaloka arrived in Colombo on August 27, 1909, to spearhead a two-month tour with Dharmapala during which he gave forty-eight talks, interpreted into Sinhalese by Maha Bodhi Society activist Walisingha Harishchandra.[5] Factoring in a week's illness and some planned talks that failed to materialize, the pace was close to one a day. Returning frequently to Colombo's Saraswati Hall, venues elsewhere were mostly Buddhist Theosophical Society schools, Buddhist temples and *pirivenas* (monastic seminaries), and market or municipal halls. Until mid-October, Dhammaloka toured mostly in the west around Colombo or around Galle in the south, with one trip to Anuradhapura. In late October and early November the journeys lengthened, culminating in a trip to Badulla and Bandarawala, Ratnapura, Kandy, and Rambukkana (see Map 9.1). Despite the difficulties that beset the tour, Dhammaloka was clearly felt to be a speaker worth taking around the country.

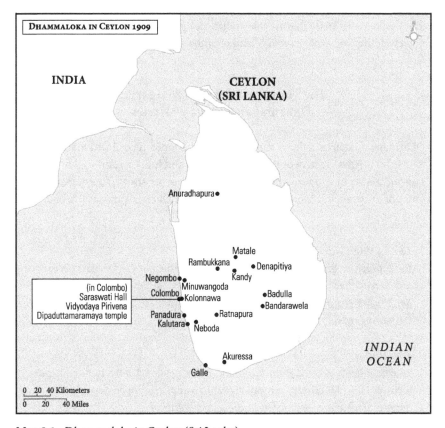

Map 9.1. Dhammaloka in Ceylon (Sri Lanka).

Dhammaloka's talks were wildly popular, often attracting audiences of thousands. Anagarika Dharmapala's diaries and the *Sinhala Bauddhaya* newspaper mention a "crowded hall" many times. We are told of "about 700" people at Saraswati Hall, "about 1,500" at Minuwangoda temple, "over 2,000" at Kolonnawa Pansala, and "about 3,000" at Dipaduttamaramaya temple and at Saraswati (again). At Galle Park, the crowd was "about five thousand" including "hundreds of English, Dutch, Tamil and Muslim people."[6]

Such figures always have to be regarded with caution, but the time and money Anagarika Dharmapala invested in Dhammaloka bears witness to the Irish monk's impact. As *Sinhala Bauddhaya* commented, "Buddhists should think of Mr. Anagarika Dharmapala and the Maha Bodhi Society who bore huge expenses and brought the reverend to the country."[7] Dhammaloka's value to the Maha Bodhi Society project is also reflected in the position of honor he occupied, being consistently the lead speaker with Maha Bodhi representatives, including Dharmapala, coming second. Dhammaloka is even found ritually administering *pansil* (vows to observe the five lay precepts) to the crowd.[8] The controversy around his visit boosted attendance, hence donations and book sales. The tour evidently helped Dharmapala's positioning of himself and the Maha Bodhi Society at the "militant reformist" end of Sinhalese Buddhist revivalism.[9]

The Tour Seen through Anagarika Dharmapala's Private Diaries

Dharmapala's diaries offer a remarkable and candid record of Dhammaloka's tour from the perspective of its main organizer and funder, reminiscent of backstage accounts of modern rock tours.[10] The excerpts show Dharmapala's clear sense of purpose, but increasing frustration with Dhammaloka as the busy tour progressed:

12 Aug 1909 [writes Dharmapala]
Recd: telegram from Dhammaloka that he is starting for Ceylon next Saturday and to send the passage money by wire . . . . Under Buddhist Rule we were a million times better off. Sent a telegram to Dharmaloka [sic] to come that I will pay the fare on arrival.

27th Friday
U. Dhammalok arrived from Rangoon, at my request. I have to pay his passage. Rs. 60/-. He is now our guest. His arrival at [sic] opportune. I hope the dying Sinhalese men will listen to the loving words of Buddha. We must work unceasingly.

Occasional asides give a flavor of the atmosphere at Dhammaloka's talks:

(August) 29th Sunday
At 2 P.M. with Dhammaloka went to lecture at Ranatta. I had never been to this village before. The Sinhalese are deteriorating. Action must be taken at once.
   At 5 P.M. Dhammaloka at the Saraswati Hall. Slavery under Christianity. Dhammaloka at Rajagiriya at 8.30. . . . The Saraswati Hall crowded. The lecture at Rajagiri was against the devil Jehovah.

(October) 29th Friday
At Bandarawala. The local Catholic padri is a Sinhalese by the name Rodrigo. He has published a pamphlet attacking the Lord Buddha. At 2 P.M. D. lectured against Catholic Christianity and I followed suit. It was a regular bombarding.[11]

Sinhala Bauddhaya describes Dhammaloka's enthusiastic reception there:

Buddhist gents of Bandarawala welcomed the reverend with lamps, torches and choirs at the railway station and escorted him to the temple by the procession of drummers. He stayed at a place specially prepared for him.[12]

(October) 30th Saturday
Started in the morning for Badulla. Reached B. at 11 A.M. Dhammaloka stayed at the Parivena. H[arischandra] and I had rooms at J. Kotalawala's Office. Lecture at 7 P.M. at the Buddhist School. The Hall was crowded.

(November) 3rd Wednesday
In the afternoon U.D. lectured agst: Christianity at the Sangharaja Pirivena [Kandy]. I bombarded at the Christian ramparts.

Dhammaloka's Sermons

Anagarika Dharmapala intended Dhammaloka's tour to shore up Buddhism against Christian missionary threats as a public display of the Maha Bodhi Society's position and a rallying cry for Buddhists across the island. For Dhammaloka, it was a new audience for the message already proclaimed in his Burmese tours and through his Buddhist Tract Society publications.

   Between *Sinhala Bauddhaya* and Dharmapala's diaries, we have a fair record of the topics of Dhammaloka's talks, including two full transcriptions.[13] This is the only period of his career for which we have such detailed information. Dhammaloka's lectures all revolved around his challenge to Christianity. Titles included "What has Christianity done to the world?" "Falsity of Christianity," "Slavery under Christianity, "A reply to my critics," and "The myths of the Salvation Army."

Dhammaloka had always said that his role was not to replace his fellow monks' exposition of the Dhamma but to challenge Christian missionaries. This challenge could be launched from various angles.[14] He could decry the textual underpinnings of Christian religion, point to failings in its practice (just as some Christians compared actual Buddhism unfavorably to textual ideals), or both at once—arguing that the failings of Christianity reflected its flawed biblical basis. He could also attack Christianity on ethical grounds, where many agreed that Buddhism was strongly positioned, or on its scientific credibility, challenging the widespread claim that Christianity underpinned Western scientific and intellectual superiority and instead emphasizing its "superstitious" character, in contrast to Buddhism.

Dhammaloka also argued that Christianity was declining throughout Europe in the face of scientific developments, the rise of freethought, and the decline of religious-authoritarian states. Like Dharmapala, he identified missionary activity as a tool of colonialism. Both criticized the apparent apathy of most monks and called for laity and monks alike to take action.

Dhammaloka's transcribed (and translated) talks convey their tone as well as their content. A lecture on September 3 identified the targets of his polemic:

> At Vidyodaya Pirivena[15] on Friday, addressing a crowd of about 2000 at 8.30 pm, Rev. Dhammaloka said . . . that destroying the building named Christianity built on a weak foundation called the Bible was an important task. Considering the current situation in Ceylon, a precious, momentous cure had to be given to treat the mythical Christian illness. . . . Pastors who come to Ceylon from countries like France carry four dangerous items in their pockets: in the first pocket they carry the Bible, the second pocket contains a bottle of Whiskey, the third pocket has a gun and the fourth pocket has a plan to get a plot of land, albeit small, and build a house.[16]

This unusual riff on Dhammaloka's usual trio of "the Bible, the whiskey bottle, and the Gatling gun" evokes nineteenth-century colonial legislation allowing large amounts of land in Ceylon to be auctioned off cheaply for British-owned plantations.[17] The island had been massively changed by these plantations and the influx of Tamil migrant labor to work them.[18] The effect, Dharmapala lamented, was economic devastation for the locals:

> *Everywhere there is desolation. The villagers after having sold their ancestral property to the British planters have become coolies in the Estates.*[19]

On Wednesday, September 8, Dhammaloka addressed "a crowd of about 800" in Rajagiri Buddhist College, by invitation of "the Student society of Welikada Lady Dharmayopana" on "Christianity and the Study of Theory." He opened by declaring that

> [s]ayings in the Bible contradict one another. One can see that in one instance one is advised not to murder, and then in about 300 instances murders take place.... In the Book of Exodus, Chapter 32: 27, the Israelite God Jehovah says this: "Everyone should take a sword and go from door to door of the entire camp and murder one's siblings, supporters and neighbours." In the same Book, the 3rd and 4th verses of Chapter 15 say "Jehovah was a warrior, his name was Jehovah and he drowned pharaoh's troops and chariots in the ocean." Are these not murders? . . . Christian priests mislead the Sinhalese by screaming that the Bible, which is full of such facts, is a holy book! See if any book that is a part of our Tathagatha's Tripitaka [the Buddha's teachings] has such cruel sayings. Not so![20]

In these talksDhammaloka highlights biblical encouragements to breach all five of the major Buddhist precepts, not just killing:

> According to your main religion [Buddhism], there are five precepts that you need to obey. You should abstain from murder, theft, sexual promiscuity, lying and intoxication. But the Bible teaches us to do those very five things.[21]

He decries the Bible's encouragement of warfare and killing, contrasting the religiously sanctioned ethnic violence of the Bible with his own multiethnic and anti-militarist Buddhist perspectives. Then he moves from a critique of the text to its use in justifying present-day militarism and colonialism:

> They lecture about peace on Christmas Day when Jesus was born. On that day, Christianity is a "peaceful" religion. But the "peace" of this day is, once the sermon is over, to go home, eat meat, and make merry drinking whiskey, brandy, gin and schnapps. Isn't this a wonderful "peace"? Look at the government records to see the amount of alcohol Lankans consumed before Christianity came to Ceylon and after it has come. They say Ceylon was "civilised" by Christians, who brought colourful coats, collars and hats and said "what you are wearing is uncivilized, wear these and become civilized," and they praise Three Star Brandy, Beehive Brandy and White Horse Whiskey. They scheme to send whatever little money the gullible Sinhalese have got back to their [home] country. What can you say about the "civilization" you get from drinking alcohol?[22]

At Negombo temple two days later, Dhammaloka's lecture on the same topic, "Christianity and Study of Theory" was judged worth serializing over three issues of *Sinhala Bauddhaya*. Dhammaloka argued that scientific knowledge undermines the authority of any Christian text:

> The Bible says that the earth rests on four pillars. I would like know what those four poles themselves stand on. Chapter 7:1 reveals the answer. "Then, I have seen that four corners of the earth are borne by four angels who protect the earth, the sea and the trees from winds blowing from four directions." The earth is a globe. Have you ever heard or seen a globe with four corners?[23]

Dhammaloka's Politics

Dhammaloka offered his sharpest political analysis in Minuwangoda on September 6 to a 1,500-strong audience "of Buddhists, Christians and nonbelievers." Again serialized in *Sinhala Bauddhaya*, this lecture gives the clearest surviving account of Dhammaloka's political position.[24] He began:

> When Christianity rose in Europe, the conditions there were completely different to the conditions of today. . . . Christianity spread amongst them when they were thus unintelligent and uncivilized. They were like infants; they did not possess a developed intellect. It is no surprise that amongst such people a religion [like Christianity] spread strongly. A child can easily be taught any religion. Since children do not possess the intellect to allow them to analyze things, they will believe in whatever religion they are taught until the day they die. This is the main reason for Christianity being prevalent in Europe.[25]

Dhammaloka's point was that if Europe had seen scientific and political progress, this was in spite of Christianity, not because of it:

> Today the situation is quite different. . . . Theoretically developed intelligent Europeans have directed their intellect to studying the Bible closely. When they did so, they found out that the Bible is full of unacceptable, contradictory statements and various points of view developed about the Bible. What happened to Christianity as a result of all these views? Christianity was splintered into many sects.[26]

Highlighting how Christianity usurped the power of the state to survive in Europe, Dhammaloka now turned to contemporary events:

Today, I am going to read you a passage . . . about the conflict between the Spanish government and the Christian Church of that country, [which] points out the travails Christianity has landed in, saying that if they are not solved soon, this conflict could result in the Spanish government expelling the padres and sisters from the country. In Spain, for about a thousand years when the Church reigned, thousands of people were tortured and killed. Why does the Spanish government act differently now? What is the reason? The reason is that there is freethinking in that country.[27]

This was a month after the *Setmana Tràgica* ("tragic week") in Catalonia, a military intervention against radical workers in Barcelona and elsewhere, which led to a liberal shift in Spanish politics. It saw the execution of Francesc Ferrer, founder of the Modern School, his killing subsequently commemorated by anarchists and freethinkers in Europe and North America setting up secular schools in his name.[28] Dhammaloka was clear which side he was on and that the struggle was international. In this context, Christian missionary incursions into Buddhist spaces required direct redress:

These days, while padres are trying to spread Christianity in the country in different ways, it is important to look at where Buddhism stands in Ceylon. Compared with the efforts the Christian padres are making to spread Christianity in Ceylon, Buddhist bhikkhus seem to be making little effort. Buddhism is a *dhamma* [teaching] that could help build intellect and good character in the world. If the Buddhist clergy of a country where there is such a great religion acted effectually, there would be no reason for Christianity to spread. If the Buddhist bhikkhus were not just concerned about the lodges and *pirikara* [donated items] but instead worked to save their religion from criticisms thrown at the religion by those who believe in myths, Buddhists would not have to face this danger. . . .

Right now there are Buddhist missionaries in different parts of the world. The intention of these missionaries is to eliminate the threats Buddhists face from other religions and to develop their own religion by overcoming the obstacles opponents throw in their way.[29]

The criticism of apathetic Buddhist monks was echoed in Dharmapala's accompanying talks. The "Buddhist missionaries" are not Ananda Metteyya's 1908 mission to London but those defending existing Buddhists from Christian missionaries, such as Dhammaloka and his ordinands. As in Ceylon, Burmese Buddhists had been slow to respond to the threat:

A few years ago, there were riots in Burma because of Christian missionaries. In Rangoon, those missionaries began to stalk the streets and crossroads preaching Christianity and attacking Buddhism. They distributed thousands of leaflets and pamphlets amongst Burmese Buddhists. Not content with this, they distributed pamphlets attacking Buddhism at Buddhist temples and at Buddhist festivals, attacked Buddhism in every possible way and worked effectively to deceive Buddhists and convert them to Christianity. Burmese Buddhists could not get away from the activities of these Christian padres and were helpless. Burmese bhikkhus too were concerned only about their temple, robes and *dana* and did not make any effort to save Buddhists from the threats.[30]

This, he declares, was the spur for his own radicalization and emergence as Irish Buddhist monk and campaigner.

It is around this time that I became a novice. Although Burmese bhikkhus did not accept me as a friend at first, I realised that if we were to eliminate the threats to Burmese Buddhism, the lectures of the padres should be stopped and I resolved to do this. I knew the only way to destroy the power of the padres. I realised that the only way to attack Christianity is to expose the Christian holy book, the Bible, to the whole world.[31]

Thus freethinking arguments from the shelves of the hobo's bookshop or sailor's home could be enrolled in the service of Buddhism.

So in Burma, I prepared to attack Christianity through the Bible itself and proved the falsity of Bible through its phrases. I began to print and distribute leaflets with snippets from the Bible in the very same foul language that was used in the Bible. Then the padres got frightened.[32]

This, he argues, was the origin of his massive success in Burma, a project that could be translated to Ceylon, which had had its own struggle.

About 30 years ago, Buddhists in Colombo too faced a lot of hardships because of Christians. Often Buddhists were ashamed to acknowledge their religion. Christian priests insulted Buddhism daily, weekly, monthly. Christian padres had learned not only their own religion, but had learned a little Buddhism and on this basis attacked Buddhism. At that moment, Kotahene Migettuwatte Thero came forward and conducted lectures to protect Buddhism.[33] Christianity still has not recovered from Migettuwatte Thero's attacks.[34]

He claimed to be continuing this fight with new weapons, with evidence that Buddhists were winning the battle.

> As soon as I arrived here, the *Ceylon Independent, Catholic Messenger* and other local Christian papers growled at me. Barked at me. That's all they could do. We all know that all a scared, toothless dog can do is to bark when it sees someone at a distance. What has happened to the commotion of those papers now? They are silent. I have shown up the state of Christianity in European countries and the nature of their padres. Now they are quiet. . . .
>
> I attacked Christianity successfully in Burma. The padres could not burn me at the stake or send me to jail. I distributed leaflets there proving the pointlessness of Christianity in which I included intriguing phrases from the Bible.[35]

Looking to build on these successes and drive the point home, Dhammaloka returned to the critique of colonialism. War was in the air in Europe in the lead-up to World War I, but in Asia the impact of European militarism had already been felt.

> Some Christians claim that the speech Jesus made on top of the mountain is a very good one. But it is certain that those Christians who know what it is about would not act accordingly. An ordinary Christian would not know what it is all about. Most of the time, they have not even read it. One of the phrases in it is "those who submit will own the earth." . . .
>
> Look at countries like Burma and Ceylon who have been colonised by Europeans. Would more subservient Sinhalese own the earth? Can't you see how the plots of land that were in the hands of Sinhalese for about two thousand years are falling into the hands of European planters? When you look at Burma, India, Ceylon or any other such country, does it not prove that the phrase from the Bible quoted above is a lie? What the colonised get from Europeans is the missionary padres, a bottle of whisky and a packet of opium.[36]

Colonialism was violence in Dhammaloka's world, and Christianity was the tip of the sword. But the colonized need not be duped.

> There is a group of natives in New Zealand called Maori. The Christian missionaries who came to them advised them to "look up at the sky and pray to God. Then you will be blessed." Maori people responded saying "when we look up and pray, you steal the earth below our feet."[37]

Dhammaloka deftly aligned South Asian and Maori experiences of colonialism. This unusual move underlines the pan-ethnic nature of his anti-imperialism.

The violence of colonialism in Ceylon or Burma was intimately linked to the re-pression of indigenous populations by European settler colonials throughout their empires in Dhammaloka's broad ethnic solidarity. With eyes opened to the threat, something could be done. Dhammaloka turns to the importance of education:

> Buddhism imposes no ban or hindrance on critical examination. Buddhists should learn Buddhism well. They should examine everything. If there is any-thing they don't understand, they should clarify it by speaking to a bhikkhu or another learned person. In the meantime, if a white-faced padre approaches, some think that just because he has a white face, his religion would have an ex-otic taste and they would start running after him. Just like a spider who spins his web around his prey, he will offer hospitality to the stranger and very quickly turn him into a slave. So, what is the advice the priest gives the poor man? "Don't think. Don't read. Do as you are told. Thinking and reading are our re-sponsibility. We will do that for you. All you have to do is to do as you are told." Today Roman Catholic people are like slaves. What is the advice Buddhism gives? "Learn and develop your intellect." Buddhism teaches that ignorance is the cause of suffering. It is true. When he develops his intellect, man tries to break free. The British governing system today is an example. That is why the padres advise one "not to look at books, not to read and to do as they are told."[38]

Knowledge, in other words, is power. And the Buddhist religion, uniquely in Dhammaloka's view, encourages critical reflection.

> When Buddhist infants are sent to Christian schools, their soft minds are poi-soned. In a very short time, those children lose feelings of nationalism and pa-triotism. They lose their religion too. They practice foreign habits. Do Christian parents send their children to Buddhist schools? No. So why do Buddhists send their own children to Christians' schools? Buddhists should realise that chan-ging the minds of children is the main means through which Christianity is spread in a country and they should set up Buddhist schools in every village.[39]

This was the rationale for the Buddhist Theosophical Society schools where Dhammaloka regularly spoke, as well as the Buddhist schools he frequented in Burma and founded in Bangkok and Singapore.[40]

In these sermons we see Dhammaloka fleshing out his slogan of "the Bible, the whiskey bottle, and the Gatling gun" to critique the combination of actually existing Christianity, alcohol or drug addiction, colonial militarism, land grabs, and the "civilizing" process. His strategy involves a polemic against a waning but still-dangerous "foreign" faith, debate, organization ("a hundred heroic men" such as Dharmapala), and promotion of critical thinking as a way forward to—what? If not the political independence that a later generation of nationalists would demand, then certainly self-confidence, assertion of religious identity, collective action, and the prospect of a non-repressive future free of colonialism and Christianity.

Traveling with the Irish Monk: Conflicts and Egos

While Dhammaloka's controversial performances gained notoriety for the tour, behind the scenes it was not easy sailing. The schedule was grueling, and traveling companions did not always get along. Dhammaloka got sick, and was sometimes grumpy with his hosts and even his audiences. As Dharmapala's diaries reveal, Dhammaloka was no angel. From the outset there was rivalry between Dhammaloka and Harishchandra, the Maha Bodhi Society activist who served as his translator, and Anagarika Dharmapala was uncertain how to mediate this.

> (August) 27th Friday [Dhammaloka's first day in Ceylon]
> *Saraswati Hall lecture. I introduced M. [sic] Dhammaloka. He addressed the audience for a few minutes. There was enthusiasm manifest. Harishchandra has not learnt to be courteous.*

An entry four days later is disturbing but ambiguous:

> 31st Tuesday
> *It was 2.30 this morning the Arakanese student and Nagahawatta entered into my room and woke me up and the former complained that last night Dhammaloka insulted him indecently etc. This came like a shock to me. The student had also told Jayasinha. On inquiry Dhammaloka denies ever having done anything indecent. It is impossible to believe that he would do anything mean after having worked in Burma for 10 years. It is easy to destroy the character of a man of religion.*

It is not clear whether "insulted" in this context referred to words or actions. The comment about working in Burma for ten years suggests that it may have been the kind of thing which could otherwise have been ascribed to a cultural misunderstanding. We have found no other references of this kind.[41]

The rest of the tour had its conflicts and showed that Dhammaloka was struggling physically (whether because of health, climate, the pace of the tour, or all three):

(September) 17th Friday
Started for Gorakana, 2.20 P.M. There were lots of women. Dhammaloka spoke and he suddenly sat down and then I commenced. We returned by the 7 P.M. train.

Dharmapala's diaries show Dhammaloka as increasingly stubborn and intransigent, causing trouble for the tour and his sponsor.

(October) 8th Friday
Arriving at the M.B. Office I was thunderstruck when U. Dhammaloka told me that he is leaving us for good this evening as it is impossible to do good to a people who do not appreciate good. He was inflexible and insisted that he must leave this evening. After much coaxing we succeeded.

At Saraswati Hall @ 5PM there was a large gathering to hear Dhammaloka, but he declined to go and I had to take his place & spoke for ½ hour, and MCP for another ½ hour.

Dharmapala nevertheless found a solution:

(October) 12th Tuesday
Presented a Gillette Razor to U. Dhammaloka.

A razor is one of the few "requisites" a bhikkhu may possess. Gillette had recently patented their disposable double-edged safety razor blade, and the gift enabled Dharmapala to restore Dhammaloka's wounded pride. However, Dharmapala was now less sympathetic to his traveling companion:

(October) 15th Friday
Passed the night at Akuressa. Dhammaloka for hours & hours will continue talking agst: Ananda Maitreeya[42] [sic] & shows an abnormal spirit of vengeance.

(October) 16th Saturday
Partition Day.[43] Started from Akuressa in the morning. Pouring rain, got wet. All the way for three hours he talked agst: A.M. and Mrs. Besant.[44]

Reached Denipitiya at 10.30. Dhammaloka had good dana. He declined to speak at Denipitiya. We reached Weligama and when asked to speak he declined and having insulted the people he walked off! The man has revengeful temper. I sent Harishchandra with him to Colombo and I got off at Ahangama . . . .

Samaraweera Mohandiram felt greatly insulted by Dhammaloka.

The pressures of the tour soon left Dharmapala as disaffected with his Maha Bodhi associate Harishchandra as with Dhammaloka:

(October) 18th Monday
The Dodanduwa building started 2½ years is incomplete. What a shame? Nobody comes to do the work. Harishchandra starts a work and leaves it off before its culmination.

Passed the night at Nagoda. . . . Harishchandra thinks that we should not have anything to do in the future, with U. Dhammaloka. He is ignorant of Buddhism; is very unclean and is easily provoked to anger. His good qualities are that he can rattle away for hours agst: Christianity and is not idle in clear weather.[45]

There is an irony in two modernist Asian Buddhists with an essentially self-invented "anagarika" [semi-monastic] status questioning the Buddhist credentials of a fully ordained white bhikkhu of the Burmese sangha.[46] Despite all, Dharmapala seems to have managed his star Dhammaloka well, and they continued the wildly popular tour.

(October) 25th Monday
The Badulla trip will I hope not have to be abandoned. It is a pity that Dhammaloka has a very bad temper. Our priests who are incumbents of temples are a demoralised lot. They are only active when they want to chew betel and take dana. What a pity that they are so indolent.

U. Dhammaloka is now quite well and he is able to undertake the trip to Badulla, Ratnapura, Kandy & Neboda.

This last paragraph was presumably added later, Dharmapala perhaps breathing a sigh of relief.

The Political Context

By 1909, the Sinhalese Buddhist sangha's initially relaxed response to Christian exclusivism and contempt for Buddhism had long been abandoned.[47] Dhammaloka's tour followed nearly fifty years of revivalist responses, public debates, and polemics in which Anagarika Dharmapala's Maha Bodhi Society had recently provided the sharpest edge.[48] Dharmapala's critique of Christianity, albeit over a longer period, paralleled Dhammaloka's. The two activists, who had met in 1900 and maybe before, had closely allied starting points.[49] "Higher Buddhism," wrote Dharmapala, has no place for theology, and it has got nothing to do with creator gods and fighting lords. It rejects the phantom of a separate soul entity residing somewhere in the body. It rejects a saviour by whose favour one can go to heaven, it rejects the superstitions of an eternal hell and an eternal heaven, it rejects the idea of prayer to bribe the god, and it repudiates the interference of priests.[50]

Of an earlier phase of Buddhist revival in Ceylon, Richard Young and G. P. V. Somaratna write that "the imported anti-Christian and anticlerical ideologies of Europe, especially the Free-Thought of Britain's 'Victorian Infidels,' increasingly found its way into the productions of the revivalist press."[51] Figures such as Migettuwatte Gunananda Thera were not simply name-dropping when citing "Carlile, Holyoake, Bradlaugh, and other secularists, agnostics, or 'atheists,'" but were familiar with their works.[52] As we saw in Chapter 8, Gunananda's own mid-1880s Buddhist Tract Society series comprised "mostly reruns of Bradlaugh."[53] Dhammaloka's expertise in freethinker arguments thus worked well in Ceylon.

For the ruling classes in Burma and Ceylon, converting Buddhists to Christianity was an acceptable activity. Only when matters went the other way did criticism arise. Dharmapala highlighted this double standard in a letter to the *Ceylon Independent* defending Dhammaloka's right to speak out:

It was only a few months ago that Sir Joseph Hutchinson delivered an oration against Buddhism when he presided at the opening ceremony of the British and Foreign Bible Society's House, and again Justice Middleton presiding at the Anglican synod several weeks ago gave hints as to what the Clergy should do to convert the Buddhists, and he was surprised seeing the activity of the Buddhists at Baddegama!! . . .

A solitary Buddhist priest of the white race comes to Ceylon and opens fire at the "mighty fabric" of Christianity, and the black-robed sentinels are panic-stricken and are meeting in solemn conclave how to destroy the Irish Buddhist priest! It only shows the Buddhists that the Christian foundations in Ceylon have not the strength to bear the attack of a single yellow-robed monk.

Let us have fair play, and it is not fair that you should ask the Buddhists to keep quiet, while the Christian padres are active in the villages in trying to convert Buddhists to Christianity.[54]

The Establishment Fights Back

Dhammaloka's outspoken assaults on Christian truths unsurprisingly won him enemies across the colonial establishment. The press, police, governmental authorities, and even some of the more respectable Buddhist organizations opposed him. The pro-missionary *Ceylon Observer*, owned and edited by Scottish Baptist John Ferguson, and the twice-weekly *Catholic Messenger* published scathing attacks almost as he arrived.[55] The *Messenger* ran this mocking piece on September 4:

> An Irish Buddhist Priest must assuredly be a *rara avis* and well worth seeing; for Pat is noted for his attachment to the Faith of his forefathers—the faith that was preached in the Emerald Isle by St. Patrick several centuries ago—and would never dream of bartering it away for any other creed unless he is actually "reduced to shavings." Hence we are at a loss to understand what sort of an Irishman we have in the person of the Rev. V Dhammaloka who is now in our midst. This white yellow-robed personage arrived from Burma on Friday last. When asked by the "Times'" reporter what it was that led him to Buddhism, Dhammaloka replied that he had been a free thinker before he read Buddhism and that rationalist and free thought literature led him to the new faith. Now Pat is a "Yellow robe" and the President of the Buddhist Tract Society to boot—a society whose sole aim is to attack Christianity. "We don't trouble much," said the white bonze to the "Times'" reporter, "about preaching Buddhism in Burma. The best method of converting the people is to attack Christianity and stop them embracing that faith." . . . That is how Dhammaloka looks at the matter. A queer doctrine, is it not? . . .
>
> Hence Dhammaloka [does] not care a pin about what J. Wettha Sinha told us some time ago in the Ceylon National Review, that "Buddhism enforces the cultivation of peace and good will towards all living beings (including even cows and dogs) denouncing the distinctions of caste, creed, colour, race and species." This is too tame a doctrine for bellicose people like Dhammaloka. We are going to see hard times, then. A new valiant Irish Bonze is come from Burma with the set purpose of attacking and overthrowing the mighty fabric of Christianity by the power of his "gab," and of making Buddhism reign supreme in Ceylon! A grand sight it will be for the Y.M.B.A. and Mr. D. B. Jayatilaka![56]

Dharmapala's diaries track other media controversies around the tour. The *Ceylon Independent* joined the attack. Dharmapala's late August and September diary entries describe a flurry of attacks on both Dhammaloka and himself in the *Independent*.

A *Sinhala Bauddhaya* report of September 18 reveals that the *Independent* had called for Dhammaloka to be deported:

> Many ill-informed persons harbouring hatred towards Rev U Dhammaloka who has been active and has been giving lectures in cities and villages in Colombo, Negombo and Panadura since 27th August have been trying to

deceive the public by spreading various lies in the *Independent* and *Catholic Messenger*. Saying that he delivers seditious speeches and that he uses harsh words when speaking about Christianity, the editor of the *Independent* urges the English government to deport the reverend. We are shocked by this naive statement of the editor who has not been to listen to a single lecture of the reverend. What is the reason for European padres to give up their countries and villages and come to countries like Ceylon and Burma? We advise all not to be misled by false articles produced by the padres and their supporters who oppose Rev Dhammaloka's attempt to demonstrate the ways of those who try to destroy Buddhism for the sake of their own salary and the misleading editorial based on such articles.

    . . . [We] heard that the Superintendent of Southern Province Police too heard the lecture well. We could even check with the high officials of the government if the reverend delivers seditious lectures, as accused by the *Independent*. We say it is the responsibility of the government to do what is appropriate to journalists who publish misleading articles and editorials.[57]

Touché: we see your call for deportation and we raise you a call for action on misreporting! Further attacks included a cartoon against Dhammaloka in the *Amicus* newspaper.[58] He responded publicly:

24th Friday
Saraswati Hall. Dhammaloka "A reply to my Critics." The hall was crowded. We have to adopt such tactics as would put the Christians to shame. K.B.B. suggests that respectable people should send a signed protest agst: the Indpt: C.P. Wijeratne.

This gives us a sense of the variety of tactics Dharmapala and Dhammaloka used in response to media attacks. The next day's *Sinhala Bauddhaya* offered:

A Lament
It is a known fact in the country that European Rev U Dhammaloka's lectures on Christianity delivered in many parts of the country have instilled fear into the minds of Christians. In the meantime, newspaper editors . . . have tried to gratify the Christian lamb by publishing a lament in the paper on the 22nd of this month. Since there are signs of bad times to come, as the proverb goes, "in catastrophic times, darkness is everywhere" they babble on about nonsense that they have picked up from here and there about Dhamma [Buddhism] in order to make a peculiar profit out of this situation.[59]

Lectures and Counter-Lectures

Dhammaloka's opponents did not rely only on the newspapers; a high-profile Christian lecture series was hastily arranged after the start of Dhammaloka's tour. Dharmapala notes that the two series clashed: A. G. Fraser and Kenneth Saunders, Christian missionaries, lectured opposite Dhammaloka between October 4 and 10. Fraser's talk was countered by a tract, "The Credentials of Christianity Examined in the East," published by Ceylon YMBA activists. Dharmapala thought Fraser's and Saunders's lectures effective:

(October) 7th Thursday
The local [Colombo] papers are giving in full reports of the lectures delivered by Fraser & Saunders. The wonder is that Christianity is not spreading fast in Ceylon, when we think of the stupendous efforts made by the Christians.

The *Ceylon Observer*, reporting the first talk, highlighted a supposed contrast between Christians promoting Christianity without saying a word against Buddhism and Dhammaloka's provocative method of promoting Buddhism by criticizing Christianity:

Lectures in Christianity: First Lectures at the Public Hall Yesterday
Mr. A G Fraser, M.A. Principal of Trinity College, Kandy, delivered the first of a series of lectures [. . .]
    "Ladies and gentlemen—The present course of lectures will be altogether—and I take it upon myself the responsibility to say exclusively—Christian. They shall be constructively Christian, they shall be reverentially Christian, they shall be moreover apologetically Christian." . . . Mr. Fraser then delivered his lecture which is published in our daily issue and he prefaced it by saying that he was not going in the course of his lectures to refer in any way to Buddhism, for he had not the slightest degree any quarrel with Buddhism and those he knew were all his friends and friendly with him. He was not going to touch on Buddhism at all.[60]

The report described Dhammaloka's supporters poised at the lecture to distribute pro-Buddhist leaflets with questions for the missionaries, to take notes, and to intervene.[61] Such interruptions were the bread and butter of religious debate, and, as Dharmapala's diaries show, Christians gave as good as they got:

(September) 4th Saturday
Dhammaloka quoted the Bible and showed the diabolism of Christianity. Simon Silva, the Wesleyan Kapurala [preacher] disturbed the meeting. He was hooted by the audience.

Sinhala Bauddhaya adds that Silva "representing the Church Missionary Society in Kalutara debated about the Bible with the European reverend and left soon after he was defeated."[62]

Another time, the Christian who interrupted was so thoroughly defeated that he handed over his own weapon:

5th Sunday
At the lecture a tom-tom beater dressed in the garb of a Catechist came & disturbed the meeting.[63] *The man had a Sinhalese Bible in his hand and I tackled him and put him to shame. The Bible that was in his hands, he gave it to me.*

In *Sinhala Bauddhaya*'s account:

There was a Sinhala Christian who had come with a Bible to ask the reverend [Dhammaloka] questions. Taking him to be someone who has come to make trouble, he was ordered to sit by the preacher's seat. Since he could not ask any questions, he asked the reverend to clarify [a] few verses from the Bible. Then the reverend ordered him to read from the Bible he was carrying and he read a few verses that were marked by someone else. When the reverend asked him to read this verse or that verse, he turned the pages this way and that way and said he could not find the specified verse and that he does not have a lot of practice on reading the Bible. Answering the questions Mr. Dharmapala asked, he said he was a cart-puller and that he came to this meeting with the Bible that was given by pastor Simon Silva. The Bible was given to Rev Dhammaloka.[64]

Such trophies were a common feature of religious controversies:

6th Monday
Left Kalutara, by the 8 A.M. train. At the Station we had another tussle with the Wesleyan Minister, Silva. He came to get the Bible and we drove him away. If Truth is to triumph we shall be victorious this time, and we shall drive the Catholics and the Protestants out of Ceylon.

Under Surveillance

Others, too, saw Dhammaloka as a threat. The police were aware that Buddhist revival rhetoric might pose a threat to the stability of colonial rule. Sedition was a concern for the British authorities across colonial Asia at the time, with nationalist agitation growing in Burma, India, and Ceylon. The Ceylon police, though more interested in Dharmapala's politics than in Dhammaloka's, seem to have been alerted to Dhammaloka's presence by his opponents in Burma. A letter from "a gentleman who occupies a high position in Burma . . . and whose veracity is above all suspicion"[65] was printed in the *Catholic Messenger* and the *Ceylon Observer* in September, offering:

Interesting Details Concerning the Irish Bikshu
I am writing this to let you know that, a certain Buddhist priest, by name U Dhammaloka left Rangoon by the SS. "Bangala" for Madras where he will probably land today. He is on his way via Tuticorin to Ceylon to start an anti-Christian Mission having been specially invited by the Ceylon Buddhists who stated in their letter of invitation that "The Roman Catholics are converting too many Buddhists to Christianity in their schools"; and he was asked to start

An Anti-Roman Catholic Crusade
throughout the Island of Ceylon. U Dhammaloka has taken along with him some cases full of books written against the faith which he imported some time ago from America, along with a lot of "Free thought" trash; and unless I am absolutely certain of my facts, I would not write them to you in this way. But, evidently he intends to give trouble in Ceylon; and he will endeavour to incite the native infidels against the native Christians.

This man is one of the Europeans who have lately put on the yellow robe. There are about half a dozen of these, most of them old sailors, who find it very convenient to be fed and clothed by the poor Burmese whom they easily make their dupes.[66]

This letter, with its references to "inciting" the natives, clearly sought to position Dhammaloka's activities as seditious. The *Catholic Messenger* joined this call, and the Ceylon Observer reprinted its remarks without comment:

Buddhists Bent on War
Notwithstanding the appeal we lately made to the Buddhist Community in the cause of peace, Dharmapala and his clique are bent upon boring Catholics. We hear that copies of a supplement to the Buddhist paper known as [*Sinhala*] "*Bouddhaya*" patronised by Dharmapala himself in which several villainous and blasphemous speech[es] of U Dhammaloka are reproduced are being circulated over Colombo. How is this going to end?[67]

The *Messenger* repeated the allegation of sedition, reporting that the police were making their presence known:

> Dhammaloka Dogged by Police
> We learn from the local press that the Irish Bonze, who goes about abusing Christianity and preaching "sedition" is being accompanied by an Inspector and two Constables told off to watch his movements. Is not this a great shame for the Buddhists of Colombo who got this strange individual out of Burma?[68]

Other newspapers continued the reports that Dhammaloka was being followed by the police:

> The Irish Buddhist Priest arrived here yesterday and met the Buddhists in the Buddhist English Schoolroom. Inspector Collett, specially deputed by the police, travelled at the same time from Colombo and watched proceedings.[69]

Not only the regular police kept Dhammaloka under surveillance. The Galle government agent Charles Lushington mentioned in his diary for September 17 that he was keeping an eye on the "Irish Priest."[70] Other public officials also got in on the act:

> **(October) 6th Wednesday**
> *There were the station house officer and the post master taking notes of the Irish priest's lecture. He spoke for 2 hours; then I started and when I began to attack the renegades and the traitors, both of them quietly sneaked out.*[71]

These interlopers were evidently interested in Dhammaloka rather than Dharmapala. But not every official saw Dhammaloka as a problem:

> Moratuwa resident Criminal investigator, Mr. Karunatilaka praised [Dhammaloka's] lecture and said people should try to reap the benefits from it.[72]

The Tour's Unexpected End

Just when Dharmapala thought he had sorted out Dhammaloka's complaints, the tour suddenly fell apart:

> **(November) 5th Friday**
> *U.D. came to see me and said that he has to leave Ceylon this evening and that on no account he could prolong his stay. This is bad for he had promised to go to*

Neboda and the poor people had twice made arrangements to receive him. The Irish nature manifests itself most unexpectedly. Had he only finished the course as promised all would have been pleased. He arrived in Colombo on the 29th August last [27th according to earlier entries] *and has worked unceasingly for the welfare of Buddhism. But the end is a tragedy. Dhammaloka priest left for India this afternoon. We paid him Rs. 50/- and Dr. Perera 50/-.*

Writing the next day, *Sinhala Bauddhaya* put the best face possible on events:

European reverend U Dhammaloka who arrived in Colombo on the invitation of the Maha Bodhi Society's founder Mr. Anagarika Dharmapala on the 27th of August travelled with Mr. Dharmapala and Mr. Harishchandra in Colombo and the regions and conducted public lectures on the falsity of Christianity and truth of Buddhism with clarity. In the meantime, due to important reasons, the reverend left the island on the evening of Friday the 5th of this month. . . . The ability to come to the midst of a large crowd and speak the truth like a war hero is one of the reverend's natural qualities. We know that we have not benefited this much from anyone who has been giving anti-Christian lectures in recent times. It is praiseworthy that, in this short time, the reverend travelled to rural parts of the island and spoke until late, sacrificing his sleep. Bhikkhus from our country should learn from the reverend and act in the same way. . . . Though he had accepted invitations to conduct lectures in places like Ratnapura, he had to abandon them as he had to leave the country due to an important need.

Devout persons like reverend Dhammaloka are a true rarity in the world. Unlike padres who act out of their selfish interests, reverend Dhammaloka tired himself out to promote the *sasana* [Buddhism] and the stupid Christians who inappropriately accused him like a dog barking at a mountain did nothing more than tarnish their own conscience.[73]

Dharmapala wrote a similar piece in the same edition:

Reverend U Dhammaloka and Public Lectures
Thousands of Buddhists in places like Neboda, Balapitiya, Ratnapura, and Matale were preparing to listen to the priest's lectures. He could not grace these places as he had to leave Colombo in a hurry. He could not give his body comfort as he was tiring himself day in day out to give lectures. Buddhists in Neboda, Ratnapura and Matale should not defile their minds about [his] inability to conduct [planned] lectures and remember that all things are uncertain.[74]

The intelligence and police surveillance may have prompted Dhammaloka to leave, amid rumors of sedition charges. His departure took place on the day the Ceylon Legislative Council reportedly passed a bill "providing that open air preachers vilifying other people's religion were liable to imprisonment," a new law seemingly aimed squarely at Dhammaloka.[75] His opponents were certainly happy to see him go. The *Observer* exulted in Dhammaloka's sudden departure:

The Irish "Buddhist Priest"—A Hurried Departure from Ceylon
The curtain has at last fallen on the scene of activity selected by the Irish "Buddhist Priest" Collin (*alias* Upasaka Dhammaloka) for a furtherance of his blasphemous and virulent opposition to all religions outside the pale of Buddhism. His advent in Ceylon was hailed with a great degree of enthusiasm by only a section of the local Buddhists; but the attitude he adopted in proclaiming his mission soon attracted the attention of the Police and he was practically under their surveillance during his brief stay in Ceylon. It is an open secret that the Police even ventured so far as to seek the assistance of a short hand reporter to take down *verbatim* his "lectures." Dhammaloka has doubtless the keenness of perception to realise that his stay, perilous as it was, would be short-lived, and he made a most unceremonious exit yesterday when he sailed by the Tuticorin steamer and was seen off by a few of his "admirers"—and the Police. While in Colombo, he proposed writing a book on the "Convent and Confessional"—and it is no breach of faith to mention this fact—his idea being to throw out to the public another outrageous volume that would eclipse even the repulsive and abhorrent book entitled "The Credentials of Christianity."[76]

Missing the final few lectures did not lessen the impact of the tour as a whole. Dhammaloka had spent more than two months in Ceylon attracting huge crowds to hear forty-eight impassioned speeches in support of Anagarika Dharmapala's modernizing Buddhist cause. Little wonder that the colonial establishment was relieved to see him depart.

If Dhammaloka's premature departure offended his allies, this was not irreparable. As we have seen, Dharmapala and *Sinhala Bauddhaya* smoothed over supporters' concerns, and the paper serialized two of Dhammaloka's sermons over three later issues. A year later, when Dharmapala, back in Calcutta, was proposing a Maha Bodhi–organized "Pan Buddhistic Congress," he listed national Buddhist organizations that would field inquiries. On this list were modernist Buddhist luminaries including Paul Carus of Illinois, the Hon. Secretary of the Buddhist Society of Great Britain and Ireland, Sakurai Gicho in Tokyo, and Prince Vivit Varnapreeja in Bangkok. In Burma—with more addressees than anywhere except India—the names included the Society for Promoting Buddhism, Rangoon, Ananda Metteyya's International Buddhist Society, the distinguished Hindu-Buddhist U Ohn Ghine—and "The President, Buddhist Tract Society, Tavoy Kyoung, Godwin Road, Rangoon," namely Dhammaloka.[77] In the following year, Dhammaloka and Dharmapala were still in correspondence and apparently in accord, as Dharmapala's diaries reveal:

27 March 1911
The <u>Hindu</u> of Feb: 14 had my letter against Theosophy. There is also the letter of Dhammaloka giving extracts of my private letter to him. There can be no union with occultists.

Dhammaloka's Ceylon tour had been highly eventful, contested internally (within Anagarika Dharmapala's circles) as well as externally (colonial and Christian media, counter-lectures, police and other authorities), and it was physically and emotionally demanding. Probably much the same could be said of Dhammaloka's activities elsewhere, if we had this level of documentation from independent sources. As it is, the variety of recorded perspectives on this tour offers an unparalleled insight into the daily realities of organizing contentious religious politics in early twentieth-century colonial Asia.

Events in Ceylon reveal the backstage Asian networks that enabled celebrities like Dhammaloka (or Dharmapala) to play the part they did. While the work of the Maha Bodhi Society claimed explicitly to be international, Dhammaloka's time in Ceylon reveals exactly how such work relied on concrete cross-cultural interactions and more mundane and plebeian exchanges—ones Dhammaloka was well accustomed to from his work in the Tavoy networks through Rangoon, Penang, and Bangkok. We see Sinhalese Buddhist modernists working to bring a poor white to speak to rural and urban crowds—and publishing the results. We can see the direct ties and parallels between anti-colonial and freethought activism across Asia and as far as Spain. Movements of this nature created not just dramatic discord, but also new kinds of interconnection.

10

Dhammaloka's Last Years and a Mysterious Death

1909–12

We opened this book with Dhammaloka on trial in January 1911 for sedition. This chapter returns to the courtroom, setting events not only in religious context, but in a wider drama of colonial power and subaltern political organizing. We see Dhammaloka at the center of multiple encounters between different ethnic networks and social movement activities in a moment of political crisis. We then explore the mysterious events that follow.

There are few records of Dhammaloka's activities in 1909 after his precipitate departure from Ceylon. He went to India for "a short visit," but we have no records of dates or places.[1] Letters from Dhammaloka to the freethinking US newspaper *Blue Grass Blade* were published in December 1909, and he was evidently building the work of the Buddhist Tract Society (BTS). The BTS published several pamphlets in 1909 and 1910, and Dhammaloka was probably in Rangoon overseeing the process.

By February 1910, a hostile Christian article "Buddhism on the Warpath" complained that the "Buddhist Tract Society is sending out its books and leaflets by the millions" and went on to describe the thriving BTS bookstall at the Shwedagon Pagoda.[2]

Confrontation in Moulmein

In October 1910, Dhammaloka traveled to the bustling urban port of Moulmein. Moulmein was north of Tavoy, on the same shipping routes. A British colonial capital before 1852, the city had since grown in prominence and prosperity. It was home to numerous Christian missions, including the American Baptists, an Anglican Society for the Promotion of the Gospel, and the large St. Patrick's Catholic school and brotherhood. At the same time, a burgeoning Burmese and Mon middle class had made Moulmein an important center of modern Buddhist

The Irish Buddhist. Alicia Turner, Laurence Cox, and Brian Bocking, Oxford University Press (2020) © Alicia Turner, Laurence Cox and Brian Bocking.
DOI: 10.1093/oso/9780190073084.001.0001

organizing activities with the first Buddhist associations and the first independent Buddhist school founded there in 1899. By 1910 the town could boast three English-language Buddhist schools.[3]

October was not a traditional time of year for a preaching tour, and it seems Dhammaloka had come especially to Moulmein to give a series of three lectures on Saturday October 29, Tuesday November 1, and Saturday November 5. Their content was nothing unusual, simply his standard strident warnings to Burmese Buddhists about the threat of Christianity, and a recitation of the freethinking critique of Christian beliefs typical of his BTS publications. As always, he attracted large and appreciative audiences, but on these three nights there were others less friendly in attendance, including on November 5 a shorthand writer sent by Christian missionaries to record Dhammaloka's words *verbatim*.

Three days later Dhammaloka received this summons:

> In the Court of the District Magistrate of Amherst.
> Criminal Miscellaneous Case No. 71 of 1910, to U Damaloka [*sic*] alias Colvin resident of Peygyaung, Moulmein. Whereas it has been made to appear to me that you (1) U Damaloka alias Colvin, should be called upon to show cause why you should not furnish security for your good behaviour. You are hereby required to attend in person at the Court of the District Magistrate of Amherst on the 18th day of November 1910 at 10 o'clock to show cause in accordance with the annexed order (2), Given under my hand and the Seal of the Court this 8th day of November 1910.
> E. N. DRURY
> District Magistrate, Amherst[4]

The charges rested on complaints brought by two missionaries, one Anglican and the other American Baptist.[5] Dhammaloka indirectly names the Baptist, while indicating the degree of religious tension in Moulmein:[6]

> It seems to be a strange irony of fate that twenty inhabitants of the institute for the blind in the town of Moulmein, as soon as I was charged, sent a petition to the police magistrate accusing pastor H. Darrow, the director of the said institution, of cruelty, immorality and other misdeeds against the poor blind people. Pastor H. Darrow is a missionary, sent by the American Baptist church.[7]

The district magistrate should have sought government sanction before deciding these "preventive" charges against Dhammaloka were worthy of prosecution.[8] Such cases were understood as politically sensitive, and Dhammaloka had been making much the same public speeches for years. Why bring him to court only now?

Colonial officials would have been aware that in the previous year he had been on an autumn speaking tour of Ceylon, organized by the most celebrated Buddhist campaigner of the day, Anagarika Dharmapala. In Ceylon, Dhammaloka's vehement denunciations of Christianity, delivered to appreciative crowds of thousands, had generated widespread controversy and attracted the attention of the police and government. British officials observed some of these talks, and the police hired a stenographer to take notes, so it is likely that charges were being prepared with a view to arresting Dhammaloka in Ceylon.[9]

Perhaps Moulmein Christians simply acted against Dhammaloka for their own purposes, but it may also be significant that Dhammaloka had demonstrated in his 1909 Ceylon tour that he could incite anti-Christian feeling in Ceylon with impunity by retreating to his safe Burmese base. Did the authorities in Ceylon perhaps demand of those in Burma that something be done about this disruptive, border-hopping monk? As usual with Dhammaloka, the three Moulmein talks attracted an audience of thousands, so the colonial authorities had good reason to be nervous of his influence.

When Dhammaloka appeared to answer the summons on Friday November 18, he was "accompanied by a large number of Phongyis and his numerous Buddhist admirers." His case was promptly adjourned until the 23rd, probably because of the scale of popular mobilization.[10] As the radical newspaper *United Burma* noted of the 23rd,

> From early in the morning, the town hall was full to bursting of curious people, but most were disappointed in their hopes of getting good seats, because soldiers and civilian police were stationed everywhere.[11]

Writing to the American freethinking *Truth Seeker*, Dhammaloka was dismissive of his missionary foes, while identifying the British attempt to silence him as part of a wider international malaise:

> If the missionaries alone had power, they would doubtless do with me as the clerical Spanish government did on 13 October 1909 with the great and noble martyr Francesc Ferrer [the executed anarchist educator mentioned in Chapter 9].[12]

The magistrate's decision to proceed with charges reflected the unequal balance of power in the colonial context. As Dhammaloka's Western freethinking supporters commented:

> In this case, the accusers have wealth and religious influence on their side as well as a press that does not sympathize with the natives. On the other side

are strength in numbers, justice and it seems not a little learning. But they are poor.[13]

Why so much popular support for Dhammaloka? It was not just that he was a revered monk. The Indian newspaper *Amrita Bazar Patrika* explained that

[d]uring 1901 and 1902, Mr. U Dhammaloka started an agitation against the practice of European Government officials keeping Burmese women without having been legally married to them. As the reader is aware, Lord Curzon in 1902 issued instructions to the Government of Burmah, to require all officials who had formed such matrimonial alliances to at once go through the ceremony under the Christian Marriage Act and, in case of refusal, to require them to resign. This reform had much to do with the agitation set up by Mr. U Dhammaloka. He also took up for agitation another matter of public grievance, namely, inadequate payment or non-payment for articles taken from villagers for the table of officials on tour in the interior. He brought the case of the aggrieved before Lord Curzon with the result that officials were enjoined to make out a monthly report of the amount of food supplied by each village or house, which, they had to get certified by the headmen of the villages they travelled in. So one can see that U Dhammaloka is above the ordinary run of mankind and no wonder that his case has caused more than ordinary interest.[14]

Officials abandoning a "native wife" and children on returning to Britain, or touring officials appropriating food and supplies without payment, aroused strong feelings. In 1904 Dhammaloka had intervened in Singapore to prevent a "Eurasian Buddhist priest" from selling two Burmese boys to a Manila pearlfishing boat for $1,500 each.[15] When we also recall his naming-and-shaming of members of the Rangoon establishment over the kidnapping of a Japanese woman and his successful campaigns against corrupt Singapore officials, we can get a sense of why he attracted so much popular support—and why colonial officials might see him as a potentially dangerous figure, to be handled carefully.

Dhammaloka's defense of Buddhism against missionaries spoke not just to his multiethnic plebeian base but to the elite of the Burmese Buddhist reformers of the day. Even for this police court hearing, he was represented, as later in the Rangoon Chief Court, by the well-known Burmese barrister U Chit Hlaing. Chit Hlaing was the son of a prominent Moulmein family; his father had helped create the Buddhist association and school in 1899. In 1895, aged twenty, Chit Hlaing had left Burma for England to study for the bar, returning in 1902 as a lawyer, in time to help establish the Moulmein Young Men's Buddhist Association (YMBA) in 1906.

U Chit Hlaing would become one of the most famous Burmese figures of the early twentieth century. By 1914 he was leading the YMBA in resisting the British, and by 1920 he was part of the politicized group forming the General Council of Burmese Associations. He ultimately became a nationalist hero and one of the most recognizable names in Burma, earning him a substantial intelligence file in the British archives. He practiced little as a lawyer, focusing mainly on politics, but here, before the start of his nationalist career, he put his legal credentials to work in aid of Dhammaloka.[16]

In the Moulmein magistrate's court, the prosecution produced five witnesses to Dhammaloka's lecture. These witnesses testified for two hours, before Chit Hlaing and the prosecutor made closing statements. The magistrate, having heard the evidence, issued his ruling the following day: Dhammaloka was "convicted and bound over to keep the peace for one year"[17] on two sureties of Rs. 1,000 each.[18] In other words, if he fell short of the court's idea of "good behavior" at any time these substantial sums (approximately US$10,000 each in today's money) provided by supporters would be forfeited to the court.

Word of the trial soon spread across Burma and India.[19] It was clear, however, that this was not the end of the story; Dhammaloka was resolved to appeal against the order. The radical *United Burma* newspaper chose its words carefully:

> We do not intend to make this case the subject of any commentaries, but we would encourage the people of Burma to give U Dhammaloka all the moral and pecuniary support they can, in order to overturn the judgement of the Moulmein police magistrate if possible. This police magistrate interprets paragraph 108 CPC in his own way. Hundreds of Christians have preached and published blasphemous books, pamphlets and leaflets about non-Christian religions, but in all these years no-one has yet been arrested or bound over.[20]

A lengthy letter from "Buddhist *dayakas*" (patrons or sponsors) in defense of "our esteemed brother U Dhammaloka, Buddhist Phongyee" accompanied the article, citing the names of prominent international freethinkers. Its Moulmein correspondent added:

> The Buddhists in Moulmein are very embittered. They are considering collecting a defence fund in order to submit the case for trial in the highest court. It was well known what the police court's judgement would be. The newspapers in Moulmein have barely mentioned the trial. I cannot understand their silence. The judgement is a slap in the face for every Buddhist in the province, and what the consequences will be is not so easy to predict. However, the Christian missionaries' propaganda in this part of Burma has now been rendered impossible for the next fifty years.[21]

In this politicized context, Chit Hlaing immediately ordered a complete transcript of the proceedings and applied to the Chief Court in Rangoon for an appeal.[22]

Why the Rangoon Appeal Mattered

The nearly three months between his sentencing in Moulmein and the appeal hearing in Rangoon offered time for Dhammaloka and his supporters to mobilize for action. If he could attract a crowd of monks and Buddhist laypeople at a few days' notice in distant Moulmein, the response was much greater—and involved more than just Burmese Buddhists—in his home base of Rangoon. Dhammaloka had repeatedly warned the Burmese that the British were a threat to their religion, and here was that threat to religion—potentially to any non-Christian religion—made manifest, with the full might of the British Crown coming down on one brave Buddhist monk who dared to speak out in defense of Buddhism.

The victimization of Dhammaloka was consequently not just a Buddhist issue. "This case," said the Indian papers, "is creating a great sensation amongst not only the Burmese community whom it principally concerns but also among the general public."[23] Why? Because in cosmopolitan and multi-religious Rangoon, as the census later that year would show, 56.4 percent of Rangoon's population was Indian, particularly laborers in this colonial port.[24] In other words, well over half the general public in the early 1900s was neither Buddhist nor Burmese. If the British were prepared to silence Dhammaloka, a much-loved Burmese-ordained Buddhist, where would this repression of religion stop? The forthcoming case was enough to make the colonial authorities very nervous indeed.

United Burma, which skirted contempt of court in its call to contribute to Dhammaloka's defense fund, was no ordinary Rangoon newspaper. Its proprietor, Dr. Pranjivan Mehta, was a close collaborator of Gandhi. In 1908 Mehta had founded the Burma branch of the Indian National Congress,[25] and in 1909 Gandhi wrote *Hind Swaraj*, articulating his strategy for independence, for Mehta.[26] *United Burma* was thus associated with the radical wing of the Indian nationalist movement. Its readership was relatively small (by 1910 over 700) but highly politicized. Mehta was well known as a public advocate on behalf of Rangoon's Indian population. *United Burma* and its readership were happy to ally with Burmese Buddhists against the colonial power.

Even in embryo, such an alliance was significant.[27] By 1920, Mehta would work with Chit Hlaing to link then-moderate Burmese nationalism and the Indian National Congress; the connection between these two was made around the Dhammaloka trial. Later in the 1920s Mehta would organize Rangoon dock workers into trade unions. All this was some years in the future, but Mehta was already a figure of concern to the authorities.[28] This alliance stood behind Dhammaloka who even in 1901 was already "very popular with both the Buddhists and Hindus of Rangoon."[29]

The forthcoming Chief Court hearing thus brought together the as yet unorganized power of Rangoon's multiethnic poor, the visible development of Burmese Buddhist nationalism, and popular support for Dhammaloka's challenge to the everyday injustices of colonialism. If we ask why Dhammaloka was targeted more determinedly in 1910–11 than in 1900–1, when the authorities had backed off over the shoe question, the answer probably lies in the widening threat to colonial power in British India.

In 1905 the British had partitioned Bengal into a broadly Hindu west and Muslim east, to weaken Bengali support for nationalism. In this case, divide and rule backfired. Partition boosted "Swadeshi and boycott," the strategy of boycotting British goods and buying Indian-made to hasten independence. The 1907 "Surat split" divided moderates and radicals in the Indian National Congress over these tactics: Gandhi and Mehta supported Swadeshi. A government report said that Mehta's *United Burma* newspaper was "[a]n ardent advocate of Swadeshi and boycott; hence needs watching."[30] Indian radicals including Lala Lajpat Rai were exiled without trial to Mandalay, enabling *United Burma* to make use of this Indian cause on its own doorstep.[31]

The Surat split enabled increased government repression of the radicals, including the banning of seditious meetings in 1907, increased censorship in 1908 and 1910, and a general trend toward coercive measures.[32] The attempt to suppress Dhammaloka fit this trend. In fact, his case would be used as legal precedent in later repression of Indian nationalists. The combustible combination of a popular campaigner, Buddhist nationalism, Indian dock workers, and Indian National Congress radicals would be enough to make the authorities cautious. They needed to defeat Dhammaloka in court, but could not afford to make a martyr of someone who so clearly fit the part.

In 1910–14 the metropolitan and imperial center, the UK, was also itself wobbling. The 1910 parliamentary election saw Irish nationalist MPs holding the balance of power and promises of Home Rule. "Black Friday" saw police violence and sexual assaults on suffragettes. The "Great Labour Unrest" of 1910–14 had already seen troops deployed and a striking miner killed; railway workers joined the strike, an international dock strike was threatened, and a warship deployed.

In this context, instability and repression were in the air. While the sorts of connections represented by Dhammaloka were only a shadow of the alliances that would defeat empire in Ireland and later in Asia, strategic authorities could hardly ignore them: Irish, Indian, and Sinhalese nationalism; dock workers in Liverpool and Rangoon. In this context, Dhammaloka as beachcombing Irish bhikkhu (and ex-dock worker), and his many connections and networks, held a dangerous potential.

Supporting Dhammaloka

Burmese, Indians, and Chinese all rallied to Dhammaloka's side and created a defense fund. On January 5 and 6, 1911, "good offices of the proprietors of the Edison Bioscope stationed at the corner of Godwin and Canal Streets" donated takings from the new motion picture cinema, a technology invented only ten years previously.[33] The proprietors likely knew Dhammaloka well—their cinema adjoined the Thayettaw monastic complex housing Dhammaloka's Tavoy monastery, which appears on the map of downtown Rangoon (Map 10.1) adjacent to the new general hospital and the jail. The multiethnic community of the surrounding Chinatown sprang to support Dhammaloka, as did much of the rest of the city.

Dhammaloka's appeal in the Chief Court before Justice Twomey was initially scheduled for Friday, January 13. The newly completed Chief Courthouse (see Figure 10.1; it still stands today) overlooked Fytche Square, the colonial park,

Figure 10.1. The newly built Chief Court of Burma on Fytche Square, Rangoon, about 1910—the venue for Dhammaloka's January 1911 hearing before Judge Twomey. Color postcard, probably by D. A. Ahuja.
From the New York Public Library, digitalcollections.nypl.org/ Image ID 4044351.

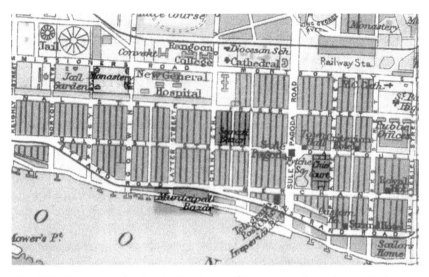

Map 10.1. Support in the streets: Street map of Rangoon in the early twentieth century, edited to highlight the breadth of public support for Dhammaloka during the hearing: the Tavoy monastery on Godwin road in Chinatown/Lanmawdaw, the Municipal Bazar, the Surati Bazar, and the Chief Court building on Fytche Square.
© Source: John Murray Co. London. *A Handbook for Travellers in India, Burma and Ceylon* (1924).

faced by the Sule Pagoda, the central Buddhist edifice, and by the Rangoon Town Hall, the central symbol of colonial authority.

That day,

> The Burmese stall-keepers of the Iron Bazar in Lanmawdaw, Suratee Burra Bazar and the Strand Municipal Bazar closed down their stalls and wended their way to the Chief Court to witness how their popular Irish priest was to be tried.[34]

From Chinatown (Lanmdawdaw/Godwin Road) in the west to the Indian quarters, down to the riverfront, all native commerce ground to a halt that day.

> There was a big crowd of spectators of all grades blocking the Court, and the yellow robe of the Burmese Phongyee was everywhere in evidence. . . . The Fytche Square gave scant accommodation to the people that poured in from all directions.[35]

Dhammaloka's supporters reflected his wide appeal. He had made himself a friend not just to Burmese Buddhists, but to the plebeian population of Indians,

Chinese, sailors, soldiers, and beachcombers, and not just those from the cosmopolitan city of Rangoon, but across the colonial province and much of Southeast Asia. That day they turned out to return the friendship.

> U Dhammaloka himself was parked in the street in a gaily decorated landau drawn by men women and children amidst great applause. That is an ovation which is very rarely accorded even to the most distinguished men . . . .[36]

Dhammaloka had been greeted as a hero on his preaching tours to the small towns and villages of Burma, but here the urban capital carried him along in a fashion reserved for royalty and the most senior monks on their way to prestigious rituals.

The public display of support and the background concerns we have sketched out evidently had an impact. Like the Moulmein trial, the hearing was postponed until January 20.[37] And thus the stage was set for the confrontation between Buddhist monk and colonial judge that began this book.

Sentence Is Passed

Following the trial, judgement was deferred in turn until January 31. Judge Daniel Twomey backed the Crown lawyer Rutledge to the hilt, dismissing all Chit Hlaing's arguments and observing that a statement "may be highly inflammatory when translated into an Oriental language and served out with spicy comments to an audience of Orientals in a public address."[38] Twomey was almost certainly correct in his interpretation of the intention of the law. His arguments held sway—and indeed the record of this case survives partly because it set a precedent for interpreting this section of the Penal Code in sedition trials against Indian nationalists.

Twomey's judgment epitomizes the mounting concerns felt by the colonial authorities around issues of race, education, language, and the transgressive power of popular religion. Summing up, he observed that

> in estimating the intention and probable effect of such utterances it is proper to consider not only the personality of the speaker but the circumstances in which he spoke. The majority of the audience were presumably uneducated persons with no means of checking the extravagant statements that were made. They would be the more inclined to believe them as the speaker was by birth a European and presumably a Christian. . . . The lurid picture of horrors done in the name of Christianity and the attacks on Christian ministers as a class

were, in my opinion, calculated to excite ill-feeling in the minds of such audience towards Christians in general. From the tone and spirit of the speeches there can be little doubt that this result was contemplated by the speaker. . . . This appears to be the language of spleen rather than that of true missionary ardour.[39]

Dhammaloka had hit a nerve. He was European, by Twomey's standards also "uneducated," but nevertheless a powerful orator and an effective campaigner. Yet, reading Twomey's lament, what seems to have given offense above all is that Dhammaloka lacked an English sense of fair play in matters of religion. Dhammaloka really *did* intend the Burmese to rise up and reject Christianity. Appeal dismissed!

Twomey's decision seems not to have succeeded in clipping Dhammaloka's wings. Reflecting on the case shortly afterward, Dhammaloka wrote to an old friend in Calcutta:

My case has exercised a great stir in Burma, but my reputation has not suffered in the least by the prosecution. It in fact has given me a big boost in the eyes of the Burmese people, and Buddhists in general.[40]

Fleeing the Country?

Yet, after all the publicity surrounding Dhammaloka's case, Twomey's rejection of the appeal seems to have had at least one of its desired effects. While Dhammaloka held that the charge of sedition had boosted his popularity, which was clearly true, for the rest of 1911 the public record is silent on Dhammaloka's activities. Then, on February 1, 1912, exactly a year and a day after Twomey's judgement, Dhammaloka quietly left Rangoon for Singapore, where on February 8 he boarded the passenger steamer SS *Charon*, bound for the west coast of Australia. The *Charon* dropped off many of its passengers, British, Japanese, and Malay, at pioneer Australian gold rush or pearl-diving settlements scattered along the northwest coast. At Fremantle, the seaport for Perth, Dhammaloka disembarked after sixteen days at sea. He had sailed as a paying passenger with no companion. The Fremantle immigration report lists him as "Mr. Dhammaloka," nationality "British" and occupation "Priest (Buddist)" [*sic*].[41] Clearly, he was not traveling *incognito*.

Dhammaloka would spend ten days in Perth before the next leg of his voyage. Disembarking as a European Buddhist monk, where might he go to find food and shelter? Among Europeans, those most likely to warm to a European Buddhist visitor were the members of the well-established Theosophical Society lodge in Perth.[42] Among Asians, of the 154 individuals in Perth identified as "Buddhist" in the previous year's census, most would have been migrant workers from China, Japan, and Ceylon.[43] Or, as a temperance campaigner, Dhammaloka may have contacted one of the three local IOGT lodges.[44] Perhaps one of Perth's many "coffee palaces" (temperance hotels) took him in.

On Tuesday, March 5, 1912, Dhammaloka boarded another and far larger vessel, the Orient Line's 1,200-passenger RMS *Otranto*, for the voyage to Melbourne, then Australia's capital. Thus it was that U Dhammaloka arrived at Melbourne on Tuesday, March 12, 1912, in some style.

The Sad Death of Dhammaloka

Within two days, an extraordinary letter was posted to the *Englishman* newspaper in Calcutta.

> Dear Sir,
> Would you kindly publish in your paper an account of the death of a European Buddhist Monk that had resided in this hotel for the last few months or so. I am informed by people here that he belongs to the same religion as the people of Ceylon and that they are called Buddhists or some other curious name. We are not able to find any clue to his friends, if he has any, and perhaps by a small paragraph in your paper they may be able to know of his death in the Melbourne General Hospital, from beri-beri. He gave his name here as U Dhammaloka, or something similar. Perhaps I have not spelled it right, but that is how it was registered on the hotel register. The agents of the Orient Steam Ship Co. are willing to carry his boxes back to Ceylon, provided we can get in communication with any of his friends or relations. He seemed to be a strange character, as he wore a peculiar garb made of yellow cotton, and he would not wear any shoes, which I think was the cause of his death.
> Trusting that I am not intruding upon your time and space.
> —I remain, yours faithfully,
> John Larkins, Proprietor, Melbourne, Australia.
> Neale's Temperance Hotel, Lonsdale and Queen Streets, Melbourne, March 14th.[45]

This letter reporting the death of a well-beloved character was a hoax, and an effective one. It can only have been written by Dhammaloka himself, newly arrived from Perth. There was indeed a temperance hotel on the corner of Lonsdale and Queen Streets (see Figure 10.2). Its official name was "Tankard's Temperance

Figure 10.2. Sober travelers only: Tankard's Temperance Hotel (left center), at the corner of Queen and Lonsdale Streets, Melbourne, about 1880. By 1912 the hotel was known locally as Neale's.
State Library, Victoria.

Hotel" after its original owner, but by 1912 it was owned by a Mrs. C. E. Neale. An aging two-story brick building, it was "convenient for the tram stop, the law courts, various government buildings and the telephone exchange."[46] There was no "Melbourne General Hospital" in 1912, nor a hotel proprietor called John Larkins, though the name might strike a chord with anyone familiar with Irish politics; Jim Larkin (1876–1947) was well known for organizing Irish dock workers, and would shortly lead the trade unions in the momentous "Dublin Lockout" of 1913.[47]

The letter from Melbourne appeared in the Calcutta *Englishman* on April 11 in an article with the (comprehensively misleading) title "From Catholic Priest to Buddhist Monk—DEATH OF DHAMMALOKA—The Story of a Strange Character." The article included a substantial obituary of Dhammaloka by an unnamed Calcutta "correspondent" who had met Dhammaloka about ten years before in Singapore, when Dhammaloka was establishing the school there, and who had attended the 1904 novice ordination of Dharmatrata described in Chapter 6. The writer, who described Dhammaloka as "a terror to evildoers," fond of hounding corrupt officials, was well aware of Dhammaloka's adventures in Ceylon and Burma, including the recent court case. The two had met most recently the previous year in Calcutta, where Dhammaloka "created a stir one evening at the Eden Gardens when, clad in his yellow robes, hatless and shoeless, he unassumingly and quietly wended his way among the throng that had assembled to listen to the music."[48]

The *Englishman*'s report prompted further obituaries well beyond India. Few were flattering, but as an indication of just how well-known Dhammaloka's name had become, news of his death from beri-beri in Melbourne was reported as far afield as Los Angeles[49] and London.[50] The *Singapore Free Press and Mercantile Advertiser*, reporting the Calcutta *Englishman* story, added its own note of veracity in recalling that Dhammaloka had looked "very grey and worn out" when he passed through Singapore a few weeks earlier.[51]

When Dhammaloka reappeared in Singapore a couple of months later, we find only one brief retraction of the report of his death, in the same Singapore newspaper that had described him as "grey and worn out." Dhammaloka's visit to their offices encouraged the paper to report that he was now "in the best of health."[52]

Back in March, as the letter from "John Larkins" was wending its way to Calcutta, Dhammaloka left Melbourne for his next destination, the city of Brisbane, several more days' voyage up the eastern coast of Australia. By his own account, Dhammaloka was in Brisbane on Easter Monday, April 8, 1912. He later said he had attended a special reception of the Queensland Grand Lodge meeting of the IOGT. We have only his word that he was at this major temperance event, but he had an entrée into temperance circles, and he very probably was there, invited or not.[53] Dhammaloka may have hoped to be reunited in Brisbane with the wealthy Irish-Australian Theosophist Letitia Jephson, who had supported him in Japan a decade earlier and had talked of establishing a Brisbane branch of the IYMBA (see Chapter 4). If so, he was disappointed, for Jephson had died in 1908.[54]

A Visit to Thursday Island?

For the six-week period between April 8 when Dhammaloka was in Brisbane, and May 22 when, back in Fremantle, he embarked on the *Charon*'s sister ship *Minderoo* to return to Singapore, we have found no evidence of Dhammaloka's activities. We can speculate that he spent perhaps three to four weeks traveling somewhere beyond Brisbane. His most likely destination would be Thursday Island, a tiny island in the Torres Strait in the far north of Queensland. He was somehow familiar with Thursday Island: back in December 1904, the local *Torres Straits Pilot* newspaper had announced that

[w]e are requested by J. M. Dohertson, Secretary of Buddhist Missions, Singapore, to mention that the Revd. Lord Abbot U Dhammaloka will arrive at Thursday Island in about a month or so, with the object of opening up a

Buddhist mission "for the propagation of the sublime doctrine of Buddha." We are told that the Rev. U Dhammaloka is an Irishman by birth, and has been at Thursday Island before, so that he is no stranger to the place, and, as the laws prevent the entrance of Asiatics into the country, it has been deemed desirable to send his reverence.[55]

In the late nineteenth century, Thursday Island had developed a significant pearl-diving industry relying on large numbers of Japanese and Sinhalese workers. By 1900 there were 3,600 Japanese on the island, with a Buddhist cemetery and an annual *Obonmatsuri* ancestors lantern festival. Sinhalese Buddhists had lived on Thursday Island since at least 1876; by the 1890s they numbered around 500. A temple was constructed, with two bodhi tree saplings. Maybe Dhammaloka was the Buddhist monk who, a Sinhalese Thursday Islander born in 1888 recalled, had visited the island around the turn of the century.[56]

The larger context of this economic activity by white settlers in the Torres Straits area involved the ongoing massacre, abuse, and starvation of thousands of indigenous Torres Straits islanders and Aboriginal people of northern Australia.[57] By the early 1900s, the "White Australia" policy also prevented Asians from traveling between Thursday Island and the rest of Australia. While Dhammaloka had signaled his intention of visiting the island in 1904, he had not made the journey then. Perhaps he had been there in some capacity in his pre-monastic days (he claimed in 1902 to have been a mining engineer in Australia).

Though gone from Australia once he had embarked on the *Minderoo* at Fremantle, Dhammaloka was not forgotten, at least not by the Australian police, for on June 27 the *Victoria Police Gazette* published the following notice in its "Missing Friends" section

> WILLIAM COLVIN, *alias* W. Damaloka, is inquired for by the Deputy general of Police, for Railways, Criminal Investigation, Burma, India. Description:— About 42 years of age, 5 feet 5 inches high, small grey eyes, grey hair, clean shaven, slightly stooped, speaks quickly; wears a yellow robe. He left Burma for Australia on the 1st February, 1912. —O.4282A. 14th June, 1912.[58]

This early Interpol notice was in vain, for by this time Dhammaloka (older than 42) was back in Singapore and resuming his former activities.

Why Did Dhammaloka Come to Australia?

So much for Dhammaloka's itinerary and untimely death. We know he liked to travel, but the question remains, *why* Australia? And, having arrived there, why send a false report of his own death to a major Calcutta newspaper? As with so much of Dhammaloka's life, we have only fragments of information, of varying reliability, to provide clues. On this uncertain basis we can offer two possible answers, though neither may be correct.

One is that he was reconnoitering a first "mission to the West," in rehearsal for a visit to America. In this scenario, Dhammaloka traveled to Australia to discover what reception awaited a European Buddhist monk in a "European" country. Australia in 1912 was a British dominion, but unlike other British colonial possessions such as Burma, India, Ceylon, and the Straits Settlements where the Irish Buddhist had won the hearts of the majority Asian population, Australia's populace was overwhelmingly European.[59] The notorious "White Australia" policy, intended to strengthen white settler colonial identity, was introduced from 1901 onward, and by the time of Dhammaloka's visit, race-based immigration restriction laws were in place.

The declared motive for this openly racist policy was fear of competition. Alfred Deakin, three times prime minister between 1903 and 1910 and the architect of the "White Australia" policy, had been a keen Theosophist with a high regard for "Eastern" culture but a closed vision of Australia as a "white" nation.[60] He believed that Asian immigrants to Australia, being more highly skilled, energetic, and motivated than whites, would, if unchecked, come to dominate trade and industry and thus threaten the privileged position of the Europeans.

In "White Australia," then, being a European certainly helped Dhammaloka when it came to immigration and travel, but wearing the Buddhist robe conferred no benefits. Immediately on his return from Australia, Dhammaloka told a Singapore newspaper that "he had proposed visiting America, but postponed his trip owing to the presidential election and other unforseen [sic] difficulties."[61] Maybe Dhammaloka really did believe that America could not cope with a presidential election and his own advent at the same time, but more likely he had learned from his Australian trip that in America, whose governing white immigrant population was similarly bent on restricting Asian immigration,[62] Dhammaloka's position as a white Buddhist monk would carry no advantage at all.[63]

On the Run?

A second possible answer to the question "why Australia?" is that, as suggested by the notice in the *Victoria Police Gazette*, Dhammaloka was on the run from the police in Burma and, like many another fugitive from colonial justice in those times, he had fled to the vastness of Australia. The false report of his own death, then, was intended to put the police off his trail.

For some reason it was the Burma Railway Police who were eager to lay their hands on Dhammaloka. A likely explanation is that, following the 1910 Indian Press Act, the Burma Railway Police had been empowered to search for seditious literature "in the custody of the Post Office," which included mail trains. In Burma, Dhammaloka may have been hindered by the court's 1911 order from speaking in public for the following twelve months, but he may nevertheless have continued to circulate his ideas via tracts and other writings. In December 1910 he told a freethinking correspondent that a plan "some months" old to change the name of the Buddhist Tract Society to "Burma Freethought Association" had now been implemented, as evidenced by new headed stationery. This may have been an attempt to circumvent the Press Act.[64]

Having been bound over on January 31, 1911 for a year, against monetary sureties, to desist from any "seditious" activities, he probably knew that the police would look for a reason to re-arrest him on February 1, 1912, the minute he was free again. If any of his publications found on the mail trains during the 1911–12 period when he was bound over seemed seditious, this could be construed as breaching the terms of the existing order. This would mean the forfeiture of his supporters' sureties and a further period of constraint, and possibly jail. In the wider context of intensifying repression primarily shaped by the radicalization of Indian nationalism, he may also have felt that the longer-term outcome would not be determined by the local balance of forces in his favor and that he could easily be an incidental casualty of a broader wave of repression. Discretion might be the better part of valor.

The idea of a Dhammaloka on the run is plausible, but only up to a point. For one thing, he seems to have bought a return steamer ticket. And if he wanted to disappear, he could easily have traveled to (or at least within) Australia under a European name and in civilian clothes. He could have used an alias. Yet he sailed on both the *Charon* and *Otranto* as Rev. Dhammaloka, Buddhist priest, so he was making no effort to pass unnoticed. Quite the reverse: the Victoria police probably thought it would not take much asking around to find a European who "wears a yellow robe."

And if he was intent on disappearing, why did he return, and so soon? Back in Asia he was instantly recognizable, and practically Dhammaloka's first act on disembarking was to march into the offices of the *Singapore Advertiser* to tell the world that he was alive—and this under the very noses of the colonial police whose Rangoon colleagues were ostensibly pursuing him under a criminal investigation.

Either Dhammaloka was not in fear of arrest by this point, or conceivably he wanted to be arrested again, to give his career a further boost. Either way, no arrest happened, and the Burma police pursued their inquiries no further. However, we have no further record of Dhammaloka returning to Burma after

1912, so perhaps the Rangoon authorities were simply trying to make it difficult for him to operate in Burma and it was enough for them that he stayed away; they may even have preferred this to having an imprisoned "martyr" on their hands.

The faked death letter from Melbourne seems to offer evidence for the "on the run" theory. It is a classic ruse to put pursuers off one's scent and hopefully have the police file closed for good. But Dhammaloka came back, and even announced his return. So if the letter was not meant to put the police off his trail, then why send it? Was it done just as a joke—"for the craic," as the Irish say? The letter could have caused Mrs. Neale back in Melbourne some real problems if one or more enterprising individuals had taken up the offer of Dhammaloka's belongings via free return, courtesy of the Orient Line. Maybe Dhammaloka went to the hotel anticipating free board and accommodation from a temperance-supporting proprietor with an Irish-sounding name, was turned away, and this was his ingenious revenge?

Perhaps a better clue to his intention in writing the hoax letter lies in the final sentence of the obituary written by the Calcutta *Englishman*'s correspondent, who knew Dhammaloka both in private and in public. While the obituary largely praises Dhammaloka's virtues, the last sentence reads: "Withal, he was an egoist R.I.P." Maybe Dhammaloka, like most of us, was curious to know what others would say about him after he was dead. Unlike most of us, being Dhammaloka, he decided not to wait until it was too late.

Why Dhammaloka Matters

This is not (quite) the end of the story. But before saying farewell to Dhammaloka, why should his many lives—as sailor and hobo, in Burma and Japan, Singapore and Siam, Ceylon and Australia—matter, more than a century later? Here we want to bring out three possible answers: his unexpected personal consistency, the challenge of making a new world, and his plebeian cosmopolitanism.

Personal Consistency

Many readers may wonder, as we did when we first began to research him, how sincere Dhammaloka really was—or even how much of a Buddhist he was. He clearly made up stories about himself, he used pseudonyms, and he attacked his opponents, though only ever verbally, in a far from monk-like way. Yet what

Dhammaloka achieved as a pioneering European Buddhist monk was by any standards remarkable. He was innovative, inventive, unorthodox, and unpredictable. He played fast and loose with Buddhist tradition at times and to some extent made it up as he went along. He was always far more than "just" a monk. Yet we did find some constant and clearly deeply held values that underpinned his words and actions.

Dhammaloka certainly displayed a convert's zeal. He seldom had anything bad to confess about himself as a monk, but he admitted to Harry Franck that in his pre-Buddhist life he had been a drunk and a drifter who cursed and fought his way across the world.[65] It was through Buddhism that he had overcome his old habits and become a new man. Training as a monk had been for Dhammaloka a transformative and liberating experience, after a life which he now saw as chaotic and aimless. Of course we should take converts' starkly contrasting "before" and "after" narratives with a pinch of salt. Whatever his shortcomings in his earlier life, he had obviously acquired skills and experiences that proved useful after 1900. These included a seaman's knowledge of Asian geography and shipping routes, organizing and speaking skills perhaps learned from political activism, and the know-how and confidence to exploit the press to his own advantage. He used these skills after he became a monk, in the service of a number of strongly held principles and values.

One of these values was temperance. Campaigning against the evils of alcohol was not just an aspect of Dhammaloka's Buddhism; he was willing to call a truce even with Christians in the cause of temperance. The movement's broadly Christian but non-sectarian ethos gave organizers the latitude to invite temperance campaigners—even controversial ones—to address a temperance audience, as Dhammaloka did in Singapore in February 1903. In Bangkok, he joined forces with the Anglican Canon Greenstock to open a temperance club.[66] In Japan in 1902, Dhammaloka's attacks on Christianity had been pointedly ignored by the Japanese press, while "Dhammaloka's lectures on temperance were, however, reported and favorably commented upon."[67]

Temperance was institutionalized in associations like the IOGT and its lodges across the world, as well as numerous temperance hotels and bars (Tankard's is only one of several similar establishments visible in the photograph in Figure 10.2). The movement constituted a public, political, and global "war on drink" which sought to mobilize the authorities as well as ordinary people to eradicate the alcohol trade. IOGT lodges indulged in a fair amount of public rivalry and included their fair share of grandstanders, con artists, hypocrites, and secret drinkers—according to hostile accounts of lodges in Burma and elsewhere. While not slow to criticize lodges he found wanting, Dhammaloka was a sincere and consistent ally of the movement. Arriving in Melbourne in 1912, he evidently headed for the temperance hotel, and in Brisbane he attended the annual IOGT Grand Lodge meeting.[68] As a monk in Burma, Dhammaloka would never be offered alcohol. Speaking to the *Nipon* newspaper, he compared Burmese monks with the priests he encountered in Japan, saying:

> I have been a monk for ten years, but I have not even once heard, not even a rumor, that monks of the turmeric color have their hands on alcohol. But after I have come to Japan, I hear Japanese monks drink alcohol (sake), so I am astonished very much. . . . Even in Japan, Buddhist teachings do not say we should drink alcohol, they say it is bad to drink, but they are exceedingly corrupt. I am extremely surprised to know that even though these rules exist, monks have arbitrarily made up their own rules [. . .] Lay people of Japan are far purer. I can therefore live with lay people. . . . I have lived together with monks, but it was a monk who once encouraged me to drink whisky.[69]

A second principle was Buddhist monastic discipline, whether alms-collecting (see Figure 10.3 for a particularly modern take on this) or eating one meal a day, a code of conduct which, as far as we know, Dhammaloka adhered to willingly from the time of his ordination until the day he died, while other Europeans of the period, including Ananda Metteyya, joined and then left the order within a few months or years. Admittedly, Dhammaloka bent the rules at

Figure 10.3. Buddhism and modernity: Phongyis [monks] in a tram car going out collecting alms, Rangoon. Color postcard by D. A. Ahuja, ca. 1910.
© Collection of Sharman Minus.

times, for example wearing his black Japanese priestly robe—reportedly with a Good Templar-style collar, and over a white suit, and boots—though only outside Burma. Within the country, he was scrupulous in conforming to people's expectations of a monk. His public addresses, delivered in an energetic and declamatory style hitherto unknown in the Burmese sangha, were unusual, but went down very well with his Burmese audiences. The British may have charged him with sedition, but even they did not accuse him of being un-Buddhist. He believed in the power of argument, but as a monk, and a humanitarian, he opposed any kind of physical violence. Contemplating a trip through China, where Christian missionaries had been murdered, Dhammaloka explained he would "advocate tolerance to Christianity, and will ask the Buddhist priests to counsel the people not to attack Christian missions or to murder native and foreign Christians."[70]

A third was Dhammaloka's commitment to root out corruption, especially among those holding public office. We have seen numerous examples, including his reportedly persuading the Viceroy that British-Burmese sexual relationships should be regularized by marriage and that food requisitioned from villages by government officials should be duly receipted and paid for; his exposure of corrupt officials, and saving two boys from being sold into slavery. In Japan in 1902, the Indian secretary of the Japan & India Club in Tokyo described how, during his time in Japan, Dhammaloka had campaigned fearlessly to expose the moral failings of Japanese Buddhist priests. His (premature) obituarist in the Calcutta *Englishman* of April 1912 recorded that

> Dhammaloka was, indeed, a terror to evil-doers, and many have been the sensational exposures that he has been instrumental in effecting. He always kept in touch with the highest officials, and, through information acquired and supplied by him, the malpractices of many unscrupulous men have been laid bare and condign punishment meted out to the offenders.[71]

Finally, education was dear to Dhammaloka's heart. In his *Nipon* interviews he explained how Burmese monasteries provided free education, contributing to Burma's high literacy level, and to Franck he recounted that he had taught in the Tavoy monastery before becoming a "bishop" and starting his travels. In Bangkok and the Straits Settlements, he worked to establish free schools welcoming pupils of every background, and we find him presiding at the opening of a Tamil school in Rangoon. He was no doubt keenly aware of the deficiencies in his own education. However, we know that he read widely, that he spoke well, and that he circumvented his limited writing skills by making effective use of secretaries and amanuenses. Dhammaloka evidently believed that learning English as a *lingua franca* and studying modern subjects while (at least in the case of Buddhist children) adhering to Buddhist values was the best gateway for youngsters in Asia to employment, scientific knowledge, and rational thought.

In each of these areas, Dhammaloka probably appreciated their value because he had experienced their absence. In forty-five years of living hand-to-mouth around the world, he had seen the effect of alcohol on himself and on others. Before becoming a Buddhist and entering the path to happiness, he had led an undisciplined and aimless life. As a drifter, he must often have suffered injustice and humiliation at the hands of corrupt officials. In Dublin as a child he had received an unsatisfactory education before having to make his way in the world, and as a result he was vulnerable to the sneers of better-educated but morally questionable characters.

Clearly, too, these values formed a personal basis for his solidarity—alcohol symbolized the cultural destruction of traditional Asian ways of being under colonialism, while the figure of the monk represented an ideal Buddhist way of life. Corruption could stand for the reality of colonial rule as experienced by the poor and powerless, while education could offer a way forward for young Asians—as indeed it would for the generation that would make the new postcolonial states.

Inventing the Modern World

A reader might also ask: but weren't Dhammaloka's efforts ultimately failures? As we have seen, Dhammaloka was in part forgotten because he did not serve as a founding figure for later organizations. This of course was true for most of his contemporaries. In fact we may need to pay *more* attention to failure in understanding pan-Asian and globalizing Buddhism: just as most monks disrobe, most Buddhist organizations do not survive for long.[72] Too often the history of religions is told in terms of what succeeded, but what worked is often only a small part of what was tried. Something can be learned from efforts made in vain, from the organizations that did not last, and from the experience of failure as well as the rarer moments of success.[73]

Dhammaloka's life shows him wrestling with the questions "how can we organize internationally?" and "what does a Buddhism for the modern world look like?" Like his contemporaries, Dhammaloka was often making it up as he went along. With hindsight, we can have reasonably accurate expectations of what a successful global Buddhist organization might look like, but this is largely because of the trials and errors of Dhammaloka and others. For example, it seemed entirely reasonable for Buddhist revivalists to follow the apparently successful "modern" model of Christianity. Hence the Young Men's *Buddhist* Association, the Society for the Promotion of *Buddhism*, the *Buddhist* Tract Society, and so on. Both Christians and Buddhists in the early 1900s believed in the effectiveness of preaching, tracts, and polemics.

Ananda Metteyya pursued a different strategy from Dhammaloka, but his missionizing efforts had little more purchase in the long run, and he is remembered largely because the Buddhist Society of Great Britain and Ireland was later absorbed by London's Buddhist Society as the latter emancipated itself from British Theosophy.

So, too, with Dhammaloka's organizing strategies: the standard strategy of ordaining monks proved of limited effectiveness.[74] Constructing schools, publishing tracts, the preaching tour, newspaper polemics—all had their value, but consistently fell short of their intended goals. We could say that Dhammaloka and his contemporaries had to "fail" to pave the way for today's more effective global Buddhist organizations. Perhaps no matter what he did, the conditions were simply not ripe for his efforts to have a greater impact.

However, it was not only Buddhists who were struggling to understand cross-national organizing. None of the founders of Theosophy expected their own movement to have the immense impact it did on cultural change in the West and political organizing in Asia—or that its syncretic *religious* strength would wane precisely as it gave birth to religion-specific successor organizations, from Dharmapala's Maha Bodhi Society to the London Buddhist Society.

The temperance organizations would remain an effective networking tool (and a good way to find a host in a new city) for some decades to come, but their goal of universal temperance remained determinedly out of reach. In the political realm, the Second (socialist) International, then bringing together most of the world's left parties, enjoyed massive organizational strength in 1913, yet its working-class member organizations would, virtually without exception, capitulate to the war between empires and capitalists that they had sworn to resist as late as summer 1914.

Transnational organizing in Dhammaloka's time certainly meant embracing what the new times offered. We see Dhammaloka on steamships and railways, writing to telegraph-fed newspapers and working with cheap printing, corresponding with Buddhist and freethought journals abroad, moving through a world of congresses and conferences, forming and joining organizations structured by branches and periodicals, being photographed and interviewed, exploiting his "celebrity" to meet the expectations of the Burmese monks who had ordained him. But, then as now, the existence of new technological or organizational possibilities was no guarantee of their effectiveness.

Nor was the post-imperial future easy to imagine.[75] In Dhammaloka's lifetime, most of the atlas was marked by the colors of a handful of European empires.

246 THE IRISH BUDDHIST

Asia, where more than half the human race lived, and lives, was dominated by the British, French, Dutch, Ottoman, and Russian empires. Within a quarter-century of Dhammaloka's death, the first three would crumble in the face of Japanese expansion, and yield up their colonial possessions more or less rapidly after World War II.

After the Russian Revolution of 1917 and Irish independence in the 1920s, it would be increasingly clear—not least to nationalist elites educated under the colonial powers—that the future was one of independent nation-states with a developmentalist orientation. This had not been obvious a few years previously, even to those who ardently longed to see an end to empire. This fact reminds us that a world of ethnically defined nation-states was not the only possible future for post-colonial Asia, and helps explain some of the complexities and contradictions of Dhammaloka's own practice.

Pan-Asian Buddhist revival, like pan-Islamic organizing, imagined a different kind of future, in some ways perhaps more similar to the multinational empires it was seeking to displace. With no caliphate to look back to, and millenarianism largely confined to single-country perspectives, Buddhist revivalist imaginings were necessarily vague, where such a future could even be imagined. The image of Japan as Buddhist "big brother," or of India as the home of Buddhism, enabled some intellectuals in these regional centers to envision themselves as playing a leading role in a future Buddhist Asia; while Dharmapala's Bodh Gaya–centric vision has found a limited reality in its role today as a pan-Buddhist pilgrimage center, albeit with monasteries and temples largely divided by nationality.

In Dhammaloka's international activism—pitched as it was against the image of a globe ruled by "the Bible, the bottle, and the Gatling gun"—we do not find a concrete imagining of a post-colonial Asia. But the development of a global Buddhism as a different kind of present—like the everyday internationalism of freethinkers, temperance activists, or Theosophists—involved an organizational practice that felt like a possible universal future. Its shaping by immediate, practical realities and the looseness of its wider vision both indicate just how hard it was to imagine that future, in the last few years before the collapse of the German, Austro-Hungarian, Ottoman, and Russian empires and the appearance of the Irish Free State as the first successor state to the British empire since 1776.

Asian decolonization would be one of the largest social movement outcomes of the twentieth century. The difficulty of imagining that process—and the multiplicity of earlier visions of the future—may be worth recalling today, when we are trying to imagine pathways to an ecologically sustainable world not structured around runaway carbon consumption.

A Plebeian Cosmopolitanism

Lastly, a reader might ask, what about race? Are we not just celebrating another white hero—and were his politics not simply another kind of exclusivist racism, which is too often seen in Buddhist communities today?

Dhammaloka's life lets us see not only his own vision of Buddhist modernity and the intersection of movements in the twentieth century: it also offers a window into networks and interconnections between social worlds that rarely come to light in histories of colonialism. With a few exceptions, his world was not the literary, intellectual, or middle-class life usually associated with the Buddhist revival. Instead, his associates included sailors, traders, villagers, and laborers, Asians and Europeans.

His story keeps reminding us that despite the way colonials viewed themselves and wrote their histories, Europeans were often not the agents of change in Asia, but at times the "front men" or even stage props for Asian initiators. At their best moments they were recognized as allies and accomplices in Asian movements. Ironically, writing the history of a European man in Asia helps us use what sources survive to shed some light on the agency of local networks everywhere Dhammaloka traveled.

His life also demonstrates the lie behind stories that empires told to construct and maintain their power—the idea of a radical gulf between colonizer and colonized, the myth of racial difference, or the belief in solidarity based on race or religion. Barefoot, bareheaded, in Asian clothes and begging, he embodied a disruption of such hierarchies, while the "shoe controversy" explicitly challenged them.

The story of an Irish Buddhist monk agitating against Christianity and, through it, colonialism draws attention to the fault lines of class and nation in Europe that lay hidden behind the colonial project, as well as to the possibility of radical solidarity between Asians and Europeans fostered by Buddhism, or by common cause in any number of other fronts: education, anti-alcohol, anti-corruption, freethought, anti-colonialism.[76]

Dhammaloka was connected to an eclectic range of patrons, friends, sponsors, and supporters. These links share a common theme of disregarding and devaluing exactly those divisions which colonial and contemporary discourse alike presume to be fundamental elements of human identity. Of course, Dhammaloka himself breached colonial and racial difference, but repeatedly in his work and interactions we see those around him equally indifferent to supposed distinctions of ethnicity, culture, and religion.

From the moment of his ordination sponsored by a Chinese businessman, Dhammaloka seems surrounded by people who find concepts of strict religious and ethnic identity irrelevant to their purposes and their daily lives. Perhaps

ironically for a religious figure whose main weapon in the fight against colonialism was championing Buddhism, even the supposed unbreachable and fundamental factor of religious identity seems to matter little to Dhammaloka and his
allies (so long as you weren't a Christian missionary). From Chinese supporters
via a Hindu social club to the "stout Punjabees" who accompanied him, ethnic
and religious difference do not seem to matter much to the people around
Dhammaloka, or to define the scope of their affiliations or actions in the ways in
which those reporting on them in these terms presumed they should.

Dhammaloka's travels and projects reveal networks between Asians that are
deeply eclectic in their backgrounds and trajectories (from a Burmese gem merchant, via a Shan saopha trying to reinvent Buddhist kingship, a Singaporean
Chinese intellectual trying to invent Confucian modernity, or a Chinese doctor
in Penang crusading against opium, to a Singaporean opium baron family, and
so forth).

The Tavoy network of monasteries from Rangoon to Bangkok to Penang,
too, reflects not just the well-known story of how ethnic networks enable mobility in Southeast Asia. Within the Tavoy "family" of monasteries, affiliation
could be based as much on an attitude toward inclusion as on an ethnic or regional identity, defined by their hospitable attitude to all comers at a polyglot
and multicultural crossroads. The Rangoon Tavoy monastery was as much
defined by the black sailor who turned up looking for a bed as by the Chinese
sponsor at Dhammaloka's ordination or any Tavoyan monks who welcomed and
accommodated them.

Moreover, Dhammaloka's massive popular appeal, whether in port cities or
small towns and villages, points to how widespread this attitude of indifference
to ethnic, racial, and religious difference seems to have been. Dhammaloka was
welcomed often not because he was an oddity, but because he was "one of us"—
he could hold his bowl correctly on alms rounds and navigate the plebeian side of
an urban port with ease, but more than this, he shared the view that differences
in identity were not fundamental or important, and he performed this on a
daily basis.

As we have seen, the bazaars of Rangoon closed to support him; Indians,
Chinese, and Burmese came out in his defense. This does not mean that
Dhammaloka or his friends and supporters were color blind: to the contrary, he
seems particularly attuned to the ways in which constructions of difference were
drawn into the violent service of colonialism, poverty, and exclusion—and he
was popular for his opposition to blatant injustice.

This natural disregarding of difference is all the more remarkable, given
how Dhammaloka drew attention to religion as a divider, but also how the
movements that followed later from the work that he and his collaborators did
coalesced so swiftly around particularly rigid ideas of identity—the imagining

and construction of national identity and the increasing conflation of religion, nation, and ethnicity.

In an earlier draft we considered titling this conclusion "Plying between Worlds." This metaphor seems a good one on which to end—or almost end—our story. As a sailor, Dhammaloka plied his way in the sense of sailing and navigating. But he also plied between worlds in the sense of braiding and connecting, bringing together the things which both the earlier world of empires and the later world of nation-states, in their different ways, have sought to keep apart.

Epitaph

When last seen, in June 1912, Dhammaloka was in a Singapore newspaper office disavowing reports of his death. This is one of the last things we know about him. He claimed that he would stay in Singapore only a few days before proceeding to Penang. Having left Ceylon in November 1909 under a cloud after his tour with Dharmapala, and following his conviction for sedition in Burma in 1910–11, Dhammaloka seems to have chosen to return from Australia not to Burma but to the other centers in Southeast Asia that had welcomed him in 1903–5: first Singapore, then Penang, and soon enough Bangkok. His assertion in Singapore that he was "in the best of health" perhaps foreshadowed troubles to come. The next report we have of him a few weeks later, on July 4, 1912, records that he is "an inmate of the District Hospital, Penang."[1] Ill health may once again have put a substantial damper on his activities and travels, as it did in Burma in early 1907 when he spent months in the Rangoon General Hospital.

There are no reports during 1912 of any activities of the schools or missions he had founded in these places, but he must have had sufficient well-wishers to welcome him back to his old haunts. At the end of October 1912, he was once more on the move, the *Singapore Free Press* reporting that

[t]he Rev. Dhammaloka, the Irish Buddhist priest who was on a visit to Ipoh, left for Penang by the mail train yesterday, en route to Bangkok.[2]

Ipoh had been included in Dhammaloka's last tour of the Federated Malay States (now Malaysia) in 1905, when we also lost track of his whereabouts for a year and a half. This could easily be explained by the lack of newspapers preserved from that area, or perhaps he had a lower public profile there. However, in late 1912 he was traveling again. A week after the report of his leaving Ipoh, it was reported in Singapore that

[t]he Rev. U Dhammaloka, the Irish Buddhist monk, arrived [here] from Penang yesterday by the "Klang" and is proceeding to Bangkok where he will probably make a long stay.[3]

The Irish Buddhist. Alicia Turner, Laurence Cox, and Brian Bocking, Oxford University Press (2020)
© Alicia Turner, Laurence Cox and Brian Bocking.
DOI: 10.1093/oso/9780190073084.001.0001

This was November 6, 1912. He was in Singapore only for a brief stopover to change ships for Bangkok. For all we know, back in Bangkok, Dhammaloka may have rejoined Wat Ban Thawai and the work of the school he founded. The school has survived to the present day, but has no record of his time there. In the newspapers we have been able to search in Bangkok there are no reports of his activities during 1912 or 1913, so whatever he did, it cannot have gained the same public attention as in 1903.

It seems that he did revive some of his previous zeal for founding organizations during this time. A 1914 book on the state of Buddhism in Burma, based on a survey of Christian missionaries, specifically asked the missionaries about the Burmese people's opinion of European Buddhist monks. The emphasis is largely on the missionaries' own negative opinions of Dhammaloka. However, the editor added in square brackets, "It is interesting to note that though a notice of his death appeared in Burma he is very much alive in Siam as President of the Buddhist Free Thought Association."[4] Presumably this refers to 1912 reports of the death in Melbourne. There are no other records of this freethought association, but it is consistent with the rhetoric of the Buddhist Tract Society, renamed "Burma Freethought Association," that Dhammaloka promoted before his trial.

On October 18, 1913, almost a year after Dhammaloka left Singapore for Bangkok, a lone report appears in the Singapore *Weekly Sun*:

> The Rev. U. Dhammaloka has returned to Singapore after a stay of several months in Cambodia, where he was the guest of the King and delivered a series of dissertations. He is staying at present with Mr. B. P. de Silva and his friends will like to hear that he is looking well.[5]

The account is tantalizing in the few but remarkable details it offers. It seems to be a return to the Dhammaloka of nearly a decade earlier—the hubristic recounting to Harry Franck of pioneer missions to Buddhist kingdoms (first Lhasa, then Nepal, now Cambodia) with a warm welcome by royalty and popular fame and respect for Dhammaloka's wisdom. Given what we know of his missions to Singapore, Bangkok, and Penang, it would be tempting to fill in the outlines of this Cambodia report with visions of Dhammaloka preaching against Christianity, opening a school or a mission, and rallying local Buddhists to his cause. And it is easy to see a return of the Captain Daylight persona—the self-promoter, unburdened by modesty and convinced of the unquestioned support of Buddhist elites. Unfortunately, we have not found any contemporary records from Cambodia to confirm or disprove this tale. It stands in historical limbo—plausibly true, but equally plausibly an exaggerated wish-fulfilling dream, like Dhammaloka's tall stories of Tibet and Nepal.

But this short report also brings Dhammaloka back to familiar and well-known spaces that we can cross-check in the archives: to Singapore, the site of some of his greatest early successes and to the home of émigré Sinhalese jeweler B. P. de Silva—the faithful Maha Bodhi supporter who provided Dhammaloka with an address and connections in his early days in the city. It ends, however, with another reference to Dhammaloka's good health, suggesting that his friends had reason to be concerned.

There is one further fragmentary report, also from mid-October 1913, this time indicating an encounter of some kind between Dhammaloka and the indefatigable campaigner Anagarika Dharmapala. Dharmapala, sailing from Singapore to Bangkok, wrote on October 14, "U Dhammaloka intends visiting Ceylon next month."[6] On the 16th, Dharmapala's diaries show him

> [a]t Penang. I did not go ashore as I had no idea of the whereabouts of the Sinhalese. I spent the whole day on board. Wrote a few letters. I am sorry to hear that Prince Jinawaravongsa[7] has reverted to his old immoral ways. U Dhammaloka told me that he is indulging in intoxicating liquor. I wrote to the Prince to go back to Ceylon.[8]

Two days later, the Singapore *Weekly Sun* carried the report that Dhammaloka had just returned to Singapore from Cambodia. Dharmapala and Dhammaloka's paths had presumably crossed in Singapore. In any case, it is clear that their relations had been repaired after the challenging Ceylon tour of 1909. De Silva in Singapore was an obvious connection to both: he had funded Dhammaloka's school in Singapore, and had been mentioned in Dharmapala's diaries as early as 1889, when de Silva had been president of the Singapore branch of the Theosophical Society, and Olcott and Dharmapala visited him there en route for Japan.

Dhammaloka's Last Days

Dhammaloka's stay with de Silva in Singapore is our last sighting of the Irish Buddhist. If he did travel to Ceylon, we have found no record of it, and after October 1913, the trail finally goes cold. Having so deftly documented his fake death from beri-beri in a Melbourne hotel, ensuring that news of it would spread around the world, there is no report anywhere of Dhammaloka's actual death. Perhaps the illness that put him in hospital in Penang in July 1912 eventually proved fatal—hence the October 1913 reference to his health. On the principle of "once bitten, twice shy," newspapers may have been reluctant to publish a second obituary of someone they had already pronounced dead—even if they had something new to say. A death off the beaten track (or where newspapers have not survived or have not yet been digitized) might also explain the silence around his demise.

We could, of course, equally imagine Dhammaloka robustly continuing his work in Southeast Asia for years to come, albeit with a diminished profile as newspaper attention turned after 1914 to the spreading World War. Perhaps he died quietly, sometime after the outbreak of war, in a remote monastery. Given the choice, Dhammaloka would almost certainly have lived out his days in Asia. As he told Franck in 1905: "'Twas hard, the first months, eating nothing but curry and rice. Now, bless you, I'd not eat European food if 'twas set down before me."

But with Dhammaloka we can never know. Perhaps the colonial authorities did eventually come after him, and this finally pushed him to change his identity again—in which case, as the rest of his life attests, he could have finished up anywhere in the world: in Australia's radical underworld, or masquerading as the Catholic priest he was sometimes mistaken for. He might even have returned to Dublin, or Liverpool, or San Francisco, to live out his last days.

Unless new discoveries are made, Dhammaloka's ending is one for each reader to write differently, in keeping with the interpretation of his life that seems most convincing. In death, as in life, Dhammaloka continues to challenge and charm us in equal measure.

The Irish Buddhist: Timeline

Year		See Chapter(s)
Before 1900	Dhammaloka's first 40-odd years of life (under one or several names) before emerging as a monk and public figure in Rangoon. Born in Dublin (possibly Booterstown Avenue, Blackrock), crossed America as an itinerant worker (probably), became a trans-Pacific sailor (probably), lived and worked in Australia (possibly), may have been political radical / alcoholic / Salvation Army officer, worked his way to South Asia, lived in Ceylon, then Burma, and found Buddhism sometime between 1880 and 1900.	1
1900	July: Full (Upasampada) ordination in Rangoon. The first Western Buddhist monk?	2
	Circulates English-Burmese pamphlet "Buddhists of Burmah!" throughout Burma.	
	October: Warns missionaries not to distribute Christian literature at the Shwedagon Pagoda.	
	December: First tour to Toungoo and Mandalay; meets the Society for Promoting Buddhism.	
1901	January: Dispute with fellow temperance campaigners in Rangoon.	2, 3
	February–March: Preaching tour of South/ Southeast Burma. Wins debate with a Christian missionary.	
	March–July: "Shoe controversy" and Shwedagon pagoda confrontations in Rangoon. Police involvement.	
	December: Interviewed for a *Harper's Magazine* article at the novice ordination of an Englishman.	

Year		See Chapter(s)
1902	January–March: To Mandalay again after the Viceroy's visit. Addresses crowds of thousands in tour of Upper Burma.	2, 4
	Two surviving photographs taken in Mandalay and Rangoon.	
	April–May: Multiple invitations from throughout Burma and preaching visits.	
	July: Departs unexpectedly for Japan.	
	August: Arrives in Japan.	
	September–December: Appears at IYMBA launch and other gatherings, lengthy newspaper interviews.	
1903	January–February: Returns via Kobe, Hong Kong, and Penang to Singapore. Sails with the ruler of Kengtung for Bangkok, proposing to visit Tibet.	5
	March: Starts a free school at Wat Bantawai.	
	June: Announces new international Buddhist conference center to be built.	
	August: Invited to Singapore by Chinese philanthropists. Establishes a successful school for poor Chinese boys and the English Buddhist Mission, on Havelock Road.	
1904	March: Singapore; starts publishing Buddhist literature.	5, 6
	April: Organizes innovative New Year's celebrations involving different Buddhist communities.	
	May–June: Sends two Europeans from Singapore to Burma for ordination.	
	October: Performs his first ordination.	

Year		See Chapter(s)
1905	January: Singapore *Straits Times* editor Edward Morphy denounces Dhammaloka as a "fraud."	5, 7
	February–April: Travels extensively in India and/or Nepal.	
	May: Tells the story of his life and trip to Lhasa to "vagabond writer" Harry Franck.	
	June–October: Travels to Penang and other parts of the Malay States, fundraising for Buddhist schools/missions.	
1906	No reports discovered for this year.	
1907	Spring: Ill in hospital and convalescing, 3–4 months.	8
	June: Says work restricted to temperance movement.	
	October: Launch of Buddhist Tract Society, publishing atheist, Buddhist, and radical texts.	
	November: Trip to Mandalay.	
1908	January: Mandalay; disrupts annual meeting of American Baptists.	8
	February–March: Successful reprise of 1901 and 1902 tours of Upper Burma, attracting thousands at every stop.	
	Buddhist Tract Society (BTS) sets up several branches, is increasingly active up to 1910, and attracts international attention.	
1909	August–November: Wide-ranging tour of Ceylon with Anagarika Dharmapala.	9
	November: Leaves Ceylon suddenly.	
1910	BTS work continues with several publications; Dhammaloka probably in Burma.	10
	October: Visits Moulmein, gives talks, and is charged by the local magistrate with sedition.	
	November: Tried and sentenced in Moulmein.	

Year		See Chapter(s)
1911	January: Appeal in the Rangoon High Court against the Moulmein magistrate's sentence. Huge crowds gather in support.	1, 10
	No reports of his activities for the rest of 1911.	
1912 onward	1 February: Leaves Burma, sails via Singapore for Australia, visiting Perth, Melbourne, Brisbane, and possibly Thursday island.	10, Epitaph
	News of his death in Australia prompts obituaries in India, UK, and USA. Various final sightings of Dhammaloka add to the mystery.	

Glossary

Amherst British name for the colonial administrative region containing Moulmein

anagarika lit. "homeless one," Buddhist celibate

beachcomber European in Asia living from casual labor, begging, often ex-sailors

bhikkhu, bikkhu, bhikshu, bikshu Buddhist monk

Bodh Gaya place of the Buddha's enlightenment in Bihar, India

bodhisattva vows vows to become a Buddha for the sake of all beings

bonze Buddhist priest or monk (Japan)

brahmacharya lay celibate

Buddham saranam gacchami "I go for refuge to the Buddha"; the first of the "three refuges" (along with the Dhamma and the Sangha) invoked by Buddhists

Dana generosity, donations

dana generosity, donations

Dhamma the Buddha's teaching, truth, or law

Fenians radical Irish nationalists in Ireland (Irish Republican Brotherhood), the US and elsewhere

Fourierism a form of utopian socialism

freethinker, freethought synonymous with "atheism" in the 1900s; more broadly, one who rejects conventional or revealed (religious) truth and seeks social progress through reason and logic

gaungbaung headscarf (Burma)

Gautama Sakyamuni, the historical Buddha

Hinayana Theravada, Southeast Asian Buddhism (derogatory); see also Mahayana

kyaung, kyoung monastery (Burma)

Lanmawdaw Godwin Road, site of Tavoy monastery in Rangoon, synonymous with Chinatown

Mahayana predominant Buddhism of East Asia and Tibet; see also Hinayana, Theravada

Mohammedan common term for Muslim in the 1900s

myook town leader (Burma)

Otani branch of Japanese "True Pure Land" Buddhism; see Shinshu

Pali the sacred language of Theravada Buddhist texts

pansala monastery (Ceylon)

pansil vows to obey the five Buddhist lay precepts

phongyi (hpongyi, hpoongyee, phoongyi, etc.) Buddhist monk (Burma)

Sakyamuni Gautama, the historical Buddha

samanera, samenera Buddhist novice

sasana the dispensation, Buddhism

sangha the Buddhist monastic order

sayadaw High status monastic title, similar to chief abbot (Burma)

Shinshu Jodo Shinshu or "True Pure Land" form of Japanese Buddhism, focusing on the Buddha Amida

Sinhala, Sinhalese, Singalese, Singhalese majority language of Buddhists in Sri Lanka

swadeshi Indian nationalist strategy of producing local goods and boycotting Western products

taik monastery complex (Burma)

tathagatha the Buddha

Tavoy, Thawai, Dawai, Dawei port town in Southeast Burma, ethnic group from the town, and associated monasteries in Rangoon, Penang, and Bangkok

thathanabaing head of the Burmese royal Thudhamma monastic lineage

Thayettaw Kyaung Taik Rangoon monastery complex containing the Tavoy monastery and many others

Theosophy Founded in New York in 1875 and subsequently centered in India, Theosophy was by 1900 a global esoteric movement. Notable leaders included Helena Blavatsky, Henry Steel Olcott, and Annie Besant.

Theravada predominant Buddhism of Southeast Asia and Sri Lanka

Tripitaka the collection of Buddhist scriptures

upasaka Buddhist lay devotee

upasampada full (higher) ordination

Vesak, Wesak festival (usually April) celebrating the Buddha's enlightenment, birth, and passing

Vinaya the rules of monastic discipline

wat –monastery (Siam)

zayat monastery rest house for visitors (Burma)

Notes

Introduction

1. "The Appeal Case of U Dhammaloka," *Amrita Bazar Patrika*, January 13, 1911, 7.
2. Franck, *A Vagabond Journey*, 364; "A Pioneer Buddhist Monk," *American Theosophist & Theosophic Messenger* 14 (September 1913): 1023; "From Catholic Priest to Buddhist Monk," *Englishman*, April 11, 1912, 7; "Missing Friends," *Victoria Police Gazette*, June 20, 1912, 317.
3. "From Catholic Priest to Buddhist Monk," *Englishman*, April 11, 1912, 7.
4. Ba U, *My Burma*, 67–8.
5. Twomey, "Thathanabaing, Head of Burmese Monks in Burma." Twomey's 1904 paper in *The Imperial and Asiatic Quarterly Review* was abridged anonymously as: A Correspondent, "Burmese Buddhism and the British Raj," *Times*, October 9, 1904. Twomey was grandfather of the eminent anthropologist Prof. Mary Douglas.
6. Donogh, *History and Law of Sedition*, 165–67; Huxley, "Positivists and Buddhists: The Rise and Fall of Anglo-Burmese Ecclesiastical Law." He could have been charged under laws against insulting religion, but instead they chose this section.
7. Reported in : "En Hädelseprocess i Bortre Asien," *Forskaren [The Investigator]* 19 (January 1911): 105–9. Translation by Laurence Cox.
8. "En Hädelseprocess i Bortre Asien," *Forskaren [The Investigator]* 19 (January 1911): 105–9. Translation by Laurence Cox.
9. "Bound over" was a precautionary measure; the sureties (bonds) from his supporters would be forfeit if Dhammaloka misbehaved. *United Burma*, December 4, 1910.
10. Twomey's January 31st judgment with a summary of the arguments on both sides appeared shortly afterward in the *Criminal Law Journal of India*. Chaudhri, "Criminal Revision No. 378B of 1910."
11. Turner, "The Bible, the Bottle and the Knife."
12. Chaudhri, "Criminal Revision No. 378B of 1910."
13. Burma (6): Account of Mr Dhammaloka," Nipon, December 21, 1902, 3. We are indebted to Dr. Naoko Gunji for her detailed work in translating these interviews.
14. "Burma (6): Account of Mr Dhammaloka," Nipon, December 21, 1902, 3; "An Open Letter to U Dhammaloka," *Times of Burma*, April 10, 1901, 5; Dhammaloka, "The Open Letter," *Times of Burma*, April 13, 1901, 5.
15. Chaudhri, "Criminal Revision No. 378B of 1910," 249.
16. See Chapter 8.
17. "En Hädelseprocess i Bortre Asien," *Forskaren [The Investigator]* 19 (January 1911): 105–9. Translation by Laurence Cox.
18. "From Catholic Priest to Buddhist Monk," *Englishman*, April 11, 1912, 7.
19. Kirichenko, "Between Thathanadaw and Theravada."
20. Cotes, "The Ordination of Asoka," 753–54.

21. "The Irish Buddhist Returns," *Straits Times*, August 26, 1903, 2.

22. Kemper, *Rescued from the Nation*; Suzuki, *Selected Works of D. T. Suzuki*.

23. Braun, *The Birth of Insight*; Anne Blackburn, *Locations of Buddhism*.

24. Jaffe, "Seeking Sakyamuni: Travel and the Reconstruction of Japanese Buddhism."

25. Ober, "Like Embers Hidden in Ashes."

26. Fischer-Tiné, *Low and Licentious Europeans*.

27. Mizutani, "Historicising Whiteness."

28. Cox, "Rethinking Early Western Buddhists."

29. Amrith, *Crossing the Bay of Bengal*.

30. Mizutani, "Historicising Whiteness," 6; Fischer-Tiné, *Low and Licentious Europeans*, 4; Arnold, "European Orphans and Vagrants in India"; Fischer-Tiné, "Britain's Other Civilising Mission," 302–303.

31. Lewis, *Cities in Motion*.

32. Cox, *Buddhism and Ireland*, 113–14.

33. Ignatiev, *How the Irish Became White*.

34. Kipling, *Kim*; Croker, *Road to Mandalay*.

35. Franck, *Vagabond Journey*, 362.

36. Lopez, *Prisoners of Shangri-La*. See also: Osto, *Altered States*, chapter 3.

37. Kerouac, *The Dharma Bums*.

38. "European Ordained as Buddhist Priest," *Straits Times*, October 3, 1904, 4.

39. Braddell, Brooke, and Makepeace, *One Hundred Years of Singapore*; Dumoulin and Maraldo, *Buddhism in the Modern World*.

40. Tweed, *Crossing and Dwelling*.

41. Gandhi, *Affective Communities*; Viswanathan, *Outside the Fold*; O'Malley, *Ireland, India and Empire*.

42. Bocking, "Flagging up Buddhism"; Cox, *Buddhism and Ireland*; Deslippe, "Brooklyn Bhikkhu."

43. Franklin, *Lotus and the Lion*.

44. Dhammaloka, "A Hindu on Paine," *Blue Grass Blade* 23 (December 12, 1909): 7.

Chapter 1

1. Thompson, *Witness against the Beast*, 69.

2. Fischer-Tiné, *Low and Licentious Europeans*, 15, 20.

3. "An Irish Buddhist Priest: Discovered in the Crowded Precincts of Asakusa," *The Voice: An Independent Journal of Christian Civilization*, August 23, 1902, 1–2. We have no evidence for anything like a Buddhist church in nineteenth-century Ireland. Like many things about Dhammaloka, it makes a good tale.

4. "Solved!" *Atlanta Constitution*, July 30, 1911, B6; "Solved—the Riddle of Dama Laku 'the Wise One,' the Buddhist Abbot of Rangoon—Once an American Tramp," *San Francisco Examiner*, July 30, 1911, 56–57.

5. "A Pioneer Buddhist Monk," *American Theosophist & Theosophic Messenger* 14, (September 1913): 1023. Theosophy, founded in New York in 1875, was by 1900 (and still is) a global esoteric movement. Of its early leaders, Helena Blavatsky and

Henry Steel Olcott went to India and embraced Buddhism, particularly in Ceylon. Annie Besant, president of the Theosophical Society from 1907, became a key figure in Indian nationalist politics.

6. Cotes, "The Ordination of Asoka."

7. Cotes misnames Dhammaloka, her interviewee at the ordination of Asoka, as "Oo Dhamma-nanda." "Burma," *Homeward Mail*, January 20, 1902, 77. A colourized version of this photograph appears on the cover.

8. Fisher, *A Woman Alone in the Heart of Japan*, 201–09.

9. This Irish Research Council for the Humanities and Social Sciences–funded project identified worlds into which Dhammaloka could easily have fitted, but without locating him in any specific context. This is not surprising; he probably used aliases, and poor people simply left few traces.

10. "Solved!" *Atlanta Constitution*, July 30, 1911, B6.

11. Of course, we cannot assume that Franck's account is accurate either.

12. Franck, *A Vagabond Journey*, 361.

13. "Missing Friends," *Victoria Police Gazette*, June 20, 1912, 317; "From Catholic Priest to Buddhist Monk," *Englishman*, April 11, 1912, 7.

14. Dhammaloka is frequently referred to as English or Irish. The sole exception is at the "Opening Ceremony of the Inauguration of the International Buddhist Young Men's Federal Association," *Takanawa Gakuho [Takanawa University Gazette]* (October 5, 1902): 78–79, where he is said to be Scottish, the Irish/Scottish distinction being of little significance in Japan.

15. Morphy, "Editorial," *Straits Times*, February 19, 1905, 4. "Solved!" *Atlanta Constitution*, July 30, 1911, B6.

16. Both Franck and Cotes represent Dhammaloka speaking a (rural/emigrant) "stage Irish" typical of writings of the period, but the Dublin accent is very different from this caricature. We should not read any *local* meaning into the way Americans such as Cotes and Franck represent Dhammaloka's speech.

17. "The Irish Buddhist Returns," *Straits Times*, August 26, 1903, 2.

18. Rachel Pisani found that arrest records for San Francisco in the early 1870s, if they listed more than one name, gave an average of five aliases.

19. Fischer-Tiné, *Low and Licentious Europeans*.

20. "Missions," *Times of Burma*, February 16, 1901, 4.

21. "Dhammaloka v. Emperor."

22. "Colvin" is Scottish and indicates Northern Irish families from settler backgrounds. "William" evokes the Protestant hero William of Orange.

23. "Rev. U Dhammaloka," *Singapore Free Press and Mercantile Advertiser*, April 23, 1912, 7.

24. Franck, *A Vagabond Journey*, 364. Stage Irish adjusted.

25. "An Irish Buddhist Priest," *Catholic Advance*, October 28, 1905, 5; "Mayor Fitzgerald's Breezy Interview with Sir Thomas," *Boston Sunday Post*, December 22, 1912, 33. Notably, most of these names (Colvin, Calvin, Collin[s], Kelly, Carroll) begin with a hard "c."

26. "A Pioneer Buddhist Monk," *American Theosophist & Theosophic Messenger* 14, (September 1913): 1023.

27. Genealogist Dr. Fiona Fitzsimons confirms that this identification is as secure as can be hoped for in this period (pers. comm.).
28. Our own researches in this area were complemented by Dr. Fitzsimons's *Eneclann* genealogy researchers, Prof. Thomas Tweed (Tweed, "Toward the Study of Vernacular Intellectualism"), and our research assistant Rachel Pisani, who spent a year tracing Dhammaloka's US travels.
29. His siblings were Edmond (1845); another Laurence (1848, presumably died in infancy); Timothy (1850); Ned (c. 1850); and Hannah (1853). Catherine's name is given elsewhere as Horan or Horgan. Carroll family historian Ken Lennan pers. comm., citing DLHRC Booterstown B5, 0, 143 Baptism.
30. Family details from http://www.lennan.be/len007b.htm and http://www.lennan.be/len007c.htm and from the St. James RC parish register.
31. Family memory says that Catherine ran or owned a nursing home, perhaps in Williamstown. *Thom's Directory*; email from Ken Lennan, December 14, 2009.
32. Cox, *Buddhism and Ireland*, Chapter 3.
33. Cox, "Dhammaloka as Social Movement Organizer." Cox, *Buddhism and Ireland*, 237.
34. Email from Colm Breathnach, March 1, 2011.
35. Dun Laoghaire Genealogical Society, *Irish Genealogical Sources*, 6: Booterstown Register 6/98. Reference from Ken Lennan. Seven years of schooling left Dhammaloka writing like a child, according to Morphy in 1905. Morphy, "Editorial," *Straits Times*, February 19, 1905, 4.
36. Whelan, "The Long Shadow of the Great Hunger." *Irish Times*, September 1, 2012.
37. "Solved!" *Atlanta Constitution*, July 30, 1911, B6.
38. Tweed, "Toward the Study of Vernacular Intellectualism," 286 n 2.
39. Two Lawrence Carrolls are found in Trow's New York City directories for the period, but neither seems likely to be our man. *Trow's New York City Directory 1872/3; Trow's New York City Directory 1873/4.* Rachel Pisani suggests (pers. comm.) that he found sailing work and so does not appear in directories.
40. "Solved!" *Atlanta Constitution*, July 30, 1911, B6.
41. "Solved!" *Atlanta Constitution*, July 30, 1911, B6.
42. Avrich, *Haymarket Tragedy*, 2:17.
43. Franck, *A Vagabond Journey*, 361.
44. DePastino, *Citizen Hobo*, 17.
45. DePastino, 15.
46. DePastino, 28; Higbie, *Indispensable Outcasts*, 85.
47. DePastino, *Citizen Hobo*, 4. DePastino is one of the few scholars of hobo social history to focus on the 1870s.
48. "Solved!" *Atlanta Constitution*, July 30, 1911, B6.
49. Franck, *A Vagabond Journey*, 361. Stage Irish adjusted.
50. "Solved!" *Atlanta Constitution*, July 30, 1911, B6. Rachel Pisani found that arrests for petty larceny and assault were far more common in San Francisco in this period than those for drunkenness. However, the 1906 fire destroyed many police records.
51. Langley, *The San Francisco Directory for the year 1874*, 514.
52. A quartermaster (i.e., responsible for a watch), equivalent to 3rd mate, did not require a license so was paid less. Normally progress from ordinary seaman via able seaman

to 3rd mate took four years. Dhammaloka could not have been an ordinary sailor on a Pacific Mail ship; this role was now only available to Chinese at lower wages. Interview with Ted Rausch, San Francisco Maritime Society.

53. "Solved!" *Atlanta Constitution*, July 30, 1911, B6.
54. Franck, *A Vagabond Journey*, 362. Stage Irish adjusted.
55. If true, he was in the US until at least the *Catechism*'s publication date of 1881. The *China Mail* in 1903 told a similar tale, but set in Australia. "An Irish Buddhist: Bound for Thibet," *Japan Times*, February 13, 1903, 5.
56. "A Pioneer Buddhist Monk," *American Theosophist & Theosophic Messenger* 14 (September 1913): 1023.
57. "Burma (5): Account of Mr Dhammaloka," *Nipon*, December 19, 1902, 3.
58. "Solved!" Atlanta Constitution, July 30, 1911, B6.
59. Franck *Vagabond Journey*, 362.
60. Cotes, "The Ordination of Asoka," 754.
61. Cotes, 754. Stage Irish adjusted.
62. Franck, *A Vagabond Journey*, 273. A claim in February by Dhammaloka that he was off to Nepal may have been reported in Colombo. The Nepalese regime at the time was famously averse to modernist Buddhists, and Dhammaloka was likely traveling in India instead. Bocking, "U Dhammaloka The Irish Pongyi (1856–1914) in India, Nepal and Tibet."
63. Dhammaloka subsequently told Harry Franck he had just spent three months in Nepal.
64. "Burma (3): Account of Mr Dhammaloka," *Nipon*, December 17, 1902, 3.
65. "Burma (1): Account of Mr Dhammaloka," *Nipon*, December 14, 1902, 3.
66. "Solved!" *Atlanta Constitution*, July 30, 1911, B6. The *Dhammapada* is a well-known scripture.
67. Cotes, "The Ordination of Asoka," 753.
68. "Burma (2): Account of Mr Dhammaloka," *Nipon*, December 16, 1902, 3. The interpreter for the interviews was the then-Unitarian Hirai Kinza.
69. Franck, *A Vagabond Journey*; "Solved!" *Atlanta Constitution*, July 30, 1911, B6; "Solved—the Riddle of Dama Laku 'the Wise One,' the Buddhist Abbot of Rangoon—Once an American Tramp," *San Francisco Examiner*, July 30, 1911, 56–57; "A Pioneer Buddhist Monk," *American Theosophist & Theosophic Messenger* 14 (September 1913): 1023.
70. DePastino, *Citizen Hobo*, 15.
71. "Bassein," *Times of Burma*, February 16, 1901, 5.
72. Also known as the Independent Order of Good Templars. For a history of the IOGT and temperance internationalism see: Fahey, *Temperance and Racism*; Fahey, "Temperance Internationalism."
73. Conrad, *The Shadow-Line*; Cox, "Rethinking Early Western Buddhists."
74. "European Buddhist Priest," *Hong Kong Telegraph*, August 14, 1902, 4; "An Irish Buddhist: Bound for Thibet," *Japan Times*, February 13, 1903, 5; "Burma (5): Account of Mr Dhammaloka," *Nipon*, December 19, 1902, 3.
75. "France and Siam: Position of the Treaty," *London Evening Standard*, April 2, 1903, 5; "Horn Island," *Northern Miner*, August 31, 1899, 2. Steve Mullins, pers. comm.

76. He claimed as a former engineer to have drawn the plans for a recent Burmese-funded building at Bodh Gaya, but we have found no confirmation. "Burma (5): Account of Mr Dhammaloka," *Nipon*, December 19, 1902, 3.

77. "Religious," *Brisbane Courier*, January 7, 1905, 16.

78. Franck, *A Vagabond Journey*, 363. Stage Irish adjusted.

79. "Solved!" *Atlanta Constitution*, July 30, 1911, B6.

80. "European Buddhist Priest," *Hong Kong Telegraph*, August 14, 1902, 4.

81. Cotes Ordination of Asoka, 753–54.

82. "From Catholic Priest to Buddhist Monk," *Englishman*, April 11, 1912, 7; *Buddhist Review* 4, no. 3 (1912): 240; "A Pioneer Buddhist Monk," *American Theosophist & Theosophic Messenger* 14 (September 1913): 1023.

83. "Life in the Churches: A Buddhist Propaganda," *Christian Advocate* 76, no. 39 (September 26, 1901): 1552.

84. He might have been an informer: the 1883 murder of James Carey, who had informed on Irish nationalist assassins, while traveling to South Africa under another name, was well known.

85. Dunne, "Cultures of Resistance in Pre-Famine Ireland."

86. Breathnach, "Resistance in Pre-Famine Dublin," 9–19.

87. Conan Doyle's "The Valley of Fear" reflects popular images. For the actual history, see: Kenny, *Making Sense of the Molly Maguires*.

88. Hallgrimsdottir and Benoit, "From Wage Slaves to Wage Workers," 1403.

89. This was the world in which the young Greek-Irish Lafcadio Hearn (1850–1904) was sent out from Ireland to Cincinnati, was abandoned by his distant relations, and became a freethinker c. 1870, working for a Fourierist printer and writing about Eastern philosophy. Cox, *Buddhism and Ireland*, 237.

90. DePastino, *Citizen Hobo*, 24.

91. Gandhi, *Affective Communities*.

92. DePastino, *Citizen Hobo*, 32–33.

93. Higbie, "Unschooled but Not Uneducated," 104.

94. Cox, "Dhammaloka as Social Movement Organizer."

95. Anderson, *The Hobo: The Sociology of the Homeless Man*.

96. Anderson, *The Hobo*, 8–10.

97. Anderson, *The Hobo*, 186.

98. Anderson, *The Hobo*, 187; "What a Hobo Reads," *Ernest Watson Burgess Papers 1866-1966*, document 150, Special Collections Research Center, University of Chicago Library.

99. Saxton, *Indispensable Enemy*, 114–18.

100. Chandler, "Chinese Buddhism in America," 16.

101. "Butte's Far Eastern Influences," http://www.butteamerica.com/fareast.htm (accessed April 24, 2019).

102. Cross, *History of the Labor Movement in California*, 71.

103. Saxton, *Indispensable Enemy*.

104. By 1878 miners were becoming organized in the Butte Workingmen's Union.

105. DePastino, *Citizen Hobo*, 15.

106. DePastino, 20.

107. Ignatiev, *How the Irish Became White*.

108. Cox, *Buddhism and Ireland*, 243.

109. Ignatiev, *How the Irish Became White*; McVeigh, *Racialization of Irishness*.

110. "Burma (1): Account of Mr Dhammaloka," *Nipon*, December 14, 1902, 3.

111. A Sailor, "How I Became a Buddhist," *British Buddhist* 2, no. 9 (1927): 7–8.

Chapter 2

1. "Ordination of English Novice," [in Burmese] *Hanthawaddy Weekly Review*, July 14, 1900, 234. Our thanks to Pyi Phyo Kyaw for her help in translating this article.

2. Novice (*samanera*) ordination requires only one ordaining monk and can be performed at any location. In nineteenth-century Burma, most young boys spent some time as a *samanera*, which is a prerequisite for full *upasampada* ordination after age twenty. The *upasampada* ordination requires a *sima* or delimited space with a quorum of five monks. There are no clear rules for how long an adult must remain a novice before full ordination. At least two Europeans ordained in 1902 spent approximately six months as novices before full ordination, while Gordon Douglas/ Asoka in 1899 received *samanera* and *upasampada* ordination on the same day. "Mr. Gordon Douglas as Buddhist Priest," *Journal of the Maha-Bodhi Society* 7, no. 11 (March 1899): 106–7. Moreover, it is common for Burmese boys to live at the monastery even before novice ordination, in preparation. Crosby, *Theravada Buddhism*; Crosby, "Ordination and Disrobing in Theravada Buddhism."

3. *Catalogue of Books and Pamphlets Published in Burma* (Rangoon: Superintendent Government Printing), 1893–94. "Appointment of Thathanabaing Headship of the Buddhist Church," 1886 Series 1/1(A). Accession No. 1778, File 18, Myanmar National Archives, Yangon, Myanmar.

4. Today Arakan (Rakhine) is best known for the violent expulsion of the Rohingya Muslim ethnic minority, but in Dhammaloka's era its capital was known as a cosmopolitan multi-religious hub.

5. *Sinhala Bauddhaya*, November 20, 1909, 7.

6. "Burma (5): Account of Mr Dhammaloka," *Nipon*, December 19, 1902, 3.

7. Franck, *A Vagabond Journey*, 380–84.

8. "Ordination of English Novice," [in Burmese] *Hanthawaddy Weekly Review*, July 14, 1900, 234. Translation by Pyi Phyo Kyaw.

9. "A Buddhist Pilgrimage," *Ceylon Observer*, November 3, 1898, 1506. "The Buddhist Casket at Kandy," *Ceylon Observer*, January 23, 1899, 116.

10. Turner, "Irish Pongyi in Colonial Burma."

11. Dhammaloka, "Notice," *Times of Burma*, November 3, 1900, 6.

12. "Local News," *Times of Burma*, January 19, 1901, 6.

13. "Notice," *Times of Burma*, February 6, 1901, 10.

14. Dhammaloka, "Dear Brother Dharmapala," *Journal of the Maha-Bodhi Society* 9, no. 8 (December 1900): 76. In this letter Dhammaloka talks of progress "since I last saw you," implying earlier encounters. This was reported in: "A Remarkable Circular: Buddhists of Burma," *Times of Burma*, January 9, 1901, 7.

15. U Dhammaloka, "Buddhists of Burmah," *Arakan Times*, December 29, 1900, reprinted in the *Times of Burma*, on January 9.

16. "A Remarkable Circular: Buddhists of Burma," *Times of Burma*, January 9, 1901, 7.

17. Dhammaloka, "Kleine Mitteilungen," *Das Freie Wort* 1, no. 6 (June 20, 1901): 191–92.

18. "Mandalay," *Times of Burma*, January 4, 1901, 6.

19. Founded in upstate New York in 1850, in 1906 it officially changed its name to the "International Order of Good Templars" to reflect its lodges around the world.

20. "Temperance," *Times of Burma*, January 12, 1901, 4.

21. "New Mission," *Times of Burma*, January 23, 1901, 4. The tour announcements claimed he was paving the way for a new "Buddhist Mission Society from America which will arrive shortly." We have found no other record of such a society.

22. "Bassein," *Times of Burma*, February 16, 1901, 5–6.

23. "Bassein," *Times of Burma*, February 16, 1901, 5–6.

24. "Missions," *The Times of Burma*, February 16, 1901; "Bassein," *The Times of Burma*, February 16, 1901.

25. Dhammaloka normally used a translator when addressing Burmese audiences. His translators came from diverse backgrounds—Chinese, Burmese, and Punjabi, representing the ethnic diversity of his mission and audiences. "Bassein," *Times of Burma*, February 16, 1901, 5–6; "The Decadence of Heathenism," *Baptist Missionary Magazine* 82, no. 8 (August 1902): 572–73; Thaw, "Correspondence," *Maha-Bodhi and the United Buddhist World* 10 (April 1902): 119–20; "Mandalay" *Burma Echo*, January 4, 1908, 11.

26. "Bassein," *Times of Burma*, February 16, 1901, 5–6.

27. Turner, *Saving Buddhism*.

28. "Bassein," *Times of Burma*, February 16, 1901, 5–6.

29. Young and Somaratna, *Vain Debates*.

30. Franck, *A Vagabond Journey*, 365–6.

31. "New Mission," *Times of Burma*, January 23, 1901, 4.

32. *Times of Burma*, March 27, 1901, 6.

33. "Turning Christian Converts Back to Buddhism," *Literary Digest* 23 (August 1901): 199–200. "'Christianity' in Burma," *Deseret Evening News*, August 24, 1901, 4; Dhammaloka, "Kleine Mitteilungen," *Das Freie Wort* 1 (June 20, 1901): 191–92.

34. "General News," *Hackney Express and Shoreditch Observer*, January 4, 1902, 4; "Zigon," *Times of Burma*, April 2, 1902, 5.

35. "European Buddhists," *Times of Burma*, December 4, 1901, 4; "Europeans and Buddhism," *Pioneer*, December 27, 1901, 4.

36. "Burma," *Homeward Mail*, January 20, 1902, 77. The same *Rangoon Gazette* report was also carried as "Europeans and Buddhism," *Pioneer*, December 27, 1901, 4. See also Chapter 6.

37. Cotes, "The Ordination of Asoka," 758.

38. Cotes, "The Ordination of Asoka. "Dhamma-ānanda" means "bliss of the dharma." Cotes may have confused Dhammaloka's name with that of the distinguished Indian scholar monk Dharmananda Damodar Kosambi (1876-1947), ordained in Ceylon in 1902 and living in Burma by 1903. Payer, "Materialien Zum

Neobuddhismus: Die Ersten Europäischen Mönche Und Versuche Der Gründung Eines Vihâra Auf Dem Europäischen Festland"; Nyanatusita and Hecker, *The Life of Nyanatiloka Thera*, 25.

39. "An Irish Buddhist: Bound for Thibet," *Japan Times*, February 13, 1903, 5; "An Irish Buddhist in Bangkok," *Bangkok Times and Weekly Mail*, February 25, 1903, 19; "The Irish Buddhist Returns," *Straits Times*, August 26, 1903, 2.

40. Cotes, "The Ordination of Asoka," 758.

41. "In a queue" refers to the man's Chinese hairstyle; Cotes tells us he was a finance clerk.

42. Cotes, "The Ordination of Asoka," 758.

43. "Solved—the Riddle of Dama Laku 'the Wise One,' the Buddhist Abbot of Rangoon—Once an American Tramp," *San Francisco Examiner*, July 30, 1911, 56–57. "Solved!" *Atlanta Constitution*, July 30, 1911, B6; "Irish Buddhist. Dublin Man's Remarkable Career," *Sunday Independent*, August 16, 1911, 8.

44. "Burma (8): Account of Mr Dhammaloka," *Nipon*, December 24, 1902, 3.

45. Morphy, "Editorial," *Straits Times*, February 19, 1905, 4.

46. Cannadine, *Ornamentalism*.

47. "Election of the Buddhist Archbishop," *Times of Burma*, November 30, 1901, 4.

48. "Election of the Buddhist Archbishop," *Times of Burma*, November 30, 1901, 4.

49. Harry Franck recounts how in 1905 Dhammaloka showed him a newspaper clipping inviting the reader "to compare the receptions tendered Lord Curzon and the Irish Buddhist in Mandalay." Franck, *A Vagabond Journey*, 364. Subsequent newspaper stories, based on this, went further, suggesting that the Viceroy's reception was poorly attended *because* Dhammaloka's crowded reception was being held elsewhere in Mandalay at the same time, but the dates do not match. "Solved!" *Atlanta Constitution*, July 30, 1911, B6. Cotes, traveling with the Viceroy's party, describes Curzon's arrival in Mandalay, the substantial crowds present to welcome him, and many of the dignitaries present, including the Thathanabaing-elect. Cotes, "In Burma with the Viceroy."

50. "Solved!" *Atlanta Constitution*, July 30, 1911, B6. "American" meaning Irish-American.

51. "An Irish Buddhist Monk," *Maha-Bodhi and the United Buddhist World* 10 (February 1902): 91.

52. *Times of Burma*, April 23, 1902, 3.

53. Likely including the photograph of Dhammaloka by Johannes & Co. published five years later in Calcutta, with the comment that he was now stouter than in the photograph (see Figure I.1). "Rangoon—Rev. U. Dhumloka," *The Empress*, November 1907, 13.

54. Thaw, "Correspondence," *Maha-Bodhi and the United Buddhist World* 10 (April 1902): 119–20; Moung Moung, "U Dhammaloka's Tour," *Times of Burma*, January 18, 1902, 6–7. On the veracity of such reported numbers, see Chapter 9. A few popular Buddhist preachers of this era, including Ledi Sayadaw, drew similar crowds.

55. Thaw, "U Dhammaloka's Visit to Vajirama Sayadaw," *Maha-Bodhi and the United Buddhist World* 10 (April 1902): 120.

56. Maung Maung is sometimes written Moung Moung. Moung Moung, "U Dhammaloka's Tour," *Times of Burma*, January 18, 1902, 6–7.

57. Some of the information about this tour comes from Japanese sources: "Burma (2): Account of Mr Dhammaloka," *Nipon*, December 16, 1902, 3.

58. "Toungoo," *Times of Burma*, January 1, 1902, 6.

59. "U Dhammaloka," *Times of Burma*, February 12, 1902, 3.

60. "Letpadan," *Times of Burma*, March 8, 1902, 5.

61. "The Revival of Buddhism," *Times of India*, March 21, 1902, 3.

62. "Myittha," *Times of Burma*, February 8, 1902, 6.

63. "Letpadan," *Times of Burma*, June 7, 1902, 6.

64. Cotes, "The Ordination of Asoka," 758–59.

65. "Opening Ceremony of the Inauguration of the International Buddhist Young Men's Federal Association," *Takanawa Gakuho [Takanawa University Gazette]* (October 5, 1902): 78–79.

66. "Toungoo," *Times of Burma*, January 1, 1902, 6.

67. "Letpadan," *Times of Burma*, March 8, 1902, 5. Another novice, Mr. Warwick, was ordained that spring as Theeyedaza. "Letpadan," *Times of Burma*, June 7, 1902, 6.

68. U Dhammaloka, *Times of Burma*, April 26, 1902, 1; *Singapore Free Press and Mercantile Advertiser*, April 2, 1902, 2.

69. "U Dhammaloka," *Times of Burma*, March 26, 1902, 4.

70. "U Dhammaloka," *Times of Burma*, March 26, 1902, 4.

71. Daylight, "Correspondence- Shwegyin," *Times of Burma*, April 12, 1902, 5.

72. Buddhist, "Correspondence-Sandoway," *Times of Burma*, May 14, 1902, 6.

73. Daylight, "Correspondence- Zigon," *Times of Burma*, May 28, 1902, 6.

74. Daylight, *Times of Burma*, May 28, 1902, 6.

75. "Modern Preaching," *Burman Buddhist* 1, no. 3 (August 1908): 50–51.

76. The most famous was Ledi Sayadaw, who popularized lay meditation. Braun, *The Birth of Insight*.

77. "Henzada," *Burma Echo*, May 9, 1908, 9.

78. In this, he resembled Col. Olcott in Ceylon, key differences being Dhammaloka's class background and status as an ordained monk.

79. "Passengers Left by the Mails," *Singapore Free Press and Mercantile Advertiser*, July 24, 1902, 64.

80. "U Dhammaloka," *Times of Burma*, March 26, 1902, 4.

81. Skeptic, "U Dhammaloka," *Times of Burma*, April 12, 1902, 5.

82. Moung Moung, "U Dhammaloka's Tour," *Times of Burma*, January 18, 1902, 6–7. See Chapter 5 for a list of the donated items.

83. "The Decadence of Heathenism," *Baptist Missionary Magazine* 82, no. 8 (August 1902): 572–73.

Chapter 3

1. "Wearing Shoes in Pagodas," 1919, Series 1/15(D), Accession No. 1330, File 2P-45, Myanmar National Archives, Yangon, Myanmar.

2. "Shoes at Shwedagon," *Times of Burma*, March 6, 1901, 4–5.

3. "Shoes at Shwedagon," *Times of Burma*, March 6, 1901, 4–5; "Local News," *Times of Burma*, March 6, 1901.
4. See Turner, *Saving Buddhism*, Chap. 5.
5. "Shoes at Shwedagon," *Times of Burma*, March 6, 1901, 4–5.
6. "The Open Letter," *Times of Burma*, April 13, 1901, 5.
7. A high-ranking assistant commissioner.
8. A Burmese, "A Wonderful Vision," *Times of Burma*, March 20, 1901, 5, written on March 18.
9. Candier, "Conjuncture and Reform in the Late Konbaung."
10. Justice, "A Wonder of the 20th Century," *Times of Burma*, March 20, 1901, 5.
11. Daylight, "Wonderful Vision," *Times of Burma*, March 23, 1901, 5.
12. Famous for his books including: White, *Burma*; White, *A Civil Servant in Burma*.
13. "The Shwe Dagon Pagoda," *Times of Burma*, June 15, 1901, 4.
14. "An Open Letter to U Dhammaloka," *Times of Burma*, April 10, 1901, 5.
15. Dhammaloka, "The Open Letter," *Times of Burma*, April 13, 1901, 5.
16. Dhammaloka, *Times of Burma*, April 13, 1901, 5.
17. "The Shoe Question: The Vernacular Press," *Times of Burma*, June 5, 1901, 5.
18. "The Pagoda Case: Prosecution in Rangoon," *Times of India*, May 16, 1901, 5.
19. "Rangoon Pagoda Case: Prisoner's Appeal Dismissed," *Times of India*, May 24, 1901, 5.
20. "Rangoon Pagoda Case: Prisoner's Appeal Dismissed," *Times of India*, May 24, 1901, 5.
21. "The Pagoda Case: Accused Released," *Times of India*, July 4, 1901, 5.
22. *Lutheran Observer*, August 23, 1901, 15.
23. "The Shoe Question," *Time of Burma*, May 29, 1901, 5.
24. "Rangoon Pagoda: Further Trouble Reported," *Times of India*, August 1, 1901, 5.
25. Dhammaloka, "The Open Letter," *Times of Burma*, April 13, 1901, 5.

Chapter 4

1. "U Dhammaloka," *Times of Burma*, March 26, 1902, 4.
2. Sight-seer, "Mandalay," *Burma Echo*, January 18, 1908, 11.
3. Singh, *Story of Swami Rama*, 194; Burris, *Exhibiting Religion*.
4. Bocking, Cox, and Yoshinaga, "First Buddhist Mission to the West; Bocking, "Flagging up Buddhism."
5. Japanese names are given family name first, as in Japan.
6. Vivekananda supporter Narendranath Sen (1843–1911), president of the Bengal section of the Theosophical Society and owner-editor of the *Indian Mirror* newspaper, was instead proposed as chairperson on the Indian side.
7. We are indebted to Yoshiko Okamoto for most of this information. See Bandyopadhyay, "Japanese Scholar Traces History of Kolkata," *Times of India*, November 13, 2014. http://timesofindia.indiatimes.com/city/kolkata/Japanese-scholar-traces-history-of-Kolkata/articleshow/45127933.cms and Okamoto, "An Asian Religion Conference Imagined."

8. Shackle, "After Macauliffe."

9. Swami Vivekananda's close disciple, the Irish-born Hindu Margaret Noble.

10. Singh, *Story of Swami Rama*, 190–91. According to Vivekananda's *Reminiscences*, a parallel invitation arrived from the Japanese emperor. Vivekananda declined this invitation also. Medhasananda, *Vivekananda and Japan*.

11. The patron was the Raja of Tehri. Singh, *Story of Swami Rama*, 194.

12. Virk, "Professor Puran Singh."

13. Franck, *A Vagabond Journey*, 362.

14. "Burma (5): Account of Mr Dhammaloka," *Nipon*, December 19, 1902, 3. "Osutoria" [in phonetic Japanese], here meaning Australia.

15. *Times of Burma*, September 3, 1902, 4; "European Buddhist Priest," *Hong Kong Telegraph*, August 14, 1902, 4. "An Irish Buddhist Priest: Discovered in the Crowded Precincts of Asakusa," *The Voice: An Independent Journal of Christian Civilization*, August 23, 1902, 1–2.

16. "Mr Dhammaloka's Visit (*Damaroka-shi no korai*)," *Asahi Shimbun*, October 10, 1902. Okamoto Yoshiko pers. comm. August 6, 2013.

17. *Times of Burma*, September 3, 1902, 4.

18. "Burma (5): Account of Mr Dhammaloka," *Nipon*, December 19, 1902, 3; *Takanawa Gakuho (Takanawa University Gazette)* (October 5, 1902): 78.

19. "Burma (8): Account of Mr Dhammaloka," *Nipon*, December 24, 1902, 3.

20. "Opening Ceremony of the Inauguration of the International Buddhist Young Men's Federal Association," 79 *Takanawa Gakuho [Takanawa University Gazette]* (October 5, 1902): 78–79; "Burma (5): Account of Mr Dhammaloka," *Nipon*, December 19, 1902, 3.

21. Theravada is the predominant form of Buddhism in Southeast Asia. Jaffe, "Seeking Sakyamuni: Travel and the Reconstruction of Japanese Buddhism."

22. *Maha-Bodhi and the United Buddhist World*, Vol. 12, (1903) Nos. 5–6, inside cover. Unsho is listed in the journal as "Lord Abbot Unsiyo Vajo, *Mejiro*, Tokio, Japan" ("Vajo" is *wajo*; a Shingon Abbot).

23. "Burma (5): Account of Mr Dhammaloka," *Nipon*, December 19, 1902, 3. Dhammaloka says he had recommended Unsho for vice president of the BPS "about seven years ago."

24. Takanawa Buddhist University was a very short-lived institution. It was originally the Tokyo branch of *Bukkyo Daigaku* ("The Buddhist University") in Kyoto, which is now Ryukoku University (not to be confused with today's *Bukkyo Daigaku*). Takanawa Buddhist University lasted only two years in Tokyo, closing in 1904 in a very public debacle involving protests, a mass staff resignation, parental distress, and deep acrimony. "The Closing of Takanawa Buddhist University," *Yomiuri Shimbun*, January 13, 1904; "The Takanawa Buddhist University Incident and Nishi Honganji," *Yomiuri Shimbun*, January 20, 1904. See Iwata, "Takanawa Bukkyō University and the IYMBA."

   The Ryukoku University website records that in 1904 the Takanawa and Kyoto institutions were "unified" to form *Bukkyo Daigaku* in Kyoto, renamed Ryukoku University in 1922. http://www.ryukoku.ac.jp/english/university/rekishi/index.html (accessed June 20, 2010).

25. Literally, "All-countries Buddhist Youth Alliance Association" reflecting the intention to found not just a local *kai* (association) but a *rengo-kai*, a "federation" or higher-level umbrella group, based in Japan and fostering national associations worldwide. The Constitution and Rules of the IYMBA were published in English and Japanese because English was to be the *lingua franca* of the global network. Iwata, "Takanawa Bukkyō University and the IYMBA."

26. In Japanese, *Takanawa Gakuho.* We are indebted to Prof. Yoshinaga Shin'ichi, who alerted us to this material. The information from *Takanawa Gakuho* was provided by PhD researcher Mami Iwata. We are also very grateful to John Breen and Yoshinaga Shin'ichi for help with the following translations; any errors are of course our own.

27. "Opening Ceremony of the Inauguration of the International Buddhist Young Men's Federal Association," *Takanawa Gakuho [Takanawa University Gazette]* (October 5, 1902): 78–79. We are grateful to Taylor & Francis for permission to reproduce translations from Bocking, "'A Man of Work and Few Words'?," November 2010. *Contemporary Buddhism* is at https://www.tandfonline.com/.

28. Sakurai had recently returned from a world tour with the head of the Otani sect. See Katayama, "Kozai Ōtani on the Way to Europe."

29. *Futsu kyoko*, a Western-style school for Japanese pupils established by Higashi Honganji.

30. The *Senkyokai*, often translated "Buddhist Propagation Society," the predecessor of the IYMBA, was a Shinshu initiative to establish overseas Buddhist missions. These included Charles Pfoundes's 1889–1892 mission in London. Bocking, Cox, and Yoshinaga, "First Buddhist Mission to the West."

31. "Opening Ceremony of the Inauguration of the International Buddhist Young Men's Federal Association," *Takanawa Gakuho [Takanawa University Gazette]* (October 5, 1902): 78–79.

32. "Opening Ceremony of the Inauguration of the International Buddhist Young Men's Federal Association," *Takanawa Gakuho [Takanawa University Gazette]* (October 5, 1902): 78–79.

33. Aged 64, Shimaji (1838–1911) was a Shinshu veteran of the 1868 Meiji Restoration.

34. "Opening Ceremony of the Inauguration of the International Buddhist Young Men's Federal Association," *Takanawa Gakuho [Takanawa University Gazette]* (October 5, 1902): 78–79.

35. "Opening Ceremony of the Inauguration of the International Buddhist Young Men's Federal Association," *Takanawa Gakuho [Takanawa University Gazette]* (October 5, 1902): 78–79.

36. "Burma (3): Account of Mr Dhammaloka," *Nipon*, December 17, 1902, 3.

37. "Some Months Ago," *Straits Times*, August 6, 1903, 6; "Buddhist Societies: The Protest from Rangoon," *Bangkok Times and Weekly Mail*, July 24, 1903, 3.

38. "Buddhist Society for Siam," *Bangkok Times and Weekly Mail*, June 6, 1903, 6.

39. Or Fujieda Nobumasa.

40. A celebrated journalist and Christian patriot.

41. Anagarika Dharmapala had most recently come to Japan in April 1902 and left in May. Puran Singh had in fact been in Japan studying since 1900. He was Indian (Sikh) and a recent convert (in Tokyo) to Buddhism. At the student conference he spoke as

a Buddhist, but just that morning had become a devotee of the visiting Hindu guru, Swami Rama.

42. Swami Rama Tirtha. See earlier discussion.

43. Sensho Murakami (1851–1929), well-known intellectual proponent of Mahayana Buddhist unity.

44. "Student Association Autumn Term Gathering," *Takanawa Gakuho [Takanawa University Gazette]* (November 5, 1902): 72–73.

45. Cotes, "The Ordination of Asoka," 758–59.

46. Fisher, *A Woman Alone in the Heart of Japan*, 201. The denunciation was not in *The Voice* itself (Yoshinaga Shin'ichi, pers. comm.). In a later (February 1903) edition of *The Voice* is an article "Dhammaloka and Rev Tribolet." We have not traced a copy, but Tribolet was an American Baptist missionary in Burma, so probably it was not an encomium.

47. See Hardacre, *Shintō and the State*, 3–6.

48. Masuzawa, *Invention of World Religions*; Josephson, *The Invention of Religion in Japan*; Thomas, *Faking Liberties*.

49. For Shimaji Mokurai's lasting influence on the "religious freedom" debate following his 1873 tour to Europe, see Hitoshi, "Shinto as a 'Non-Religion.'" On Meiji Shinto, see Bocking, "Shinto."

50. A petition to the Meiji oligarchs in defense of Buddhism's religious independence from government was written under Shimaji's influence by his close colleague Ouchi Seiran. Hitoshi, "Shinto as a 'Non-Religion,'" 255. It argues that in contrast to "religious" activities, sacred imperial rites (Shinto) belong to this world; they should be performed by the government and everyone should be required to participate, to avoid the risk of people exercising their religious freedom not to believe in Shinto.

51. Née Letitia Arabin; her English husband's distant ancestral home was Mallow Castle, County Cork. Widowed at 40, she was a successful hotel proprietor in Brisbane, visiting Japan at least twice during retirement. "Death of Mrs Jephson," *Brisbane Courier*, January 6, 1908, 7; Hagger, "Brisbane Lodge Golden Jubilee."

52. Takanawa Buddhist University offered a progressive curriculum and opportunities for female education. In Japanese, IYMBA meant "International Buddhist *Youth* Association." Its English name, like its prototype YMCA/YWCA, was gendered.

53. Foster et al., *The Encyclopedia of the Stone-Campbell Movement*, 34. Eugenese Snodgrass was by then an independent missionary in Tokyo.

54. Fisher, *A Woman Alone in the Heart of Japan*, 201–2. Stage Irish adjusted.

55. Fisher, 201–2. Stage Irish adjusted.

56. Fisher, 205–6.

57. Bocking, "'A Man of Work and Few Words'?," November 2010, misidentified katakana '*pinan*' (Penang) as Pinan, Philippines.

58. "An Irish Priest," *Straits Times*, February 3, 1903, reports that Dhammaloka is in Hong Kong (and hoping to be the first European to visit Lhasa). IYMBA developments of 1902–3 are outlined in *Ryūkoku Daigaku Sanbyakunenshi [300-Year History of Ryūkoku University]*, 822.

59. *Ryūkoku Daigaku Sanbyakunenshi [300-Year History of Ryūkoku University]*, 822.

Chapter 5

1. See Chapter 2.
2. Moung Moung, "U Dhammaloka's Tour," *Times of Burma*, January 18, 1902, 6–7.
3. Dhammaloka, "Japan and China," *Times of Burma*, January 7, 1903, 5.
4. Moung Moung, "U Dhammaloka's Tour," *Times of Burma*, January 18, 1902, 6–7. "U" here is a general Burmese title of respect and does not mean Revd. His donations to the SPB demonstrate his connections to the Maha Bodhi Society and the Bodh Gaya efforts.
5. Bodh Gaya, site of the Buddha's enlightenment under the Bodhi tree, promoted by Anagarika Dharmapala's Maha Bodhi society as a pan-Buddhist center of pilgrimage.
6. Moung Moung, "U Dhammaloka's Tour," *Times of Burma*, January 18, 1902, 6–7.
7. Dhammaloka, "Japan and China," *Times of Burma*, January 7, 1903, 5.
8. "News from the Far East: Kobe," *London and China Telegraph*, March 2, 1903, 2.
9. "Lord Abbot U Dhammaloka [Interview]," *Times of Burma*, March 14, 1903, 7.
10. "Singapore," *Times of Burma*, March 4, 1903, 5.
11. "An Irish Buddhist in Bangkok," *Bangkok Times and Weekly Mail*, February 25, 1903, 19. "The Rev U Dhammaloka," *Straits Times*, February 17, 1903, 5.
12. "The State of Kieng Tung: Our Latest Royal Visitor," *Straits Times*, February 17, 1903, 5.
13. Marshall, *The Trouser People*, 197.
14. "Shan Sawbwas Visited Gya," *Times of Burma*, January 17, 1903, 4.
15. "A Little Known but Important Potentate," *Straits Times*, February 16, 1903, 4.
16. "The State of Kieng Tung: Our Latest Royal Visitor," *Straits Times*, February 17, 1903, 5.
17. "The Irish Buddhist Returns," *Straits Times*, August 26, 1903, 2. Paul Beau was governor of French Indochina, Théophile Delcassé France's foreign minister.
18. Edwards, "Watching the Detectives: The Elusive Exile of Prince Myngoon of Burma."
19. "Visit of Kengtung Sawbwa to Colombo, Singapore and Bangkok," 1903 Series 1/1(B), Accession No. 6324, File 45–43, Myanmar National Archives, Yangon, Myanmar.
20. Marshall, *The Trouser People*, 197.
21. "The Swabwa of Kengtung: His Visit to Bangkok," *Bangkok Times and Weekly Mail*, February 25, 1903, 19; "An Irish Buddhist in Bangkok," *Bangkok Times and Weekly Mail*, February 25, 1903, 19.
22. "His Highness the Sawbwa," *Straits Times*, March 14, 1903, 3.
23. "His Highness the Sawbwa," *Straits Times*, March 14, 1903, 3.
24. "Siam," *Times of Burma*, March 28, 1903, 7.
25. "The Irish Buddhist, the Lord Abbot," *Times of Burma*, March 25, 1903, 4.
26. "U Dhammaloka," *Bangkok Times and Weekly Mail*, May 2, 1903, 6.
27. Choompolpaisal, "Tai-Burmese-Lao Buddhisms." We are indebted to Dr. Choompolpaisal for his remarkable work in tracing Dhammaloka's activities and connections in Thailand and elucidating the complex religious and political cross-currents of 1900s Bangkok. He also organized the successful 2012 "Buddhist Crossroads" conference at University College Cork during his year-long postdoctoral

research project "Continuities and Transitions in Early Modern Thai Buddhism," supported by the Dhammakaya International Society of the United Kingdom. See Bocking et al., *A Buddhist Crossroads: Pioneer Western Buddhists and Asian Networks 1860–1960*.

28. "Burma (3): Account of Mr Dhammaloka," *Nipon*, December 17, 1902, 3.
29. I.e., had become wealthy.
30. The old name for the Thai *baht*.
31. "Free Education in Bangkok," *Bangkok Times and Weekly Mail*, June 5, 1903, 3.
32. "Free Education in Bangkok," *Bangkok Times and Weekly Mail*, June 5, 1903, 3.
33. "Free Education in Bangkok," *Bangkok Times and Weekly Mail*, June 5, 1903, 3.
34. "Education in Siam," *Bangkok Times and Weekly Mail*, June 6, 1903, 6.
35. "Buddhist Society for Siam," *Bangkok Times and Weekly Mail*, June 6, 1903, 6. Dhammaloka may have regarded himself as representative of all three associations; in his *Nipon* interview, he says he is an honorary member of the Maha Bodhi Society. "Burma (5): Account of Mr Dhammaloka," *Nipon*, December 19, 1902, 3.
36. "Buddhist Societies," *Times of Burma*, July 23, 1903, 5.
37. "A Foreign Buddhist in Bangkok," *Bangkok Times and Weekly Mail*, June 10, 1903, 19.
38. "A Foreign Buddhist in Bangkok," *Bangkok Times and Weekly Mail*, June 10, 1903, 19.
39. "A Proposed Buddhist Congress," *Bangkok Times and Weekly Mail*, June 23, 1903, 15.
40. *Ryūkoku Daigaku Sanbyakunenshi [300-Year History of Ryūkoku University]*, 821. Emphasis added.
41. "Buddhist Societies," *Bangkok Times and Weekly Mail*, July 31, 1903, 3. See Chapter 7.
42. "The European Buddhist Priest," *Straits Times*, August 20, 1903, 5.
43. "Rev. Dhammaloka Delivered an Address," *Straits Times*, February 16, 1903, 4; "Singapore," *Times of Burma*, March 4, 1903, 5.
44. "The Rev U Dhammaloka," *Straits Times*, February 17, 1903, 5.
45. Ong Siang Song, *One Hundred Years' History of the Chinese in Singapore*, 534–35.
46. "Picturesque Singapore," *Straits Times*, October 1, 1897, 3.
47. Bazell, "Education in Singapore," 448; Leng, "Education in the Colony," 11–17; "'Chean Jim Hean' School," *Straits Times*, November 12, 1897, 2; *Straits Times*, March 9, 1900, 2.
48. Bazell, "Education in Singapore," 448.
49. "The European Buddhist Priest," *Bangkok Times and Weekly Mail*, August 10, 1903, 9; "The Irish Buddhist Priest," *Bangkok Times and Weekly Mail*, August 31, 1903, 12; "The Irish Buddhist Priest," *Bangkok Times and Weekly Mail*, September 2, 1903, 20; "The Irish Buddhist Priest," *Bangkok Times and Weekly Mail*, September 11, 1903, 4.
50. The pseudonym recalls "Captain Moonlight," a common signature used in agrarian struggles in the Ireland of the period. Dunne, "Cultures of Resistance in Pre-Famine Ireland."
51. "The Irish Buddhist Priest," *Bangkok Times and Weekly Mail*, September 11, 1903, 4.
52. "The Irish Buddhist Priest," *Bangkok Times and Weekly Mail*, September 11, 1903, 4.
53. "The Irish Buddhist Priest," *Bangkok Times and Weekly Mail*, September 2, 1903, 20.
54. "Buddhism in Singapore," *Straits Times*, October 3, 1904, 5.

55. Captain Daylight, "Correspondence-Buddhist Activity," *Maha-Bodhi and the United Buddhist World* 12, no. 5–6 (1903): 60–61.
56. Leng, "Education in the Colony."
57. "Buddhist Activity in Singapore," *Straits Times*, January 20, 1904, 3. See "BP de Silva." http://www.bpdesilvajewellers.com/ "BP de Silva Group of Companies." http://www.bpdesilva.com/.
58. "Notes and News," *Straits Chinese Magazine* 8, no. 3 (September 1904): 159–61.
59. "Buddhist Activity in Singapore," *Straits Times*, January 20, 1904, 3.
60. "Notes and News," *Straits Chinese Magazine* 8, no. 3 (September 1904): 159–61.
61. "Buddhist Activity in Singapore," *Straits Times*, January 20, 1904, 3; Tweed, "Tracing Modernity's Flows."
62. "Pamphlets on Buddhism," *Times of Burma*, March 26, 1902, 4.
63. "Buddhism in Singapore," *Straits Times*, October 3, 1904, 5.
64. "On the Verandah," *Straits Times*, September 30, 1899, 2; Dhammaloka, "Shiko," *Times of Burma*, September 23, 1903, 5.
65. Payer, "Materialien Zum Neobuddhismus: Die Ersten Europäischen Mönche Und Versuche der Gründung Eines Vihâra Auf Dem Europäischen Festland." See also the reference in Nyanatusita and Hecker, *The Life of Nyanatiloka Thera*.
66. "Jodo Shinshu Buddhism Celebrates 125th Anniversary in Hawaii."
67. Kawaguchi, "Hidden Thibet: Eighteen Months in Lhassa."
68. "Buddhist Activity in Singapore," *Straits Times*, January 20, 1904, 3.
69. Doran, "Bright Celestial."
70. "The Buddhist Flag," *Straits Times*, January 18, 1904, 5.
71. "Singapore Buddhists," *Straits Times*, March 9, 1904, 5.
72. "Singapore Buddhists," *Straits Times*, March 9, 1904, 5.
73. "The Buddhist New Year," *Straits Times*, May 2, 1904, 5.
74. For background on the mission see: "On the Verandah," *Straits Times*, September 30, 1899, 2.
75. "A Buddhist Festival," *Singapore Free Press and Mercantile Advertiser*, April 28, 1904, 3.
76. "The Buddhist New Year," *Straits Times*, May 2, 1904, 5.
77. "The Buddhist New Year," *Straits Times*, May 2, 1904, 5.
78. "A Buddhist Festival," *Singapore Free Press and Mercantile Advertiser*, April 28, 1904, 3.
79. *Singapore Free Press and Mercantile Advertiser*, June 14, 1904, 5.
80. "Buddhism in Singapore," *Straits Times*, October 3, 1904, 5; *Singapore Free Press and Mercantile Advertiser*, June 14, 1904, 5.
81. Evidently a mishearing of "Saviour of the Law."
82. "European Ordained as Buddhist Priest," *Straits Times*, October 3, 1904, 4. A fuller account appears in "Buddhism in Singapore," *Straits Times*, October 3, 1904, 5.
83. Iwata, "Takanawa Bukkyō University and the IYMBA," 31–32.
84. Roberts is confusingly identified as Dhammawanga on occasion. *Straits Times*, October 1, 1904, 5.
85. *Times of Burma*, February 1, 1905, 6.

86. "The Right Reverend Lord Abbot U Dhammaloka FTS," *Straits Times*, January 19, 1905, 4.

87. Morphy, "Editorial," *Straits Times*, February 19, 1905, 4.

88. "Religious," *Brisbane Courier*, January 7, 1905, 16. Reproducing an article from the *Torres Straits Pilot*.

89. "Local News," *Times of Burma*, June 7, 1905, 6; "An Irish Buddhist Priest," *Catholic Advance*, October 28, 1905, 5.

90. Franck, *A Vagabond Journey*, 361–64.

91. "Local News," *Times of Burma*, June 7, 1905, 6.

92. Franck, *A Vagabond Journey*, 361. Franck's subsequent date of May 13 for arriving in Rangoon seems to be an error. Bocking, "'A Man of Work and Few Words'?"

93. Franck, *A Vagabond Journey*, 361.

94. Franck, 363. Stage Irish adjusted.

95. Franck, 273.

96. See the over-optimistic account in Bocking, "U Dhammaloka The Irish Pongyi (1856–1914) in India, Nepal and Tibet."

97. Cox and Turner, "Maha Bodhi Society in Arakan"; Barua, "Thrice Honored Sangharaja Saramedha (1801–82): Arakan-Chittagong Buddhism across Colonial and Counter-Colonial Power."

98. Franck, *A Vagabond Journey*, 363. Stage Irish adjusted.

99. "Local News: Chittagong," *Times of Burma*, June 7, 1905, 6. "Parinirvana" (the Buddha's passing) was intended.

100. "Local News," *Times of Burma*, June 7, 1905, 6.

101. "Local News," *Times of Burma*, June 7, 1905, 6.

102. "The Irish Buddhist Returns," *Straits Times*, August 26, 1903, 2.

103. "European Ordained as Buddhist Priest," *Straits Times*, October 3, 1904, 4.

104. Our thanks to Jasmine Jasani for her assistance in researching Tan Teck Soon, G. L. Tuck, Dhammikarama monastery, and the Burmese community in Penang.

105. *History of Dhammikarama Temple Penang*.

106. "Buddhism," *Straits Echo*, July 6, 1905, 4.

107. "Buddhism," *Straits Echo*, July 10, 1905, 4.

108. "Lord Abbot U Dhammaloka," *Times of Burma*, July 19, 1905, 9.

109. Frost, "*Emporium in Imperio*."

110. Though perhaps not with the position of Dhammaloka's Singapore patron Cheang Jim Chuan, whose family wealth came from intoxicants.

111. "U Dhammaloka," *Times of Burma*, August 16, 1905, 5.

112. "U Dhammaloka," *Times of Burma*, August 16, 1905, 5. Abrams was a committee member.

113. *Straits Echo*, September 28, 1905, 4.

114. *Times of Burma*, October 21, 1905, 4.

115. *History of Dhammikarama Temple Penang*, 54–55.

116. Lewis, *Cities in Motion*; Frost, "*Emporium in Imperio*"; Frost, "Asia's Maritime Networks."

117. Choompolpaisal, "Tai-Burmese-Lao Buddhisms"; "Free Education in Bangkok," *Bangkok Times and Weekly Mail*, June 5, 1903, 3.

118. Choompolpaisal, "Tai-Burmese-Lao Buddhisms."

119. On this in Burma, see: Roberts, *Mapping Chinese Rangoon*; Ware, "Origins of Buddhist Nationalism in Myanmar/Burma"; Osada, "Housing the Rangoon Poor."

120. Ikeya, "Colonial Intimacies in Comparative Perspective"; Lewis, *Cities in Motion*.

121. "The Irish Buddhist Returns," *Straits Times*, August 26, 1903, 2.

Chapter 6

1. Allan Bennett [MacGregor] was known by several names. His monastic name is given as Ananda Maitreya, Maitriya, Mittriya, Maitreeya, Mitria, or Metteyya, and he is sometimes called Mr. MacGregor and referred to as Scots rather than English.

2. An extensive list of such figures can be found on our website: https://dhammalokaproject.wordpress.com/ We welcome further contributions.

3. Bocking, Cox, and Yoshinaga, "First Buddhist Mission to the West."

4. "Small Talk," *The Sketch*, August 7, 1895, 81.

5. "Un Chretien Converti Au Bouddhisme," *Annales de l'Extreme Orient* 2 (February 1879): 264. Versions of the lengthy Hong Kong newspaper report on this item appeared in Derby, Singapore, and Sydney, the last under the title "A Pervert from Christianity to Buddhism," *Sydney Morning Herald*, September 19, 1878, 7. An April 1879 letter about "Conversion to Buddhism (Siam)," *Yorkshire Post and Leeds Intelligencer*, March 20, 1879, 3, reveals that the convert was an alcoholic Australian, not Austrian.

6. "The Conversion of a European to Buddhism in Bangkok," *Straits Times*, September 7, 1878, 7.

7. "A Scotchman Going to Turn Buddhist Priest," *Daily Advertiser*, June 25, 1892, 3; "A Scotchman Going to Turn Buddhist Priest," *Buddhist* (June 17, 1892): 192; *The Colonies and India*, July 23, 1892, 24.

8. Kemper, *Rescued from the Nation*, 42.

9. Cox and Sirisena, "Early Western Lay Buddhists."

10. Bartholomeusz, *Women under the Bo Tree*.

11. Jaffe, "Seeking Sakyamuni: Travel and the Reconstruction of Japanese Buddhism."

12. Bocking, Cox, and Yoshinaga, "First Buddhist Mission to the West"; Bocking, "Flagging up Buddhism."

13. Yoshinaga, "Three Boys on a Great Vehicle."

14. Cox, "Rethinking Early Western Buddhists."

15. "European Loafers as Buddhist Priests," *Singapore Free Press and Mercantile Advertiser*, December 2, 1904, 3; "Loafers in Burma," *Straits Times*, December 12, 1904, 8.

16. C. D., "Calcutta," *Times of Burma*, June 7, 1905.

17. Franck, *A Vagabond Journey*, 272–73.

18. Brownlow, *The Autobiography of Louis Brownlow*, I:483.

19. Ellis, "The Revival of Buddhism in Burma," *The East and the West* 4, (1906): 61–65.

20. Reprinted in "The Irish Buddhist Priest," *Ceylon Observer*, September 11, 1909, 1366.

21. "Mayor Fitzgerald's Breezy Interview with Sir Thomas," *Boston Sunday Post*, December 22, 1912, 33; Cox, *Buddhism and Ireland*, 254–55. Another report places this encounter in China: "Sir Thomas Lipton Spends Few Hours Seeing Salt Lake," *Salt Lake Herald-Republican*, December 2, 1912, 3.

22. "Buddhism," *Burma Echo*, June 8, 1907, 9.

23. "Our Perak Contemporaries," *Straits Times*, October 13, 1904, 4.

24. "St. Thomas' College Magazine," *Ceylon Observer*, February 6, 1899, 196.

25. Ananda Maitriya, *Foundation of the Sangha of the West*; Ananda Metteyya, "Entre Nous," *Truth*, July 15, 1908, 130.

26. He could even have disrobed temporarily, perhaps, as the French diplomat Charles Lemire claimed in 1903, to spend some time in Europe before 1900. "France and Siam: Position of the Treaty," *London Evening Standard*, April 2, 1903, 5.

27. "Bhikshu Asoka or Gordon Douglas," *Tribune*, April 26, 1900, 1; "'Bhikku Asoka' Dead" *Times of India*, April 23, 1900, 3.

28. "Mr. Gordon Douglas as Buddhist Priest," *Journal of the Maha-Bodhi Society* 7, no. 11 (March 1899): 106–7; Chatterji, *Maha Bodhi Society Diamond Jubilee*; Cox and Sirisena, "Early Western Lay Buddhists"; "Here and There," *Supplement to the Ceylon Observer*, September 29, 1898.

29. Mendelson, *Sangha and State in Burma*.

30. Kirichenko, "New Spaces for Interaction."

31. Htin Aung, *Burmese Monk's Tales*.

32. Vajirarama can also be transliterated Waziyayama. Kirichenko, "New Spaces for Interaction."

33. "The Buddhist Casket," *Ceylon Observer*, January 26, 1899, 137; "The Tooth of Buddha: Casket Removed to Kandy," *Times of India*, January 28, 1899, 6; "The Buddhist Casket at Kandy," *Ceylon Observer*, January 23, 1899, 116; "The Buddhist's Casket," *Ceylon Observer*, January 21, 1899, 105.

34. "'Bhikku Asoka' Dead," *Times of India*, April 23, 1900, 3; "Mr. Gordon Douglas as Buddhist Priest," *Journal of the Maha-Bodhi Society* 7, no. 11 (March 1899): 106–7; Anne Blackburn, *Locations of Buddhism*, 167–88. We do not know why Sumangala refused to ordain Douglas. It may have been to do with problems stemming from the ordination of the Thai Prince Jinavaravamsa in the Amarapura lineage in 1896. However, Sumangala had previously participated in the novice ordination of Shaka Unsho and Shaku Soen in 1886 and 1887. Jaffe, "Seeking Sakyamuni: Travel and the Reconstruction of Japanese Buddhism." It also may have to do with how Sinhalese ordination lineages are limited by caste. Malalgoda, *Buddhism in Sinhalese Society*.

35. "Buddhism in Ceylon: A European Ordained Priest," *Times of India*, January 28, 1899, 5; "The Buddhist Casket at Kandy," *Ceylon Observer*, January 23, 1899, 116.

36. "St. Thomas' College Magazine," *Ceylon Observer*, February 6, 1899, 196.

37. "Akyab," *Times of Burma*, November 17, 1900, 6.

38. "The 'English' Buddhist Priest," *Ceylon Observer*, July 20, 1899, 1065.

39. "Bhikkhu Asoka," *Journal of the Maha-Bodhi Society* 8, no. 6 (October 1899): 59.

40. "Mr. Gordon Douglas Exhibits Himself in Benares," *Journal of the Maha-Bodhi Society* 8, no. 12 (May 1900): 118–19.

41. "Death of a European Buddhist Priest," *Ceylon Observer*, April 11, 1900, 478; "Death of an English Buddhist," *Pioneer*, April 26, 1900, 5; "'Bhikku Asoka' Dead," *Times of India*, April 23, 1900, 3; "Bhikshu Asoka or Gordon Douglas," *Tribune*, April 26, 1900, 1.

42. "Akyab," *Times of Burma*, November 17, 1900, 6.

43. "Bassein," *Times of Burma*, February 16, 1901, 5–6.

44. Our thanks to Alexey Kirichenko for helping track down these connections.

45. Crow, "White Knight in the Yellow Robe," 47.

46. Henry Steele Olcott, *Old Diary Leaves: The History of the Theosophical Society*, vol. 4, 1887–92 (Adyar: Theosophical Publishing House, 1910); Anagarika Dharmapala, "Arakan Maha-Bodhi Society," *Journal of the Maha-Bodhi Society* 3, no. 12 (1895); "Buddhist Charity in Arakan," *Journal of the Maha-Bodhi Society* 8, no. 4 (1899). Cox and Turner, "Maha Bodhi Society in Arakan."

47. "European Hpoongyis," *Times of Burma*, December 18, 1901, 4. Asoka II offers some competition to Ananda Metteyya's status as the "third" Western Buddhist. Ananda Metteyya was ordained a novice in Akyab on December 8, 1901, one week before Asoka II's novice ordination. However, both had their *upasampada* ordination on the auspicious day of Vesak (May 21) in 1902. Ananda Metteyya stands out as the clear "third" for our purposes, mainly because there are no further reports about Asoka II in any records. Ananda Maitriya, *Foundation of the Sangha of the West; Maha-Bodhi News* [in Burmese], June 5, 1902, 51–52; Cotes, "The Ordination of Asoka," October 1902.

48. Ananda Maitriya, *Foundation of the Sangha of the West.*

49. Ananda Metteyya, "Entre Nous," *Truth*, July 15, 1908, 130.

50. Harris, "Ananda Metteyya: Controversial Networker, Passionate Critic"; Crow, "White Knight in the Yellow Robe."

51. This was a false start; the organization did not actually get off the ground until November 1902 when he refounded it in Rangoon. *Revised Prospectus of the Buddhasasana Samagama*, vol. 1a, *Publications of the Buddhasasana Samagama* (Rangoon: Hanthawaddy Press, 1903).

52. Dhammaloka, "Buddhism and Journalism," *Burma Echo*, August 31, 1907, 6, esti-mated the cost over five years at 22,000 rupees, around US $20,000 in today's money.

53. Crow, "White Knight in the Yellow Robe"; Harris, "Ananda Metteyya: Controversial Networker, Passionate Critic."

54. "Buddhism in England: First 'Missionary' Arrival," *Tribune*, May 21, 1908, 5.

55. And obscured the first Buddhist mission to *London* almost two decades earlier. Bocking, Cox, and Yoshinaga, "First Buddhist Mission to the West."

56. *Times of Burma*, June 25, 1902, 6.

57. "A Scotch Buddhist Priest," *Bangkok Times and Weekly Mail*, July 7, 1903, 16.

58. "Buddhist Societies," *Times of Burma*, July 23, 1903, 5; "Buddhist Societies," *Bangkok Times and Weekly Mail*, July 31, 1903, 3.

59. "A Scotch Buddhist Priest," *Bangkok Times and Weekly Mail*, July 7, 1903, 16.

60. Dhammaloka, "Buddhism and Journalism," *Burma Echo*, August 31, 1907, 6.

61. Dhammaloka, "Entre Nous," *Truth*, July 8, 1908, 65. Ananda Metteyya, in his reply, acknowledged this. Junjiro Takakusu (Kobayashi Jun) (1866–1945) and Kasawara Kenju (1852–83) were Oxford students of Max Müller. A robed Japanese priest accompanied Pfoundes at London public lectures in 1891 Bocking, Cox, and Yoshinaga, "First Buddhist Mission to the West."

62. Dhammaloka, "Entre Nous," *Truth*, July 8, 1908, 65.

63. Ananda Metteyya, "Entre Nous," *Truth*, July 15, 1908, 130.

64. Cox, "European Buddhist Traditions"; Ananda Metteyya, "Entre Nous," *Truth*, July 15, 1908, 130.

65. Ananda Maitriya, *Foundation of the Sangha of the West*, 14.

66. Ananda Maitriya, *Foundation of the Sangha of the West*, 15.

67. C. D., "Calcutta" *Times of Burma*, June 7, 1905.

68. *Times of Burma*, June 25, 1902, 6.

69. Nyanatusita and Hecker, *The Life of Nyanatiloka Thera*, 24–25.

70. Crosby, "Ordination and Disrobing in Theravada Buddhism."

71. "Lord Abbot U Dhammaloka," *Times of Burma*, July 19, 1905, 9.

72. Quoted in "An Irish Buddhist Priest," *Ceylon Observer*, September 4, 1909, 1337.

73. "Burma," *Homeward Mail*, January 20, 1902, 77; Cotes, "The Ordination of Asoka," June 1902.

74. "Letpadan," *Times of Burma*, June 7, 1902, 6.

75. *Singapore Free Press and Mercantile Advertiser*, June 14, 1904, 5.

76. "U Dhammaloka," *Times of Burma*, August 16, 1905, 5.

77. "European Ordained as Buddhist Priest," *Straits Times*, October 3, 1904, 4.

78. "A Buddhist Festival," *Singapore Free Press and Mercantile Advertiser*, April 28, 1904, 3; "The Buddhist New Year," *Straits Times*, April 28, 1904, 5.

79. "A Buddhist Festival," *Singapore Free Press and Mercantile Advertiser*, April 28, 1904, 3.

80. His Dublin address appears in the 1904–6 subscriber list for Paul Carus's journal *Light of Asia*. Our thanks to Thomas Tweed for this information. "Local News," *Times of Burma*, June 7, 1905. "The Reverends U Damaloka and U Vara," *Straits Echo*, July 5, 1905. For more connections with Dublin Buddhists, see Cox, *Buddhism and Ireland*, 261.

81. Franck, *A Vagabond Journey*, 382–86. See Chapter 7.

82. *Times of Burma*, January 22, 1902, 6; *Times of Burma*, June 25, 1902, 6.

83. Cox, *Buddhism and Ireland*, 255–56.

84. "European Loafers as Buddhist Priests," *Singapore Free Press and Mercantile Advertiser*, December 2, 1904, 3; "Loafers in Burma," *Straits Times*, December 12, 1904, 8.

85. "Burma," *Homeward Mail*, January 20, 1902, 77.

86. "Letpadan," *Times of Burma*, June 7, 1902, 6.

87. "Letpadan," *Times of Burma*, March 8, 1902, 5.

88. *Times of Burma*, January 22, 1902, 6; *Times of Burma*, June 25, 1902, 6.

89. Ruan, Secretary of the Japan & India Club, Tokyo, "U Dhammaloka in Japan," *Times of Burma*, January 17, 1903, 5.

90. "An Irish Buddhist: Bound for Thibet," *Japan Times*, February 13, 1903, 5.
91. *Singapore Free Press and Mercantile Advertiser*, June 14, 1904, 5.
92. *Straits Times*, October 1, 1904, 5.
93. "Under the lead of the Irish Pongyi, or priest, the Buddhist Society have voted to start a 'King Edward Memorial Buddhist Boys' School' in Pyinmana [Burma]." "When Opposition Is Praise," *Missions: A Baptist Monthly Magazine* 2 (1911): 133.
94. *Amrita Bazar Patrika*, February 9, 1905, 3.
95. "Local News," *Times of Burma*, June 7, 1905, 6.
96. *Singapore Free Press and Mercantile Advertiser*, June 27, 1905, 2.
97. "U Dhammaloka," *Times of Burma*, August 16, 1905, 5.
98. "Buddhism," *Burma Echo*, July 27, 1907, 9.
99. Moung Moung, "U Dhammaloka's Tour (Continued)," *Times of Burma*, January 22, 1902, 6–7.
100. "Zigon," *Times of Burma*, April 2, 1902, 5.
101. Cotes, "The Ordination of Asoka," October 1902.
102. Cotes, 756.
103. Cotes, 757.
104. Cotes, 758.
105. Cotes, 759.
106. Reproduced in "Our Perak Contemporaries," *Straits Times*, October 13, 1904, 4.
107. *Straits Times*, October 15, 1904, 4. Freedom from debt and not being in the king's service are prerequisites for ordination.
108. "Our Perak Contemporaries," *Straits Times*, October 13, 1904, 4.
109. "Buddhism in Singapore," *Straits Times*, October 3, 1904, 5; "European Ordained as Buddhist Priest," *Straits Times*, October 3, 1904, 4.
110. "Buddhism in Singapore," *Straits Times*, October 3, 1904, 5.
111. "On the Verandah," *Straits Times*, September 30, 1899, 2.
112. "A Buddhist Festival," *Singapore Free Press and Mercantile Advertiser*, April 28, 1904, 3.
113. "European Buddhists," *Times of India*, August 11, 1904, 6.
114. "Buddhist Activities in Kyoukse," *Times of Burma*, June 29, 1904, 5.
115. "Buddhism in Singapore," *Straits Times*, October 3, 1904, 5. "Buddhism and Missionary Work," *Straits Times*, October 7, 1904, 2.
116. "Buddhism and Missionary Work," *Straits Times*, October 7, 1904, 2.
117. For example, the ordination of Countess Canavarro. Bartholomeusz, *Women under the Bo Tree*; Cox and Sirisena, "Early Western Lay Buddhists."
118. "Mr. Gordon Douglas Exhibits Himself in Benares," *Journal of the Maha-Bodhi Society* 8, no. 12 (May 1900): 118–19, citing the *Ceylon Independent*.

Chapter 7

1. Franck, *A Vagabond Journey*.
2. Franck, "Girdles the World," *New York Times*, March 20, 1910, 6.
3. Franck, *New York Times*, March 20, 1910, 6.

4. Numerous reviews survive. It was translated almost immediately into German (1912) and later into Czech (1921) and Slovak (1936).

5. He presumably recorded them by periodically mailing letters home during his journey. The level of accuracy and detail in the book varies, and several reviewers thought that he had embellished the record, but it seems improbable that he reconstructed a narrative involving hundreds of often accurate names, places, events, and conversations from memory.

6. Franck, *A Vagabond Journey*, 358–59.

7. Franck, 269.

8. Perhaps "Askins (William James), M. A., Vern. [Spring] 1869" as listed in Todd, *Catalogue of Graduates University of Dublin*.

9. Franck, *A Vagabond Journey*, 272.

10. "Even the beachcomber does not walk in India. To ride is cheaper. Third class fare ranges from two-fifths to a half cent a mile, and on every train is a compartment reserved for 'Europeans and Eurasians only,' into which no native may enter on penalty of being frightened out of his addled wits by a bellowing official." Franck, 291.

11. Franck, 360–61. Stage Irish adjusted. Dhammaloka later claimed he enjoyed "special saloon accommodation" courtesy of the Raja of Hill Tippers. "Local News," *Times of Burma*, June 7, 1905, 6. See Chapter 6.

12. The Lhasa story appeared in the Singapore *Straits Times*, the Dublin *Sunday Independent* (subsequently summarized in many other Irish papers), and the *San Francisco Examiner* and Atlanta *Constitution*. The Indian missionary story appeared in the *Hackney Express* (London) and many other regional papers, such as the *Monmouthshire Beacon*. "East and West," *Monmouthshire Beacon*, August 26, 1910, 8.

13. Stowaways.

14. Railway police.

15. Handling cargo.

16. Implying a date before 1885.

17. A scam, a clever way to get money for nothing.

18. Franck, *A Vagabond Journey*, 361–62. Stage Irish adjusted.

19. A display of market goods on the ground.

20. Franck, *A Vagabond Journey*, 362–63. Stage Irish adjusted.

21. The 1903–4 British military expedition to Tibet led by future new age mystic Lt. Col. Francis Younghusband.

22. Franck, *A Vagabond Journey*, 363. Stage Irish adjusted. As we have seen, Dhammaloka had probably not been to Nepal, but rather was traveling in India during the previous three months.

23. Franck, 363–64. Stage Irish adjusted.

24. Franck, 364.

25. "Solved—the Riddle of Dama Laku 'the Wise One,' the Buddhist Abbot of Rangoon—Once an American Tramp," *San Francisco Examiner*, July 30, 1911, 56–57.

26. Franck, *A Vagabond Journey*, 365–66. Stage Irish adjusted.

27. Franck, 380–84.

28. Franck, 382.

29. Franck, 380–84.

Chapter 8

1. *Times of Burma*, January 2, 1906, 2.

2. *Burma Echo*, May 18, 1907, 10; "Rangoon Debating Society," *Burma Echo*, June 8, 1907, 9.

3. "Anglo Vernacular School," *Burma Echo*, July 6, 1907, 9.

4. Dhammaloka, "Medical," *Burma Echo*, September 14, 1907, 12.

5. "The Irish Hpoongyi the Only One in the World," *Rangoon Times*, July 6, 1907, 13–14.

6. "Buddhist Tract Society," *Burma Echo*, September 14, 1907, 12.

7. "Mandalay," *Burma Echo*, December 28, 1907, 9.

8. "Mandalay," *Burma Echo*, December 28, 1907, 9.

9. Sight-seer, "Mandalay," *Burma Echo*, January 18, 1908, 11.

10. "Mandalay," *Burma Echo*, January 4, 1908, 11.

11. A Sympathizer, "Myingyan," *Burma Echo*, February 8, 1908, 7.

12. "Henzada," *Burma Echo*, May 9, 1908, 9.

13. "Henzada," *Burma Echo*, May 9, 1908, 9.

14. "Minbu," *Burma Echo*, March 14, 1908, 9.

15. "Pakokku," *Burma Echo*, March 7, 1908, 8.

16. A Sympathizer, "Myingyan," *Burma Echo*, February 29, 1908, 8.

17. "Henzada," *Burma Echo*, May 9, 1908, 9.

18. A Sympathizer, "Myingyan," *Burma Echo*, February 8, 1908, 7.

19. A Sympathizer, "Myingyan," *Burma Echo*, February 29, 1908, 8.

20. "Pakokku," *Burma Echo*, March 7, 1908, 8.

21. "Shwegyin: U Dhammaloka Robbed," *Times of Burma*, April 19, 1902, 5.

22. "Book Money Found," *Singapore Free Press and Mercantile Advertiser*, May 8, 1902, 13.

23. "European Loafers as Buddhist Priests," *Singapore Free Press and Mercantile Advertiser*, December 2, 1904, 3.

24. "An Ex-Phoongyi Gets His Discharge," *Rangoon Times*, December 3, 1910, 10.

25. *Times of Burma*, January 4, 1905, 4.

26. "Advertisement: Revival of Buddhism," *Times of Burma*, April 17, 1901, 7.

27. "Singapore Buddhists," *Straits Times*, March 9, 1904, 5; "The Right Reverend Lord Abbot U Dhammaloka FTS," *Straits Times*, January 19, 1905, 4.

28. Purser, *Christian Missions in Burma*, 217.

29. "Buddhism." *Burma Echo*, September 7, 1907, 12.

30. "Buddhist Tract Society," *Burma Echo*, September 14, 1907, 12.

31. "Missions," *Lucifer* 6, no. 34 (June 15, 1890): 349; Dukes, *Everyday Life in China*, 214; Richard, *Forty-Five Years in China*, 272; "A Buddhist Tract Society," *Journal of the Maha-Bodhi Society* 5, no. 8 (December 1896): 57; Morris, *Life of John Murdoch LLD:*, 136; Young and Somaratna, *Vain Debates*, 210.

32. Dhammaloka, "A Hindu on Paine," *Blue Grass Blade* 23, no. 3 (December 12, 1909): 7.

33. "Buddhist Lent," *Burma Echo*, October 12, 1907, 12.

34. "Mandalay," *Burma Echo*, January 4, 1908, 11.

35. A Sympathizer, "Myingyan," *Burma Echo*, February 8, 1908, 7.

36. "Henzada," *Burma Echo*, May 9, 1908, 9.

37. Clark, "Buddhism on the Warpath"; Clark, *Memories of Many Men in Many Lands*, 387.

38. Clark, "Buddhism on the Warpath," 248.

39. Presumably Arthur Veitch White, a hydroelectric engineer and "flat earther." Schadewald, "Scientific Creationism, Geocentricity, and the Flat Earth."

40. Dhammaloka, "From Far-Off India," *Blue Grass Blade* 23, no. 3 (December 12, 1909): 6–7.

41. Dhammaloka, "A Hindu on Paine," *Blue Grass Blade* 23, no. 3 (December 12, 1909): 7. The description "Hindu" reflected the editor's limited knowledge of Asian religions.

42. MacDonald, *Fifty Years of Freethought*, 335.

43. "Letter to The Humanitarian Review," *Humanitarian Review* 9, no. 8 (March 1911): 507.

44. Dhammaloka's name also occurs in other Western freethinking publications without evidence of direct contact, such as the *Freie Wort*'s translation of his Akyab declaration.

45. Quoted in Remsburg, *Thomas Paine: The Apostle of Liberty*, 192.

46. Egoroff, *Buddha-Sakya-Muni*. Sakyamuni is a name of the Buddha.

47. "Madame Egoroff at Vidyodaya College," *Ceylon Observer*, January 31, 1909, 166.

48. "Russian Lady Artist Action for Damages against the Maha Bodhi Society," *Ceylon Observer*, July 22, 1912, 1255.

49. "Russian Lady Artist's Action v. Maha Bodhi Society," *Ceylon Observer*, June 10, 1912, 984; "Grievances of a Russian Lady and Her Mother," *Ceylon Observer*, March 2, 1912, 373.

50. Egoroff, *Buddhism: The Highest Religion*. Ganga is marijuana.

51. There is a reference on page 2 to another title by Brown: *Researches in Oriental History*.

52. In fact the Emanuel Temple was (and still is) a Chicago synagogue; the Jewish authorities ultimately canceled the event: "Girls Will Kiss Away the Debt," *Logansport Semi-Weekly Reporter*, December 3, 1909, 3; "Girls to Kiss $5000 Debt from Temple Emanuel Sunday Night," *The Inter Ocean*, December 1, 1909, 1; "Show Girls Offer to Replace Those Forbidden in Kissing Bee," *The Inter Ocean*, December 5, 1909, 11; "Kiss Sale Is Stopped," *San Francisco Examiner*, December 23, 1909, 17.

53. I.e., "Address to the Uncouth God."

54. "From Catholic Priest to Buddhist Monk," *Englishman*, April 11, 1912, 7; *Amrita Bazar Patrika*, November 26, 1910, 6.

55. The Burmese Young Men's Buddhist Association, not affiliated with the IYMBA in Japan or Dhammaloka's YMBAs in Southeast Asia. Its leadership was associated with educated elites in this period.

56. Ananda Metteyya's organization.

57. Christian preachers. In this period, "sky pilots" suggested harbor pilots guiding souls to a safe berth in heaven (as in Dhammaloka's "hymn" parody).

58. *The Teachings of Jesus Not Adapted to Modern Civilization*, 64.

59. Clark, "Buddhism on the Warpath," 247–48.

60. Coleman, *Bible God Disproved by Nature*.
61. Purser, *Christian Missions in Burma*, 217.
62. Peebles, *What Is Buddhism*.
63. Ingalls, *History of Atchison County, Kansas*.
64. Cox, "Dhammaloka as Social Movement Organizer."
65. Royle, *Victorian Infidels*, 70.
66. Coulter, *Hidden Tradition*.
67. Barnard, "Reading in Eighteenth-Century Ireland."
68. Our thanks to Keith Flett and Bob Jones for help in this area.
69. Taylor, *From Self-Help to Glamour*, 44.
70. Rothstein, *A House on Clerkenwell Green*, 35, 40, 45, 49.
71. Rothstein, 49–51.
72. Shipley, *Club Life*, 21.
73. Rogers, *Labour, Life and Literature: Some Memories of Sixty Years*, 69.
74. Shipley, *Club Life*, 37–38.
75. "The Far East: France and Siam, Position of the Treaty," *Homeward Mail*, April 4, 1903, 449.
76. Ben Reitman, who shared column space with Dhammaloka in *The Truth Seeker*, was involved in the Modern School movement. A college-educated newcomer found him "a vulgar and unstable character," evoking hostile missionaries' comments on Dhammaloka. Avrich, *Modern School Movement*, 126.
77. Higbie, *Indispensable Outcasts*, 191; citing: Flynt, *Notes of an Itinerant Policeman*, 216–18; see also: Flynt, *Tramping with Tramps*.
78. Higbie, *Indispensable Outcasts*, 191–92.
79. Hapgood, *The Spirit of Labor*, 413.
80. "The Truth Seeker (Masthead)," *The Truth Seeker*, January 1874, 1.
81. Murray, *A Fantastic Journey*, 26.
82. Franck, *A Vagabond Journey*, 375.
83. Sailors' homes (as opposed to missions) were provided by secular organizations, whether state, trade unions, or voluntary societies. Kennerley, "Merchant Seafarer Education."
84. "Christian Missions in China," *National Reformer*, September 20, 1891, 187–88.
85. "Bombay Secularists Meet Bradlaugh," *National Reformer*, January 26, 1890, 51.
86. Peebles, *What Is Buddhism*, 32.
87. Young and Somaratna, *Vain Debates*, 210.
88. Ingalls, *History of Atchison County, Kansas*, 505.
89. Ananda Metteyya, "International Freethought Congress," *Buddhism: An Illustrated Quarterly* 1, no. 4 (November 1904): 667–68. In fact the first had been held around 1860. This may refer to the Geneva meeting of 1903 or the Rome one of 1904. Batchelor, "The Other Enlightenment Project."
90. "Freethinkers in Rangoon," *The Burma Echo*, October 12, 1907, 12.
91. Taylor, *From Self-Help to Glamour*, 93.

Chapter 9

1. Much of the information in this chapter draws on research carried out in India and Sri Lanka for the Dhammaloka project by Dr. Mihirini Sirisena, who has also published an article on the tour: Sirisena, "Dissident Orientalist." We are deeply grateful for her work in obtaining and translating Dhammaloka's sermons from the *Sinhala Bauddhaya*. In addition, we owe a deep debt to Steven Kemper, author of the definitive biography of Anagarika Dharmapala, for his help with Dharmapala's diaries. His work has laid the historical groundwork for this chapter. Kemper, *Rescued from the Nation*.

2. Dhammaloka, "Dear Brother Dharmapala," *Journal of the Maha-Bodhi Society* 9, no. 8 (December 1900): 76.

3. "Burma (3): Account of Mr Dhammaloka," *Nipon*, December 17, 1902, 3; Cotes, "The Ordination of Asoka."

4. "From Catholic Priest to Buddhist Monk," *Englishman*, April 11, 1912, 7.

5. "Passengers to and from Ceylon," *Ceylon Observer*, August 27, 1909, 3; "Reverend U Dhammaloka's Lectures," *Sinhala Bauddhaya*, October 9, 1909, 3; Sirisena, "Dissident Orientalist."

6. *Sinhala Bauddhaya*, September 4, 1909; "Letters: A Lecture by Irish Priest U Dhammaloka," *Sinhala Bauddhaya*, November 20, 1909, 7; "The Speech European Rev Dhammaloka Gave at the Deepadruttama Temple," *Sinhala Bauddhaya*, September 25, 1909, 9; "Rev Dhammaloka Lectures and False Statements of Ill-Informed," *Sinhala Bauddhaya*, September 18, 1909, 3. Dharmapala diaries, September 24 and October 4, 1909.

7. "Reverend U Dhammaloka," *Sinhala Bauddhaya*, November 6, 1909, 5.

8. "Rev. U Dhammaloka and Mr. Anagarika Dharmapala Lectures," *Sinhala Bauddhaya*, September 11, 1909, 8; "Rev U Dhammaloka's English Lectures," *Sinhala Bauddhaya*, September 11, 1909, 9.

9. Harris, *Theravada Buddhism and the British Encounter*, 168.

10. Dharmapala's diaries were transcribed into typewritten volumes by the Anagarika Dharmapala Trust, Colombo, and copies are housed at the Sri Lankan National Archives and the Maha Bodhi Society Library in Colombo. For more on Dharmapala's diaries, see: Kemper, *Rescued from the Nation*, appendix 1.

11. The military metaphors resemble the language of the Salvation Army at the time.

12. "Regional Travels," *Sinhala Bauddhaya*, October 30, 1909, 9.

13. Translations by Mihirini Sirisena. The *Sinhala Bauddhaya* texts reflect notes of Harishchandra's interpreting of Dhammaloka's talks. We thus have the gist rather than any nuances.

14. Harris, *Theravada Buddhism and the British Encounter*, 203–4.

15. A leading site of Buddhist revival movements in Ceylon. Anne Blackburn, *Locations of Buddhism*, chapter 2.

16. "Rev U Dhammaloka's English Lectures," *Sinhala Bauddhaya*, September 11, 1909, 9.

17. Sirisena, "Dissident Orientalist."

18. Amrith, *Crossing the Bay of Bengal*.

19. Dharmapala diaries, October 12, 1909.

20. "Rev U Dhammaloka's English Lectures," *Sinhala Bauddhaya*, September 11, 1909, 9. Translation by Mihirini Sirisena.

21. "Christianity and the Study of Theory (Continued)," *Sinhala Bauddhaya*, October 2, 1909, 8.

22. "Rev U Dhammaloka's English Lectures," *Sinhala Bauddhaya*, September 11, 1909, 9.

23. "Christianity and Study of Theory (Continued)," *Sinhala Bauddhaya*, October 2, 1909, 8. This incidentally suggests that Arthur White, the Canadian flat earther who contacted Dhammaloka, would have gotten a dusty answer in the envelope we found (see Figure I.3 in the Introduction).

24. "Letters: A Lecture by Irish Priest U Dhammaloka," *Sinhala Bauddhaya*, November 20, 1909, 7; "U Dhammaloka: A Lecture Given by the Irish Priest," *Sinhala Bauddhaya*, November 27, 1909, 3; "U Dhammaloka: A Lecture Given by the Irish Priest," *Sinhala Bauddhaya*, December 11, 1909, 3. Translations by Mihirini Sirisena.

25. "A Lecture by Irish Priest U Dhammaloka," *Sinhala Bauddhaya*, November 20, 1909, 7. Translation by Mihirini Sirisena.

26. "A Lecture by Irish Priest U Dhammaloka," *Sinhala Bauddhaya*, November 20, 1909, 7. Translation by Mihirini Sirisena.

27. "A Lecture by Irish Priest U Dhammaloka," *Sinhala Bauddhaya*, November 20, 1909, 7. Translation by Mihirini Sirisena.

28. Avrich, *Modern School Movement*.

29. "A Lecture by Irish Priest U Dhammaloka," *Sinhala Bauddhaya*, November 20, 1909, 7. Translation by Mihirini Sirisena.

30. "A Lecture by Irish Priest U Dhammaloka," *Sinhala Bauddhaya*, November 20, 1909, 7. Translation by Mihirini Sirisena.

31. "A Lecture by Irish Priest U Dhammaloka," *Sinhala Bauddhaya*, November 20, 1909, 7. Translation by Mihirini Sirisena.

32. Continuation of the sermon in "U Dhammaloka: A Lecture Given by the Irish Priest," *Sinhala Bauddhaya*, November 27, 1909, 3. Translation by Mihirini Sirisena.

33. The reference is presumably to the 1873 Panadura debate and earlier debates in the 1860s. Dhammaloka praised "the work of world famous Migettuwatte Gunananda Thero," on the twenty-ninth anniversary of his death, suggesting familiarity with this bit of Ceylonese history. "The Speech European Rev Dhammaloka Gave at the Deepadruttama Temple," *Sinhala Bauddhaya*, September 25, 1909, 9; Malalgoda, *Buddhism in Sinhalese Society*, 225; Young and Somaratna, *Vain Debates*, 155.

34. "U Dhammaloka: A Lecture Given by the Irish Priest," *Sinhala Bauddhaya*, November 27, 1909, 3. Translation by Mihirini Sirisena.

35. "U Dhammaloka: A Lecture Given by the Irish Priest," *Sinhala Bauddhaya*, November 27, 1909, 3. Translation by Mihirini Sirisena.

36. "U Dhammaloka: A Lecture Given by the Irish Priest," *Sinhala Bauddhaya*, November 27, 1909, 3. Translation by Mihirini Sirisena.

37. "U Dhammaloka: A Lecture Given by the Irish Priest," *Sinhala Bauddhaya*, November 27, 1909, 3. Translation by Mihirini Sirisena. The story had been around for a while.

At an 1884 meeting with Christian missionaries in London, the Maori secretary of King Tawhiao told the same story, to the discomfiture of his audience. *Auckland Star*, October 12, 1894, 5.

38. Continuation of the sermon in "U Dhammaloka: A Lecture Given by the Irish Priest," *Sinhala Bauddhaya*, December 11, 1909, 3. Translation by Mihirini Sirisena.

39. "U Dhammaloka: A Lecture Given by the Irish Priest," *Sinhala Bauddhaya*, December 11, 1909, 3. Translation by Mihirini Sirisena.

40. In his lecture of November 4, Dhammaloka mentioned "the need to open a women's school in the region," as he had envisaged also in Singapore, Bangkok, and Penang. "Bringing Reverend U Dhammaloka to Rambukkana," *Sinhala Bauddhaya*, November 6, 1909, 9. Translation by Mihirini Sirisena.

41. A later entry may relate to this incident. On November 5, Dharmapala records "*a dream that I was beating a man for having used obscene words.*"

42. See Chapter 6.

43. Anniversary of the controversial partition of Bengal in 1905. See Chapter 10.

44. Annie Besant had become president of the Theosophical Society two years earlier.

45. I.e., in favorable circumstances, probably referring to Dhammaloka's health; he was ill from November 16–23.

46. Harishchandra was one of only two "anagarika brahmacharyas" (lay celibates) ordained by Dharmapala himself. Kemper, *Rescued from the Nation*, 43 n 94.

47. Harris, *Theravada Buddhism and the British Encounter*, chapter 21.

48. Kemper, *Rescued from the Nation*.

49. Dhammaloka, "Dear Brother Dharmapala," *Journal of the Maha-Bodhi Society* 9, no. 8 (December 1900): 76.

50. Dharmapala, "Our Duty to the Peoples of the West," *Maha-Bodhi and the United Buddhist World* 35, no. 9 (September 1927): 424. Cited in Harris, *Theravada Buddhism and the British Encounter*, 204.

51. Young and Somaratna, *Vain Debates*, 45.

52. Young and Somaratna, 139.

53. Young and Somaratna, 210.

54. *Ceylon Independent*, September 11, 1909; reproduced in: Dharmapala, "The Irish Buddhist Priest," *Maha-Bodhi and the United Buddhist World* 17, no. 10 (October 1909): 257–59. Thanks to Adrian Hermann for this reference.

55. Spitz, "The Catholic Church in Ceylon," *Tablet*, April 28, 1906, 8–10. Young and Somaratna describe an 1874 *Messenger* editorial as "characteristically offensive" and "disingenuously claiming to be above reproach." Young and Somaratna, *Vain Debates*, 182–83.

56. "An Irish Buddhist Priest," *Ceylon Observer*, September 4, 1909, 1337. D. B. Jayatileke of the local Young Men's Buddhist Association wrote to the *Observer* and *Catholic Messenger* denying responsibility for the tour: Jayatileke, "Correspondence: The Irish Buddhist Priest," *Ceylon Observer*, September 14, 1909, 1376.

57. "Rev Dhammaloka Lectures and False Statements of Ill-Informed," *Sinhala Bauddhaya*, September 18, 1909, 3. Translation by Mihirini Sirisena.

58. The cartoon appeared around September 18–19, 1909, and possibly in a 1909 *Amicus Annual*, but so far we have been unable to find a copy.

59. "A Lament," *Sinhala Bauddhaya*, September 25, 1909, 10. Translation by Mihirini Sirisena.

60. "Lectures on Christianity," *Ceylon Observer*, October 5, 1909, 1491.

61. "Lectures on Christianity," *Ceylon Observer*, October 5, 1909, 1491.

62. "Rev. U Dhammaloka and Mr. Anagarika Dharmapala Lectures," *Sinhala Bauddhaya*, September 11, 1909, 8. Translation by Mihirini Sirisena.

63. Buddhist drumming, perceived as intrusive and disruptive of Christian places of worship, was the object of constant complaint from missionaries and civil servants. Young and Somaratna, *Vain Debates*, 191.

64. "Rev. U Dhammaloka and Mr. Anagarika Dharmapala Lectures," *Sinhala Bauddhaya*, September 11, 1909, 8.Translation by Mihirini Sirisena.

65. "The Irish Buddhist Priest," *Ceylon Observer*, September 15, 1909, 1386.

66. "The Irish Buddhist Priest," *Ceylon Observer*, September 11, 1909, 1366.

67. "The Irish Buddhist Priest," *Ceylon Observer*, September 11, 1909, 1366. The September 4 supplement to *Sinhala Bauddhaya* summarized two of Dhammaloka's talks: "Where Did the Bible Come From?" and "What Has Christianity Done to the World?" and outlined a third, on his mission and the contradictions of the Bible, *in extenso.* Two further lectures were published in full, in installments.

68. *Catholic Messenger*, September 17, 1909, reprinted in: "Dhammaloka Dogged by Police," *Ceylon Observer*, September 18, 1909, 1404.

69. "Outstation News: Badulla," *Ceylon Observer*, November 1, 1909, 1629.

70. Powell, *Manual of a Mystic*.

71. Dharmapala diaries, October 6, 1909.

72. "Reverend U Dhammaloka's Lectures," *Sinhala Bauddhaya*, October 9, 1909, 3. Translation by Mihirini Sirisena.

73. "Reverend U Dhammaloka," *Sinhala Bauddhaya*, November 6, 1909, 5. Translation by Mihirini Sirisena.

74. "Bringing Reverend U Dhammaloka to Rambukkana," *Sinhala Bauddhaya*, November 6, 1909, 9. Translation by Mihirini Sirisena.

75. "Ceylon," *Woodstock Letters* 39, no. 2 (1910): 255.

76. "The Irish 'Buddhist Priest': A Hurried Departure from Ceylon," *Ceylon Observer*, November 6, 1909, 1654. The book is presumably De Souza, *Credentials of Christianity*. During this period the Buddhist Tract Society was indeed publishing (short) books.

77. "Pan Buddhistic Congress," *Tribune*, April 7, 1910, 2.

Chapter 10

1. Chatterji, *Maha Bodhi Society Diamond Jubilee*, 78–79.

2. Clark, "Buddhism on the Warpath."

3. Turner, *Saving Buddhism*, 67–69.

4. "J. Dhammaloka Bound Over," *Amrita Bazar Patrika*, December 3, 1910, 8.

5. *Truth Seeker*, December 24, 1910, quoted in: "En Hädelseprocess i Bortre Asien" *Forskaren [The Investigator]* 19, no. 1 (January 1911): 105–9.

6. The Irish-run St. Patrick's School in Moulmein was at this point struggling with a student Buddhist Association that no doubt challenged its Catholic rituals in various ways.

7. "En Hädelseprocess i Bortre Asien," *Forskaren [The Investigator]* 19, no. 1 (January 1911): 105–9. Translation by Laurence Cox. Darrow was convicted (so the charges were not mere retaliation) but was fined, in today's money, a mere US $250 compared with Dhammaloka's US $20,000. (Rs 2,000).

8. Under paragraph 153a of the Indian Penal Code.

9. "The Irish 'Buddhist Priest': A Hurried Departure from Ceylon," *Ceylon Observer*, November 6, 1909, 1654.

10. "J. Dhammaloka Bound Over," *Amrita Bazar Patrika*, December 3, 1910, 8.

11. "En Hädelseprocess i Bortre Asien," *Forskaren [The Investigator]* 19, no. 1 (January 1911): 105–9. Translation by Laurence Cox.

12. "En Hädelseprocess i Bortre Asien," *Forskaren [The Investigator]* 19, no. 1 (January 1911): 105–9. Translation by Laurence Cox.

13. "En Hädelseprocess i Bortre Asien," *Forskaren [The Investigator]* 19, no. 1 (January 1911): 105–9. Translation by Laurence Cox.

14. *Amrita Bazar Patrika*, November 26, 1910, 6.

15. "A 'Relic' Hawker," *Singapore Free Press and Mercantile Advertiser*, January 12, 1904, 5.

16. Maung Zeyya, *Myanmar lu kyaw taya* [One hundred exceptional Myanmar men and women], 28–29; Chatterjie, *Meeting the Personalities*, 18–19; "Burma List No. 32 History Sheet of U Chit Hlaing," 1933. BL IOR/M/1/1. India Office Records, British Library, London.

17. "J. Dhammaloka Bound Over," *Amrita Bazar Patrika*, December 3, 1910, 8.

18. *Amrita Bazar Patrika*, December 10, 1910, 8; Chaudhri, "Criminal Revision No. 378B of 1910."

19. Although the extant Rangoon papers are remarkably silent on the issue at this point—perhaps encouraged by colonial officials. "Buddhist Priest Prosecuted," *Amrita Bazar Patrika*, November 26, 1910; "European Buddhist Charged with Sedition," *Times of India*, November 28, 1910, 10.

20. *United Burma*, December 4, 1910. Translation by Laurence Cox from "En Hädelseprocess I Bortre Asien," *Forskaren [The Investigator]* 19, no. 1 (January 1911): 105–9.

21. "En Hädelseprocess i Bortre Asien," *Forskaren [The Investigator]* 19, no. 1 (January 1911): 105–9. Translation by Laurence Cox.

22. *Amrita Bazar Patrika*, December 10, 1910, 8.

23. "The Appeal Case of U Dhammaloka," *Amrita Bazar Patrika*, January 13, 1911, 7.

24. Coclanis, "Welfare of the Weak: Dr P J Mehta," 10.

25. Hunt, *Gandhi in London*, 133.

26. Mehrotra, "The 'Reader' in Hind Swaraj, Dr. Pranjivan Mehta, 1864–1932"; Mehrotra, *The Mahatma & the Doctor*.

27. Coclanis, "Welfare of the Weak: Dr P J Mehta," 52–54.

28. By 1918 he would be ordered to leave Burma—and able to defeat this order publicly. Coclanis, 51–52.
29. *Times of Burma*, March 27, 1901, 6.
30. Mehrotra, "The 'Reader' in Hind Swaraj, Dr. Pranjivan Mehta, 1864–1932." In 1907 *United Burma* would "frankly confess that we are in line with the views of the Indian National Congress."
31. Cutting from *The Panjabee*, June 12, 1907, cited in Singh, *Deportation of Lala Lajpat Rai*, 103.
32. Sarkar, *Modern India*, 138.
33. "The Appeal Case of U Dhammaloka," *Amrita Bazar Patrika*, January 13, 1911, 7.
34. "The Appeal Case of U Dhammaloka," *Amrita Bazar Patrika*, January 13, 1911, 7.
35. "The Appeal Case of U Dhammaloka," *Amrita Bazar Patrika*, January 13, 1911, 7.
36. "The Appeal Case of U Dhammaloka," *Amrita Bazar Patrika*, January 13, 1911, 7.
37. "The Appeal Case of U Dhammaloka," *Amrita Bazar Patrika*, January 13, 1911, 7.
38. Chaudhri, "Criminal Revision No. 378B of 1910," 250.
39. Chaudhri, 250.
40. "From Catholic Priest to Buddhist Monk," *Englishman*, April 11, 1912, 7.
41. The "White Australia" policy required passenger lists to identify race and nationality.
42. Thompson and Thompson, "A Brief History of the Perth Lodge of the Theosophical Society 1897 to 1976."
43. Those professing as Buddhist rose from 761 in 1901 to almost 2,000 in 1911. "The Australian Census," *West Australian*, May 20, 1912, 8. The history of Buddhism in Perth today looks back only as far as the 1970s. Croucher, *Buddhism in Australia 1848–1988*, 11–12.
44. Loreley A. Morling, genealogist; pers. comm. November 15, 2011.
45. "From Catholic Priest to Buddhist Monk," *Englishman*, April 11, 1912, 7.
46. According to the sale particulars in the following year. *Argus*, October 25, 1913, 3. Originally built by a John Tankard, in 1912 and 1913 Melbourne Directories it is shown as Tankard's, with Mrs. C. E. Neale's name after it. Our thanks to archival researcher Helen Doxford Harris for this and other information.
47. See, e.g., Newsinger, "Jim Larkin, Syndicalism and the 1913 Dublin Lockout."
48. "From Catholic Priest to Buddhist Monk," *Englishman*, April 11, 1912, 7.
49. "A Pioneer Buddhist Monk," *American Theosophist & Theosophic Messenger* 14, (September 1913): 1023.
50. *Buddhist Review* 4 (1912): 240.
51. "Rev. U Dhammaloka," *Singapore Free Press and Mercantile Advertiser*, April 23, 1912, 7.
52. "Rev. U Dhammaloka," *Singapore Free Press and Mercantile Advertiser*, June 13, 1912, 378.
53. "Rev. U Dhammaloka," *Singapore Free Press and Mercantile Advertiser*, June 13, 1912, 378. The meeting of the Grand Lodge occupied several days over the Easter weekend. "Good Templars," *Brisbane Courier*, April 6, 1912, 6.
54. "Death of Mrs Jephson," *Brisbane Courier*, January 6, 1908, 7.

55. "Religious," *Brisbane Courier*, January 7, 1905, 16. "Dohertson" is a rare name and probably a best guess by the editor at the signature of "Roberts," the Welsh-American novice (see Chapter 6).

56. Croucher, *Buddhism in Australia 1848–1988*, 4–6; Adam and Hughes, *The Buddhists of Australia*, 7.

57. See the digital humanities website documenting these atrocities: Ryan, "Colonial Frontier Massacres in Central and Eastern Australia 1788–1930." https://c21ch.new-castle.edu.au/colonialmassacres/introduction.php

58. "Missing Friends," *Victoria Police Gazette*, June 20, 1912, 317.

59. The 1911 census records 4.5 million inhabitants, mainly whites. In 1911, 3,699,478 of the total population ("excluding full-blooded aborigines") had been born in Australia and almost 600,000 were immigrants from the UK (including Ireland), with far smaller numbers from other European countries. Knibbs, *Census of Australia*, 2073.

60. Norris, "Deakin, Alfred (1856–1919)."

61. "Rev. U Dhammaloka," *Singapore Free Press and Mercantile Advertiser*, June 13, 1912, 378.

62. The Chinese Exclusion Act of 1882 had been made permanent in 1902; a later Immigration Act in 1917, the Asiatic Barred Zone Act, would prevent immigration from the Asia-Pacific region including British India.

63. Even thirty years later, the Italian-American monk Ven. Lokanatha's mission to the USA was met with "mocking indifference." Deslippe, "Brooklyn Bhikkhu."

64. "En Hädelseprocess i Bortre Asien," *Forskaren [The Investigator]* 19, no. 1 (January 1911): 105–9.

65. "Solved!" *Atlanta Constitution*, July 30, 1911, B6.

66. "The Irish Buddhist Priest," *Bangkok Times and Weekly Mail*, September 11, 1903, 4.

67. Ruan, Secretary of the Japan & India Club, Tokyo, "U Dhammaloka in Japan," *Times of Burma*, January 17, 1903, 5.

68. "Rev. U Dhammaloka," *Singapore Free Press and Mercantile Advertiser*, June 13, 1912, 378.

69. "Burma (4): Account of Mr Dhammaloka," *Nipon*, December 18, 1902, 3.

70. "An Irish Buddhist: Bound for Thibet," *Japan Times*, February 13, 1903, 5.

71. "From Catholic Priest to Buddhist Monk," *Englishman*, April 11, 1912, 7.

72. See Cox, *Buddhism and Ireland*, chapter 6 for recent examples.

73. Cox, "Researching Transnational Activist Lives."

74. Skilton, "Elective Affinities."

75. Mishra, *From the Ruins of Empire*.

76. Gandhi, *Affective Communities*.

Epitaph

1. "Here & There," *Ceylon Observer*, July 5, 1912, 1205.

2. *Singapore Free Press and Mercantile Advertiser*, October 31, 1912, 276.

3. *Singapore Free Press and Mercantile Advertiser*, November 7, 1912, 298.

4. Purser and Saunders, *Modern Buddhism in Burma*, 87.

5. *Weekly Sun*, October 18, 1913, 3.

6. Dharmapala diaries, October 14, 1913.

7. For a discussion of the Thai Prince monk Jinavaravamsa, see: Anne Blackburn, *Locations of Buddhism*, 178–80.

8. Dharmapala diaries, October 16, 1913.

Bibliography

Newspapers

Amrita Bazar Patrika (Calcutta)
Arakan Times (Akyab)
Argus (Melbourne)
Asahi Shimbun (Osaka)
Atlanta Constitution
Auckland Star (New Zealand)
Bangkok Times and Weekly Mail
Blue Grass Blade (Lexington, KY)
Boston Sunday Post
Brisbane Courier
Burma Echo (Rangoon)
Ceylon Independent (Colombo)
Ceylon Observer (Colombo)
Christian Advocate (New York)
Colonies and India (London)
Daily Advertiser (Singapore)
Das Freie Wort (Frankfurt)
Deseret Evening News (Salt Lake City)
Empress (Calcutta)
Englishman (Calcutta)
Forskaren [The Investigator] (Minneapolis)
Hackney Express and Shoreditch Observer (London)
Hanthawaddy Weekly Review [in Burmese] (Rangoon)
Homeward Mail (London)
Hong Kong Telegraph
Inter Ocean (Chicago)
Japan Times (Tokyo)
Literary Digest (New York)
Logansport Semi-Weekly Reporter (Indiana)
London and China Telegraph (London)
London Evening Standard
Lutheran Observer (Philadelphia)
Maha-Bodhi News [in Burmese] (Rangoon)
Monmouthshire Beacon (Monmouth, UK)
New York Times
National Reformer
Nipon (Tokyo)
Northern Miner (Queensland)
Pioneer (Allahabad)

Rangoon Times
Salt Lake Herald-Republican
San Francisco Examiner
Singapore Free Press and Mercantile Advertiser
Sinhala Bauddhaya (Colombo)
Straits Echo (Penang)
Straits Times (Singapore)
Sunday Independent (Dublin)
Supplement to the Ceylon Observer (Colombo)
Sydney Morning Herald
Takanawa Gakuho [Takanawa University Gazette] (Tokyo)
Times (London)
Times of Burma (Rangoon)
Times of India (Bombay)
Tribune (Lahore)
United Burma (Rangoon)
Victoria Police Gazette (Melbourne)
Weekly Sun (Singapore)
West Australian (Perth)
Yomiuri Shimbun (Tokyo)
Yorkshire Post and Leeds Intelligencer

Buddhist Journals and Their Contemporaries

American Theosophist & Theosophic Messenger (Los Angeles)
Annales de l'Extrême Orient (Paris)
Baptist Missionary Magazine (Boston)
British Buddhist (London)
Buddhism: An Illustrated Quarterly Review (Rangoon)
Buddhist Review (London)
Burman Buddhist (Rangoon)
Catholic Advance (Wichita)
Christian Advocate (New York)
East and the West: A Quarterly Review for the Study of Missions (London)
Humanitarian Review (Los Angeles)
Indian World (Calcutta)
Journal of the Maha-Bodhi Society/Maha-Bodhi and United Buddhist World/Maha-Bodhi
    (Calcutta)
Lucifer (London)
Missions: A Baptist Monthly Magazine (New York)
Straits Chinese Magazine (Singapore)
Tablet (London)
Sketch (London)
Truth (London)
Voice: An Independent Journal of Christian Civilization (Tokyo)
Woodstock Letters (Maryland)

Archival Sources

Adyar Library and Research Centre, Adyar.
Anagarika Dharmapala Trust, Maha Bodhi Society, Colombo.
India Office Records, British Library, London.
Myanmar National Archives, Yangon, Myanmar.
Public Record Office Victoria, Melbourne, Australia.
Special Collections, Criss Library, University of Nebraska, Omaha.
Special Collections Research Center, University of Chicago Library, Chicago.

Books, Tracts, and Articles

Adam, Enid, and Philip J. Hughes. *The Buddhists of Australia*. Canberra: Australian Government Publishing Service, 1996.

Amrith, Sunil S. *Crossing the Bay of Bengal: The Furies of Nature and the Fortunes of Migrants*. Cambridge, MA: Harvard University Press, 2013.

Ananda Maitriya. *The Foundation of the Sangha of the West; Being an Account of the Upasampada Ordination of Bhikkhu Ananda Maitriya (Allan Bennett MacGregor)*. Rangoon: Hanthawaddy Printing Works, 1902.

Anderson, Nels. *The Hobo: The Sociology of the Homeless Man*. Chicago: University of Chicago Press, 1923.

Arnold, David. "European Orphans and Vagrants in India in the Nineteenth Century." *Journal of Imperial and Commonwealth History* 7, no. 2 (January 1979): 104–27.

Avrich, Paul. *The Haymarket Tragedy*. Vol. 2. Princeton, NJ: Princeton University Press, 1984.

Avrich, Paul. *The Modern School Movement: Anarchism and Education in the United States*. Oakland, CA: AK Press, 2006.

Ba U. *My Burma: The Autobiography of a President*. 2nd ed. New York: Taplinger, 1959.

Barnard, Toby. "Reading in Eighteenth-Century Ireland: Public and Private Pleasures." In *The Experience of Reading: Irish Historical Perspectives*, edited by Bernadette Cunningham and Máire Kennedy, 60–77. Dublin: Library Association of Ireland, 1999.

Bartholomeusz, Tessa J. *Women under the Bo Tree: Buddhist Nuns in Sri Lanka*. New York: Cambridge University Press, 1994.

Barua, D. Mitra. "Thrice Honored Sangharaja Saramedha (1801–82): Arakan-Chittagong Buddhism across Colonial and Counter-Colonial Power." *The Journal of Burma Studies* 23, no. 1 (2019): 37–85.

Batchelor, Stephen. "The Other Enlightenment Project." In *Faith and Praxis in a Postmodern Age*, edited by Ursula King, 112–27. New York: Cassell, 1998.

Bazell, C. "Education in Singapore." In *One Hundred Years of Singapore*, edited by Roland St. John Braddell, Gilbert Edward Brooke, and Walter Makepeace, 427–76. London: Murray, 1921.

Blackburn, Anne. *Locations of Buddhism: Colonialism and Modernity in Sri Lanka*. Chicago: University of Chicago Press, 2010.

Bocking, Brian. "'A Man of Work and Few Words'? Dhammaloka beyond Burma." *Contemporary Buddhism* 11, no. 2 (November 2010): 125–47.

Bocking, Brian. "Flagging up Buddhism: Charles Pfoundes (Omoie Tetzunostzuke) among the International Congresses and Expositions, 1893–1905." *Contemporary Buddhism* 14, no. 1 (2013) 17–37.

Bocking, Brian. "Shinto." In *Encyclopedia of Religion*, 2nd ed., edited by Lindsey Jones, 8356–71. Detroit: Gale Macmillan, 2005.

Bocking, Brian. "U Dhammaloka: The Irish Pongyi (1856–1914) in India, Nepal and Tibet." *South and Southeast Asia Culture and Religion* 6 (2012): 73–86.

Bocking, Brian, Phibul Choompolpaisal, Laurence Cox, and Alicia Turner. *A Buddhist Crossroads: Pioneer Western Buddhists and Asian Networks 1860–1960*. London: Routledge, 2014.

Bocking, Brian, Laurence Cox, and Shin'ichi Yoshinaga. "The First Buddhist Mission to the West: Charles Pfoundes and the London Buddhist Mission of 1889–1892." *DISKUS* 16, no. 3 (2014): 1–33. http://mural.maynoothuniversity.ie/5629/1/LC_first%20bud-dhist.pdf

Braddell, Roland St. John, Gilbert Edward Brooke, and Walter Makepeace. *One Hundred Years of Singapore: Being Some Account of the Capital of the Straits Settlements from Its Foundation by Sir Stamford Raffles on the 6th February 1819 to the 6th February 1919*. 2 vols. London: Murray, 1921.

Braun, Erik. *The Birth of Insight: Meditation, Modern Buddhism and the Burmese Monk Ledi Sayadaw*. Chicago: University of Chicago Press, 2013.

Breathnach, Colm. "Working-Class Resistance in Pre-Famine County Dublin: The Dalkey Quarry Strikes of the 1820s." *Saothar* 30 (2005): 9–19.

[Brown, George W.] *The Teachings of Jesus Not Adapted to Modern Civilization*. Rangoon: Printed and published by the Buddhist Tract Society, at the Burma Echo Press, 1910.

Brownlow, Louis. *The Autobiography of Louis Brownlow*. Vol. I. Chicago: University of Chicago, 1958.

Burris, John P. *Exhibiting Religion: Colonialism and Spectacle at International Expositions, 1851–1893*. Charlottesville: University Press of Virginia, 2001.

Candier, Aurore. "Conjuncture and Reform in the Late Konbaung Period: How Prophecies, Omens and Rumors Motivated Political Action from 1866 to 1869." *Journal of Burma Studies* 15, no. 2 (December 2011): 231–62.

Cannadine, David. *Ornamentalism: How the British Saw Their Empire*. Oxford: Oxford University Press, 2002.

Chandler, Stuart. "Chinese Buddhism in America: Identity and Practice." In *The Faces of Buddhism in America*, edited by Charles Prebish and Kenneth Tanaka. Berkeley: University of California Press, 1998.

Chatterjie, S. *Meeting the Personalities: Burma Series*. Rangoon: Rasika Rajani Press, 1956.

Chatterji, Suniti Kumar, ed. *Maha Bodhi Society of India: Diamond Jubilee Souvenir 1891–1951*. Calcutta: Devapriya Valisinha, Maha Bodhi Society, 1952.

Chaudhri, S. D. "Lower Burma Chief Court Criminal Revision No. 378B of 1910, January 31, 1911." *The Criminal Law Journal of India: Containing Full Reports of All Reported Criminal Cases of the High Courts and Chief Courts, &c. in India* 12 (1911): 248–50.

Choompolpaisal, Phibul. "Tai-Burmese-Lao Buddhisms in the 'Modernizing' of Ban Thawai (Bangkok): The Dynamic Interaction between Ethnic Minority Religion and British–Siamese Centralization in the Late Nineteenth/Early Twentieth Centuries." *Contemporary Buddhism* 14 (2013): 94–115.

Clark, Francis E. "Buddhism on the Warpath." *The Independent . . . Devoted to the Consideration of Politics, Social and Economic* 68, no. 3192 (February 3, 1910): 246–49.

Clark, Francis E. *Memories of Many Men in Many Lands: An Autobiography.* Boston and Chicago: United Society of Christian Endeavor, 1922.

Coclanis, Angelo. "Welfare of the Weak: Dr PJ Mehta and the Fight for Improved Conditions for Indian Labour Migrants in Rangoon, 1899–1932." Master's thesis, Columbia University and The London School of Economics, 2015.

Coleman, Wm Emmette. *The Bible God Disproved by Nature.* New York: D. M. Bennett, 1875.

Conrad, Joseph. *The Shadow-Line: A Confession.* London: Dent, 1917.

Cotes, Mrs. Everard [Sara Jeanette Duncan]. "In Burma with the Viceroy." *Scribner's Magazine* 32 (July 1902): 58–72.

Cotes, Mrs. Everard [Sara Jeanette Duncan]. "The Ordination of Asoka." *Harper's Monthly Magazine* 105 (October 1902): 753–59.

Coulter, Carol. *The Hidden Tradition: Feminism, Women, and Nationalism in Ireland.* Cork: Cork University Press, 1993.

Cox, Laurence. *Buddhism and Ireland: From the Celts to the Counter-Culture and Beyond.* Sheffield, UK: Equinox, 2013.

Cox, Laurence. "European Buddhist Traditions." In *Oxford Handbook of Contemporary Buddhism*, edited by Michael Jerryson, 332–45. New York: Oxford University Press, 2016.

Cox, Laurence. "Researching Transnational Activist Lives: Irish Buddhists and the British Empire." *Interface: A Journal for and about Social Movements* 8, no. 2 (2016): 171–83.

Cox, Laurence. "Rethinking Early Western Buddhists: Beachcombers, 'Going Native' and Dissident Orientalism." *Contemporary Buddhism* 14, no. 1 (2013): 116–33.

Cox, Laurence. "The Politics of the Buddhist Revival: U Dhammaloka as Social Movement Organizer." *Contemporary Buddhism* 11, no. 2 (November 2010): 173–227.

Cox, Laurence, and Mihirini Sirisena. "Early Western Lay Buddhists in Colonial Asia: John Bowles Daly and the Buddhist Theosophical Society of Ceylon." *Journal of the Irish Society for the Academic Study of Religions* 2 (2016): 108–39.

Cox, Laurence, and Alicia Turner. "International Religious Organisations in a Colonial World: The Maha Bodhi Society in Arakan." In *Theosophy across Boundaries*, edited by Hans-Martin Krämer and Julian Strube. Albany: State University of New York Press, forthcoming.

Croker, Bithia Mary. *The Road to Mandalay: A Tale of Burma.* London: Cassell, 1917.

Crosby, Kate. *Theravada Buddhism: Continuity, Diversity and Identity.* Chichester: Wiley-Blackwell, 2014.

Crosby, Kate. "Ordination and Disrobing in Theravada Buddhism: The Sangha as a Barometer of the Community." *Religions of South Asia* 8, no. 1 (2014): 97–108.

Cross, Ira Brown. *A History of the Labor Movement in California.* Berkeley: University of California Press, 1935.

Croucher, Paul. *Buddhism in Australia 1848–1988.* Kensington: New South Wales University Press, 1989.

Crow, John L. "The White Knight in the Yellow Robe: Allan Bennett's Search for Truth." Master's thesis, University of Amsterdam, 2009.

De Souza, Armand. *The Credentials of Christianity Examined in the East.* Colombo: Young Men's Buddhist Association, 1909.

DePastino, Todd. *Citizen Hobo: How a Century of Homelessness Shaped America.* Chicago: University of Chicago Press, 2003.

Deslippe, Philip. "Brooklyn Bhikkhu: How Salvatore Cioffi Became the Venerable Lokanatha." *Contemporary Buddhism* 14, no. 1 (May 2013): 169–86.

"Dhammaloka v Emperor." *Criminal Law Journal of India* 12 (1911): 248–50.

Donogh, Walter Russell. *The History and Law of Sedition and Cognate Offences, Penal and Preventive, with a Summary of Press Legislation in India and an Excerpt of the Acts in Force Relating to the Press, the Stage, and Public Meetings.* London: W. Thacker, 1917.

Doran, Christine. "Bright Celestial: Progress in the Political Thought of Tan Teck Soon." *Sojourn: Journal of Social Issues in Southeast Asia* 21, no. 1 (2006): 46–67.

Dukes, Edwin. *Everyday Life in China: Or, Scenes along River and Road in Fuh-Kien.* London: Religious Tract Society, 1885.

Dumoulin, Heinrich, and John C. Maraldo. *Buddhism in the Modern World.* New York: Macmillan, 1976.

Dún Laoghaire Genealogical Society, ed. *Irish Genealogical Sources.* Vol. 6. School Registers 1861–1872 and 1891–1939. Dún Laoghaire: Dún Laoghaire Genealogical Society, 1997.

Dunne, Terry. "Cultures of Resistance in Pre-Famine Ireland." PhD thesis, National University of Ireland Maynooth, 2015.

Edwards, Penny. "Watching the Detectives: The Elusive Exile of Prince Myngoon of Burma." In *Exile in Colonial Asia: Kings, Convicts, Commemoration*, edited by Ronit Ricci, Jerry H. Bentley and Anand A. Yang, 248–78. Honolulu: Hawai'i University Press, 2016.

Egoroff, Sophia. *Buddha-Sakya-Muni: A Historical Personage Who Lived Towards B.C. 390–320 The Divine Socialist. His Life and Preachings, His Salutary Influence and the Civilization of the Whole World.* Ceylon: Partially Published at Maha Bodhi Press, 1910.

Egoroff, Sophia. *Buddhism: The Highest Religion.* Rangoon: Buddhist Tract Society and Burma Echo Press, 1909.

Fahey, David M. *Temperance and Racism: John Bull, Johnny Reb, and the Good Templars.* Lexington: University Press of Kentucky, 1996.

Fahey, David M. "Temperance Internationalism: Guy Hayler and the World Prohibition Federation." *Social History of Alcohol and Drugs* 20 (Spring 2006): 247–75.

Fischer-Tiné, Harald. "Britain's Other Civilising Mission: Class Prejudice, European 'Loaferism' and the Workhouse-System in Colonial India." *Indian Economic & Social History Review* 42, no. 3 (September 1, 2005): 295–338.

Fischer-Tiné, Harald. *Low and Licentious Europeans: Race, Class, and "White Subalternity" in Colonial India.* New Delhi: Orient BlackSwan, 2009.

Fisher, Gertrude Adams. *A Woman Alone in the Heart of Japan.* Boston: L. C. Page, 1906.

Flynt, Josiah. *Notes of an Itinerant Policeman.* Boston: L.C. Page, 1900.

Flynt, Josiah. *Tramping with Tramps: Studies and Sketches of Vagabond Life.* New York: Century, 1899.

Franck, Harry Alverson. *A Vagabond Journey Around the World: A Narrative of Personal Experience.* New York: Century, 1910.

Franck, Harry Alverson. "Girdles the World Without a Cent: Harry A. Franck, Sociologist, Tells How He 'Beat' His Way Around the World." *New York Times*, March 20, 1910.

Franklin, J. Jeffrey. *The Lotus and the Lion: Buddhism and the British Empire.* Ithaca, NY: Cornell University Press, 2008.

Frost, Mark Ravinder. "Asia's Maritime Networks and the Colonial Public Sphere, 1840–1920." *New Zealand Journal of Asian Studies* 6, no. 2 (December 2004): 63–90.

Frost, Mark Ravinder. "Emporium in Imperio: Nanyang Networks and the Straits Chinese in Singapore, 1819–1914." *Journal of Southeast Asian Studies* 36 (February 2005): 29–66.

Gandhi, Leela. *Affective Communities: Anticolonial Thought, Fin-de-Siècle Radicalism, and the Politics of Friendship*. Durham, NC: Duke University Press, 2006.

Hagger, Florence. "Brisbane Lodge Golden Jubilee." *Theosophy in Australia* 10, no. 2 (June–August 1945): 16–18.

Hallgrimsdottir, H. K., and C. Benoit. "From Wage Slaves to Wage Workers: Cultural Opportunity Structures and the Evolution of the Wage Demands of the Knights of Labor and the American Federation of Labor, 1880–1900." *Social Forces* 85, no. 3 (March 2007): 1393–1411.

Hapgood, Hutchins. *The Spirit of Labor*. With notes and introduction by James R. Barrett. Urbana: University of Illinois Press, 2004.

Hardacre, Helen. *Shintō and the State, 1868–1988*. Princeton, NJ: Princeton University Press, 1989.

Harris, Elizabeth. "Ananda Metteyya: Controversial Networker, Passionate Critic." *Contemporary Buddhism* 14, no. 1 (2013): 78–93.

Harris, Elizabeth. *Theravada Buddhism and the British Encounter: Religious, Missionary and Colonial Experience in Nineteenth Century Sri Lanka*. London: Routledge, 2006.

Higbie, Frank Tobias. *Indispensable Outcasts: Hobo Workers and Community in the American Midwest, 1880–1930*. Urbana: University of Illinois Press, 2003.

Higbie, Frank Tobias. "Unschooled but Not Uneducated: Print, Public Speaking, and the Networks of Informal Working-Class Education, 1900–1940." In *Education and the Culture of Print in Modern America*, edited by Adam R. Nelson and John L. Rudolph, 103–25. Madison: University of Wisconsin Press, 2010.

History of Dhammikarama Burmese Buddhist Temple Penang, Malaysia B.E. 2347–2535 A.D. 1803–1991. Penang: Dhammikarama Burmese Buddhist Temple, 1972.

Hitoshi, Nitta. "Shinto as a 'Non-Religion': The Origins and Development of an Idea." In *Shinto in History: Ways of the Kami*, edited by John Breen and Mark Teeuwen, 252–71. Richmond, UK: Curzon, 2000.

Htin Aung. *Burmese Monk's Tales*. New York: Columbia University Press, 1966.

Hunt, James D. *Gandhi in London*. Springfield, VA: Nataraj Books, 1993.

Huxley, Andrew. "Positivists and Buddhists: The Rise and Fall of Anglo-Burmese Ecclesiastical Law." *Law & Social Inquiry* 26, no. 1 (Winter 2001): 113–42.

Ignatiev, Noel. *How the Irish Became White*. New York: Routledge, 1995.

Ikeya, Chie. "Colonial Intimacies in Comparative Perspective: Intermarriage, Law and Cultural Difference in British Burma." *Journal of Colonialism and Colonial History* 14, no. 1 (2013).

Ingalls, Sheffield. *History of Atchison County, Kansas*. Lawrence, KS: Standard, 1916.

Iwata, Mami. "Takanawa Bukkyō University and the International Buddhist Young Men's Association: International Networks at the Turn of the Twentieth Century." *Japanese Religions* 41, no. 1–2 (2016): 25–42.

Jaffe, Richard. "Seeking Sakyamuni: Travel and the Reconstruction of Japanese Buddhism." *Journal of Japanese Studies* 30, no. 1 (2004): 65–96.

"Jodo Shinshu Buddhism Celebrates 125th Anniversary in Hawaii." Buddhist Door Global, November 28, 2014. https://www.buddhistdoor.net/news/jodo-shinshu-buddhism-celebrates-125th-anniversary-in-hawaii.

Josephson, Jason Ānanda. *The Invention of Religion in Japan*. Chicago: University of Chicago Press, 2012.

Katayama, Akio. "Kozai Ōtani On the Way to Europe." *Proceedings of the Faculty of Letters of Tokai University* 76 (2001): 175–94.

Kemper, Steven. *Rescued from the Nation: Anagarika Dharmapala and the Buddhist World*. Chicago: University of Chicago Press, 2015.

Kennerley, Alston. "Writing the History of Merchant Seafarer Education, Training and Welfare: Retrospect and Prospect." *Northern Mariner* 12, no. 2 (2002): 1–22.

Kenny, Kevin. *Making Sense of the Molly Maguires*. New York: Oxford University Press, 1998.

Kerouac, Jack. *The Dharma Bums*. New York: Buccaneer Books, 1958.

Kipling, Rudyard. *Kim*. London: Macmillan, 1901.

Kirichenko, Alexey. "New Spaces for Interaction: Contacts between Burmese and Sinhalese Monks in the Late Nineteenth and Early Twentieth Centuries." Unpublished paper. Asia Research Institute Working Paper Series. Singapore: Asia Research Institute, National University of Singapore, 2015.

Kirichenko, Alexey. "Between Thathanadaw and Theravada: The Constructions of Buddhism and Transformation of Buddhist Identity in Myanmar." In *Casting Faiths: Technology and the Creation of Religion in East and Southeast Asia*, edited by Thomas DuBois, 23–45. New York: Palgrave Macmillan, 2009.

Knibbs, G. H. *Census of the Commonwealth of Australia: Part XIV–Summary*. Melbourne: Minister of State for Home Affairs, 1911.

Langley, Henry G. *The San Francisco Directory for the Year 1874, Embracing a General Directory of Residents and a Business Directory*. San Francisco: Henry G. Langley, 1874.

Leng, Siow Poh. "Education in the Colony." *Straits Chinese Magazine* 8, no. 1 (March 1904): 11–17.

Lewis, Su Lin. *Cities in Motion: Urban Life and Cosmopolitanism in Southeast Asia, 1920–1940*. Cambridge, UK: Cambridge University Press, 2016.

Lopez, Donald S. *Prisoners of Shangri-La: Tibetan Buddhism and the West*. Chicago: University of Chicago Press, 1998.

MacDonald, George E. *Fifty Years of Freethought: Being the Story of The Truth Seeker, with the Natural History of Its Third Editor*. New York: Truth Seeker, 1929.

Malalgoda, Kitsiri. *Buddhism in Sinhalese Society, 1750–1900: A Study of Religious Revival and Change*. Berkeley: University of California Press, 1976.

Marshall, Andrew. *The Trouser People: The Quest for the Victorian Footballer Who Made Burma Play the Empire's Game*. New York: Penguin Putnam, 2002.

Masuzawa, Tomoko. *Invention of World Religions: Or, How European Universalism Was Preserved in the Language of Pluralism*. Chicago: University of Chicago Press, 2005.

Maung Zeyya. *Myanmar lu kyaw taya* [One hundred exceptional Myanmar men and women]. Yangon: Unity Press, 2010.

McVeigh, Robbie. *The Racialization of Irishness: Racism and Anti-Racism in Ireland*. Vol. 3: *Ireland between Two Worlds*. Belfast: Centre for Research and Documentation, 1996.

Medhasananda, Swami. *Vivekananda and Japan*. Zushi, Kanagawa, Japan: Vedanta Society of Japan, 2009.

Mehrotra, Sri Ram. *The Mahatma and the Doctor: The Untold Story of Dr. Pranjivan Mehta, Gandhi's Greatest Friend and Benefactor 1864–1932*. Mumbai: Vakils, Feffer and Simons, 2014.

Mehrotra, Sri Ram. "The 'Reader' in Hind Swaraj, Dr. Pranjivan Mehta, 1864–1932." *Dialogue: A Quarterly Journal of the Astha Bharati* 12, no. 2 (December 2010). Accessed December 3, 2019. https://www.asthabharati.org/Dia_Oct%20010/s.r.%20meh.htm

Mendelson, Michael. *Sangha and State in Burma: A Study of Monastic Sectarianism and Leadership*. Edited by John P. Ferguson. Ithaca, NY: Cornell University Press, 1975.

Mishra, Pankaj. *From the Ruins of Empire: The Intellectuals Who Remade Asia.* New York: Farrar, Straus and Giroux, 2012.

Mizutani, Satoshi. "Historicising Whiteness: From the Case of Late Colonial India." *Australian Critical Race and Whiteness Studies Association Journal* 2, no. 1 (2006): 1–15.

Morris, Henry. *Life of John Murdoch LLD: The Literary Evangelist of India.* London: Christian Literature Society, India, 1906.

Murray, Paul. *A Fantastic Journey: The Life and Literature of Lafcadio Hearn.* Folkestone, Kent: Japan Library, 1993.

Newsinger, John. "Jim Larkin, Syndicalism and the 1913 Dublin Lockout." *International Socialism: Quarterly Journal of the Socialist Worker's Party* 2, no. 25 (Autumn 1984): 3–36.

Norris, R. "Deakin, Alfred (1856–1919)." In *Australian Dictionary of Biography.* Canberra: National Centre of Biography, Australian National University, 1981. http://adb.anu.edu.au/biography/deakin-alfred-5927.

Nyanatusita, Bhikkhu, and Hellmuth Hecker. *The Life of Nyanatiloka Thera: The Biography of a Western Buddhist Pioneer.* Kandy, Ceylon: Buddhist Publication Society, 2008.

Ober, Douglas. "'Like Embers Hidden in Ashes, or Jewels Encrusted in Stone': Rāhul Sāṅk Tyāyan, Dharmānand Kosambī and Buddhist Activity in Colonial India." *Contemporary Buddhism* 14, no. 1 (May 2013): 134–48.

Okamoto, Yoshiko. "An Asian Religion Conference Imagined: Okakura Kakuzō, Oda Tokunō, Swami Vivekananda and Unwoven Religious Ties in Early Twentieth-Century Asia." *Japanese Religions* 41, no. 1–2 (2016): 1–24.

O'Malley, Kate. *Ireland, India and Empire: Indo-Irish Radical Connections, 1919–64.* Manchester: Manchester University Press, 2009.

Ong Siang Song. *One Hundred Years' History of the Chinese in Singapore.* London: J. Murray, 1923.

Osada, Noriyuki. "Housing the Rangoon Poor: Indians, Burmese, and Town Planning in Colonial Burma." IDE Discussion Papers. Institute of Developing Economies, Japan, March 2016.

Osto, Douglas. *Altered States: Buddhism and Psychedelic Spirituality in America.* New York: Columbia University Press, 2016.

Payer, Alois. "Materialien zum Neobuddhismus: Die ersten europäischen Mönche und Versuche der Gründung eines Vihâra auf dem europäischen Festland." Accessed April 12, 2019. http://www.payer.de/neobuddhismus/neobud0203.htm.

Peebles, J. M. *What Is Buddhism.* Colombo: Sri-Dharma-Sri, Maha Bodhi Press, 1907.

Powell, Michael. *Manual of a Mystic: F. L. Woodward, a Buddhist Scholar in Ceylon and Tasmania.* Historical Survey of Northern Tasmania 5. Canberra: Karuda Press, 2001.

Purser, William Charles. *Christian Missions in Burma.* Westminster: Society for the Propagation of the Gospel in Foreign Parts, 1911.

Purser, William Charles, and Kenneth James Saunders. *Modern Buddhism in Burma: Being an Epitome of Information Received from Missionaries, Officials and Others.* Rangoon: Christian Literature Society, Burma Branch, 1914.

Remsburg, John E. *Thomas Paine, the Apostle of Liberty; an Address Delivered in Chicago, January 29, 1916. Including the Testimony of Five Hundred Witnesses.* New York: Truth Seeker, 1917.

Richard, Timothy. *Forty-Five Years in China: Reminiscences.* London: Fisher Unwin, 1916.

Roberts, Jayde Lin. *Mapping Chinese Rangoon: Place and Nation among the Sino-Burmese.* Seattle: University of Washington Press, 2016.

Rogers, Frederick. *Labour, Life and Literature: Some Memories of Sixty Years.* London: Smith, Elder, 1913.

Rothstein, Andrew. *A House on Clerkenwell Green.* 2nd ed. London: Marx Memorial Library, 1983.

Royle, Edward. *Victorian Infidels: The Origins of the British Secularist Movement, 1791–1866.* Manchester: Manchester University Press, 1974.

Ryan, Lyndall. "Colonial Frontier Massacres in Central and Eastern Australia 1788–1930." University of Newcastle Australia, Center for 21st Century Humanities. Accessed April 12, 2019. https://c21ch.newcastle.edu.au/colonialmassacres/introduction.php.

Ryūkoku Daigaku Sanbyakunenshi [300-year history of Ryūkoku University]. Kyoto: Ryūkoku Daigaku Shuppanbu [Ryukoku University Publications Dept.], 1939.

Sarkar, Sumit. *Modern India.* New York: Palgrave Macmillan, 1989.

Saxton, Alexander. *The Indispensable Enemy: Labor and the Anti-Chinese Movement in California.* Berkeley: University of California Press, 1995.

Schadewald, Robert J. "Scientific Creationism, Geocentricity, and the Flat Earth." *Skeptical Inquirer* 6, no. 2 (Winter 1981–82): 41–48.

Shackle, Christopher. "After Macauliffe: The Wondrous Liberty of Puran Singh." *Journal of the Irish Society for the Academic Study of Religions* 4 (2017): 74–89.

Shimatsu, Yoichi. "A Hidden History: 'Free Tibet, the Lost Crusade of Buddhist Japan.'" *Japanese Religions* 33, no. 1–2 (2008): 91–95.

Shipley, Stan. *Club Life and Socialism in Mid-Victorian London.* History Workshop Pamphlets 5. London History Workshop Centre. London: Journeyman, 1983.

Singh, Gandha. *Deportation of Lala Lajpat Rai and Sardar Ajit Singh.* Patiala: Dept. of Punjab Historical Studies, Punjabi University, 1978.

Singh, Puran. *The Story of Swami Rama: The Poet-Monk of the Punjab.* Madras: Ganesh, 1924.

Sirisena, Mihirini. "The Dissident Orientalist: An Interpretation of U Dhammaloka's 1909 Tour of Ceylon." *Interventions: International Journal of Postcolonial Studies* 19, no. 1 (2017): 126–43.

Skilton, Andrew. "Elective Affinities: The Reconstruction of a Forgotten Episode in the Shared History of Thai and British Buddhism—Kapilavaḍḍho and Wat Paknam." *Contemporary Buddhism* 14, no. 1 (2013): 149–68.

Suzuki, Daisetz Teitaro. *Selected Works of D. T. Suzuki.* Edited by Richard M. Jaffe. Oakland: University of California Press, 2015.

Taylor, John. *From Self-Help to Glamour: The Working Man's Club, 1860–1972.* History Workshop Pamphlets 7. Oxford: History Workshop, 1972.

Thomas, Jolyon Baraka. *Faking Liberites: Religious Freedom in American Occupied Japan.* Chicago: University of Chicago Press, 2019.

Thompson, Clare, and Keith Thompson. "A Brief History of the Perth Lodge of the Theosophical Society 1897 to 1976." The Theosophical Society in Perth. Accessed January 21, 2019. http://tsperth.com.au/index.php/Main/HistoryOfThePerthBranch.

Thompson, Edward P. *Witness against the Beast: William Blake and the Moral Law.* Cambridge, UK: Cambridge University Press, 1994.

Todd, James Henthorn. *A Catalogue of Graduates Who Have Proceeded to Degrees in the University of Dublin: From the Earliest Recorded Commencements.* Dublin: Hodges, Smith, and Foster, 1869.

Trow's New York City Directory 1872/3. New York: Trow City Directory Company, 1872.

Trow's New York City Directory 1873/4. New York: Trow City Directory Company, 1873.

Turner, Alicia. *Saving Buddhism: The Impermanence of Religion in Colonial Burma.* Honolulu: University of Hawaii Press, 2014.

Turner, Alicia. "The Bible, the Bottle and the Knife: Religion as a Mode of Resisting Colonialism for U Dhammaloka." *Contemporary Buddhism* 14, no. 1 (May 2013): 66–77.

Turner, Alicia. "The Irish Pongyi in Colonial Burma: The Confrontations and Challenges of U Dhammaloka." *Contemporary Buddhism* 11, no. 2 (November 2010): 149–71.

Tweed, Thomas. *Crossing and Dwelling: A Theory of Religion.* Cambridge, MA: Harvard University Press, 2009.

Tweed, Thomas. "Toward the Study of Vernacular Intellectualism: A Response." *Contemporary Buddhism* 11, no. 2 (November 2010): 281–86.

Tweed, Thomas. "Tracing Modernity's Flows: Buddhist Currents in the Pacific World." *The Eastern Buddhist* 43, no. 1–2 (2012): 35–56.

Twomey, D. H. R. "Thathanabaing, Head of Burmese Monks in Burma." *Imperial and Asiatic Quarterly Review* 17, no. 34 (April 1904): 326–35.

Virk, H. S. "Professor Puran Singh (1881–1931): Founder of Chemistry of Forest Products in India." *Current Science* 74, no. 11 (1998): 1023–24.

Viswanathan, Gauri. *Outside the Fold: Conversion, Modernity, and Belief.* Princeton, NJ: Princeton University Press, 1998.

Ware, Anthony. "The Origins of Buddhist Nationalism in Myanmar/Burma: An Urban History of Religious Space, Social Integration and Marginalization in Colonial Rangoon after 1852." In *Religion and Urbanism: Reconceptualising Sustainable Cities for South Asia*, edited by Yamini Narayanan, 27–43. New York: Routledge, 2015.

Whelan, Kevin. "The Long Shadow of the Great Hunger." *Irish Times*, September 1, 2012.

White, Herbert Thirkell. *A Civil Servant in Burma.* London: Edward Arnold, 1913.

White, Herbert Thirkell. *Burma.* Cambridge, UK: Cambridge University Press, 1923.

Yoshinaga, Shin'ichi. "Three Boys on a Great Vehicle: 'Mahayana Buddhism' and a Trans-National Network." *Contemporary Buddhism* 14, no. 1 (May 2013): 52–65.

Young, Richard Fox, and Gintota Parana Vidanage Somaratna. *Vain Debates: The Buddhist Christian Controversies of Nineteenth-Century Ceylon.* Vienna: Sammlung De Nobili, 1996.

Index

For the benefit of digital users, indexed terms that span two pages (e.g., 52–53) may, on occasion, appear on only one of those pages.

Figures and Maps are indicated by *f* and *m* following the page number